PRIMITIVE LAW, PAST AND PRESENT

PRIMITIVE LAW
PAST AND PRESENT

A. S. DIAMOND

METHUEN & CO LTD
London

First published 1971 by Methuen & Co Ltd
11 New Fetter Lane, London, EC4
© 1971, A. S. Diamond
Printed in Great Britain by
T. and A. Constable Ltd
Hopetoun Street, Edinburgh

SBN 416 66080 0

Distributed in the USA
by Barnes & Noble Inc.

Contents

Preface   *page* vii
Table of Abbreviated References   ix
A Short Glossary   xxiii

PART I

1   Introduction   3
2   The Legal Legacy of the Past   9
3   The Legal Legacy of the Past (*continued*)   24
4   The Earliest Literature and the Codes   39
5   The Early Codes of the Past – Barbarism   55
6   The Central Codes of the Past – Early Civilization   70
7   The Late Codes of the Past – The Flowering of   82
     Civilization
8   The Late Codes of the Past (*continued*)   92
9   The Early Law of India   104
10   The Roman Twelve Tables   114
11   The Law of the Hebrews   124
12   The Hebrew Code   139

PART II

13   The Food Gatherers   157
14   Early Hunters, Agriculturists and Pastoralists   172
15   Agriculturists, Hunters and Pastoralists of the Second
     Grade   198
16   Cattle Keepers – The Third Agricultural Grade, First
     Stage   225
17   Cattle Keepers – The Law   244

18 Cattle Keepers – Crimes and Civil Injuries 260
19 The Recent Peoples of the Early Codes – Third Agricultural Grade, Second Stage 271
20 The Recent Peoples of the Early Codes – The Law 288
21 Trial by Ordeal in the Early Codes 297
22 The Recent Peoples of the Central Codes – Third Agricultural Grade, Third Stage 313
23 The Recent Peoples of the Central Codes – Feudalism 328
24 The Recent Peoples of the Central Codes – The Law 336
25 The Recent Peoples of the Late Codes 347
26 The Recent Peoples of the Late Codes – Kinship, Marriage, Property and Inheritance 364
27 The Recent Peoples of the Late Codes – Transactions and Contract 378
28 The Recent Peoples of the Late Codes – Religion, Letters and Procedure 389
29 The Recent Peoples of the Late Codes – Crimes and Civil Injuries 395

Index 401

Preface

This book began as a third edition of *Primitive Law*.[1] But thirty-five years have elapsed since the first edition was published, and the second was little more than a copy of the first, and I hope that during the intervening period I have bettered my knowledge of the subject. In the result, although the theme is much the same, and the method and conclusions are not in essence different, there is hardly a sentence in common between this and the first edition, though I have taken a few pages from my *Evolution of Law and Order* (London, 1951).

The chief differences are in the volume of the evidence presented of the legal usages of peoples of recent times, and the more detailed references to authorities, especially the skilled monographs of social anthropologists, of a quality which was still new in 1935. I have also added much in the way of description of the economies of all these peoples. Less space is devoted to the examination and criticism (hardly necessary in these days) of the hypothesis, made famous by Sir Henry Maine, that 'law is derived from pre-existing rules of conduct which are at the same time legal, moral and religious in nature', and that 'the severance of law from morality and religion from law belong only to the later stages of mental progress'.[2] And I have also made a change, or development, in presentation, by dividing the book into two sections, one examining the evidence afforded only by the legal remains of the past, and the other the legal usages of present and recent peoples and the light they throw on past laws and legal

[1] *Primitive Law*. 1st edn, London: Watts & Co., 1935. 2nd edn, London: Longmans, Green & Co., 1950.
[2] *A.L.* 14, 16 and *passim*.

vii

systems. In effect this is also a division between the laws of literate and pre-literate peoples, and this has a certain importance of its own.

Because of these changes I have altered the title of the book to 'Primitive Law, Past and Present'. I have retained the term 'primitive' partly because the book is known under this name, and partly because I know of no satisfactory substitute. Professor Max Gluckman, in his *Politics, Law and Ritual in Tribal Society* (1965), writes (p. xv): 'By "tribal society" I mean the kind of community which was once described by the term "primitive society", a term now rightly rejected.' I would venture to doubt, on the other hand, whether there are any expressions used by social anthropologists more inconsistently or with vaguer meaning than 'tribe' and 'tribal', and to think that if the term 'primitive' is now under a cloud, the same cloud has extended itself to those expressions. I hope it will be seen that in this book the term 'primitive' is used with a precise meaning.

I have been at pains, in a book intended for the lawyer and the anthropologist, to aim at simplicity, and to avoid as far as possible both the technical terms and analyses of the lawyer and the sophisticated language and conceptions of the modern British social anthropologist, which serve to render each unintelligible to the other, and especially the latter to the former.

The statement of a rule or custom is usually in the historic present, whether it still exists or not, but unless the contrary is indicated the dates are those referred to in the authorities cited.

I have taken the opportunity to correct some errors of fact and, on better knowledge, modified my views of the evidential value of one or two ancient documents, but I have no doubt that in a book of this kind it is impossible to avoid error. Indeed, I sometimes doubt if anyone will ever have sufficient knowledge to write such a book, so vast is the volume and variety of the phenomena of human societies and legal systems.

August 1970   A. S. D.

Table of Abbreviated References

(All other references in the book are in full)

A.1, A.2 and A.3	First, Second and Third Agricultural Grades.
A.A.S.O.R.	Annual of the American Schools of Oriental Research (New Haven).
A.C.	Middle-Assyrian Code of Laws relating to Women. Text, translation and commentary in Driver & Miles (1935), 382f.
Aeth.	Laws of Aethelberht. Text, translations and commentaries in Liebermann and in Attenborough (1922).
Aghbougha	The Georgian Code of Aghbougha, ed. J. Karst, in Corpus Juris Ibero-Caucasici, Première Section, Droit National Géorgien Codifié, Tome II, vol. 6. Strasburg: Heitz & Cie, 1938.
Akiga's Story	Translated and edited by R. East. Oxford University Press, 1939.
A.L.	Sir Henry Maine, *Ancient Law*. London: Murray, 1861.
Alabaster (1899)	E. Alabaster, *Notes and Commentaries on Chinese Criminal Law and Cognate Topics.* London: Luzac & Co.
Alf.	The Laws of Alfred. Text, translations and commentaries in Liebermann and in Attenborough (1922).
Anderson (1951)	J. N. D. Anderson, *Homicide in Islamic Law*, in B.S.O.A.S., 1951, xiii, 4.
Anderson (1955)	J. N. D. Anderson, 'Tropical Africa, Infiltration and Expanding Horizons' in *Unity and*

Variety in Muslim Civilisation, ed. Grünebaum. University of Chicago Press.

Anderson (1959a) J. N. D. Anderson, *Conflict of Laws in Northern Nigeria: A New Start*, International and Comparative Law Quarterly, VIII (July 1959), 442f.

Anderson (1959b) J. N. D. Anderson, *Islamic Law in the Modern World*. London: Stevens & Sons.

A.P.S. (1940) *African Political Systems*, ed. Fortes and Evans-Pritchard. Oxford University Press.

Arth. *The Arthaçastra of Kautilya*, trans. R. Shamasastry. Mysore, 2nd edn, 1923.

Attenborough (1922) F. L. Attenborough, *The Laws of the Earliest English Kings*, with English translation and commentary. Cambridge University Press.

B.A.E.B. Bulletin of the Bureau of American Ethnology, Washington D.C.

B.A.E.R. Bulletin of the Bureau of American Ethnology Annual Reports, Washington D.C.

Barnett (1955) H. G. Barnett, *The Coast Salish of British Columbia*. University of Oregon.

Beech (1911) M. W. H. Beech, *The Suk*. Oxford: Clarendon Press.

Berndt (1964) R. M. & C. H. Berndt, *The World of the First Australians*. London: Angus & Robertson.

Bird (1946) J. Bird, 'The Alacaluf', in *H.S.A.*, I, 55f.

Birket-Smith (1929) Kaj Birket-Smith, *The Caribou Eskimo* (Report of the 5th Thule Expedition). Toronto.

Birket-Smith (1959) *The Eskimos* (trans. from the Danish, 2nd edn, 1959). London: Methuen.

Bloch (1961) Marc Bloch, *La Société Féodale*, trans. L. A. Manyon as *Feudal Society*. London: Routledge.

Bohannan (1953) L. & P. Bohannan, *The Tiv of Central Nigeria*. London: International African Institute.

Bohannan (1957) P. Bohannan, *Justice & Judgment among the Tiv*. Oxford University Press

Bohannan (1968)	P. & L. Bohannan, *Tiv Economy*. London: Longmans.
Bowers (1965)	A. W. Bowers, *Hidatsa Social and Ceremonial Organisation*, B.A.E.B. 194.
B.S.O.A.S.	Bulletin of the School of Oriental & African Studies, London.
Burns (1947)	Sir A. Burns, *History of Nigeria*, 4th edn. London: George Allen & Unwin.
Bushnell (1922)	David I. Bushnell, *Villages of the Algonquin, Siouan and Caddoan Tribes West of the Mississippi*, B.A.E.B. 77.
Caesar *D.B.G.*	Julius Caesar, *De Bello Gallico*.
Can.	Canute.
Cape Commission	Cape of Good Hope, Report & Proceedings with Appendices of the Government Commission on Native Laws & Customs. Cape Town: Richards, 1883.
C.H.	Code of Hammurabi. Text, translation and commentary in Driver & Miles (1952 and 1955).
Champion (1967)	A. M. Champion, ed. Middleton, *The Agiryama of Kenya*, Occasional Paper No. 25, R.A.I.
C.H.I.	Cambridge History of India.
Ch'ü (1961)	T'ung-Tsu Ch'ü, *Law & Society in Traditional China*. Paris and The Hague: Mouton & Co.
Civil (1965)	M. Civil, *New Sumerian Law Fragments, O.I.P.*, Assyriological Studies No. 16, 1965.
Clapham (1949)	Sir John Clapham, *A Concise Economic History of Britain from the Earliest Times to 1750*. Cambridge University Press.
Cod. Theod.	*Theodosian Code*. Translation and commentary in C. Pharr, *The Theodosian Code*. Princeton University Press, 1952.
Cooper (Tierra del Fuego)	J. M. Cooper, *Analytical & Critical Bibliography of the Tribes of Tierra del Fuego and Adjacent Territory*, B.A.E.B., 63.
Cooper (Yahgan)	J. M. Cooper, 'The Yahgan', in *H.S.A.*, I, 81f. (1946).

Cooper (Chono)   J. M. Cooper, 'The Chono', in *H.S.A.*, I, 47f. (1946).

Cooper (Ona)   J. M. Cooper, 'The Ona', in *H.S.A.*, I, 107f. (1946).

Cooper   J. M. Cooper, 'The Patagonian and Pampean
(Patagonia)   Hunters', in *H.S.A.*, I, 127f. (1946).

Danquah (1928)   J. B. Danquah, *Akan Laws & Customs*. London: Routledge.

Dasent (1861)   G. W. Dasent, *The Story of Burnt Njal* and *Njal's Saga*. Also trans. Magnasson and Palsson. London: Dent, 1960.

Deacon (1934)   A. B. Deacon, *Malekula. A Vanishing People in the New Hebrides*. London: Routledge.

Delhaise (1909)   Delhaise, *Les Warega*. Brussels: De Wit.

De Vaux (1961)   Roland de Vaux, O.P., *Ancient Israel, Its Life & Institutions* (Eng. trans.). London: Darton, Longman & Todd.

D.H.R.   Darest-Hausoullier-Reinach, *Inscriptions Juridiques Grecques*, Paris (vol. I, 1895; vol. II, 1898-1904).

Diamond (1951)   A. S. Diamond, *The Evolution of Law & Order*. London: Watts.

Dig.   Digest.

Diringer (1948)   David Diringer, *The Alphabet*. London: Hutchinson.

Doke (1931)   C. M. Doke, *The Lambas of Northern Rhodesia*. London: Harrap.

Dornan (1925)   S. S. Dornan, *Pygmies & Bushmen of the Kalahari*. London: Seeley, Service & Co.

Driberg (1923)   J. M. Driberg, *The Lango, A Nilotic Tribe of Uganda*. London: T. Fisher & Unwin.

Driver & Miles   G. R. Driver & Sir John Miles, *The Assyrian
(1935)   Laws*. Oxford University Press.

Driver & Miles   G. R. Driver & Sir John Miles, *The Babylonian
(1952)   Laws*, vol. I. Oxford University Press.

Driver & Miles   G. R. Driver & Sir John Miles, *The
(1955)   Babylonian Laws*, vol. II. Oxford University Press.

E.A.L.   East African Protectorate Law Reports, *Notes*

	on *East African Native Laws & Customs*, vols I to III.
Ed. Roth.	Edictus Rothari, in *M.G.H.*, Legum XV, 4, 3f.
Ed. Theod.	Edictum Theoderici, in *M.G.H.*, Legum XV, 5, 145f.
Eggan (1937)	Fred. R. Eggan (ed.), *Social Anthropology of North American Tribes*, 2nd edn. Chicago University Press, 1955.
E.L. & C.	Sir H. Maine, *Early Law & Custom*. London: Murray.
Elias (1951)	T. U. Elias, *Nigerian Land Law & Custom*. London: Routledge & Kegan Paul.
Elkin (1964)	A. P. Elkin, *The Australian Aborigines*, 4th edn. Sydney: Angus & Robertson, 1964.
Elmendorf (1960)	W. W. Elmendorf, *The Structure of Twana Society, with Comparative Notes on the Structure of Yurok Culture by A. L. Kroeber*. Washington State University Press.
Evans (1937)	I. H. W. Evans, *The Negritos of Malaya*. Cambridge University Press.
Evans-Pritchard (1937)	E. E. Evans-Pritchard, *Witchcraft, Oracles & Magic* among the Azande. Oxford University Press.
Evans-Pritchard (1940)	E. E. Evans-Pritchard, *The Nuer*. Oxford University Press.
Evans-Pritchard (Anuak)	E. E. Evans-Pritchard, *The Political System of the Anuak of the Anglo-Egyptian Sudan*. London: Percy Lund Humphries, 1940.
Evans-Pritchard (1948)	E. E. Evans-Pritchard, *The Divine Kingship of the Shilluk of the Nilotic Sudan*. Cambridge University Press.
Evans-Pritchard (1951)	E. E. Evans-Pritchard, *Kinship and Marriage among the Nuer*. Oxford University Press.
Evans-Pritchard (1954)	E. E. Evans-Pritchard, *Nuer Religion*. Oxford University Press.
Finkelstein (1965)	J. J. Finkelstein, 'Some New Misharum Material & Its Implications', *O.I.P.*, Assyriological Studies No. 16, 233f.

Firth (1936)   Raymond Firth, *We, the Tikopia*. London:
                        Allen & Unwin.

Fletcher & La   A. C. Fletcher & F. La Flesche, *The Omaha
Flesche (1911)   Tribe*, B.A.E.R., 27.

Forde (1934)   C. D. Forde, *Habitat, Economy and Society*.
                        London: Methuen.

Forde & Scott   C. D. Forde & Richenda Scott, *The Native
(1946)   Economies of Nigeria*. London: Faber &
                        Faber.

Forde (1952)   C. D. Forde, *The Yoruba-Speaking Peoples of
                        South-Western Nigeria*. London: International
                        African Institute.

Fortes (1940)   M. Fortes, 'The Political System of the
                        Tallensi', in *A.P.S.*

Fortes (1945)   M. Fortes, *The Dynamics of Clanship among the
                        Tallensi*. Oxford University Press.

Fortes (1949)   M. Fortes, *The Web of Kinship among the
                        Tallensi*. Oxford University Press.

Fortes (1950)   M. Fortes, 'Kinship & Marriage among the
                        Ashanti', in *African Systems of Kinship &
                        Marriage* ed. Radcliffe-Brown & Forde.
                        Oxford University Press.

Fortune (1932)   R. F. Fortune, *The Sorcerers of Dobu*. London:
                        Routledge.

Frostathing   Frostathing Law, trans. L. M. Larson, *The
                        Earliest Norwegian Laws*. Oxford University
                        Press, 1935.

Ganshof (1952)   F. L. Ganshof, *Qu'est-ce que La Féodalité*
                        (trans. by Grierson as *Feudalism*). London:
                        Longmans Green.

Gaud (1911)   F. Gaud, *Les Mandja*. Brussels: De Wit.

Gifford (1929)   E. W. Gifford, *Tongan Society*. B. P. Bishop
                        Museum, Honolulu.

Gluckman (1969)   M. Gluckman (ed.) *Ideas and Procedures in
                        African Customary Law*. Oxford University
                        Press.

Gulathing   Gulathing Law, trans. L. M. Larson, *The
                        Earliest Norwegian Laws*. Oxford University
                        Press, 1935.

Gulliver (1963)   P. H. Gulliver, *Social Control in an African Society*. London: Routledge & Kegan Paul.

Gurney   O. R. Gurney, *The Hittites*. London: Penguin Books, 1961f.

Gurney & Kramer   O. R. Gurney & S. N. Kramer, *Two Fragments (1965)   of Sumerian Laws*, Oriental Institute of the University of Chicago, Assyriological Studies No. 16, p. 13f.

Gusinde (1937)   M. Gusinde, *Die Feuerland Indianer, II Die Yamana*. English translation by P. Schütze, *The Yamana*. New Haven: Human Relations Area Files, 1961.

Gusinde (1946)   M. Gusinde, *Urmenschen in Feuerland*. Vienna: Mödling.

H. & E.   The Laws of Hlothere & Eadric. Text, translations and commentaries in Liebermann and in Attenborough (1922).

Harrison   J. J. Harrison, *Life among the Pygmies of the Ituri Forest*.

H.C.   Hittite Code. Text and translations by J. Friedrich. Leyden: E. J. Brill, 1959.

Hessels & Kern   J. M. Hessels & H. Kern (ed.), *Lex Salica: (1880)   The Ten Texts with the Glosses & The Lex Emendata*. London: John Murray.

Hobley (1910)   C. W. Hobley, *Ethnology of the A-Kamba and Other East African Tribes*. Cambridge University Press.

Hodgkin (1935)   R. H. Hodgkin, *A History of the Anglo-Saxons*. Oxford University Press.

Hoebel (1954)   E. A. Hoebel, *The Law of Primitive Man*. Harvard University Press.

Hernlé (1937)   A. Winifred Hernlé, 'Social Organisation'. Chap. IV of *The Bantu-Speaking Tribes of South Africa*. London: Routledge.

Hogbin (1934)   H. I. Hogbin, *Law and Order in Polynesia*. London: Christophers.

Hollis (1905)   A. C. Hollis, *The Masai*. Oxford: Clarendon Press.

Hollis (1909)   A. C. Hollis, *The Nandi*. Oxford: Clarendon Press.

Howard (1965)   J. M. Howard, *The Ponca Tribe*. B.A.E.B., 195, 1965.

Howell (1954)   P. P. Howell, *A Manual of Nuer Law*. Oxford University Press.

H.S.A.   *Handbook of South American Indians*, ed. Julian H. Steward. B.A.E.B., 143; 6 vols; Washington D.C., 1946.

Humphreys (1926)   C. B. Humphreys, *The Southern New Hebrides. An Ethnological Record*. Cambridge University Press.

Ine   *The Laws of Ine*. Text, translations and commentaries in Liebermann and in Attenborough (1922).

Jenness (1934)   Diamond Jenness, *The Indians of Canada*. Department of Mines, Bulletin 65, Anthropological Series No. 15, National Museum of Canada, Toronto.

Joyce (1914)   T. A. Joyce, *Mexican Archaeology*. London.

Klima (1965)   'Bibliographisches zu den Keilschriftrechten VI' in the *Journal of Juristic Papyrology* (University of Warsaw Institute of Papyrology & Ancient Law, vol. XV, 367f.).

Kraus (1965)   F. R. Kraus, 'Ein Edikt des Königs Samsu-Iluna von Babylon', *O.I.P.* Assyriological Studies No. 16.

Krieger (1943)   H. W. Krieger, *Island Peoples of Western Pacific, Micronesia and Melanesia*. Washington D.C.

Kroeber (1925)   A. L. Kroeber, *Handbook of Indians of California*, B.A.E.B., 78. Washington D.C.

Krzywicki (1934)   L. Krzywicki, *Primitive Society and Its Vital Statistics*. London: Macmillan.

Larson (1935)   L. M. Larson, *The Earliest Norwegian Laws*. Oxford University Press and Columbia University Press.

L. Alam.   Lex Alamannorum. *M.G.H.*, Leg. XV, 3, 1f.

L. Angl. et Werin. Lex Anglorum et Werinorum, *M.G.H.*, Leg. XV, 5, 103f.

L. Bai. Lex Baiuvariorum, *M.G.H.*, Leg. XV, 3, 183f.

L. Burg. Lex Burgundionum, *M.G.H.*, Leg. XV, 3, 497f.

L.E. The Laws of Eshnunna.

L. Fris. Lex Frisionum, *M.G.H.*, Leg. XV, 3, 631f.

L. Fr. Cham. Lex Francorum Chamavorum, *M.G.H.*, Leg. XV, 5, 269f.

L.I. The Laws of Lipit Ishtar. See F. R. Steele, *The Code of Lipit Ishtar*, American Journal of Archaeology, 51, 158f.; 52, 425f. (1947-8); and Civil (1965).

L. Rib. Lex Ribuariorum, *M.G.H.*, Leg. XV, 5, 185f.

L. Sal. Lex Salica. See texts in Hessels & Kern (1880).

L. Sax. Lex Saxonum, *M.G.H.*, Leg. XV, 5, 1f.

L. Thuring. Lex Thuringorum (L. Angl. et Werin).

L. Vis. Lex Visigothorum. See Leges Visigothorum Antiquiores, ed. Zeumer (1894).

Les Bangala Van Overbergh & De Jonge, *Les Bangala*. Brussels, 1904.

Les Mangbetu Van Overbergh & De Jonge, *Les Mangbetu*. Brussels, 1909.

Lewis (1966) *Islam in Tropical Africa*. Oxford University Press.

Liebermann F. Liebermann, *Die Gesetze der Angelsachsen*. Halle, 1903-16.

Lindblom (1920) Gerhard Lindblom, *The Akamba in British East Africa*. Upsala. 2nd edn, 1920.

Llewellyn & Hoebel (1941) K. N. Llewellyn & E. A. Hoebel, *The Cheyenne Way*. University of Oklahoma Press.

Lloyd (1962) P. C. Lloyd, *Yoruba Land Law*. Oxford University Press.

Lowie (1948) Robert H. Lowie, *Some Aspects of Political Organisation among the American Aborigines*. Huxley Memorial Lecture for 1948: Royal Anthropological Institute.

L.Q.R. Law Quarterly Review.

MacDowell (1963)   D. M. MacDowell, *Athenian Homicide Law in the Age of the Orators*. Manchester University Press.

McKennan (1959)   R. A. McKennan, *The Upper Tanana Indians*. Yale University Publications in Anthropology, No. 55.

Mair (1934)   L. P. Mair, *An African People in the Twentieth Century*. London: Routledge.

Malinowski (1922)   B. Malinowski, *Argonauts of the Western Pacific*. London: Routledge.

Malinowski (1926)   B. Malinowski, *Crime & Custom in Savage Society*. London: Kegan Paul & Trubner.

Manu   The Code of Manu. English translation by G. Bühler, in *The Sacred Books of the East*, XXV.

Maybury-Lewis (1967)   D. Maybury-Lewis, *Akwě-Shavante Society*. Oxford: Clarendon Press.

Mead (1920)   M. Mead, *Social Organisation of Manua*.

Meek (1925)   C. K. Meek, *The Northern Tribes of Nigeria*. Oxford University Press.

Métraux (1946)   A. Métraux, 'The Botocudo', in *H.S.A.*, I, 435f.

M.G.H.   *Monumenta Germaniae Historica*. Hanover: Hahn, 1863-89.

Mooney (1928)   James Mooney, *The Aboriginal Population of America North of Mexico*. Smithsonian Misc. Coll., vol. 80, No. 7. Washington D.C.

Moore (1958)   Sally Falk Moore, *Power and Property in Peru*. New York, Columbia University Press.

Nadel (1942)   S. F. Nadel, *A Black Byzantium*. Oxford University Press.

Nimuendajú (1946)   C. Nimuendajú, 'Social Organisation and Beliefs of the Botocudo of Eastern Brazil', *South-Western Journal of Anthropology*, vol. II.

Oberg (1940)   K. Oberg, 'The Kingdom of Ankole in Uganda', in *A.P.S.*

O.I.P.   *Oriental Institute Publications*, Chicago.

Opler (1955)   M. E. Opler, 'An Outline of Chiricahua Apache Social Organisation', in Eggan (1937).

P. & M.   Sir F. Pollock and F. W. Maitland, *History*

of English Law before the Time of Edward I, 2nd edn, Cambridge University Press.

Perham (1969)	M. Perham, *The Government of Ethiopia*. 2nd edn. London: Faber & Faber.
Peristiany (1939)	J. G. Peristiany, *The Social Institutions of the Kipsigis*. London: Routledge.
Peristiany (1954)	J. G. Peristiany, *Pokot Sanctions and Structure*, in *Africa*, XXIV, No. 1, 17-25. Oxford University Press.
Plomley (1968)	N. J. B. Plomley, *An Annotated Bibliography of the Tasmanian Aborigines*. London: R.A.I., Occasional Paper No. 28.
Pospisil (1958)	L. Pospisil, *Kapauka Papuans and Their Law*. Yale University Publications in Anthropology, No. 54.
Pozo	H. C. Pozo, 'Social and Economico-Political Evolution of the Communities of Central Peru, in *H.S.A.*, II, 483f.
Prescott (Mexico)	W. H. Prescott, *History of the Conquest of Mexico*. New York, 1843.
Prescott (Peru)	W. H. Prescott, *History of the Conquest of Peru*. Philadelphia, 1847.
Provinse (1937)	J. H. Provinse, *The Underlying Sanctions of Plains Indian Culture*, in Eggan.
Radcliffe-Brown (1922)	A. Radcliffe-Brown, *The Andaman Islanders*. Cambridge University Press.
Radin (1923)	Paul Radin, *The Winnebago Tribe*, B.A.E.R., 37.
R.A.I.	Royal Anthropological Institute of Great Britain.
Rattray (1923)	R. S. Rattray, *Ashanti*. Oxford: Clarendon Press.
Rattray (1929)	R. S. Rattray, *Ashanti Law and Constitution*. Oxford University Press. Republished 1956.
Reay (1959)	Marie Reay, *The Kuma*. Melbourne University Press.
Richards (1939)	Audrey I. Richards, *Land, Labour and Diet in Northern Rhodesia*. Oxford University Press.

Richards (1940)   Audrey I. Richards, 'The Political System of
                     the Bemba Tribe in Northern Rhodesia', in
                     A.P.S.

Richardson (1940)   J. Richardson, *Law and Status among the Kiowa
                     Indians.* American Ethnological Society,
                     Monograph I.

Rivers (1914)   W. H. R. Rivers, *History of Melanesian Society.*
                     Cambridge University Press.

Robertson (1925)   A. J. Robertson, *The Laws of the Kings of
                     England from Edmund to Henry I.* Cambridge
                     University Press.

Roscoe (1911a)   J. Roscoe, *The Baganda.* London: Macmillan.

Roscoe (1911b)   J. Roscoe, *The Banyankole.* Cambridge Univer-
                     sity Press.

Roscoe (1923)   J. Roscoe, *The Bakitara or Banyoro.* Cambridge
                     University Press.

Roth (1899)   H. Ling Roth, *Aborigines of Tasmania,* 2nd
                     edn. London: Kegan Paul, Trench & Trubner.

Routledge (1910)   W. S. & K. Routledge, *With a Prehistoric
                     People.* London: Edward Arnold.

Rowe   J. Rowe, 'Inca Culture at the Time of the
                     Spanish Conquest', in *H.S.A.*, II, 183f.

San Nicolò (1931)   Marian San Nicolò, *Beiträge zur Rechtsgeschichte
                     im Bereiche der Keilschriftlichen Rechtsquellen.*
                     Oslo: H. Aschehoug.

S.B.E.   *Sacred Books of the East.*

Schapera (1930)   I. Schapera, *The Khoisan Peoples of South Africa.*
                     London: Routledge.

Schapera (1937)   I. Schapera, *The Bantu-Speaking Peoples of South
                     Africa.* London: Routledge.

Schapera (1938)   I. Schapera, *A Handbook of Tswana Law
                     & Custom.* Oxford University Press, 2nd
                     (enlarged) edn, 1955.

Schapera (1969)   I. Schapera, *Contract in Tswana Law,* in
                     Gluckman (1969), 318f.

Schebesta (1929)   P. Schebesta, *Among the Forest Dwarfs of
                     Malaya.* London: Hutchinson.

Seligmann (1932)   C. G. & B. Z. Seligmann, *Pagan Tribes of the
                     Nilotic Sudan.* London: Routledge

Skeat & Blagden (1906) Skeat & Blagden, *Pagan Races of the Malay Peninsula*. London: Macmillan.

Stair (1897) J. B. Stair, *Old Samoa*. London: The Religious Tract Society.

Stenton (1943) Sir Frank M. Stenton, *Anglo-Saxon England*. Oxford: Clarendon Press.

Steward (1938) Julian H. Steward, *Basin-Plateau Aboriginal Sociopolitical Groups*. B.A.E.B., 120.

Steward (1949) Julian H. Steward, 'The Native Population of South America', *H.S.A.*, V, 655f.

Swanton (1928) J. R. Swanton, *Social Organisation and Social Usages of the Indians of the Creek Confederacy*. B.A.E.R. 42.

Swanton (1946) J. R. Swanton, *The Indians of the South-Eastern United States*. B.A.E.B., 137.

Swanton (1952) J. R. Swanton, *The Indian Tribes of North America*. B.A.E.B., 145.

Tabeau P.-A. Tabeau, *Narrative of Loisel's Expedition to the Upper Missouri*.

Tac. Germ. Cornelii Taciti, *De Origine et Moribus Germanorum* (A.D. 98).

Talbot (1926) P. A. Talbot, *The Peoples of Southern Nigeria*, 4 vols. Oxford University Press.

Tanner (1789) John Tanner, *An Indian Captivity* (1789-1822).

Thomas (1959) E. M. Thomas, *The Harmless People*. London: Secker & Warburg.

Turnbull (1966) Colin M. Turnbull, *Wayward Servants*. London: Eyre & Spottiswoode.

Turner (1884) Geo. Turner, *Samoa 100 Years Ago*. London: Macmillan.

Uberoi (1962) J. P. Singh Uberoi, *Politics of the Kula Ring*. Manchester University Press.

Vaillant (1944) G. C. Vaillant, *The Aztecs of Mexico*. London: Penguin Books, 1950.

Vanderlinden (1969) *Réflections sur l'Existence du Concept de Propriété Immobilière Individuelle dans les Droits Africains Traditionnels*, in Gluckman (1969) 236f.

Van der Sprenkel (1962) S. Van der Sprenkel. *Legal Institutions in Manchu China*. London: Athlone Press.

V.C.R.   Visigothic Code of Reccesswinth.
Vernadsky (1947)   G. Vernadsky, *Medieval Russian Laws*. New
                    York: Columbia University Press.
Wagner (1949)   Gunter Wagner, *The Bantu of North Kavirondo*,
                    2 vols. Oxford University Press.
Walker (1862)   *The Life & Labours of G. W. Walker.*
Walker (1933)   C. H. Walker, *The Abyssinian at Home*.
                    London: Sheldon Press.
Wallace & Hoebel   E. Wallace & E. A. Hoebel, *The Comanches,*
(1952)   *Lords of The South Plains*. University of
                    Oklahoma Press.
Whitelock (1952)   Dorothy Whitelock, The *Beginnings of English
                    Society*. London: Penguin.
Wih.   The Laws of Wihtred. Text, translations and
                    commentaries in Liebermann and in Atten-
                    borough (1922).
Williams (1936)   F. E. Williams, *Papuans of the Trans-Fly*.
                    Oxford University Press.
Williamson (1924)   R. W. Williamson, *Social & Political Systems
                    of Central Polynesia*, 3 vols. Cambridge
                    University Press.
Wissler (1916)   Clark Wissler, *Societies and Ceremonial Associa-
                    tions in the Oglala Division of the Teton Dakota*.
                    American Museum of Natural History, 11
                    Ap. 1916.
Worsley (1957)   P. Worsley, *The Trumpet Shall Sound – a
                    Study of Cargo Cults in Melanesia*. London:
                    MacGibbon & Kee.
Yaron (1969)   Reuven Yaron. *The Laws of Eshnunna*.
                    Jerusalem: Magnes Press.
Zeumer (1894)   K. Zeumer, *Leges Visigothorum Antiquiores*
                    (Fontes Iuris Germanici Antiqui ex *M.G.H.*,
                    sep. ed.). Hanover: Hahn.

A Short Glossary

AFFINES – persons related by marriage (e.g a man and his wife's sister or father).

AGE-GRADE SYSTEM – a formal classification or organization of members of a community in groups of the same age and sex, often consisting of persons who were initiated together.

AGNATES – persons related exclusively through the male line of descent.

AMBILATERAL – descent reckoned for some purposes through the male line and for others through the female line.

BILATERAL – descent reckoned through both lines.

BRIDEWEALTH or BRIDEPRICE – goods (or currency) transferred on a marriage from the bridegroom's family to the bride's under a law or custom so to do.

CLAN – a group of persons putatively related to one another by descent from one common ancestor, through the male line (a patrilineal clan) or through the female (matrilineal) and usually exogamous.

CLASSIFICATORY KINSHIP TERMS – those applied not merely to the relatives to whom they primarily refer, but also to other relatives, considered to occupy a similar relationship to the speaker (e.g. 'father' applied also to his brothers, or 'mother' applied also to her sisters).

COGNATES – persons related not through one line exclusively.

COMMUNITY – a term used in this book without any precise political connotation. So too, *group, people* and sometimes *society*.

CROSS-COUSIN MARRIAGE – the practice whereby a man marries his mother's brother's daughter, or father's sister's daughter.

ENDOGAMOUS – said of a social or territorial group, the members of which only marry within it.

EXOGAMOUS – said of a group the members of which may not marry within it.

EXTENDED FAMILY – a term of vague meaning, properly signifying a joint family (q.v.) not necessarily occupying one homestead or household.

JOINT FAMILY – relatives, extending beyond the biological or nuclear family of parents and children, and occupying one household or homestead (e.g. brothers, with their families, cultivating land together after their father's death, before division of the inheritance).

LEVIRATE – system under which a widow (in certain conditions) must marry a brother (or other near male agnate) of her deceased husband. Strictly, only applies where any offspring of this union is accounted the child of the deceased: otherwise it is merely the 'inheritance' of a widow by such brother.

LINEAGE – whether patrilineal or matrilineal, differs from a clan (q.v.) in that the ancestors up to the common ancestor can be named, and a lineage consists of all descendants in one line (i.e. male or female) of a particular person through their named ancestors. Lineages are therefore of different depths of descent, and shallower lineages may co-exist with deeper. The deepest is often called a maximal lineage, and the shallowest a minimal lineage.

MATRILINEAGE – a lineage based on descent through females only.

MATRILINEAL – said of a relationship reckoned through females only.

MATRILOCAL (or UXORILOCAL) MARRIAGE – where by custom the pair take up residence with her people.

MOIETY – one of two exogamous halves into which a community may be divided.

PARALLEL COUSINS – the children of two brothers or two sisters.

PATRILINEAGE – a lineage based on descent through males only.

PATRILINEAL – said of a relationship reckoned through males only.

PATRILOCAL (or VIRILOCAL) MARRIAGE – where by custom the pair take up residence with his people.

POLYGYNY – marriage system under which a man is permitted

to have more than one wife. (Polygamy refers to marriage by both sexes.)

RELIGIOUS RULE – a rule of conduct the sanction of which is religious (e.g. the apprehension of ill from a supernatural source, or divine displeasure).

SACRAL OFFENCE – a criminal offence which is also a religious offence.

SANCTION – the apprehension of good (reward) or ill (punishment) which furnishes the reason for obeying a law.

SEGMENTARY – a political society which is not administered or governed by a central authority, extending over the whole society, but consists of a number of co-existing parallel social groups (usually clans or lineages), often without authority in these segments.

SORORATE – practice of marrying a wife's sister.

TOTEMISM – a form of social organization in which certain groups, within a larger community (and usually exogamous clans) have a special relation with classes of animate or inanimate things (commonly an animal or a natural phenomenon). Such clans are totemic.

UNILINEAL – either patrilineal or matrilineal.

UXORILOCAL – see *matrilocal*.

VIRILOCAL – see *patrilocal*.

PART I

CHAPTER I

Introduction

The purpose of this book is to attempt an account of the general course of development of law from its beginnings until maturity. In some part or other of the world all stages of this development can be seen either in history or in recent times. In some parts of the world the beginnings can still, or could recently, be witnessed; in others law can be observed in a mid-course of development and part of the story is hidden in an unrecorded past; in others the whole story, except its closing stages, belongs to an age before the dawn of history.

But a pre-history, like a history, requires some kind of time-scale if it is to have meaning and value, even though at any moment the clock of pre-history may show a different hour in different lands. It is not to be supposed that if law can be divided into two periods, a primitive and a mature, there is no development and no change in the primitive law as, to our knowledge, there is, and must be, in the mature. If we can recognize certain general differences between a primitive and a mature law, this is only a beginning of any knowledge of either. The English law of today is remotely different from what it was only a thousand years ago, and the law cannot, in its beginnings, have sprung complete like Pallas from the head of Zeus. We may look at a distant range of mountains and seem to see a line of peaks; as we approach, the line disappears and we begin to learn the nature of the country. There is great depth between the foreground and the distance, and a progression of heights of which we had no knowledge, and there are valleys previously hidden from sight. So with the law: it is distance and lack of knowledge that create the apparent oneness in the nature of primitive law.

But how can a time-scale be discovered or imagined? We have good reason to believe that the development of civilization has moved ever more quickly since the beginning of history, so that the acceleration has been plain to see in our own lifetime; likewise changes that took place over millennia in the Near East of five thousand years ago took only a century or two in England and Western Europe of a thousand years ago and take only decades in peoples of today. We also seem to see periods of quiescence interspersed, here and there, with great strides forward in inspired ages, such as the third dynasty of Egypt, or the fifth century B.C. in Athens, or the Renaissance in Italian cities, and again we know nothing directly of events in the growth of law before history and even less of the dates of such events.

There is only one time-scale, to call it so, that can be attempted, and that is the economic, using the word in its widest sense – the progression of development of visible, measurable, material culture. We know from archaeology, as well as history, the main steps in that development in the past and they can be seen in the present. They are relevant to our study because we can see in history a correlation between the economic development and the legal, and we are entitled to expect that there was such a correlation in pre-history. Employing, then, such a time-scale, our purpose is to find the changes in the growing law that appear at every step in the scale.

We must not expect to find by this means a unilinear course of legal development. In detail it is too much to expect always to find that each step was reached from the same step in the scale. The scale is not a ladder but a tree with branches, or perhaps a forest. It is not to be expected that at each step the law of all peoples will be found to be the same. It must be rarely, if ever, that the economies of two peoples are identical, and it is not common that any rule of law of one people is the same as any rule of another. But where economies are less complex and the laws fewer and simpler, we may expect to find greater resemblances, or to find resemblances more easily. It is important to note, so far as possible, differences in economy and law, as well as resemblances, to obtain a true picture. But resemblances are more significant than differences, for differences are in the nature of things: if there is no reason to the contrary the economies and laws of two peoples can be expected to be different, and if they are similar the question arises whether this is by reason of copying or similar circumstances of origin.

There are a number of considerations by which our conclusions as to the law or economy of a particular people can be tested and confirmed. For reasons of convenience our story ends at the stage of development of law represented by that greatest of legal monuments, the Code of Hammurabi (1752 B.C.), which almost begins the history of the world's law, and at the economy of his day, and therefore similarly ends at the parallel degrees of development of law and economy in England about A.D. 1250 and at other dates in several civilizations of the past, and in a few places in modern Africa; and we can observe in the present and in the records of the past most of the stages, which constitute our story, being approached and reached and passed in the same people. We can also see large culture areas in the past and present sharing similar law and economies, and on their outskirts descending gradations of law and economy as we move towards more backward areas.

But it must be made clear that there is no necessary implication of moral progress from the expression 'stages of development of law'. It can merely mean that law has changed with a new economic system. There are some horrors in early civilization, as in modern civilization, that exceed what went before.

Although this is primarily a study in the field of historical and not analytical jurisprudence, and the concentration is on description rather than analysis, here are materials which may help in some degree to answer a number of difficult questions of legal and sociological importance. What are the factors that cause change in the law? To what extent are they the result of original invention by rulers or legislators, and to what extent learned from other peoples or brought about by economic or other changes? If they are the result of invention or learning, are they only adopted if the economy is appropriate? What is meant by the common phrase of the influence of one system of law upon another? Can law be recognized as existing where there are no courts, and is it sufficient if there are rules of conduct considered by a community to be binding? What, in the course of pre-history and in historical times, are the forces, other than of law, which effect social control? And what rules of conduct preceded the rise of law and what sanctions enforced them?

The book begins, then, with a brief account[1] of the legal legacy of the past – an outline history, by date, of the Codes and other legal documents that survive. After a discussion of the nature of Codes and their relation to early literature,[2] there follow descriptions, in the order of our economic time-scale, of the law of the Codes of past peoples in different lands and ages – the Early Codes[3] (that is to say, the most primitive), the Central Codes,[4] and the Late Codes[5] (which end with the Code of Hammurabi and parallel Codes). There follow more detailed discussions of the Code of Manu,[6] the Roman XII Tables,[7] and the Hebrew Law,[8] all belonging to the stage of the Late Codes. This then,[9] is a brief legal history of the literate peoples of the past, from the stage of the Early Codes onwards, in the order not only of our economic time-scale but also of date, in that our Early Codes represent the law (*inter alios*) of the English from A.D. 600 to 900, our Central Codes the English of A.D. 900 to 1100, and our Late Codes the English of 1100 to 1250, and corresponding dates in each case usually about a century earlier, on the continent of Western Europe.

In the remaining part of the book (Part II) we turn to the recent primitive peoples of the world, of whom we choose and describe representative samples, relying for the most part on the published accounts of these peoples by skilled social anthropologists, and selecting as examples peoples whose economy and law (where law exists) or pre-legal phenomena (where it does not) are both well attested. Following in outline the methods of Nieboer[10] and Hobhouse, Wheeler and Ginsberg[11] we define economic grades of peoples by the degree of control over their environment, in which the method of subsistence is the primary test. So we divide them into the following grades. The first is that of the Food Gatherers,[12] who live mainly by gathering their food where they find it. The second is that of the First Agricultural Grade,[13] who have added to the gathering (or hunting) of food a rudi-

---

[1] Chaps. 2 and 3.   [2] Chap. 4.   [3] Chap. 5.
[4] Chap. 6.   [5] Chaps. 7 and 8.   [6] Chap. 9.
[7] Chap. 10.   [8] Chaps. 11 and 12.   [9] Part I.
[10] H. J. Nieboer, *Slavery as an Industrial System*, 2nd edn, The Hague, 1910.
[11] L. T. Hobhouse, G. C. Wheeler and M. Ginsberg, *The Material Culture and Social Institutions of the Simpler Peoples* (1915).
[12] Chap. 13.   [13] Chap. 14.

mentary agriculture as a secondary means of livelihood. Then comes the Second Agricultural Grade,[1] that of peoples among whom agriculture (usually better called horticulture) is the main means of subsistence, and who possess no metals; and the Third Agricultural Grade is that of the peoples who combine with agriculture the keeping of cattle and possess and work metals and usually have law and courts of justice.[2]

But there are also developments parallel with these: those peoples, first, who add to food gathering a specialized hunting way of life and do not cultivate the land, and these we call the Hunters, and mark them in two grades;[3] and there are the Pastoralists, who domesticate cattle but do not cultivate the land. They are few, and of them, for reasons of space, we shall have little to say until they acquire the rudiments of agriculture and enter the Third Agricultural Grade.[4]

This is the general outline, but in the course of this classification we note the development of various aspects of material culture in addition to the method of subsistence, and observe that within each of these grades are peoples of less and more developed economies, in some respects overlapping those of later grades. This difference between more and less development increases as we mount our scale. In the Second Agricultural Grade we have included (for there is difficulty in excluding) all peoples without metals or cattle, whose principal subsistence is by horticulture, and among them the Tongans, Hawaiians and Samoans, who approach in important respects some of the most forward economies of the Third Agricultural Grade. And in the latter grade (which is of chief importance in this study) there is so much difference in degree that we have divided the peoples into four stages. The first, A (3) (1)[5] represents, for example, the economy of the Germans of Tacitus; the second, A (3) (2), corresponds closely to England of A.D. 600 to 900, the stage of the Early Codes;[6] the third, A (3) (3), which we call that of the Recent Peoples of the Central Codes,[7] corresponds to that of England from A.D. 900 to 1100, and the fourth A (3) (4), corresponds to England of the Late Codes, from A.D. 1100 to 1250 or thereabouts.[8] At the last-

[1] Chap. 15. [2] Chaps. 16f. [3] Chaps. 14 and 15.
[4] Chaps. 16 to 18. [5] Chaps. 16 to 18. [6] Chaps. 19 to 21.
[7] Chaps. 22 to 24. [8] Chaps. 25 to 29.

B

mentioned stage there is again a wide difference in degree of development between people and people. In our treatment of these recent peoples we shall also notice the light thrown on the corresponding peoples of the past, their economy and law, and the sociology of their law.

This then, is the scheme of the book. We must not expect too much precision – man and society are not numerical functions, and the process of reducing humanity to grades is, in a measure, abhorrent to man – but the more precision we are able to use, the more light may be thrown on the intangible and elusive functions and relations of man in society.

CHAPTER 2

The Legal Legacy of the Past

We begin by surveying the legal relics of the past in their historical and local perspective; that is to say, in order of time and place. We shall later arrange them in a less familiar but more significant succession – namely according to the degree of economic development reached by the peoples who produced them.

So far as is known the main centres of the development and diffusion of civilization were in areas strikingly alike. They were alongside great and permanent rivers,[1] most of which spread water and silt over the neighbouring lands in seasonal or irregular flooding; they were in latitudes free from harsh winter cold, where the temperate and sunny climate and the fertile and irrigated soil could produce more than one crop a year. It was necessary that these regions should be semi-arid and therefore free of rain-forest (which could not have been cut down with the available tools of stone or soft metal) and for this reason also these homes of civilization were alongside great rivers. In the rivers there was a generous source of further food and the best roads, namely moving roads – waterways for trade and communications. In the absence of rain-forest and tsetse-fly it was possible to rear cattle, if they were to be found in those areas,[2] and the surrounding deserts gave a certain defence, in depth, against invasion. All these conditions could exist near sea-level between latitudes of 25° and 35° north, and in high altitudes at correspondingly lower latitudes. Here, then, were the chief concentrations of population, in a world of which the total of humanity was an insignificant fraction of what it is today. These conditions were especially favourable in situations near the sea.

[1] They had been preceded in the Near East by similar but smaller and less favourable areas, alongside permanent springs.
[2] They were substantially to be found in all these areas except Mexico and Peru.

Within the cultural field of Western Asia, Europe and Africa, these sites were to be found chiefly in the Lower Nile Valley, in Southern Mesopotamia (chiefly on the banks of the Euphrates), in Elam, in the valley of the Kerkha (which flowed into the Persian Gulf east of the Euphrates), and in the Indus valley – all in latitudes between 25° and 35° north. In China somewhat similar conditions were to be found in the valley of the Yellow River, at its great eastern bend between Shensi, Shansi and Honan (about 35° north), where it comes down from the dry highlands to the plain. Man reached America, by way of the frozen north, late in his history, and civilization bloomed only in recent times; there the corresponding sites, for reasons of local geography, could only be found nearer the equator and at correspondingly greater altitudes – namely, the valley of Mexico, with its five lakes at a latitude of 18° north and a height of some 7,500 feet, the Guatemala tableland, and in the Central Andes, the valley of Cuzco and Lake Titicaca and the river basins of that region, at an average height of some 11,500 feet and a latitude of about 13° south.

Town life had however begun in the Near East at least as early as 7000 B.C., and by about 3200 B.C. systems of writing had been evolved in Mesopotamia, Elam, Egypt and elsewhere, but from Egypt there are hardly any surviving legal records throughout the whole age of primitive law – that is, until about 700 B.C., when they begin to be plentiful.[1]

At the commencement of the Old Kingdom (about 3188 B.C.) it appears that Upper Egypt has for some time been a land of small, independent feudal princedoms. Lower Egypt, in its rural areas, presents a similar picture but the prosperous towns of the Nile Delta, drawing their wealth from commerce, enjoy a certain degree of autonomy and are ruled largely by their richest citizens. During the first three dynasties the kings of the south campaign

---

[1] For summaries of the little that is known of the law of Ancient Egypt, see Jacques Pirenne, *Histoire des Institutions et du Droit Privé de l'Ancienne Egypte* (Brussels, 1932-5) – a brilliant work (much drawn on here) but necessarily based to a large extent on conjecture; E. Seidl, *Einführung in die ägyptische Rechtsgeschichte* (2nd edn, Hamburg 1951); and by the same author Chap. 8 of *The Legacy of Egypt*, ed. Glanville (1942).

against the northern towns and unite Egypt under their authority, and the political power of the feudal nobility makes way for a centralized Kingdom of Egypt. The king, though not above the law, wields supreme executive, legislative and judicial authority, governing with the assistance of a new cadre of officials, whose training is that of scribes, as well as leading members of powerful families. In spite of the divine character of the kingship the state is essentially secular in the sense that the functions of priesthood and administrative officers are separate and distinct. Yet land remains the chief source of support for the bulk of the inhabitants, and the royal officials are given estates for their maintenance. The feudal character of the rural economy remains, especially in Upper Egypt, and even in the Delta towns the wealth that comes from trade is turned into land. The free peasant is losing status and land may be transferred with its occupiers, but there are few, if any, slaves except prisoners-of-war in the service of the state.

Under the fourth and fifth dynasties (about 2690 to 2420 B.C.) it appears that the strength of the monarchy is at its height. The new administrative class have become hereditary nobles and, by the enormous gifts of land and goods to the temples, and their exemptions from taxes, the priesthood has become a wealthy, ennobled, privileged and hereditary class. But the nobles are the lieges of the king. Landed estates grow larger and larger and the status of the free peasant, whose duty of service to his lord had been limited and defined in character and extent, deteriorates towards that of a serf. Cadastral surveys, which had existed in the Delta for a long time, are heard of also in the south, together with some registration of transfers of land and censuses. There appear to be important legal developments and reforms. The Court of the Six, presided over by the vizier in the name of the king, is the supreme court of the realm and the court of appeal from the local court of the nome or district, presided over by the provincial governor assisted by local notables. We hear of laws as written in books, archives recording judgments, written petitions and complaints, and writing in use for certain important transactions.[1] We hear of corporal punishment, mutilations and hanging for serious

[1] There have been since the third dynasty papyrus deeds (the *house document*) for sales and gifts of valuable property (mainly land, the occupiers and cattle). From the sixth dynasty there is a surviving judgment.

offences, but have no information as to the sanctions for homicide.[1] The paternal authority grows and the status of the wife
deteriorates. The eldest son advances in the law of succession
against his brothers.

In short, there are marked resemblances to the political and
social economy of England in the late twelfth century and early
thirteenth, at the close of our period of the primitive law. But
with the sixth dynasty begins a diminution in the power of the
kingship leading to its dissolution and the renewal of the feudalism
that still lay below the surface. The viziers capture the high offices
of the palace and the administrative powers of the Great Council
of the Six. The central administration, with its specialization of
functions, decays. The princes of the nomes oust the authority of
the vizirate and capture the local priestly and civil offices; the
royal governors disappear from the nomes which, in the rural
districts, become hereditary benefices. The central administration
of justice and the Court of the Six decay and disappear, the written
process of petition and record fades. In the towns of Lower Egypt
the place of the governor is resumed by the local plutocracy and
their families. The authority of the king in the feudal system of the
country diminishes to a lordship over such lieges as acknowledge
it, but soon the feudal princes are independent and by about 2250
B.C., the kingdom disappears.

There are later periods when anarchy and local powers give way
again to a Kingdom of Egypt and an advance in wealth and the
arts. After a brief interlude of this kind under the twelfth dynasty
(about 2000 to 1800 B.C.) the New Kingdom (from about 1575
B.C.) witnesses great material advancement and artistic achieve-
ment, and there survive a few written contracts and, in the time
of the nineteenth dynasty (about 1300 B.C.) a fragmentary penal
statute of Haremheb. So far as the evidence goes there is some
general continuity in the law and the forms of the deeds.

Nevertheless, as contrasted with the rich Mesopotamian legacy,
the extreme scantiness of the Egyptian legal remains until the
Persian period requires explanation. It cannot wholly be explained
(even in the wetter districts of the Delta) by the lesser durability

---

[1] In the field of procedure there is a case in which three oath-helpers are
required where there is no evidence save the defendant's (as to the genuineness
of a document).

of papyrus as against the clay tablets of Babylonia, for papyrus is plentiful in later ages and ostraca and limestone sheets were also in use. It seems likely that writing was only employed exceptionally, for transactions of peculiar importance and during these few periods of the early history, and that the official records were not retained save by such permanent corporations as the temples. We can also hazard a guess that the study of law was not pursued with the interest evinced by the Babylonians, and that the laws of Egypt had no great influence outside its borders.

The northern half of the lands of the Tigris and Euphrates came in time to be known to history as Assyria and the southern half as Babylonia. At the close of the fourth millennium B.C. the southern part of Babylonia, known as Sumer, was occupied chiefly by Sumerians, that is to say a population speaking the Sumerian tongue and with an advanced cultural tradition, and the northern part, known as Accad, chiefly by Semites, that is, a population speaking Semitic dialects and of a Semitic tradition of culture. From the Sumerian culture the Accadians first acquired, among other things, their system and practice of writing and their advances in the realm of law. But from early times populations of both groups were to be found in both Sumer and Accad. In the third millennium now one and now another of the chief city-states, situated along the banks of the Euphrates, held a temporary supremacy over its neighbours. Their kings appreciated the truth that it is a necessary condition of the power and popularity of a ruler that he should enjoy the reputation of a good lawgiver and judge, and several issued to their subjects of both races, for the guidance of the judges, legislative codes, with prologue and epilogue in familiar forms, providing often for similar problems in similar language. Urukagina of Lagash (c. 2750 B.C.) claims that he has established the ordinances of former times; Ur-Engur, king of Ur (c. 2400 B.C.) boasts that he has made justice to prevail according to the just laws of Shamash (sun-god and god of light and learning) and others used similar language. From Urukagina survive records of administrative reforms[1] but as yet no code of general law. From Ur-Nammu, founder of the great Sumerian third dynasty of Ur, who began his reign about 2050 B.C., survive

[1] See Maurice Lambert, 'Les Réformes d'Urukagina', in *Revue d'Assyriologie* (Paris), L, 1956, 169f.

some newly discovered fragments of a code of laws;[1] and of the
same dynasty (*c.* 2050 to 1930 B.C.) are numerous clay contract-
tablets,[2] judgments of the courts, and other documents of legal
interest. Dating from about 1900 B.C. comes one of the most
valuable of the ancient codes, the laws (in sixty clauses) of the
feudal kingdom of Eshnunna,[3] which covered most of the East
Tigris region and part of Assyria. The tablets were found at Tell
Harmal in 1947, and are written in Accadian. Many other documents of legal interest survive from the same place. Almost contemporary with the Laws of Eshnunna is a large group of laws
written in Sumerian, and issued by Lipit-Ishtar, the Accadian
King of Isin (*c.* 1930 B.C.).[4] Most of the tablets were found at
Nippur before A.D. 1900, but were only recently recognized for
what they are. In the prologue and epilogue the king describes
himself as the wise shepherd who has established justice in Sumer
and Accad in accordance with the word of the gods. Of the code
of about a hundred clauses, less than half is legible, dealing with
a variety of topics of the general law.

From the early third millennium B.C. groups of Amurru
(Amorites, Westerners), Semite invaders from the Syro-Arabian
desert, had made sporadic attacks in increasing numbers on the
peasants and city dwellers of Mesopotamia and Syria, settling
everywhere, establishing small kingdoms of their own and helping
to cause the downfall of the older states. Ultimately they created
a largely uniform culture over the whole area. The powers of the
rival city-states gave way to an Amorite dynasty of Babylon, which
ruled for three hundred years and under Hammurabi, the sixth
king of the dynasty, all Babylonia, as far even as Nineveh and

---

[1] See S. N. Kramer, Or.N.S. (1954), 40-51; and *From the Tablets of Sumer*
(1956); E. Szlechter, 'Le Code d'Ur Nammu', in *Revue d'Assyriologie*, xlix,
1955, 169-77; and for further fragments, O. R. Gurney and S. N. Kramer,
Two Fragments of Sumerian Laws, Oriental Institute of the University of
Chicago, Assyriological Studies No. 16, p. 13f. (1965).
[2] The term 'contract-tablets' is used in this book to denote clay tablets
containing records of legal or commercial transactions.
[3] A. Goetze, 'The Laws of Eshnunna' (A.A.S.O.R., xxxi, 1951-2, 1956);
R. Yaron, *The Laws of Eshnunna* (Jerusalem, 1969).
[4] See F. R. Steele, *The Code of Lipit Ishtar*, American Journal of Archaeology,
51, 158f.; 52, 425f. (1947-8): E. Szlechter, 'Le Code de Lipit-Ištar', in *Revue
d'Assyriologie*, li, 1957, 57-82; and for new texts of parts of the Code, Civil
(1965).

Asshur, was united under one rule. Now the legal history of this so-called Old Babylonian period reaches its culmination. The Sumerian language, still the language of learning but no longer in common use, remains for a long time in the phraseology of the clay contract-tablets. These number several thousands and together with the official letters that survive are enough to furnish a detailed knowledge of contemporary legal and commercial practice.[1] In about the fortieth year of his long reign of forty-three years, Hammurabi issued (*c.* 1752 B.C.) his great Code. Its prologue and epilogue are of familiar form and content, and indeed the closing sentences of the epilogue are but a version in Accadian of the corresponding portion of the epilogue of Lipit-Ishtar. Of the substance of Hammurabi's legislative provisions (numbering 282 clauses) some are of the same general character as earlier provisions, and the topics treated, the language and the content are sometimes closely similar, but there is no doubt that here is a palpable advance on all earlier law and legislators that are known or can be surmised. The central power of the state and its organization are stronger, the number of the provisions of the code is greater, its sanctions are founded largely upon a new, talionic, principle, the arrangement of the topics is new and systematic, and the language reaches perfection. As in the preceding codes the contents are purely secular, and though the prologue and epilogue pay homage to gods, the authorship is claimed by the king for himself. And alone of all the codes of primitive law – the rest of which are represented often by school copies – Hammurabi's survives on the stone on which it was published, and the authenticity of the text is unquestionable.[2]

The dynasty fell when the last king, Samsu-ditana, met his death about 1600 B.C. at the hands of Hittite invaders from the north, and after a period of confusion Cassites from the hills north

[1] There also survive later (Neo-Assyrian) copies of a large school book of the Old Babylonian period, known from its commencing words as *ana ittišu*. Like the Roman XII Tables (known to Cicero presumably from its initial words as the 'si in jus vocat', De Leg. II, 4, 9; 23, 59) it was a textbook long in use in the schools of scribes to teach legal terminology and practice rather than substantive law, but it includes the text of a small group of family laws comparable with C.H. 192, 195 (just as the XII Tables included old laws). See translation, Driver & Miles (1955), 308.

[2] The Laws of Gortyn (see *post* p. 22) also survive on the stone on which they were published, but they are no longer 'primitive'.

B*

of Elam ruled Babylonia for five hundred years. It was a dark age
of political and economic weakness and recession, and from this
Middle Babylonian period few documents survive, though they
do betoken some legal continuity.[1] For knowledge of the law of
the Near East we must look further to the north.

Contemporary with the reign of Hammurabi and for two
centuries later, there flourished on the west bank of the middle
Euphrates the Amorite kingdom of Mari, in whose palace archives
more than two hundred thousand cuneiform tablets have been
found, including commercial and legal transactions, but as yet no
text of laws. Further north, east of the Tigris and near the modern
Kirkuk there flourished at Nuzi about 1500 B.C. a kingdom from
which tablets containing family laws survive,[2] as well as some
legal and commercial transactions.

In Syria early in the eighteenth century B.C. began a great migra-
tory movement from the north-east of Hurrians and Indo-Euro-
peans and this continued south into Egypt under the leadership
of Amorite princes known there as the Hyksos. Between the
eighteenth and fourteenth centuries B.C. a kingdom flourished at
Alalakh, on the plain of Antioch, which has left some five hundred
clay tablets embodying (*inter alia*) treaties and transactions in the
field of land law. On the northern coast of Syria, opposite Cyprus
and near the modern Ras Shamra, there flourished from about
1400 to 1200 B.C., under Egyptian suzerainty, the Canaanite kingdom of Ugarit, which has yielded a great harvest of documents
shedding light on almost every aspect of national life and international relations, but as yet containing no laws.[3]

Though the Assyrian remains are not of the same value as
those of Babylonia, at intervals they supply ample and important
information. The earliest Assyrian documents of legal interest are
the fragments of Old Assyrian Laws (approximately of the period
of the Amorite Dynasty of Babylon), which come from an Assyrian fortified trading station in the region of Eastern Asia Minor

---

[1] The so-called 'Seisachtheia' (or moratorium) may be of the first Babylonian
dynasty or may be Cassite. See Driver and Miles (1955), 319. The surviving
fragments are too small to be significant.
[2] E. A. Speiser, 'New Kirkuk documents relating to family laws', in
A.A.S.O.R., X, 1930.
[3] G. Boyer, 'La place des textes d'Ugarit dans l'histoire de l'ancient droit
oriental' in J. Nougayrol (ed.), *Le Palais royal d'Ugarit*, III (Paris, 1955).

subsequently known as Cappadocia.[1] They appear to relate to the organization of a court for settling commercial disputes.[2] It is in the later, so-called Middle Assyrian period, that the Assyrian remains are of chief importance. About the twelfth century B.C., when our knowledge of Babylonia is of the scantiest, Assyria proper yields not only some collections of clay tablets of legal interest but also a copy, almost complete, of a lawbook consisting of fifty-nine paragraphs of laws relating to women,[3] a smaller tablet (of twenty paragraphs) containing land laws, a tablet (of eleven paragraphs) of laws of theft and other fragments. All these Middle Assyrian remains betoken a degree of legal and economic development hardly behind that represented by the Code of Hammurabi.[4] Of the same period is a collection of clay tablets of legal interest found in the neighbourhood of Arraphar (near the northeastern boundary of Babylonia) belonging partly to the Babylonian and partly to the Assyrian legal tradition.[5]

We must now move still further to the north, and further from the chief centres of civilization, and find in the highlands of Central and South-Eastern Asia Minor the legal remains of the feudal monarchy of the Hittites at about the same period. Here conditions are more primitive. The Hittite state as known to us was apparently established by Indo-European-speaking invaders ruling non-Indo-European native peoples. It would seem from names in the tablets of the Old Assyrian traders to whom reference has been made, that Hittites[6] were already settled there by about 1900 B.C. After a struggle between city states for ascendancy, Hattusas gained the mastery and from 1750 B.C. was the capital of a growing Hittite kingdom. It spread its conquests into northern Syria and, as we have seen, in about 1600 B.C. burst upon the stage of world history when its forces slew Samsu-ditana, the last king of the Semitic dynasty of Babylon, and captured Babylon itself. During

[1] Hence the tablets, of which these form part, are known as the Cappadocian tablets.
[2] Driver & Miles (1935), 1-3, and 376-9.
[3] Referred to in this book as the Assyrian Code (A.C.).
[4] All the Babylonian and Assyrian laws so far referred to represent the advanced stage of development of primitive law termed in this book the Late Codes.
[5] Driver & Miles (1935), 5.
[6] For a valuable account in English of what is known of the Hittites, see Gurney.

the century that followed, the Hittite kingship was torn by internecine war and murder between members of the royal house, and
reduced to impotence. About 1525 B.C. Telepinus, a usurper,
restored law and order to the state, and an edict of his survives,
laying down a law of succession and rules of conduct for the royal
family. Under succeeding monarchs the Hittite power (from now
on sometimes called the Hittite Empire), largely by its excellence
in the use of the new military arm – the fast horse-drawn chariot
with a crew of three – reduced its neighbours into vassalage and
conquered Syria, and for a few centuries shared with Babylonia
and Egypt the hegemony of the Middle East. There survives from
this period the document known as the Hittite Laws,[1] an invaluable code in Hittite cuneiform on clay tablets, which perhaps had
its origin in legislation of the fifteenth century B.C. Beyond this,
treaties, administrative decrees and other state documents survive
but no private documents, and it seems now unlikely that many
such will be found, or even existed; and therefore the means by
which the interpretation of the codes of Babylon and Assyria can
be checked is wanting in the land of Hatti. The Hittite ascendancy
ended at the beginning of the twelfth century, when the peoples
of whom we hear in the later Greek records – Phrygians, perhaps
Achaeans, and other peoples pressing from the west and north –
overcame the Hittite power and drove populations from the lands
of the Hittites southward into Syria. Here small kingdoms bearing
the name of Hittite are heard of for another five centuries till they
are submerged in the rising flood of the new Assyria, but they
have left no legal remains.

Still further south we meet peoples and individuals bearing the
name of Hittites in the records of the Hebrews that cover the
same period – namely from the time of Abraham, in the first half
of the second millennium, down to the eighth century B.C.[2] Here
the Hebrews, a Semitic-speaking group of tribes mainly of the
same Mediterranean race that populated the area from Egypt to
Elam, but including large Hittite and Philistine elements,[3] built

---

[1] Of the degree of development referred to in this book as 'the Central
Codes'.
[2] Gen. 15^{19}, 23, 26^{34}, 36^1; Num. 13^{29}; Josh. 1^4, 3^{10}; 1 Kings 11^1, 2 Kings 7^6;
2 Chron. 1^{17}.
[3] 'Thy birth and thy nativity is of the land of the Canaanite; the Amorite
was thy father, and thy mother was a Hittite'. (Ez. 16^3).

finally under David (*c.* 1011 to 972) a kingdom whose wide limits were never subsequently attained. It reached the height of its prosperity under his son Solomon (971 to 932) but after his death broke into a northern kingdom of Israel that fell to the Neo-Assyrian Empire in 721 B.C., and a smaller southern kingdom of Judah that fell to the Neo-Babylonian Empire in 587. The great Hebrew literature surviving in the Old Testament contains much that relates to their law, especially in the Pentateuch, a book edited early in the fourth century B.C., out of documents of earlier centuries. No contracts survive, but supreme in its legal interest – at least for our present purposes – is an ancient code of true law (that is, of secular law) embedded in the Pentateuch and contained in the book of Exodus, Chap. 21[1] to 22[17]. It shows in its precisely drafted clauses clear evidence of development, amendment and addition over a succession of centuries. The Hebrew Code,[1] though brief, is little less advanced than that of Hammurabi, and is perhaps nearer in its degree of development to the Laws of Eshnunna (of a millennium earlier) than to any other of the codes to which reference has been made. Yet it is true to say that all these codes give evidence of belonging to one great field of culture, for there are resemblances between them in language and content.

The next Assyrian supremacy – the so-called Neo-Assyrian period – which lasts only from the accession of Tiglath Pileser III in the middle of the eighth century to the fall of that empire about 612 B.C., produces a plentiful harvest of tablets relating to private transactions, but no legislation or law-book. It is from the rise of the ensuing Babylonian empire – or the so-called Neo-Babylonian period – that our familiarity with the life and commerce of the region reaches its summit. In the century that witnesses the fall of little Jerusalem in 587 B.C., the capture of Babylon and destruction of its empire by Cyrus of Elam in 539, and the close of the reign of Darius of Persia in 485 B.C., we have so detailed a picture from the clay documents of Babylon as is unequalled in the history of the ancient world. The names and indeed the fortunes are known of many of the most important families and commercial houses of Babylon, and a brief, unfinished

---

[1] This also is one of our Late Codes.

draft of a Neo-Babylonian Code or law-book is also extant.[1] And though there is strong evidence of development and advance in the contract-tablets of the period, yet there is still, as there was thoughout this Babylonian history of two millennia beginning with the earliest Sumerian documents, much continuity in commercial and conveyancing usage; and even under the Persians the general forms of the Babylonian contract-tablets remain. But we have chosen to mark the closing stage of primitive law with the Code of Hammurabi, and this is beyond the period of our study.

The feudal age of China seems to have begun many centuries before the dawn of history in the tenth century B.C., and to have continued thoughout the period of the Chou dynasty (1122 to 256 B.C.). Throughout these centuries the territory of the kingdom steadily widened from the Yellow River, but the number of feudal states was gradually reduced as one absorbed the other. About 250 B.C. one aggressive state, that of Ch'in, swallowed the rest and created the pattern of the culture and law that survived till the present century. Dynasty after dynasty issued a Code of statutory law, usually adapted from that of a predecessor. The Code of Li K'uei in the fourth century B.C. was something of a model for those that followed, but all codes have perished before that of the T'ang dynasty (A.D. 618 to 906) and ancient histories and annals must be relied upon for the earlier law. The code of the emperor Yang Lo of the Ming dynasty (about A.D. 1430) had something of the completeness of a code in the modern sense. Upon it were based the Ta Ch'ing Lü Li, the statutes of the Ch'ing (or Manchu) dynasty, which remained in force till 1912. All codes, from the beginnings of history, belong to our Late Codes.[2] They are chiefly codes of criminal law, but outside them is the whole of the civil law of marriage, inheritance, property and commercial transactions, the subject of much research and an expanding literature in this century.[3]

---

[1] British Museum, 82-7-14, 988. The first five clauses consist of rules relating to land; §§ 6 and 7 are miscellaneous; § 8 is described as being unfinished and therefore not included; and §§ 9-15 are a group of clauses relating to dowries.

[2] For a useful English summary of them, see title 'Law' in S. Couling, *Encyclopaedia Sinica* (1917).

[3] For the Chinese Criminal law, see Alabaster (1899), and for the traditional law of China generally, see Ch'ü (1961) and valuable bibliography; Van der Sprenkel (1962). For a description in English of life in the Chinese village, see Hsiao-Tung Fei, *Peasant Life in China* (1939).

The appearance of the Hittite Kingdom in Asia Minor in the early centuries of the second millenium B.C. and its destruction by other peoples in the twelfth century were incidents in a vast movement of primitive peoples. Mainly pastoral and mainly Indo-European speaking, they expanded and drove and were driven during two millennia south and west from the northern plains of hither Asia, destroying the early civilizations that lay in their path. In the middle of the second millennium they overwhelmed the civilization of the Indus valley, that had existed for nigh on a thousand years, in contact with Babylonia, in its twin capitals of Harappa and Mohenjo-Daro. As the written remains of its culture have not been deciphered, nothing is known of its law.[1] The invading peoples, the Aryas, spread slowly south and east in the ensuing centuries over the northern half of India. No writing survives from its culture before the rise of the Maurya dynasty at the close of the fourth century B.C., and the Hindus of our period seem never to have legislated in writing. The earliest surviving literature is purely religious and it was not till the next and the ensuing centuries, at the close of our primitive age, that the priestly caste of the brahmans, now active in the administration of justice, began to include in their sacred literature some rules of law real and ideal. Yet the earlier Arthasastra of Kautilya, a secular treatise on the political economy of India of the late fourth century B.C. and later, the observations of Megasthenes and other contemporary Greeks, the Code of Manu of about the first century B.C. and the subsequent literature give us much information of the law of these ages.[2]

Further west the same movements of Indo-European-speaking peoples produced the Mycenaean and Minoan cultures of Greece and Crete, of whose law at present nothing remains. After their destruction by Dorian or other invaders about 1300 B.C. an illiterate age ensued. The Homeric and other early poems, recorded after they had long passed from mouth to mouth, tell us little that is reliable of the primitive law of Greece. From the early seventh century B.C., first in the Greek colonies and then in Greece proper, most of the city-states had their legislators, and their names and periods are known but hardly anything survives of their work. In Athens, Draco's legislation of 620 B.C. or thereabouts seems to

[1] Stuart Piggott, *Prehistoric India to 1000 B.C.* (1950).   [2] See *post* Chap. 9.

have represented the close of our primitive period, but little of it remains save in the law of homicide.[1]

The valuable Gortyn Code – a body of Cretan legislation dating from about 450 B.C. and surviving on the stone on which it was published – is too advanced to represent the primitive age, but closely succeeds it and therefore by its resemblances and contrasts is of interest to our study;[2] and even in the Athenian law of homicide of the fourth century B.C. survivals of the latest primitive law are still to be seen.

But the philosophers of Greece did not deem law – as distinct from government – to be worthy of their study, nor did it ever become a science nor its rules a system. Little was promulgated or recorded in writing. Democracy demanded that the judges should be untrained laymen and therefore the advocates flourished by their eloqence and not by learning. Scribes of specialized experience drafted commercial documents with well-recognized forms and clauses, but the profession of lawyer did not exist even in the classical age.[3]

Material culture and civilization continued to spread to the north-west into the severer climate of central Italy, while the forests of central Europe offered for many centuries an impenetrable obstacle to trade and communications from the south and gave to the nascent southern cultures an effective shield against the inroads of the scanty populations of the north. Of the law of the Etruscans we know nothing, for their inscriptions are few and we can only guess at a material culture of the level of the Hittites, but we meet in central Italy the greatest of the world's powerful legal influences, namely that of Rome. Here again the evidence of

[1] D. M. MacDowell (1963).
[2] See D.H.R., I, 352f., where these laws are translated into French with a commentary; also Comparetti, Le legge di . . . Cretesi (Monumenti antichi, III, Milan, 1893). For an English translation of the longer Code, see Roby, L.Q.R., vol. II (1886), 135-42. This is of fourteen lengthy sections, each treating a separate subject-matter in some detail. It was found in 1884 on the left bank of the Lethaeos, engraved on part of a wall of a theatre of the first century A.D., but probably published (c. 450 B.C.) on the wall of a temple which was used, five hundred years later, in building the theatre. On the north wall of the same theatre, and also taken from an older building, are fragments of another Code of similar date.
[3] See J. W. Jones, The Law and Legal Theory of the Greeks (1956). For a systematic account of the family and property law of Athens in the period of the orators, see A. R. W. Harrison, The Law of Athens, vol. I (1968).

the primitive law is scanty. A group of legal rules, known to classical authors of the first century B.C. and later as the 'Twelve Tables', was regarded by them with veneration as (in the words of the historian Livy) 'the fountain-head of all law public and private', and was considered to have been promulgated in 450 B.C. as a legislative code (a view still accepted today). It is, however, here submitted[1] that the 'Twelve Tables' consisted mainly of a school book, devised or developed to teach legal practice to the pupils of the pontifical schools and (though it may have contained a few legislative provisions of the fifth century) dating mainly from the late fourth and early third century and edited and published with other matter about 190 B.C. Nevertheless the rules and maxims it contains do appear to have been drawn from law of the period of the Late Codes.

School books are familiar to us in the annals of early law, but the ensuing development of the Roman law was unique. In large measure it resulted from the increasing specialization that goes with material progress, a vast increase in population and the building of an empire; but law became a national pursuit and a philosophy and its development an art. The Babylonian ideal was the grant of even-handed justice – except as between patricians, plebeians and slaves – and judges free from corruption. The Hebrew ideal was the grant of equal justice, free from corruption, between rich and poor alike, and protection for the widow, the fatherless, and the foreigner. In Babylonia, and perhaps in Judah and Israel, the drafting of a Code of laws was both a literary exercise of the learned layman and a suggestion of ways of justice for the judge. But long before the Roman law attained its prime in the early third century A.D., its features had become those of modern law: a rule was law or was not law; it was a principle, extracted from a number of decisions, which must be applied to the new facts; law was a technical conception in the minds of lawyers, and its rules contained technicalities – it even lived to some extent a life of its own, separate from its changing surroundings and subject only to the power of a legislature to amend it. And while the Roman law attained a degree of development and a change in character not previously witnessed in the world's history, it perhaps raised the legal art to a standard never since surpassed.

[1] See *post* Chap. 10.

CHAPTER 3

The Legal Legacy of the Past

(*Continued*)

But law can only mature in health under the sun of freedom and an advancing economy, and long before Roman law reached the culmination of its development in the early third century A.D., decay had been apparent in that authoritarian state. Little was left of the institutions of democracy, and imperial legislation was the chief source of new law. The demarcation of social classes was so rigid that it had become difficult to escape from one to another. The Empire covered an area of nearly 2,000,000 square miles and its population before the end of the first century A.D. embraced some 60,000,000 souls, but its technology was backward[1] and made no progress, and the costs of government were no longer supported by a flow of slaves and booty from abroad. The middle half of the third century was a period of internecine strife between some fifty claimants to the throne, prolonged civil war and a collapse of the monetary system. Beyond the northern borders the barbarian inhabitants had been rising in economic status and vastly increasing in numbers; they expanded and were driven from behind to the south and west. In A.D. 98 the Roman historian Tacitus had published in his *Germania* a valuable, if brief, account of the customs and laws of the primitive peoples of the Germany of his day. Now tribes were amalgamating into confederacies and nations – for example, the Alemanni ('all-men') first heard of on the upper Rhine about A.D. 200, and the Franks ('freemen') some forty years later on the lower Rhine – and almost continuous war at the frontiers, invasion and devastation of provinces combined with internal dissension to strain towards breaking point the resources and government of the Empire. For

---

[1] No more advanced than that of England in A.D. 1500 and probably less so.

fifty years (A.D. 284 to 337) Diocletian, and then Constantine, restored the strength of authority, divided the Empire for its protection between a Western and Eastern ruler, and, on paper at least, doubled the army to 600,000 men and increased the size of the bureaucracy. But the land – almost the sole source of the revenue of the Empire – could not maintain the cost of the armies, the civil service, the vast multitude of those in Rome and Constantinople who were fed with public bread, and, after Christianity became the religion of the Empire, the serried ranks of the Church. Above all it could not afford the cost of resisting during 250 years the attacks upon the northern frontiers. A simple agriculture could not yield up half its crop for taxes, nor withstand the continued loss of manpower to the armies. The necessary imposts were not met and cities began to decay and farms were deserted in the outlying parts of the west and even Italy.

Some barbarian peoples had long served in the imperial forces and helped to appoint and remove emperors, sometimes themselves of barbarian origin. From time to time whole Teutonic nations, under the name of *foederati* or allies, were received and settled in this or that Roman province, were allotted lands and serfs of the provincials and governed themselves by their own primitive law, while the Roman colonials continued to live under the Roman law of the province. But the prestige of Rome was still beyond comparison and barbarian kings were long content to acknowledge her as their overlord and to rule in her name. Again and again, however, they waged war against her and were sometimes re-settled, as the price of peace, in a larger share of the same or another province.

The Visigoths had from the second century ravaged the northeastern frontiers of the Empire, and in the late fourth century, driven onwards by attacks of the Huns, were admitted to refuge and settled as *foederati* on the right bank of the Danube. Soon, however, they were again warring against the Eastern Empire and plundering its territories. In the fifth century they settled in Southern Gaul and Spain and after a long conflict of arms with the Romans, emerged under Euric as an autonomous state. They had assimilated something of the civilization of Rome and adopted Arian Christianity and there survive impressive fragments of a large code of laws of Euric[1] (king in A.D. 466 to 484), which applied between his subjects Gothic and Gothic, and Roman and Gothic. Between his Roman subjects Roman law applied, and for them his successor Alaric II in 506 provided the Lex Romana Visigothorum or Breviarium Alarici; a compendium derived from various Roman sources, which long survived in shorter versions and summaries of versions to keep alive a tradition of Roman law over a wide area of Western Europe. The place of both Codes was later taken by the Visigothic Code known as the Liber Judiciorum ('The Law Book'),[2] an enormous treatise completed and issued by their King Reccesswinth about A.D. 654, to apply to all subjects of the Kingdom. In it the code of Euric has been amended and supplemented by his successors Leovigild and, above all, Chindaswinth and his son Reccesswinth, to form, in spite of its diffuse length and pompous latinity, a fine compendium of Visigothic law, influenced by that of Rome. It was further amended and extended in a modest degree by later rulers.

The Burgundians in the first century A.D. occupied an area in north-east Germany, and in the following centuries migrated south and west. In the fifth century they were settled in Savoy, citizens, in their estimation, of the Roman Empire. On the fall of that empire in the west they emerged as an independent kingdom and extended their borders into the later Burgundy. At the commencement of the sixth century, during the reign of Gundobad (king 501 to 516) they enjoyed a period of prosperity. He was not the first legislator of his people, but about the year 502 promulgated its first code of laws, which survives, as amended by him and his son Sigismund, in a number of texts of the ninth and tenth centuries.[3] In it the native customary law and legislation has been skilfully expressed in a concise and excellent Latin, its terminology influenced by the Roman tradition. Although this code was issued to all subjects of the kingdom for disputes between his Roman subjects, Gundobad did not intend to abrogate the Roman law and soon after A.D. 506 issued to them the briefer Lex Romana Bur-

---

[1] In Zeumer (1894), who dates them between about 450 and 475. During the nineteenth century they were attributed to Reccared I, son of Leovigild.
[2] Zeumer (1894), pp. 25-313. It is one of our Late Codes.
[3] Zeumer (1894), pp. 497-578.

gundionum,[1] in which he set forth in Roman form, with commentary, the alterations which had been effected in the law by his legislation, dealing chiefly with titles of his Code and treating them chiefly in the same order. It did not continue long in general use.

The Ostrogoths had gradually settled themselves in Italy during the fifth century, having absorbed much of Roman culture here and elsewhere, and maintaining in large measure the Roman institutions they had found. Theodoric, surnamed the Great (who had spent his formative years as a hostage in Constantinople) ruled Italy, in title at least, for the Eastern Emperor as governor of Goths and Romans. About the year 500 he issued to his Italian peoples the code known as the Edictum Theoderici,[2] but it drew largely on late Roman sources, with amendments and additions in the field of civil injuries as needed by a simpler economy. Its arrangement of topics is disorderly and it exhibits unhappy contrasts between Roman law terms and primitive provisions, but is valuable as containing features characteristic of our Late Codes.

Attempts had been made in the Empire to bring some order into the vast mass of imperial constitutions, the accumulated legislation of the centuries. In A.D. 438, the Eastern Emperor, Theodosius II, promulgated a code of the statute law, and the Codex Theodosianus,[3] which was much drawn on by barbarian kings enacting codes for their Roman subjects, shows clearly how the law had retrogressed with the economy and primitive rules had been enacted.[4] Then nearly a century later, soon after his succession to the Eastern throne in 527, the Emperor Justinian completed his great compilation and consolidation of the mature and especially the classical Roman law, consisting of a Code of

[1] Zeumer (1894), pp. 579-624 (sometimes known as the Lex Papianus).
[2] *M.G.H.*, Legum XV, 5, 145f.
[3] C. Pharr, *The Theodosian Code*. Princeton University Press, 1952.
[4] For example, a law is passed for the release after a number of years, of children sold by their fathers as debt-slaves (3, 3; A.D. 391); the torture of witnesses, of low status at least, is common; a prosecutor, on a charge of homicide, must undertake in writing to be subject to the risk of the same punishment as that with which he threatens the accused (9, 1, 14; A.D. 383); other prosecutors (subject to rank) are to be kept in custody with the accused (9, 1, 19; A.D. 423); a charge of manifest violence is capital, and the unsuccessful prosecutor suffers the punishment the accused would have received (9, 10, 3; A.D. 319); the chief capital offences are adultery, homicide and sorcery, and also rape (9, 38). These are common features of Late Codes (see also 2, 27, 1; 9, 10, 2; 9, 12; 11, 39, 1).

Imperial Legislation (the Codex Justinianus), a textbook for students (the Institutes) and above all the Digest or Pandects (a compilation of extracts from the writings of the jurists).

But these were issued to a Roman Empire that had lost Italy. In 538 and again in 555 Justinian recovered it for short periods, but in 568, soon after his death, the Lombards successfully invaded the land. In the first century A.D. they had dwelt on the west bank of the lower Elbe, a people at all times small in numbers but fierce in spirit. In 547 Justinian had permitted them to settle within the northern frontiers of the Empire in Pannonia and Noricum, granting them subsidies in return for recruits to his mercenary armies. In the years following 568 they successfully established the kingdom of Lombardy, and under their king, Rothari, was promulgated in 643 the Edictus Rothari,[1] the first enactment of written Lombard law. It is perhaps the finest of all codes of barbarian law, a document of substantial length, rationally arranged and well devised and expressed, albeit in a poor Latin, and richly endowed with Teutonic law terms. It contains no rules and few terms of the Roman law and except in the final chapters (369-88) little or no evidence of later addition or amendment, but Liutprand and others separately added their own legislation in the following century.

Further to the west the crumbling frontiers of the Roman Empire had been passed by other barbarian peoples hardly affected by the culture of Rome, and when they learned the use of writing they recorded their native law unadorned and unimproved. The Salic Franks (the 'Freemen of the Sea' or perhaps 'of the Yssel') had lived for a time on the borders of the Empire between the Scheldt and the Meuse, and by that name were distinguished from the Ripuarian Franks who occupied the bank of the Rhine. In A.D. 358 the Salic Franks were defeated by Julian and left in possession of their lands as *foederati* or allies of Rome to protect the frontiers against other barbarians. But by the year 400 all trace of Roman culture and Christianity had receded from this area and the Salic Franks were pressing to the south over the ruins of the frontier and by 431 under their king, Clodio, reached the Somme. Under the conquering Clovis (who reigned from 481 to 511), after he had defeated the Romans at Soissons, subjugated the

[1] *M.G.H.*, Legum XV, 4, 3f. It belongs to our Central Codes.

Alemanni, procured or profited by the assassination of rival Salic kings and tricked or induced the Ripuarian Franks to accept him as their monarch, the whole of Gaul except Burgundy and Provence and Septimania in the south became a Frankish kingdom. On Christmas Day 496, at the height of his struggle against the Alemanni, he had astutely gained the support of the bishops of neighbouring kingdoms by adopting orthodox Christianity instead of the Arian heresy espoused by the Burgundians and Visigoths. In the last years of his life he edited and issued for his enlarged dominions a compilation of native, primitive law, now represented with amendments of the following century in that crude but celebrated code, the Lex Salica.[1]

Upon the death of Clovis the kingdom was divided equally among his four sons and there followed a fierce struggle for mastery between them and their successors, waged by the implements of guile, war and murder. For a time the boundaries of the kingdom were widened, till they embraced Burgundy and all France except Septimania and extended into Germany and Italy, and some sporadic legislation in the form of capitularies was issued by the Frankish rulers with the consent of their subjects for the government of their dominions. But this soon ceased: the period of the seventh century and the first half of the eighth was a dark age of violence and decadence. The fading light of Roman culture had been extinguished and the Frankish realm had broken up into three kingdoms, in each of which the royal authority, as it faded, was usurped by the mayor of the palace. Continuous internecine war ended only when the mayor of the palace of Austrasia, Pepin the Second, became master of all Gaul except Aquitaine (A.D. 687), and he remained its master until his death in 714.

His natural son, Charles Martel, who succeeded him (716 to 741) turned back the invading flood of Arabs at Poitiers and extended Frankish rule far into Germany. When Charles' younger son, Pepin, succeeded as mayor of the palace, a fruitful alliance ensued between him and the Bishop of Rome, for by the latter's support and encouragement Pepin had himself elected king by an assembly

---

[1] Hessels & Kern (1880). It shares with the Kentish Laws of Aethelberht and the Leges inter Brettos et Scotos the status of the most primitive of our Early Codes.

of the Franks and in 754 and 756 he in his turn brought about the surrender of the Lombard king and the deliverance of Rome from peril at his hands. What Pepin had commenced, his son Charlemagne brought to fruition, and by successful war extended the Frankish Empire till it reached from the Atlantic beyond the Elbe and from Northern Spain to the Baltic. On Christmas Day 800 he was crowned by the Pope as Emperor of the Romans.

During the three centuries that had passed since the collapse of the Roman Empire in the west, the weakness in the authority of kings, and the independence of local leaders – both characteristics of so primitive an economy – had left the main influence in the Church, which was not merely the sole repository of learning (as early priestly orders are wont to be) but also the sole inheritor of Roman culture. To hold together his vast empire, Charlemagne needed an increase in the royal authority, and this he obtained by raising himself upon the structure of the growing Church. When Leo III succeeded as Pope he did homage to Charles as his overlord. In domestic matters a number of capitularies were issued to give directions on problems of the day. Counts appointed by Charles governed their districts as his representatives and tribal society slowly faded, at least in the west. *Missi dominici* (envoys of the king) toured the realm and enquired and reported on a variety of matters requiring attention. A certain revival of letters was ushered in by this connection with Rome as early as the middle of the century and was encouraged and extended by Charles.

About the middle of the century, at the close of that Dark Age, three codes of law had appeared, the origins of which are obscure – the Lex Ribuaria[1] (the code of the Ripuarian Franks, which had been built up during a considerable period and drew on various Frankish sources including an earlier version of the Lex Salica), and the strange Lex Alamannorum[2] and Lex Baiuvariorum,[3] about which more will be said. But at the close of the century, at the behest of Charlemagne, his *missi dominici* recorded the legal rules of outlying provinces – the Lex Frisionum,[4] the typical and useful Lex Angliorum et Werinorum (i.e. Thuringorum),[5] the draft Lex Francorum Chamavorum,[6] and the advanced Lex

---

[1] *M.G.H.*, Legum XV, 5, 185f.   [2] *M.G.H.*, Legum XV, 3, 1.
[3] *M.G.H.*, Legum XV, 3, 183f.   [4] *M.G.H.*, Legum XV, 3, 631f.
[5] *M.G.H.*, Legum XV, 5, 103f.   [6] *M.G.H.*, Legum XV, 5, 269f.

Saxonum.[1] Partly his aim was to ascertain his rights and partly to reconcile inconsistencies, but his legislation to that end was little. The brief Lex Francorum Chamavorum is interesting as a record by a *missus dominicus* of Charles of the information given him by the people of their law – or rather of the respects in which their law differed from that of other Franks – before he had drafted a Code upon it. The emissary, it appears, took with him a document containing the title-headings, leaving blanks to be filled.

But when the genius of Charlemagne was removed by death, it was inevitable that in accordance with custom his realm should be divided between his successors and subdivided in every generation. Intestine strife, the scourge of Viking pirates and attacks of Hungarians and Saracens broke up the Empire. The great nobles consolidated their hold upon their districts and turned them into hereditary fiefs, building up the feudal system of the following centuries.

Meanwhile, during the fifth and sixth centuries peoples coming mainly from Frisia, and even less affected by Roman culture than the Franks and even more backward, had overrun by degrees much of Roman Britain. In the later sixth century they formed seven small kingdoms, made up of innumerable smaller chieftainships, and at the end of that century the leading kingdom was that of Kent, which Aethelberht ruled. In 597 with many of his subjects he was converted to Christianity, and during his life,[2] to meet the altered circumstances of his people, produced a remarkable code of laws, one of the most primitive and best of all our extant codes, couched in fit language and purely secular. Nearly a century later a few further laws of Kent were enacted by his descendants, Hlothhere[3] and Eadric.[4] The long succession of written Anglo-Saxon laws, stretching from the end of the seventh century to the Conquest, shows great deterioration from what precedes and little originality. The codes are often mixtures of legal and religious matter, including much of procedure and ritual and even sermons, but shedding little light on the law. The series continues under the early Norman kings, though from 1200 onwards the matter is again purely secular. Many of the documents of the whole of this English period are spurious.

[1] *M.G.H.*, Legum XV, 5, 1.   [2] He died in 616 or 617.
[3] Reigned 673 to about 686.   [4] Reigned about 686 to 687.

In other European lands the progress of material culture brought into existence other primitive codes and accompanied similar advances in the law.

In Scotland David I (1084 to 1153), who ruled from Caithness to the Tees and was reared at the English court, was the traditional first, great legislator. Amidst the mass of corrupt and spurious collections that present the earliest history of Scots law,[1] there can be attributed to him the Assisē Regis David,[2] a good and interesting body of provisions resembling the general law of feudal England of the first half of the twelfth century; and the Laws and the Customs of the Four Burghs,[2] which correspond closely to the constitutions and charters of liberties of the towns of England and even of the Continent, are partly also his work. But there also survives, wrongly attributed to his hand, a brief code of the Early Codes, the Leges inter Brettos et Scotos,[2] well known in Scotland and England and on the Continent and apparently still observed at the beginning of the fourteenth century among the mixed and unruly population of Galloway, for its use was prohibited by an ordinance of Edward I of 1305.[3] It is as primitive as the Laws of Aethelberht; a resemblance to that code and an affinity with the Welsh Laws are noticeable, and its primitive character emphasizes the truth that the degree of development of law is not essentially a matter of date but rather of the power of central authority. All these codes are wholly secular.

We turn to the Celtic world of the ancient Welsh and Irish Laws. Ireland did not suffer the breakdown of culture brought about by the Saxon invasion of Britain in the fifth century, but on the other hand took far less benefit from Roman civilization or from the economic progress of England in Norman times and the legal genius of the Plantagenets.

In Wales the traditional legislator is Hywel Dda[4] (Howell the

---

[1] For a brief account of the attempts and failures from the fifteenth to the nineteenth century to clear these mixtures of statutes and treatises from the 'fraud and guile' (to use the words of the ordinance of James I of Scotland of March 1425-6) that permeated them, see Preface, *Acts of the Parliaments of Scotland*, vol. I, published 1844, p. 21f.

[2] *Ibid.*

[3] Ordinacio facta per Dominum Regem Super Stabilitate Terre Scotie (*ibid*).

[4] The spelling varies much in the documents.

Good) who reigned over much, but not all, of Wales in the first half of the tenth century A.D.[1] and the bulk of the Ancient Laws of Wales are a lengthy Code known as the Laws of Hywel Dda.[2] It exists in three versions, the Code of Venedotia (North Wales), of Dimetia (South Wales) and Gwent (South-east Wales) – alike and different in many respects. According to one or other of the prefaces Howell summoned an enormous convocation of laics and clergy (the latter added lest anything should be ordained contrary to the holy scripture) and a code of existing law, with some amendments and some new rules, was prepared by a commission of twelve, approved by him and amended by some subsequent legislation. The laws survive in MSS. of the twelfth to the fifteenth centuries and are secular. Their value is little, for much or most is fanciful and ideal and much is nonsense, and all is compounded of the contributions of many hands and several centuries, but they do in sundry places reflect rules of law of contemporary Wales, and some later interpolations show normal progress and change.

These characteristics are magnified in the Ancient Laws and Institutes of Ireland,[3] which mainly consist of the Senchus Mor. According to its preface, in A.D. 438, the ninth year after his arrival in Ireland, St Patrick called a conference of the men of Erin; all the professors of the sciences were assembled, and the poet Dubhthach exhibited to him all the laws and poetry of Erin and nine persons arranged them, and 'what did not clash with the Word of God in the written law[4] and in the New Testament was confirmed by Patrick and the ecclesiastics and chieftains of Erin, for the law of nature had been quite right except the faith and its obligations and the harmony of the church and the people; and this is the Senchus Mor'. The manuscripts are of the fourteenth to the seventeenth centuries. In the course of a thousand years, generation after generation of teachers and students have written into the chaos of the texts their perplexities and their explanations, their commentaries upon commentaries, their legends and their

---

[1] Died about 948.
[2] Published by the Record Commissioners, 1841, and edited by Aneurin Owen with English translation. See H. D. Emanuel, *The Latin Texts of the Welsh Laws*. University of Wales, 1967.
[3] Published by the Commissioners, 1865 *et seq.*, with translation into English.
[4] i.e. the canon law.

dreams.[1] 'The Senchus of the men of Erin: What has preserved it? The joint memory of two seniors, the tradition from one ear to another, the composition of the poets, the additions from the law of the letter,[2] strength from the law of nature; for these are the three rocks by which the judgments of the world are supported.'

Few of these provisions of the Irish and Welsh laws were, or could have been, statutory, for there was no one to legislate for all their tribes, but they claimed in course of time authority over the whole country and became a university of knowledge, a school-book for the general education of the student. In Wales he might hope to become the judge or legal assessor, renumerated by fees, sitting in the court of a local lord. In Ireland he would become a Brehon, a jurisconsult who, if appointed by the lord, would similarly officiate as legal assessor, clerk of the court and keeper of the lord's records. Brehons also advised private clients for fees and acted as arbitrators when appointed by the parties. Few of these rules could ever have found a practical application, but in the common struggle against the English invader they retained and enhanced the allegiance of the people, including the English settlers, until their use was successfully prohibited in the thirteenth and fourteenth centuries in Wales and the seventeenth century in Ireland.

The earliest Norwegian law is to be found in two admirable codes known as the Gulathing Law and the Frostathing Law.[3] Both are substantial law-books, which have undergone a long process of development and change, originating probably in part in some older legislation and in part in older law-books. The oldest MS. of the Gulathing Law dates from about A.D. 1150[4] and of the Frostathing Law (which represents law of the northern province) from the mid-thirteenth century, and each can be taken to state the law of about A.D. 1100. They are among the best of

[1] Occasionally also flights of prurient fancy, a characteristic of spurious laws, see e.g. Venedotian Code, II, 1, 27 and 36, (*op. cit.*) and cf. L. Bai. 7; Lex Alam. 58.
[2] Of the bible and canon law. Yet the laws, with all their vast bulk, are secular. Religious matter is in a few later passages (e.g. *op. cit.* vol. 3, p. 31).
[3] See L. M. Larson, *The Earliest Norwegian Laws.* Oxford, 1935.
[4] There is, however, appended to the Gulathing Law a new tariff of payments attributed to Bjarni Mardsson, of the far north, dating from the early thirteenth century.

the early Central Codes of Western Europe and betoken the high legal abilities of the people, and though each contains a distinct section devoted to the laws of the Church, are otherwise entirely secular.

In Iceland the traditional legislator was Ulfyot, who was believed to have given a code of laws to the colonists in about A.D. 930, but it was not written and its contents are unknown. Writing came into use in the twelfth century, and from its close the literature of the sagas flourished, though they had long been recited orally. Prominent among them is Burnt Njal,[1] which contains, like other literature of the kind, tales of different date knitted together by an editor. Its hero, Njal, is an eminent lay lawyer.

> 'He was wealthy and handsome of face. . . . He was so great a lawyer that his match was not to be found. Wise, too, he was and fore-knowing and fore-sighted; of good counsel and ready to give it; and all that he advised men was sure to be the best for them to do. Gentle and generous, he unravelled every man's knotty points who came to see him.'[2]

It purports to tell of events of the end of the tenth century, and its subject is homicide and breathless lawsuits – the prose epic of a people delighting in violence and law. Until the latter part of the saga, when other tales, dating from after the introduction of Christianity, continue the story, it casts light upon the background of the law of homicide in the age of the Early Codes, when the slaying of a man (provided the slayer declares his deed afterwards, as he always does) is no religious nor moral offence, but merely a matter for the families affected to avenge or compromise by a money payment fixed by the social status of the slain – and homicide and lawsuits are nearly always so compromised. Indeed the payment so completely wipes out the act that in one case the father of the slayer adopts the son of the slain.[3] But referring to one heroic figure the narrator says in admiration: 'He was a strong

---

[1] See, for English translations, G. W. Dasent, *The Story of Burnt Njal* (1861); and *Njals Saga*, translated Magnusson & Palsson (1960); and see also Crougie, *The Icelandic Sagas*. Cambridge, 1913.
[2] Dasent (1861), I, 61.   [3] Dasent (1861), II, 59f.

man well skilled in arms and had slain many men and made no atonement in money for one of them.'[1] And Ragi is admired as 'a great manslayer'.[2] Yet if the slayer were to engage himself too frequently in homicide he might in the end be considered a nuisance and the community or part of it might be stirred to action against him.

Christianity was officially adopted in European Russia in A.D. 998, and the civilizing influences came at first from Byzantium in the south.[3] The earliest surviving code of the Kievan State (that is to say, of European Russia) is Jaroslav's Pravda, a brief and typical code of the close of the stage of the Early Codes, dating from the first half of the eleventh century. It was added to by Jaroslav's sons in the second half of that century, and the Expanded Version of the laws, of the latter half of the twelfth century, is a useful and interesting code of the Central Codes, containing law of an intensely feudal state. It includes the revised Pravda of Jaroslav's sons, a statute of Vladimir Monomach of the early twelfth century and some other legislation.[4] Of the many manuscript copies of the Expanded Version, the earliest date from the late thirteenth and the fourteenth centuries. The codes are wholly secular.

The Armenian Law Book[5] is an elaborate treatise of the thirteenth century and belongs to the close of the stage of the Central Codes or the beginning of the Late Codes. It is statutory in origin and sets out law of a feudal Christian state administered in its secular courts and ecclesiastical courts. Of its 175 titles[6]

---

[1] Dasent (1861), I, 30.   [2] Dasent (1861), I, 44.
[3] There are two Russian-Byzantine treaties in 911 and 945. The use of certain popular manuals of Byzantine law spread in Russia during the eleventh century. In the latter half of the twelfth century German expansion in the Baltic, and in the following centuries commercial treaties between North Russia and German cities, affected the development of Russian law.
[4] For English translation and commentary, see Vernadsky (1947).
[5] Edited with German translation by J. Karst, *Armenisches Rechtsbuch*. Strasburg, 1905.
[6] Titles 1-4, laws of the king and princes; 5-7, relations between lords and their dependents; 8-62, ecclesiastical law; 63-9, relations between clergy and laity; 70-1, jurisdiction of church and of state; 72-93, marriage, chastity, divorce and betrothal; 94-6, succession; 97-8, family law; 99-105, property law and especially mortgages; 106-12, purchase and sale; 113-14, wills; 115-18, slave law; 119-75, civil wrongs.

nearly half consists of ecclesiastical law, and the long section on civil injuries has many provisions of the Hebrew Code, quoted verbatim, and other references to the Old and New Testaments. Yet it would be far from the truth to suggest that it shows any confusion between law and religion.

Much of interest and value survives from the mediaeval law of Georgia, a feudal Christian kingdom with sharp differentiation of social ranks. The earliest code is the Laws of King George V of Georgia,[1] dating perhaps from the period A.D. 1325 to 1338, and devised for the peace of a remote and disorderly district. It is a brief code of forty-six clauses and belongs to the close of our stage of the Early Codes. The bulk, however, of the remains of the mediaeval law of Georgia is to be found in the fifteenth-century Code of Aghbougha,[2] which belongs to our Central Codes but shares with the Code of George V the special characteristics of the law of the kingdom. Aghbougha's Code is a collation and revision of three smaller codes, the Law of Beka, his grandfather, who ruled in East Georgia in the late fourteenth century; Aghbougha's own legislation (of the fifteenth century), and the Bagrato-Davidian Code (a fifteenth century revision of a code several centuries earlier). There also survives a considerable volume of legal documents of the period.

But in the meantime the peoples of England and the Continent had continued their economic advance at an increasing speed and the centralization of government proceeded apace. In Italy, for example, by the middle of the eleventh century the stage of material culture of our Late Codes, and in particular that of the Roman XII Tables, had been attained, and the classical Roman law, whose principles had largely been drawn from that compilation, now had practical meaning for its peoples. In England, too, which had taken its own way, a similar advance was apparent in

---

[1] In Corpus Juris Iberi-Caucasici, Tome II, *Législation Médiévale et Nomocanique*, vol. 6, *Code du Roi Geo. V* (original Georgian and Commentary) by J. Karst (Strasburg, 1940); and for English translation, see *J.R.A.S.*, July 1914, p. 608f., *Laws of King George V of Georgia, surnamed the Brilliant*, translated with commentary by Oliver Wardrop.

[2] Edited J. Karst, with French translation, *op. cit.*, 1938.

the following century, and from 1100, when Irnerius began to teach in Bologna, and from 1200, when the textbook attributed to Glanville appeared in England, the legal conceptions of Europe began to be transformed and the legal systems of the modern West were ushered in.

CHAPTER 4

The Earliest Literature and the Codes

Before a system of writing comes into use there are seen among many peoples mnemonic devices for keeping records and especially accounts. These include, for example, knot-devices and tally-sticks, the *quipu* in Peru and similar means in China.[1] When writing appears among a people it seems at first to be chiefly used for the same purposes – namely, for accounts, public records and administration by its rulers and the religious institutions, and soon almost everywhere, so far as our information extends, the knowledge and use of writing is the sole province of the *scribes*, a class who are not priests but are one of the religious orders. This is so, for example, in ancient Babylonia, Egypt, Hatti, India, Rome, Israel and Judah, Mediaeval Europe and Asia Minor, Mexico and Ethiopia. In the Old Testament this relation between the *kōhēn* (or priest) and the *sōphēr*[2] (or scribe) is plain to see. In some lands even the same sign or word is employed for both classes: for example, even in the Neo-Babylonian period the same ideogram still signified,[3] and in England 'clerk' and 'clerical' still denote both the writer and the priest. Writing is only taught in the temples and the churches, though at the end of the primitive age the ability to write begins to spread to the layman.

But all peoples do not acquire the art of writing at the same degree of development of material culture. It seems likely that ancient Sumer and perhaps Egypt, whose peoples had learned the mystery for themselves, had approached the stage of our Late Codes,[4] but their neighbours (for example, the Hittites)[5] were

[1] Diringer (1948).
[2] The verb signifies 'to count', 'to recount'.
[3] San Nicolò, (1931), 142.
[4] At any rate what survives appears to be already of that stage.
[5] Central Codes.

taught or copied it when they had not developed so far, and in early Mediaeval Europe and in our day the Christian missionaries brought it to peoples of our Early Codes, as they brought it to Aethelberht of Kent.[1]

Because writing is so early used for public records and administration, and legal and religious purposes are among the most necessary and general of public purposes, and legal and religious records the most likely to survive (for tradition is of the essence of both, and the perpetual corporations of kingship and temple can best maintain them), the oldest surviving literature of most peoples is its laws, written by the hand of the scribe;[2] in the ancient world they are of different stages of the Late Codes and the Central, in the mediaeval and modern worlds often also of the Early Codes. Where they are the earliest literature of the nation, and therefore there are no contemporary records to assist in their interpretation, we must look to the early history of literature elsewhere to help to elicit their nature and the circumstances in which they were produced.

Before writing appears, the oral tradition, or 'oral literature', that comes down from the past, telling of bygone events and the activities of kings and gods and heroes, is compounded of the contributions of many men and, if we may judge by the traditions of the backward peoples around us, like other oral messages, is in most cases factually unreliable and constantly changing.[3] In mature, modern communities, on the other hand, oral tradition is no longer a significant or respected source of knowledge. Its place is taken by histories of single and known authorship, printed and unchangeable documents with a written succession behind them of other histories and records by which their accuracy may be tested and secured. But this vast change comes only by degrees: at first only portions of tradition are written, and there is nothing, static or recorded, by which to test their accuracy or change.

---

[1] The Germanic people already possessed runic writing, suitable for brief inscriptions.
[2] See also H. M. and N. K. Chadwick, *The Growth of Literature* (1932-40), vol. 1, 481, 494, 500; vol. 2, 639; vol. 3, 698 and 865.
[3] The factual value, however, of the traditions of the backward peoples of the modern world is the subject of debate among social anthropologists.

Names of authors are rarely stated[1] and the rights of authors unrespected. There is no notion that a manuscript must not be supplemented because of the right of a deceased amanuensis that his work should remain unchanged. Even Cassiodorus (to whom, more than anyone else, we owe the survival of Latin texts in the sixth century), in his *Institutiones Divinarum Lectionum*, setting forth a plan of study for the monks of Vivarium, advises them that emendations in the sacred texts should be as well written as the originals, 'that they may rather be thought to have been written by the ancients'.

As oral tradition expands or alters, the copyist or possessor of a manuscript enlarges or corrects it to accord with contemporary tradition. For these and other reasons the earliest literature of all kinds is seen on examination to be the work of many authors, and is commonly attributed to a great name of the past, for others are unknown. So, great universalist prophecies are assigned to Isaiah and epic poems to Homer, just as great man-made objects in Southern Arabia and Aden are attributed to Solomon and the Queen of Sheba, or modern man attributes a painting to a great master. But tradition is not merely factual or intellectual: it expresses dreams and aspirations and is always in some measure affective and ideal. And as tradition develops and changes it does so in accordance with the aspirations and interests of the day, and similarly tradition recorded in literature is expanded and altered by the scribe in accordance with the ideals and interests of his time and especially the interests of the class of the scribe.

All this is especially true of law. It commonly grows and changes of itself without the aid of legislation. The scribe copying a code attributed to a past legislator often alters and expands it to embody rules current in his own time and attributed to the same author. Especially does this occur when the legislator did not legislate in writing and the scribe is recording the traditional version of his laws. There is perhaps one difference between the legal and other early literature, that codes and legislation are often

---

[1] For example, down to the First Exile no book of the Old Testament pretends to name its author; and the authenticity of any Anglo-Saxon charter which names its author is suspect (W. Levison, *England & the Continent in the Eighth Century* (1946) 227f.; D. Whitelock, *English Historical Documents* (1955), I, 341).

promulgated by kings by the new art of writing, while other early 'literature' is commonly handed down orally before it is written. Nevertheless, whether the code was originally issued in writing or not, the scribe will often expand or alter it to embody a contemporary rule. In varying degree, in both cases the document embodies an ideal – for law always partakes in some measure of the ideal, and the authority to enforce it is at first small. The scribe is always, till the close of our period, an ecclesiastic of sorts and expresses his interest and aspirations, and when the Hebrew faith and Christianity bring with them the almost unprecedented devotion of the people and influence of the Church, laws are recorded, as the words of a past, first legislator, which build and support its edifice and the rights and privileges of its servants. The extent, however, to which these phenomena occur varies vastly from one land to another and one document to another.

The chief fact that gives rise to this legal literature is the emergence of statutory legislation among the most primitive of the peoples mentioned in the previous chapter – that is to say, the Kentish people of Aethelberht and the Salic Franks of the Lex Salica – just as it emerges among recent peoples of similar economies.[1] Various circumstances call for legislation and make it possible: the increase in the number and density of the population and the area of its territory, the more frequent changes experienced by a less primitive economy, the growth of the authority of kings and of courts, the emergence and increase of rules of true law, relating especially to homicide and personal injuries, the appearance of a new consciousness of law and a new interest in it, the merger in one nation of several tribes, and, in a number of these cases, great changes in the fortunes of a people that have settled in a portion of the Empire of Rome, absorbed some of its culture and adopted its religion. Moreover some of these peoples, especially the Ostrogoths and the Lombards, who settled in Italy, knew and copied the practice of the Roman emperors, acquired from the magistrates of the Republic, to issue an *edict* setting out the laws and rules[2] which they would apply in their reign or office, and the Edictum Theoderici and the Edictus Rothari are the titles, so derived, of the codes of law issued by those rulers to their subjects. Others in similar situations, and notably the Visigoths

---

[1] See *post* Chap. 19.   [2] *Leges edictales* of the later Empire.

and Burgundians, promulgated codes of law to their nations, and this may be the meaning of Bede when he wrote of Aethelberht that 'among the other benefits that he conferred upon his people, he enacted legislation for it with the advice of his councillors according to the examples of the Romans'[1] – for the contents of the Laws of Aethelberht were in no way derived from Rome, nor even from its successor nations. But it may also be added that in the century that witnessed the issue of the Codex Theodosianus and the Code of Justinian, law and statutory law were in the fashion of the times. In sum, the emerging law of these primitive peoples had reached such dimensions as to make them conscious of its existence, nature and importance; the constitution of society was changing and the acquisition of the art of writing enabled the legislation to be made or recorded in that form.

That the bulk of the earliest legal literature was or originated in legislation can hardly be doubted. The whole succession of the Anglo-Saxon, Scottish and Welsh laws is attributed to the legislative acts of kings, the bulk of the contemporary continental laws are largely the work of royal legislators,[2] and so are the bulk of the ancient and mediaeval laws of the Near East.[3] Where there was no kingship, other law-givers are named. Many Greek city-states in the colonies and the mother country from about 660 B.C. onwards[4] had each their own first reputed legislator, and the names of many survive but hardly anything of their work.

Most of the laws that survive were issued as 'codes', the nature of which we shall presently examine, and this is equally true of the most primitive of these, for example the Laws of Aethelberht (which only survive in one manuscript of five hundred years later), and the most advanced, the laws of Hammurabi (which exist on the stone on which they were promulgated). Some had been drawn up by men familiar with the existence of codes, who mainly recorded the current law, either at the behest of a royal master, such as Charlemagne,[5] or because no common ruler existed with power to legislate for the whole society (and the latter is traditionally

---

[1] 'decreta illi iudiciorum iuxta exempla Romanorum cum consilio sapientium constituit' (Hist. Eccl., II, 5, completed about A.D. 731).
[2] The Visigothic, Burgundian, Ostrogothic, Lombard and Russian Codes.
[3] See the previous chapters.
[4] Of the stage, it would appear, of the Late Codes.
[5] The Lex Saxonum, Frisionum, Thuringorum, Francorum Chamavorum.

true of the earliest Irish Laws and Lex Salica)[1] but even the bulk of these were at some date issued by a ruler. Those that were not must be regarded with care as less trustworthy accounts of the law and less characteristic of law and the forms and functions of law. They include, for example, the Lex Alamannorum and Lex Baiuvariorum and the Irish Laws.

Most of the codes were handed down, by the scribes who copied or recorded them, as the corpus of the rules of the national law, and were added to and amended by subsequent legislators or the copyists and scribes to meet current needs or embody current traditions. But they remained unique and, so to say, official in each nation as long as its independence lasted, for although numerous copies survive of many of the codes, and they often vary under the hands of different scribes, they are versions of the same code and we never have knowledge of rival compilations.[2] Sometimes, indeed, as in the Frankish Empire,[3] or in ancient Judaea, where conquered peoples are permitted to live by their own law, a rule contained in a people's code might long outlive its independence.

There is a continuing tendency for a code of primitive law to become in time a history of the law and a law-book.[4] The scribe records the legislation of the king and it has then already become in a sense a history, and it is usually expanded and amended, as it is handed down, to embody other legislation or traditions. Writing materials are scant and dear, and as this is at first commonly the only literature, it is used to teach reading and writing and as a means of general education, in which law is a chief subject of study;[5] and so it becomes a law-book, especially where there are specialist law-scribes. At some few times and places it may come to embrace other genres, such as poetry in Ireland or religious teaching elsewhere according to the interests of the scribes, and throughout it remains in some measure a literary and philosophic exercise.

[1] See the introductions to those Codes.
[2] These considerations are perhaps most clearly instanced in the texts of the Lex Salica and the fragments of the Hittite Code.
[3] e.g. rules of the Burgundian Code of Gundobad.
[4] Each tended to be a *rechtsbuch* as well as a *gesetzbuch*.
[5] For example the Twelve Tables, the Code of Hammurabi and the Irish Laws.

One view, however, often expressed of the codes is that they were mere collections of judgments of the courts, but this is erroneous. Then, as now, the origin of some legislation may have been a decision of a court on a topical question, and it may have been desired to reverse its effect or clarify the law. There was less distinction than now between a decision of a court and a decision of the ruler. In the king's court sat the king or his representative along with his advisers; the decision looked like a judgment and also a legislative act; and some such decision might be of sufficient general importance to be incorporated in a code or law-book. Many early laws fixed sanctions where there was yet no general standard nor usage and opinions or judgments varied.[1] But we are often told that a rule in a code represented a change made by the king, especially an increase or decrease in the amount of a pecuniary sanction,[2] and there were other more radical amendments as we shall see. The notion, therefore, to which Maine's *Ancient Law* has given currency, that the codes were mere collections of existing customs, which were only subsequently altered, first by fictions, then by equity and last by legislation,[3] has no substance.

All genuine codes are couched in the natural language of statutory legislation, namely conditional sentences in the third person, the protasis containing the facts supposed, and the apodosis the sanction. Nowhere is there to be found a rule of law in the second person. Nowhere is there a rule of law without its sanction.[4] The arrangement of topics, such as it is, is the natural arrangement of statutory legislation, namely according to the *external* subject matter of the rule – homicide, wounding, theft (including the vouching of a vendor), sexual offences (adultery being often regarded as a species of theft), problems relating to cattle or land,

[1] Strabo VI, I, 8, preserves a remark of Ephorus to the effect that the Greek legislators fixed the sanctions and no longer left them to be assessed at the arbitrary will of the judges.
[2] See Edictus Rothari 74 (increases); Hittite Code (decreases in several places); Gulathing Law 22 (Magnus provides permanent outlawry for the offence of killing a child, for which Olaf had decreed a penalty of three marks).
[3] A.L., 25.
[4] It must be noted, however, that several codes include a few rules of inheritance and procedure, and here the sanction is implied rather than expressed.

offences by and against slaves, problems concerning women (including bridewealth), inheritance and so on. Throughout the primitive law the arrangement is never according to internal principle – but it should be added that principle, so far as it has come into existence, is generally pragmatic and materialist. And the problems handled are all the topical questions disputed in the courts: so, even in the Code of Hammurabi, because sale is generally a mutual transfer of goods and cash, there is hardly mention of barter or sale, and there is no mention of intentional homicide because it raised no problem.

We must not understand the word 'code' as referring to a complete statement of the law of a country, though many codes evidence an attempt to achieve such.

There is a mass of authority for saying that legislators copied the work of others. Ephorus says that Zaleucus[1] adopted laws from Cretan, Spartan and Athenian sources.[2] Plutarch[3] tells us that the Spartan legislator, Lycurgus, studied the legislation of Crete, Ionia, Egypt, and perhaps Libya, Iberia and India. Herodotus[4] says that Spartan institutions came from Crete, and Charondas[5] is said to have adopted the best from the laws of many peoples. Livy, following the fashion of Greek historians, tells us that the Commission of Three appointed to draft the Roman Code was 'despatched to Athens to copy the famous laws of Solon and to learn the institutions, customs and laws of other Greek states'.[6] Alfred[7] says that he collected the most just laws of the time of Ine, Offa[8] and Aethelberht, and did not dare to add many of his own; and in many peoples rulers commonly took over the code of their predecessors with or without amendment. The closing sentences of the epilogue to Hammurabi's Code are taken directly or indirectly from that of Lipit Ishtar of Isin, of a century earlier, or a common source, and the same can now be said of several of his laws, and within each field of culture there are more resemblances between the codes of peoples of similar economic status than are found elsewhere. In modern times there is a growing

---

[1] Of Achaean Locris.   [2] Strabo VI, I, 8.
[3] Lycurgus IV.   [4] Herodotus I, 65f.
[5] Of Catana about 660 B.C., traditionally the first Greek legislator.
[6] Livy 3, 31.   [7] Alf., Introd. 49, 9.
[8] These do not survive.

measure of conscious adaptation of advances made by other nations, but among primitive peoples communications are poor, and laws are not generally to be explained by conscious adoption, nor is every story of the kind to be accepted. Identical laws are rare and much similarity results from independent advances accompanying similar development in material culture.

A further misconception to which the works of Maine have chiefly given rise – and it is indeed fundamental to his theory of the history of law – is that law is derived from pre-existing rules of conduct which are at the same time legal, moral and religious in nature, 'the severance of law from morality, and of religion from law, belonging very distinctly to the later stages of mental progress'.[1] Although the acceptance of this belief seems, in part at least, to be due to a general tendency of mankind to people distant times and regions with the supernatural, and to look there for the abode of elusive gods and spirits, it was chiefly Maine who called in aid the evidence of the codes. 'Quite enough', he says, 'remains of these collections, both in the East and in the West, to show that they mingled up religious, civil and merely moral ordinances, without any regard to differences in their essential character';[2] and again, 'There is no system of recorded law, literally from China to Peru, which when it first emerges into notice, is not seen to be entangled with religious ritual and observance'.[3]

There is no reason why anyone, who does not desire to do so, should confuse religion with law, though their frontiers do touch in two places in modern as in primitive times.[4] Turning from these passages to the codes, and remembering that the scribes of the latter were ecclesiastics, it must surprise the reader to see how little is the volume of religious matter in them. The codes show no confusion between law and religion, and the presence of such religious matter as they do contain is due to the ecclesiastical office and interest of the scribes. In the most advanced of our codes, that is to say, the whole of the laws of Sumerians, Babylonians and Assyrians and the English laws from the thirteenth century onwards, although writing is still chiefly the province of

[1] A.L. 16.   [2] *Ibid.*   [3] E.L. & C. 5.
[4] Namely in the sacral crimes (e.g. sacrilege) and in the administration of the oath or other ordeal in litigation.

C*

ecclesiastics there are no religious rules.[1] But the most primitive
codes also contain no religious matter – the Laws of Aethelberht,
and of Hlothhere and Eadric, the Leges inter Brettos et Scotos,
the Pravda of Jaroslav, the Laws of George V of Georgia, and the
Salic Code. Most also of the codes of intermediate stages have
none or almost none – the Twelve Tables, the Hebrew Code and
the Hittite a word or two[2] – but in some of the intermediate codes
of England and the Continent we see religious matter entering
about A.D. 700 and later diminishing,[3] and the reasons are not far
to seek.

At first the scribe who records or copies the legislation has no
other part to play in the law. In the early days of the kingdoms of
Kent and Salic France the task of the Church was the conversion
of the heathen. It took and could take small active interest in the
secular affairs of the state: it was concerned with the City of God;
and the scribe was content to record with some faithfulness and
much ignorance the legislation of a king. But by the early eighth
century in England and the Continent the scene had changed. The
wealth and secular power of the Church and the religious foundations had been vastly enlarged by the constant gifts of the devout,
and the first clause of two large codes of that date is concerned to
maintain the flow.[4] As a great landowner[5] the Church was judging
disputes between its tenants. By its sole possession of any learning
in that ignorant age, it was becoming one of the chief advisers of
the Crown and sat upon its councils and advised upon its measures
and upon the decisions of appeals to the king. Moreover, by
churchly influence (as we shall later see)[6] the primitive ordeals of

[1] For the early law of India, see Chap. 9. There the unusual situation is to
be seen that the rulers did not legislate in writing, and accordingly the
earliest literature is purely religious, and legal matter enters as the
brahman acquires a place and practical interest in the administration of
justice.

[2] In the Hebrew Code only the words 'and its flesh shall not be eaten' (Ex.
21²⁸). In the Hittite Code perhaps, I, 44b and II, 51-5 and a clause at the
end. There is reason in both codes for thinking these words to be later
additions (see *post* pp. 151, 180).

[3] On the Continent it is confined to two codes of the eighth century – namely
the Lex Alamannorum and the Lex Baiuvariorum.

[4] L Alam., L Bai. (see below).

[5] In France already before the close of the eighth century it is estimated
that the Church held a third of all land, but this figure may be too high.

[6] *Post* Chap. 21.

litigation were now undergone upon the altar, and the ordeal by oath, administered by the priest, was beginning to supplant them (especially on the Continent) and the extent of the use of an ordeal had rapidly increased. Further the religious orders had found it necessary to lay down laws for the administration of the sanctuaries where homicides were taking refuge in growing numbers, and there to try disputed guilt. Moreover they were beginning to hear disputes among their flock on matters of special interest to the Church – marriage, inheritance, heresy and some other sacral offences[1] – and in addition a growing body of canon law governed relations between the servants of the Church and between the Church and the faithful.

In these divers ways the Church acquired a practical interest in law and its administration and in some of our codes of the eighth century it is expressed and entwined. Law was indeed employed to further the spiritual and material objects of the religious foundations, and as writing was now available to record transfers by the faithful it was important to monasteries and other ecclesiastical institutions to possess documents of title to the land they held or claimed when the gift was contested by the ruler or the donor's next of kin. Many were the forged charters, in the possession of abbeys and monasteries, conferring upon them titles to rights they claimed. All the charters of Aethelberht have been shown to be spurious.[2] Many were the false decretals which went to the building of the canon law. Collections of material from unknown sources travelled from country to country, receiving accretions as they went. The Hispana of the seventh century was finally enlarged in the middle of the ninth century into the fraudulent compilation of the pseudo-Isidore and, accepted by the Popes, formed the foundation of a great legal structure. The collection of four books of capitularies (that is to say, legislation) made about

---

[1] To some extent, however, this was probably a continuation and extension of the practice, in the fourth and fifth centuries, under which Romans of Christian faith, to avoid the jurisdiction of a pagan judge, submitted their disputes to their religious leaders as arbitrators, as the Jews to theirs (see already a law of the Emperor Constantine about A.D. 318 – Cod. Theod. I, 27 – of doubtful authenticity), but most of these subjects are the province of the ecclesiastical courts everywhere – for example among the Hebrews and in the former British possessions in the East (such as Malaya, Palestine and Aden) and still in Israel.

[2] W. Levison, *England & the Continent in the Eighth Century* (1946) 174-233.

the year 827 by Ansegisus, was expanded some thirty years later by Benedictus Levita by the addition of three further books containing fragments of the Lex Romana Visigothorum, canons of church councils and such materials as are found in the contemporary compilation of the false Isidore. Forgery is an important source of law.

To the same series of phenomena belong the two continental codes containing religious matter – the Lex Alamannorum and the Lex Baiuvariorum, the former of the first half of the eighth century and the latter of the second half, both being celebrated codes contained in numerous manuscripts of the late eighth and subsequent centuries. The prologues, in which their authors are named, are contradictory and entirely unacceptable.[1] The former commences with a section of clauses (1-23), embracing a third of the code and consisting of ecclesiastical law, in which the authors claim rights for the Church and punish wrongs against it, and in some of the other provisions of the code the sanctions are purely religious.[2] The later code goes further, and if the Lex Alamannorum is a compendium of laws of that nature conceived and drafted to enhance the status of the Church, the Lex Baiuvariorum belongs to the domain of the spurious.[3] The greater part of it is taken from the Lex Alamannorum and the Visigothic Codes of

[1] The prologue to the L. Alam. attributes that code to 'the time of Hlothar' (Hlothar II was a Frankish king of about 614 to 629) who, it alleges, published it 'together with 33 bishops, 34 dukes, 65 counts and the rest of the people' (the numbers vary a little in the texts). The prologue to the L. Bai., after a brief history of law from Moses onwards, attributes both these codes to 'Theodoric, King of the Franks', at whose instigation wise men, learned in the ancient laws of the realm, reduced to writing the customs of the Franks, Alamanni and Baiuvarii, each of which nations was in his power, but additions and corrections were made by him and other named rulers. Theodoric, one of the sons of Clovis, ruled one of the Frankish kingdoms about 511 to 534, but none of the above statements can be true.
[2] There follows a section (clauses 24-36) concerned with offences against the ruler and the state. The remainder consists mainly of civil offences, of which clauses 36-57 are of miscellaneous import, but clauses 38-42 contain purely religious offences. Patricide, matricide, perjury and working on the sabbath are declared to be sins. Clauses 58-66 are a tariff of sanctions for personal injuries, and 67-75 are again miscellaneous.
[3] Or perhaps it might be called, with equal justice and more charity, a draft of a body of laws for the Baiuvarii by private hands, taken mainly from other codes, bearing little relation to the actual law of that people, and attributing itself to ancient royal legislators laying down and amending customary rules.

Euric and Reccesswinth, and much of the rest from Roman law sources.

In the opening clause of the Lex Baiuvariorum[1] it is provided that

> 'whenever a free person makes a will and gives his property to the Church for the redemption of his soul,[2] let him have leave to do so with his own share after he has made division with his sons. Let no one prevent him; let neither king nor duke[3] nor any person have power to prevent him. And whatever he has given, houses, land, slaves or any other property, whatever he has given for the redemption of his soul, let him confirm in writing by his own hand, and let him bring 6 witnesses, or more if they are willing, and let them put their hands on the writing and mark their names at his request. Then let him put the writing on the altar, and so let him hand over the money in the presence of the priest who serves in that place. And thereafter let him have no power over it, neither he nor his posterity, unless the defender of the Church be willing to grant him the favour, but let the things of the Church be defended by the bishop, whatever is given by Christians to the Church of God.'

In the following clause it is provided that if anyone desires to defraud the Church or abstract property of the Church, whether he who has made a gift or his heirs or anyone else,

> 'first let him incur the judgment of God and the offence of the holy Church and let him pay to the earthly judge 3 ounces of gold, and let him return that property to the Church and add other like property under compulsion of the king or the prince who is judge in that region.'

In another clause,[4] relating to the privilege of sanctuary attached to the Church, it is laid down that no refugee is to be dragged

---

[1] Taken from the opening clause of the L. Alam., with few alterations.
[2] See Proverbs 13[8].
[3] L. Alam. 1, has 'let neither duke nor count'. A provision that the ruler shall have no power to do a thing is a useful criterion of false law.
[4] Tit. 1, cap. 7.

away until he has appealed to the presbyter or bishop. 'Let there be no fault so heinous that life be not granted, for fear of God and reverence of his saints, for the Lord hath said "Whosoever shall pardon, it shall be pardoned to him. Whosoever shall not pardon, neither shall it be pardoned to him ".'[1] Elsewhere is a description of the qualities of the ideal judge.[2]

With this code should be compared the Laws of Wihtred of Kent, another document of the eighth century, the earliest and best text of which is of the early twelfth century. It is the first extant English code to contain any religious matter. The prologue ascribes the laws to a date in the fifth year of his reign (about 695) when, as it states, it was issued at a deliberative council of the notables, at which were present

> Birhtwald, high bishop of Britain, and the aforesaid King and the bishop of Rochester (who was called Gybmund); and every order of the church of the province was unanimous with the laity of the realm. There the notables, with the agreement of all, drew up these laws and added them to the legal usages of Kent, as is hereafter stated and declared.

'The Church', says the first clause, 'shall be free of taxation, and the king shall be prayed for and they shall honour him freely without compulsion.' Clause 2 provides that 'The mundbyrd of the church[3] shall be 50 shillings like the king's'. Only the last four clauses (25-28) are of a secular nature[4] and would appear to be a later addition.

Contemporary with these are the Laws of Ine of Wessex. He reigned from 688 to 725, but the earliest text is of the tenth century. It is a very long, miscellaneous and disorderly collection. The quality is again poor – rules of ecclesiastical law and practice, some rules of procedure for the taking of ordeals in the churches, unlikely secular laws – and we can see the pattern of the English codes forming itself. The other Wessex code is that of Alfred

---

[1] See Matthew 6[14, 15].   [2] Tit. 2, cap. 16.
[3] i.e., the sum payable for breach of its right of protection.
[4] §§ 3-15 provide sanctions for various religious offences; §§ 16-24 lay down formalities for the taking of an oath of purgation by members of different classes of the population.

(reigned 871 to 900), contained in the same tenth-century manuscript. It is preceded by an enormous introduction of forty-eight chapters, consisting of sundry passages from Exodus, a summary of apostolic history with quotations from the Acts of the Apostles, and a brief account of the rise and growth of church law. In a passage that follows Alfred describes the Code as a collection of laws which his predecessors (Ine, Offa and Aethelberht) observed, except those of which he did not approve. 'For I did not dare to presume to set down in writing many of my own, for I do not know what will please those who come after us.' It is, therefore, a literary exercise, like those of Wihtred and Ine and the Lex Alamannorum and Lex Baiuvariorum. The contents are miscellaneous in their topics, unconvincing and disorderly, except for a long tariff of sanctions for wounds, reminiscent of that of Aethelberht, but with higher sums of compensation.[1]

The Anglo-Saxon laws which follow are, in large measure, of similar type. There can have been little general legislation after Aethelberht's day, and these documents, some brief, some long, are unconvincing records of it. They are literature rather than law: some purely religious and ecclesiastical in their subject-matter and sanctions;[2] some wholly secular;[3] some a mixture of secular and religious subjects and sanctions.[4] The quality of all is poor and has descended far from the code of Aethelberht: they evince little observation of the secular law in force, and little progress from the earlier to the later of these codes, each drawing largely on the contents of previous documents and written some decades, at least, after the reign to which it refers, recording, upon matters of interest to the religious author, what he believed or wished the king had produced.

The conquest of England by the Normans gave an impetus to the production of this Anglo-Saxon literature, and in the twelfth and thirteenth centuries the series is continued by other documents which, though purely secular after 1200, do not otherwise differ

[1] §§ 44-77 (the final clauses). After the orderly procedure from head to toe (§§ 44-64) a miscellaneous and disorderly collection is added (§§ 65-77), which is therefore presumably of later date.
[2] e.g. Aethelstan I, Edmund I, Edgar II, Aethelred V-X, Canute, Proclamation of 1027, Canute I.
[3] e.g. Edgar I and III, Aethelred I-III.
[4] Edgar IV, Canute, Proclamation of 1020, Canute II.

essentially from what precedes. Now it becomes easier to check
their accuracy as records of law, and the Leges Edwardi Con-
fessoris, the Leis Willelme, Leges Henrici I, Constitutiones de
Foresta, Rectitudines Singularum Personarum, De Veteri Con-
suetudine Promotionum, Mirror of Justices and other documents
are generally regarded by the legal historian as untrustworthy
versions of the law,[1] as are also many or most of the early legal
productions of Scotland.[2]

[1] Even as late as 1291, Britton's serious treatise on the law of England,
though largely based on Bracton, is put into the mouth of the king. But
what we do not blame in Thucydides' speeches we cannot reprehend in
peoples so much more backward. The difference is in the quality.
[2] See *ante* p. 32.

· civil to criminal

· intentional homicide

· consequential loss

· executory contract of

      sale

CHAPTER 5

The Early Codes of the Past – Barbarism

The most primitive codes that survive from the past are called in
this book the Early Codes. They are mainly the laws of the barbarian peoples of Western Europe, in England between A.D. 600
and 900 and on the Continent from 500 to 800, ending in England *dates*
with the Laws of Alfred the Great[1] (which we include) and ending
on the Continent just before the codes of Charles the Great[2]
(which we exclude and count among our Central Codes of the
next stage).[3] We must also, however, exclude for this purpose the
codes of the Visigoths, Burgundians and Ostrogoths, for they
had lived for long in the Roman Empire and absorbed much of
Roman culture, and it is therefore not surprising that their laws
are characteristic of our Late Codes. The Lombard Code of
Rothari, the law of a people who had resided for a shorter period
in the Empire and were less changed by Rome, belongs, in spite
of its early date, to our Central Codes. We define, therefore, our
Early Codes by date as being laws characteristic of peoples of the
material status of England between 600 and 900, as it slowly rose
during those centuries, and with the exceptions that we have
mentioned, the continental laws of 500 to 800 are of the same
category. So is the code of the Scottish border, the Leges inter
Brettos et Scotos, several centuries later but as primitive as any.
The Russian Code, Jaroslav's Pravda of the first half of the eleventh
century, and the Code of George V of Georgia, of the first half
of the fourteenth, belong to the close of our Early Codes.

[1] The Laws of Alfred (about A.D. 890 – he died 901) are, as he says, mainly
a collection of laws of earlier dates as amended by him, with few added laws
of his own.
[2] Died 814.
[3] For the Anglo-Saxon texts, translations and commentaries see Attenborough
(1922) and Liebermann; for the Continent see *ante* p. 29f.

economic
definition

Apart from criteria of date, we define our Early Codes, and distinguish them from codes of the next stage, the Central Codes, in the following economic terms. The material culture of these peoples is the most primitive among all who have produced written codes. They live by agriculture and cattle-keeping with subsidiary hunting, and no longer cattle-keeping with subsidiary agriculture and hunting.[1] They are settled in their territories, but their kings are still called kings of their people, not of their land.[2] Kings are almost everywhere[3] and the strength of kingship has grown, but local chiefs and the local and kinship groups wield powerful influences in the social structure. The laws contain as yet only the slightest evidence of an emerging feudalism.[4] There is no mention in the Codes of the sale of land. Till the end of this period there is no mention of markets or market towns. At first no laws fix prices,[5] for they change extremely slowly: the currency is at first tied to cattle or sheep,[6] and apart from domestic animals (including horses and their equipment) there is little of value,[7] and there is a traditional ratio between the prices of these domestic species. The only commercial transactions are barter and cash sale. There is no mention of hiring or commercial deposit. There are a few foreign traders, regarded with great suspicion. The populations are very small: at the beginning of our period the average size of one of the seven English Kingdoms is about 100,000, but the Mercian and Merovingian Kingdoms rise to some 300,000. The population is sparse – some ten persons to the square mile – and, as among the Germans of Tacitus, lives mainly in homesteads or in hamlets of three or four isolated households, in huts of wattle and daub near a spring or stream, from which it pastures its animals and practises a largely shifting cultivation.

[1] See Tac. Germ. 5 and 25.   [2] See note *post* p. 271.
[3] In Tacitus only some of the tribes had kings.
[4] In England the only signs are Ine 39 and Alf. 37 (sanction for anyone moving away without permission from his lord and stealing into another district); and Ine 57 (a nobleman who holds land and neglects to do military service). But no code contains much that relates to feudalism.
[5] Not till Ine 59, and L. Rib. 36.
[6] In Aethelberht's day the Kentish (golden) shilling was probably the price of a cow. It consisted of 20 (silver) sceattas, the sceatta being the predecessor of the penny. In Ine's Wessex (a sheep-rearing community) the (silver) shilling consisted of 4, later 5, pence and was the price of a sheep.
[7] Chiefly arms, articles of dress and personal adornment, and domestic equipment.

legal

We define the Early Codes in legal terms as follows. The *definition* sanctions imposed for civil (i.e. private) wrongs are pecuniary,[1] and among these the sanctions for homicide and wounding are pecuniary. The king takes part of the sums representing the sanctions for many of the more serious civil wrongs, but apart from this the criminal law is in its infancy and is hardly mentioned. Mutilations (except of slaves) are almost unknown. The bride-wealth marriage is everywhere, and the marriage-settlement is unknown.

The grand traditions of English law and English literature both *Laws of* commence with the Laws of Aethelberht, one of the most in- *Aethelberht* teresting and least known legal documents in the history of England and the oldest literary work (excepting translations and inscriptions) in any Teutonic tongue. At the close of the sixth century, Kent was the most advanced kingdom in England, which then and till after the Conquest was a full century behind the Continent. Aethelberht reigned in 597 when the mission from Pope Gregory arrived under the monk Augustine and in that year he was converted to Christianity with many of his Court. The laws survive only in the Textus Roffensis of the twelfth century, five hundred years later than his reign. The language is of a primitive simplicity, containing linguistic forms of various centuries between the seventh and the twelfth, but the later forms may be due to modernising copyists. 'These are the laws', runs the superscription, 'which King Aethelberht laid down in Augustine's day'[2] – obviously the words of a later scribe and ecclesiastic, for he seems as much interested in Augustine as in the king and he may well have drawn the phrase from the introduction to the Hebrew Code: 'These are the laws (*mishpatim*) which thou (Moses) shalt set before them'.[3] *Dom*, like *mishpat* and many another early word for law, judgment, justice, right and custom, marked the truth that law declared itself chiefly in the judgments of a court. The corresponding word of the contemporary Latin codes of the Continent was *judicium*, by which *dom* or a similar word was translated. Nevertheless it is a legislative code, though we do not know to what extent the laws were new. Like all true laws of all

---

[1] In terms of cattle or currency.
[2] 'þis syndon þa domas, þe Aeðelbirht cyning asette on Augustinus daege.'
[3] Ex. 21[1].

lands and ages they are couched in conditional sentences in the third person, the language of legislation. 'If a man binds a free man, he shall pay twenty shillings compensation.'[1]

There is no sufficient reason for doubting that Aethelberht legislated for the altered circumstances of his kingdom, perhaps with the advice of some continental monkish scribe with legal interests, nor for rejecting the laws as a code of the early seventh century which has sustained little alteration since. That in Bede's day, a century later, such a code existed, attributed to the king, cannot be doubted and even the most questionable clause in it is partly supported by a passage in his *Historia Ecclesiae*.[2] Indeed of all the Anglo-Saxon and early Norman laws it has the best claim to be considered authentic.[3]

The order of the clauses of the code shows an extreme consciousness of distinctions between social classes – a characteristic which it might not seem fanciful to describe as English, and is equally found in the Leges inter Brettos et Scotos. First (clause 1), as in some contemporary continental codes, come wrongs against the Church and the hierarchy of its servants: '[Theft of] God's property and the Church's [shall be paid for] 12 fold; a bishop's property 11 fold; a priest's property 9 fold; a deacon's property 6 fold; a clerk's property 3 fold. Breach of a church's peace 2 fold. Breach of peace of a meeting 2 fold.' Next (clauses 2 to 12) are wrongs against the king, not only directly (for example, 'If a freeman steals from the King he shall pay 9 fold')[4] but also against his *mund* or protection. So 'the king's *mundbyrd*' – i.e. the sum payable for a violation of his protection – 'is 50 shillings' (§ 8), and where a man is slain on the king's premises (§ 5) or a man lies

---

[1] Clause 24: 'Gif man frigne man gebindeþ, xx scill' gebete.'

[2] See *ante* p. 43. The passage continues, 'which, composed in the tongue of the English, are still kept and observed by them. In these, in the first place, he laid down how a man should pay compensation for theft of anything of the church, or a bishop or the other orders, wishing no doubt to give protection to those whom he had received and whose doctrine he had accepted.'

[3] The only doubt should be whether this is not a literary exercise by such a seventh-century scribe, based on legislation of the king, and the present author entertains such a doubt.

[4] Note that the sum is less than that paid for theft of property of the Church or a bishop, and only equivalent to that for a priest's. The authenticity of this is difficult to credit: but see note (2) above.

with a maiden belonging to the king (§ 10) 50 shillings[1] is to be paid to him in addition to any compensation to the kinship group of the person directly wronged. Clauses 13 and 14 concern offences against a nobleman (12 shillings for slaying another on a nobleman's premises or lying with his serving-maid). From clauses 15 to 72 is the general law of wrongs against a free commoner – 'A commoner's *mundbyrd* [shall be] 6 shillings '(§ 15). 'If one man slays another the usual wergeld to be paid shall be 100 shillings,' (§ 22) but only 80 for a *laet* (half-free) of the best class, 60 for one of the second class, and 40 for one of the third. Then from clauses 33 to 72 is a tariff-list of sums of compensation for injuries to the different parts of the body in order, commencing at the top of the body with 50 pence for seizing a man by the hair, and ending with a sum of 10 pence for loss of a toe-nail. From § 73 to § 84 is a group of clauses dealing with the common problems relating to women. The *mundbyrd* of a widow of the best class (the nobility) is 50 shillings – equivalent to that of the king – diminishing down to 6 shillings for a widow of the fourth class. If a man takes a widow who does not belong to him (i.e. whom he is not entitled to inherit) he pays double the value of the mund. The bridewealth marriage remains in force (§ 77). The sanction for forcibly carrying off a maiden is a fixed sum to the owner, and the bridewealth is also paid (§ 82). The share of a widow on the death of her husband, or of a wife parting from her husband, is defined. The final section (85-90) concerns wrongs by and against unfree servants and slaves.

One of the most important characteristics of this, one of the most primitive of all our codes, is that it is entirely secular and contains no religious or ethical rules or sanctions but only law. Secondly it contains no word of procedure; and thirdly, no reference to any commercial transaction.

The Kentish laws continue with a second group, contained in the same manuscript and attributed in the superscription to Hlothere and Eadric who reigned about 673 to 685 and 685 to 686, and it is said that they extended the laws[2] which their predecessors had made, by the *domas* there stated. These laws are few (sixteen in

---

[1] Equivalent to the price of 50 cows or the compensation for striking off a man's foot, or half a free man's wergeld, or £3,000 in present money.
[2] The word aew is used, which only occurs in the superscription to these laws and those of Ine.

number) and consist of additional, miscellaneous provisions, some concerned with special facts less common and simple, and others with sale and traders; the clauses are couched in later and different language[1] and in a style less terse; they begin with the topic with which the Laws of Aethelberht had ended, namely wrongs by servants. There is still no religious matter, but now a few procedural rules appear.[2] In the subsequent English Codes of Wihtred and Ine, religious matter makes its first appearance.

In the Early Codes of the Continent we see a similar succession. The Lex Salica, contained in a number of texts of which the earliest are of the late eighth century and the ninth, is a substantial code of sixty-five and more chapters, which was probably edited and published in Clovis' time, about A.D. 500, and amended by his successors of the sixth century. It is a monument of the unlettered ignorance of the Frankish scribes and there is also much variation between the different versions contained in the manuscripts, but all are couched in a barbarous Latin, the work of copyists as unfamiliar with that language as with the Frankish law-terms which they misquote. In the earlier part (that is to say, Chaps. 2 to 38) there are no provisions relating to procedure and no religious matter. Chapters 1 and 39 to the end include several descriptions of procedural practices, in a new and diffuse style.

The code of the kindred Ripuarian Franks, of which the earliest texts are of similar date, shows a like history of development. The oldest part (Chaps. 1 to 29) contains no procedural matter.[3] Chapters 32 to 56 are later, and draw heavily on an older version of the Lex Salica than we possess, whose chapters they often repeat in the same order, but without its procedural matter. Chapter 57 to the end of the Lex Ribuaria are later still and include some procedure. Religious rules and religious sanctions, as we have seen, make their first appearance in two eighth-century codes of doubtful authenticity – the Lex Alamannorum and Lex Baiuvariorum. The Scottish, Russian and Georgian Codes of this stage are purely secular and contain no word of procedure.

[1] The word riht, meaning law, custom, justice and right, now occurs – six times in these short laws, though it does not occur at all in Aethelberht.
[2] §§ 2, 4, 5 and 16 (as to witnesses and their evidence); 8, 9 and 10 (the provision of sureties for obedience to the court's decision); 5, 10 and 16 (oaths of purgation); 7 and 16 (vouching a warrantor).
[3] Though its rules have been adapted to the current state of the law.

These circumstances indicate that to the barbarian of the day rules of law and not the procedure were the essence of the matter – a simple truth that might have appeared self-evident but for a widespread view of primitive law which well-known dicta of Maine have helped to spread – namely that to early man a rule of procedure predominates in importance over a rule of substance, so that substantive law has at first the look of being gradually secreted in the interstices of procedure, and the early lawyer can only see the law through the envelope of its technical forms.[1]

More important, it is plain that in these Early Codes we are still near the beginnings of law in the full sense of that word – namely, rules of conduct enforceable by an organ of the state – and that law arises chiefly to appease dangerous resentments arising from private injuries, and thereby to preserve the peace. The main private wrongs are of four classes, namely, homicide, personal injuries short of death, wrongful sexual intercourse (that is to say, rape, adultery and seduction) and theft, and throughout the Early Codes (subject to certain special cases) the sanctions are pecuniary and the chief function of the law is to fix them. The most primitive of the Early Codes, namely the Leges inter Brettos et Scotos, provide for nothing but homicide and wounding. In the Laws of Aethelberht eighty-five out of ninety clauses provide sanctions for these four classes and a few other civil injuries, and in the early parts of the Lex Salica and Lex Ribuaria the proportion is as high.[2] Though the proportion later diminishes and the character of the sanctions changes, the provision of sanctions for private

private wrongs of four classes

---

[1] *E.L. & C.* 389. But the wide acceptance of this view requires more to explain it. All courts must have their procedure and there is an abundance of it in modern systems, wherever the jurisdiction of courts is limited. To a weak court, anxious to dismiss a claim or be excused a decision, procedural objections will be welcome. The conscience of the lawyer, disturbed by the amount of procedure in his own system, will impel him to support gladly this complaint against early systems. Rules of procedure that have become out of date, or are not fully understood in their sociological context by the historian, are apt to appear meaningless and therefore technical. There is very little of procedure in any code of primitive law, and in the ancient Near East technicalities even in the substantive law of the Late Codes were plainly very few.

[2] In Jaroslav's Pravda (short version) the provisions relate to homicide, personal injuries and offences against property. In the Code of King George V of Georgia there is practically nothing but homicide (18 clauses), wounding (11 clauses), wife stealing and desertion (7 clauses) and theft (2).

wrongs remains the chief activity of the law throughout the primitive era. It is, as it were, the foundation and centre of the legal system, so that this being the main need of the community in the sphere of law, especially in regard to homicide, we shall find so close a correspondence between economic development and the sanction for homicide in all our primitive peoples as to enable us in large measure to ascertain the one from the other.

The sanctions are overwhelmingly compensatory – that is to say, civil and not criminal – but compensatory of wounded feelings as well as bodily injury and loss, and just as, with us, the same act is often a wrong against the state or ruler (that is, a public wrong or a crime) as well as a wrong against an individual (a tort, delict or civil injury), so in the Early Codes. A sum of money is paid to the wronged individual or family group and sometimes a sum to the king in respect of the same wrong, and in addition there are a number of offences against the king or state alone, and some are serious crimes, punishable by a fine to the king or a capital sentence after trial (if a trial is necessary) before the king. The chief criminal offences are treason, desertion in battle, incest, bestiality and witchcraft causing death. The situation, therefore, remains much as it was in Tacitus' brief but accurate account of the Germans of his day:

> In the assembly are also heard criminal and capital charges. There is a distinction in the punishments according to the offence. Traitors and deserters are hung from trees, the cowards and the unwarlike and those guilty of bodily foulness are buried in the mud of the marsh with wattle over them.

Lesser wrongs, the civil injuries, are punished in proportion:

> the sanction on condemnation consists of a number of horses or cattle. Part of the amount is paid to the king or state, part to the injured man or his near relatives.[1]

But little or nothing is said of crime till we reach the more advanced of our Early Codes, and little is said of it in any primitive laws. For this there are probably two main reasons: one, that

[1] Tac. Germ. 12.

the codes are chiefly instructions for layman judges, and serious crime is heard by the king or his court: second, that trial and punishment of crime remains till long after the primitive age a matter for rough and ready methods of trial and arbitrary vengeance by king or mob, smacking in some degree of political action. The king or the people is the complainant, the judge and the executioner.

Let us look again at the civil rules in more detail. The reader will notice the advances and changes in the later of the Early Codes.

The chief civil wrong is homicide, for which the normal sanction in Kent is the sum of 100 shillings,[1] representing the value of 100 cows, and in the Lex Salica[2] and Lex Ribuaria[3] 200 solidi (shillings), but there is much variation according to circumstances.[4] The chief criterion is the social class of the slain. In Kent the noble's wergeld is 300 (golden) shillings.[5] In Wessex the common wergelds are three: 200, 600 and 1,200 Wessex (silver) shillings,[6] but less for Welshmen, for whom there is a separate grading according to the extent of their landholding.[7] The wergeld is sometimes less for artisans, employees and priests,[8] and on the Continent for Romans and other foreigners.[9] The slave is usually paid for according to his value.[10] Another criterion is the sex of the slain: a woman's wergeld is sometimes higher than that of a man of the same class,[11] at least if she is of child-bearing age[12] or with child.[13] Other aggravating features are that the slain man was in the protection (*in truste*) of the king,[14] or that it is a case of 'murder' – that is to say the killing was in secret or attempts were

---

[1] Aeth. 21; H. & E. 3.   [2] L. Sal. 15, 41.   [3] L. Rib. 7.
[4] In the Leges inter Brettos et Scotos it varies between 1,000 cows for the King of Scotland and 16 for a villein, according to social rank.
[5] H. & E. 1 (6,000 pence),
[6] 4,800 pence; see Ine 70; Alf. 10, 26, 27, 28. Certain members of the king's household had a wergeld of 1,200s. (Ine 19).
[7] Ine 32.
[8] L. Rib. 9, 10, 36[5] (for killing a king's man or priest, half the ordinary wergeld); Aeth. 7 (for slaying a smith in the king's service or one of his messengers, only the ordinary wergeld).
[9] L. Rib. 36.   [10] Ine 23.
[11] L. Sal. 41 (3) (triple sanction of 600s. for a freewoman); L. Alam. 49 (double). In the Leges inter Brettos et Scotos it is a third less than for her husband or brother.
[12] Till forty years of age, 600s. (L. Sal. 23 (6); L. Rib. 52).
[13] L. Sal 23; Alf. 9.   [14] L. Sal. 41 (3); L. Rib. 11 (600s).

made to hide the body.[1] There is no great amount of currency, however, and the sanction is often paid in cattle or other goods.[2] Its amount is enormous, and few – especially among the hot-blooded young men usually involved – could pay it out of their own resources, and it is normally provided in large measure by the nearest relatives of the male and female line[3] in such proportions as custom and means dictate, and its receipt is similarly shared.[4] If the money cannot be found and the relatives cannot or will not help – because of the offender's previous misdeeds or for other reasons – the killer is left to save his life, if possible, on whatever terms he can arrange.[5]

Briefly (for we shall return to this subject in a later chapter) the circumstances and social forces that give rise to this state of the law, and its meaning and effect, are as follows. The killing of a member of any kinship group inevitably causes resentment and a passion for revenge upon the killer and his kinship group and their livestock and homes. It is avoided and enmity is healed and pride satisfied by the payment and acceptance of an enormous quantity of cattle or its value in currency, and this is in accordance with public opinion, which expects and approves such a solution, and the policy of the law[6] which fixes the amount of the sanction, though this is primarily determined by the interplay of these forces. Any other sanction is not to be contemplated: for the weak royal authority to inflict a death sentence on the killer would not be possible – it has not the power nor would public opinion nor the pride and sensitivity of the kinship group of the slayer tolerate it nor does any religious principle call for it nor would it reduce disorder. Imprisonment is for the future: society cannot afford to

---

[1] L. Sal. 41; L. Rib. 15 (3 times). So that 'murder' of a man in the protection of the king is paid for with 1,800s.
[2] Aeth. 30 provides that the killer shall pay with his own money or unblemished cattle or goods, of whatever kind; and see Ine 54[1].
[3] Alf. 30; L. Rib. 12[2]; L. Sal 58, De Chrenecruda.
[4] L. Sal. 62; Alf. 31.
[5] 'De vita componat' (see L. Sal. 58). If a priest slays and the lord of the monastery chooses not to pay, he is unfrocked and given up (Alf. 21.)
[6] The situation is well expressed by Tacitus (*Germania* 21): 'A man must take up the enmities of a father or relative as well as the friendships, but they do not endure unappeasable. For even homicide is settled by a fixed number of cattle and sheep, to the satisfaction of the whole kin and the benefit of the people, for enmities are more dangerous where there is liberty.'

nourish malefactors in idleness nor would it wish to do so. It follows that the Early Codes do not as a rule provide lesser sanctions for unintentional homicide,[1] though we must not assume that the sanctions enumerated in the laws do not vary in some degree according to all the circumstances; but the latest of these codes do provide what is to be done with a tree, animal or other object by which the deceased met his death.[2]

Similar considerations apply to and explain the sanctions for lesser personal injuries. The codes fix amounts for the compensation for each wound and (for example in the Laws of Aethelberht) the passion of an early legislator or jurist for abstract perfection is expressed in a complete tariff providing an appropriate sum for each imaginable injury in the order of the limbs commencing with the hair of the head.[3] A break in the order and a list recommencing higher in the body shows an interpolation or rules derived from different sources.[4] But unanticipated injuries or combinations of injuries might always have occurred, and these provisions must not be regarded as invariable in practice: most codes content themselves with a few instances.[5] In a modern court some table, real or imagined, is equally observed, but the amount of the financial loss following from the injury is added. In a society less specialised and differentiated, the difference between the loss to one victim or another suffering the same injury, could not justify a distinction, and a principle that a man receives the amount of his actual financial damage is unknown. In the codes the amounts of the sanctions do not usually vary according to the sexual or social class of the offender,[6] but an assault by a man upon his lord or king or indecent assault on a woman or an injury causing the miscarriage of a woman with child, are distinct wrongs.[7]

The sanctions for rape are pecuniary,[8] and include the serious

---

[1] Alf. 36, however, excuses payment of the fine where a person is killed by a man's spear carried over the shoulder.
[2] See Alf. 13; L. Rib. 72; L. Sal. 36.
[3] Aeth. 33-72. [4] Alf. 65-77.
[5] e.g. L. Sal. 17, 29; L. Rib. 1-6.
[6] In the Georgian code, however, the tariff for injuries varies in proportion to the wergeld for each class.
[7] e.g. L. Sal. 20; L. Rib. 39; Alf. 11, 18 (double for assault on a nun).
[8] L. Alam. 51, 52, 58; L. Rib. 35.

wrong of carrying off a girl as a bride, without her 'owner's' consent, and in the latter case the law will also provide for payment of the brideprice,[1] as it will where sexual intercourse has been had with a girl without her parents' consent.[2] The sanction for adultery with or rape of a married woman is also pecuniary and sometimes amounts to a wergeld[3] and sometimes varies according to the husband's social status.[4] In the latest of these codes it is provided that the husband may be free of payment of wergeld if in a fight he kills them *in flagranti delicto*.[5] The wrong of taking a widow to whom the offender is not entitled by inheritance is also pecuniary.[6]

The sanction for theft is generally pecuniary. Theft of domestic animals and the harbouring of stolen animals and fugitive slaves are the only frequent examples, for these are the chief items of property apart from landholdings. Theft is regarded as heinous and dishonourable. The sanction is either a sum of money fixed by the law for each species of animal stolen,[7] varying with its age and other fixed indicia of value, or there is a more general provision of a stated multiple of the value.[8] Only in the same unconvincing clause of Aethelberht does it vary with the ecclesiastical rank of the owner.[9] The sanctions for robbery with violence or robbery of a corpse are also pecuniary.[10] But persistent theft is often treated as criminal (being an offence against the community) and punishable by cutting off the hand or foot.[11] Moreover to kill a thief caught in the act is generally excused,[12] and, under a corresponding rule (whether logical or not), a thief caught in the act

---

[1] Aeth. 82-4. The ravisher pays 'owner' 50s. and afterwards buys from him his consent, i.e. pays a brideprice. If a brideprice has already been paid by another man, the 'owner', i.e. father, brother or other next of kin, receives only 20s., but the payer of the brideprice will have his claim. If she is brought back, 35s. is to be paid to the 'owner'. There is also 15s. to be paid to the king. L. Sal. 13, 15, 25; L. Rib. 35; Alf. 11, 18, 25, 29.
[2] See references in previous note.
[3] Aeth. 31, which also provides (in the alternative?) for a payment of a brideprice to secure another wife.
[4] Alf. 10 (a modest proportion of the husband's wergeld).
[5] Alf. 42 (7); L. Rib. 77.
[6] Aeth. 76. The wrong probably disappears as polygyny is put down by the Church, which also prohibits marriage with the deceased husband's brother.
[7] e.g. L. Sal. 2-11, 23.   [8] Aeth. 4, 9.
[9] Aeth. 1. See *ante* p. 58.   [10] L. Sal. 61; L. Alam. 50: L. Rib. 85.
[11] Ine 18, 37.   [12] Wih. 25; Ine 16, 21, 35.

commits an offence for which he may, if convicted, be punished capitally or mutilated,[1] and a person allowing a thief to escape from his custody is severely punishable,[2] just as one who captures a thief is entitled to a reward.[3]

The other types of civil injuries for which the Early Codes provide are mainly the following: selling a freeman abroad as a slave (for which the sanction is often the same as in homicide, if he does not return);[4] laying bonds on a freeman;[5] forcible entry on a man's close and home;[6] supplying another with arms by which he inflicts injury;[7] pushing a man or woman out of the way;[8] calling him or her offensive names (especially a woman);[9] disorderly conduct in a man's house;[10] burning or felling another man's trees or stealing crops and plants;[11] falsely accusing a man before a court;[12] damage by trespassing animals.[13]

The chief exception to the rule that the sanctions for civil injuries are pecuniary is in regard to wrongs by slaves, who will usually belong to no kinship group and have no means to pay.[14] For them corporal punishment is devised, lashes,[15] castration[16] or other mutilation in cases of more serious wrongs; for the rest the master or slave pays.[17] There are difficulties in these cases in

[1] Wih. 26; Ine 12, 20; L. Rib. 79.
[2] Ine 28, 35, 36, 72, 73; L. Rib. 73.
[3] Ine 28; Wih. 26.
[4] H. & E. 5; L. Sal. 39²; L. Rib. 16; L. Alam. 46, 47.
[5] Aeth. 24; L. Sal. 32; L. Rib. 41.
[6] Especially by a gang of marauders, Aeth. 17, 27-9, 32; Ine, 45; Alf. 40; L. Sal. 11. This wrong is the historical origin of the English action of trespass.
[7] Aeth. 18-20; Ine 29; Alf. 19.
[8] L. Sal. 31.   [9] L. Sal. 30.
[10] H. & E. 11-14.
[11] L. Sal. 27; L. Rib. 76, 82.
[12] L. Sal. 48; L. Rib. 38 (before the king).
[13] Ine 40, 42, 49; L. Sal. 27.
[14] See, however, Aeth. 90 (theft by slave; he pays double the value of the stolen thing).
[15] L. Sal. 12¹ (small theft); L. Sal. 25⁸ (fornication by slave with another's female slave).
[16] L. Sal. 12² (theft over 40d., castration or 6s. paid by master or slave); 40⁴ (a similar case, and confession by the slave under torture); L. Sal. 25⁷ (slave has intercourse with another's female slave, of which she dies; castration or 6s.); Alf. 25 (rape of slave by slave 'compensation by castration').
[17] If the slave escapes without the fault of the master, or is surrendered by him, the master pays less (H. & E. 1-4 – homicide by a slave).

ascertaining guilt, for the slave is not an acceptable witness and prolonged torture to extort admissions is common.

In most cases of serious wrong it is the kinship group that acts in litigation and the enforcement of sanctions, and indeed the wrong is commonly one to the parent, the owner of the injured slave, the king or other person in whose *mund* or *verbum* (i.e. protection) the wronged person is, or there is a wrong to both; and a sum is paid for *mundbyrd* (infringement of this right of protection). The situation is provided for somewhat differently in the English and continental codes. The systematic Laws of Aethelberht, for example, see the generality of individuals as being in the *mund* of someone else, and fix a sum for the *mundbyrd* of the latter (including the king) according to his social class, while the continental codes provide for the more serious cases a payment of *fridus*[1] ('peace money') to the king in addition to the *faidus* ('feud money' or compensation) to the wronged group or individual, though '*fridus*' is sometimes used with the meaning of 'king's *mundbyrd*'. Here we mark the beginnings of an extension of the criminal law, namely that certain torts start to become crimes. In Aethelberht's laws, for example, apart from wrongs which are breaches of his *mund* because they are committed in his presence or against his servants or persons in his protection,[2] a fine is payable to him in any case of homicide of a freeman,[3] robbery from a freeman[4] and rape of a freewoman.[5]

In addition there are the other serious crimes, referred to above, which are not always named in the laws, but include treason[6] and also incest and the slaying of near kin.[7] Here the sanctions are usually corporal, including death,[8] penal slavery[9] and, in one late case, mutilation.[10]

---

[1] Or *fretus*, *fredus* or *freta*.
[2] Aeth. 2, 3, 5, 7, 10.
[3] Aeth. 6.   [4] Aeth. 9.
[5] i.e. carrying off a maiden by force (Aeth. 84).
[6] e.g. Alf. 4 (death and forfeiture of all possessions); L. Alam. 24f.
[7] e.g. L. Rib. 69. There is no room here for the usual play of an avenging and a defending kinship group, for there is only one.
[8] Ine 5; L. Sal. 18; L. Alam. 24-6.
[9] Ine 24; L. Sal. 25[5] (Frank fornicating with foreign slave); L. Sal. 13 (free marrying unfree).
[10] Alf. 32 (public slander – excision of tongue or payment of the offender's wergeld).

As in Tacitus' Germania,[1] marriage is everywhere by bride-wealth[2], the amount of which is not specified by the laws, because it varies too much and is a matter of agreement.[3] There are disputes in regard to it – cases where the bridewealth is received and the girl not given,[4] or she is carried off by another man.[5] The traditional Germanic morning-gift by the husband to the wife is mentioned,[6] but there is no marriage settlement by the wife's parents.

As the only commercial transactions are barter and cash sale[7] – evidenced at the end of the period by writing or witnesses[8] in cases of valuables – and no prior agreement to buy or sell is relevant or recognized, the only disputes that can arise are of two classes. The first is where a third person claims to recognize his goods in the purchaser's possession and alleges they have been stolen from him: unless the purchaser can vouch a warrantor – i.e. produce his vendor – or explain his failure to do so, he must deliver them up.[9] The other is the case where the goods (usually cattle) are found to have a disease or other blemish and the purchaser claims to reject them.[10]

There are only a few scattered rules of inheritance, chiefly contained in the celebrated but unconvincing Lex Salica, Chap. 59, *De Alodis*, repeated in Chap. 56 of the Lex Ribuaria.[11]

This is the bulk of the rules of law contained in the Early Codes. We shall have something to say about the procedure of trial in a later chapter.[12]

---

[1] Germ. 18, 'Dowry is not brought by wife to husband, but by husband to wife'.
[2] Aeth. 77 ('if a man buys a maiden'), 83; Ine 31.
[3] See *post* Chap. 17.
[4] Ine 31 (the brideprice to be repaid and as much again).
[5] Aeth. 82, 83.   [6] Aeth. 81.
[7] But Jaroslav's Pravda, 15, has a reference to a partnership; if the translation is correct.
[8] L. Rib. 59, 60.
[9] H. & E. 7, 16, Jaroslav's Pravda 14, 16.
[10] There is one case in Ine 56 (which turns on the question whether the vendor knew of the defect).
[11] See also Aeth. 78, 81.   [12] Chap. 21.

CHAPTER 6

The Central Codes of the Past – Early Civilization

dates *

'The Central Codes' is the name given in this book to all codes of law of the stage of economic development represented by England between A.D. 900 and 1100, as the English economy advanced during that period. They therefore include the continental codes of law of Western Europe beginning about 800 and ending about 1000, as well as the Lombard Code of Rothari of the seventh century.[1] The chief English codes are I Edward, II Aethelstan, I and III Edgar, I, II and III Aethelred and II Cnut,[2] all of poor quality, largely drawing on earlier English material, and showing little progress and few signs of practical application. The chief continental codes are those prepared at the behest of Charlemagne, around the beginning of the ninth century, to record the law of his peoples – namely the Lex Frisionum, Lex Angliorum et Werinorum (i.e. Thuringorum), Lex Francorum Chamavorum and Lex Saxonum.[3] Of these, the Lombard Code is far superior to the rest, but the Lex Thuringorum has merit.

There is also, however, the twelfth-century Scottish legislation – the Assisē of David I and the Laws of the Four Burghs – the Ancient Welsh and Irish Laws (in so far as they can be used and are of assistance), the two admirable Norwegian Codes, the Gulathing Law and Frostathing Law, representing the state of the law of that country in about 1100, and the late twelfth-century Russian Code, the Expanded Version of Jaroslav's Pravda. From further east and south comes, at the close of the Central Codes

---

[1] See *ante* p. 55.
[2] See the texts, translations into modern English and brief commentaries in Attenborough (1922) and Robertson (1925), and texts, translations into German and commentaries in Liebermann.
[3] The L. Rib., as it draws largely on laws of earlier centuries, has been included in the Early Codes.

and beginning of the Late, the Armenian Law-Book of the thirteenth century, and in the fifteenth century the less advanced Georgian Code of Aghbougha.[1] Of chief historical interest, however, is the Hittite Code of about 1300 to 1250 B.C, which comes from the fringe of the area of civilization of the ancient Near East and also belongs to this stage.[2] It is written in cuneiform on two clay tablets in a language of Indo-European affinity, and was discovered at the royal archive of Hattusas (modern Boghazköy). The two tablets are almost complete and their deficiencies have been largely supplemented from the numerous fragments of other copies and versions, which also survive. The tablets each consist of some 100 clauses[3] and they are continuous in their contents. Like most of our codes, this is not, in its present form, a code promulgated by one legislative act. For example, in the first table occurs, from clauses 39 to 56, a section concerning land held on terms of feudal services, but into the midst of it have been put four miscellaneous clauses (43, 44a, 44b and 45) which have no connection with that topic. Similarly, in table II, from clauses 150 to 161, is a section fixing rates of hire and prices, and from 177 to 186 other prices, and in between (162-76) is a group of clauses on a variety of topics.[4] Table II shows several other signs of piecemeal additions and extensions, but the clearest indications are in the clauses in both tables which record amendments in the law and the sanctions, especially the abolition of payments to the king.[5] In all probability

---

[1] See *ante* p. 37.

[2] Recovered in excavations at Boghazköy under Winckler, 1906-7. It was first read by F. Hrozný, and first translated (1922) by Hrozný (into French) and by Friedrich and Zimmern into German. See now, J. Friedrich, *Die Hethitischen Gesetze* (Leiden, 1959) (with German translation); A. Goetze, in J. B. Pritchard's *Ancient Near Eastern Texts relating to the Old Testament* (Princeton, 1950, 2nd edn, 1955) (English translation); F. Imparati, *Le Leggi Ittite* (Rome, 1964) (with Italian translation and commentary). For the Hittites generally (apart from their law) and good bibliography, see Gurney.

[3] As numbered by F. Hrozný, *Code Hittite, Provenant de l'Asie Mineure* (Paris, 1922) and as usually cited.

[4] Including an added clause on homicide (174), a topic already treated in §§1-6.

[5] e.g. 25 (for fouling a private water supply): 'the befouler pays 3 shekels of silver, and 3 shekels used to be taken for the Palace. Now, however, the King has abolished the payment to the Palace and the befouler gives 3 shekels of silver and goes free.' Or 58 (stealing a First Class Horse – i.e. a two-year-old). 'Formerly a man used to give 30 horses and now 15.'

D

the Code originated in briefer legislation and has been handed down, amended and extended by various scribes during a couple of centuries from the fifteenth to the thirteenth and therefore dates from the heyday of the Hittite Empire, and partakes now of the nature both of legislation and law-book. Like all our codes it is the work of ecclesiastical scribes and records the appropriate decision on such disputes as were prone to arise in the courts; but it is of an official nature, for many copies and versions (sometimes showing substantial variations) were found in the royal archive and there is no evidence of the existence of any other code. It is generally couched in conditional sentences in the third person, though the prevalence of the present tense in the apodosis indicates the nature of the code.[1] The phraseology is simple and brief but not apparently technical or skilled. In the present state of knowledge of the language the meaning of many clauses is still uncertain.

Apart from criteria of date and place we define our Central Codes and distinguish them from those of the previous stage (the Early Codes) and the next stage (the Late Codes) in the following terms of material culture (remembering however that there is considerable variation between one part of a country and another). If the previous stage was that of barbarism this marks the beginning of civilization. The arts have advanced and there is some good sculpture and military and civil architecture. The populations are more settled upon their territory and their rulers are commonly called kings of the land instead of the people. Agriculture affords the chief means of livelihood and includes a greater variety of crops, and as each man lives by his land, allotted originally to him or his predecessors by their chief or headman, and money is in little use[2] and tribute can only be paid and government carried on out of the produce of the land, the relation between occupier and lord, and lord and king, is the basis of military service, administration and jurisdiction. Hence, as the authority of government advances, during this stage feudalism reaches its height. In Mediaeval Europe and the land of Hatti it is

---

[1] The form is 'If a man . . . he pays x shekels', or 'the price of a . . . is x shekels.'

[2] In Mediaeval Europe there is a coinage; in Hatti silver in the form of bars or rings passing by weight, but barley for lesser purposes.

closely associated with a new, costly and formidable weapon. This, in Europe, is the heavy warhorse and the high-peaked saddle, and among the Hittites the heavy horsed chariot;[1] and in Europe (and we may be sure in the Near East) the feudal organization is partly shaped by the need to give to the 'knight' the landholding requisite to enable him to turn out properly trained with horses and other equipment and to provide the complement of attendants and food. The differentiation of ranks (e.g. in England, Georgia and Armenia) is multifarious and sharp, and in some lands (e.g. England, II Aethelstan 2; Scotland, Assisē David I, 18) it is an offence to be found without a lord. The populations and areas have expanded and the density increases. Several of these states (including those of Rothari, Charlemagne and the Hittites) include peoples of different languages and ethnic origins and can now be called states and empires. Towards the close of our period, in 1086, the population of the English Kingdom is about $1\frac{1}{2}$ millions and the density about 20 to the square mile. There are now substantial towns, of which London has a population of about 13,000, and there are several others numbering between 3,000 and 8,000; but the bulk of their inhabitants earn their living on the land. Most people live in small villages and only a very substantial village has in it 30 households – villages and hamlets of 2 to 6 households are very common.[2] Towns bring markets and in England the *port* (or market town) is administered by the *port reeve*. The control of markets involves market dues[3] and often the fixing of prices, and the Hittite Code lays down the prices of various skilled slaves, animals and other commodities, but, primitive laws being what they are, we must doubt whether the prices mentioned represent those actually charged.[4] As yet private transactions are hardly ever evidenced by writing.[5] There is an increase in the number of landless persons and classes of specialist

[1] And see Yigael Yadin, *The Art of Warfare in Biblical Times* (1963), and Carl Stephenson, *Mediaeval Feudalism* (1942).
[2] Clapham (1949), 44.
[3] For England, see IV Aethelred 2.
[4] The evidence from Babylonia in Hammurabi's time shows prices charged different from those in his Code.
[5] See Jaroslav's Pravda (Expanded Version) 47, 48 as to the requisite of witnesses on a loan of money. No Hittite documents evidencing private transactions remain (only royal charters including deeds of gift of great estates).

craftsmen, though most of the latter still earn their living partly on the land. With the increase in goods there is now a substantial amount of hiring of goods as well as of the services of artisans, and charges for hire are fixed in the Hittite Code. There is a beginning of the sale of land and of the recording of title to land,[1] partly because there is credit and debt. The pledging of dependents for debt (usually children and unmarried sisters) begins in the Near East,[2] though there is no evidence of it in the European Codes. There is a beginning of loan of money at interest.

In legal terms we define the stage of the Central Codes and distinguish it from the others as follows. As the solidarity of the state, as distinct from the kinship groups, advances and a national social conscience further develops, the field of the law of criminal offences expands, and this has two aspects. First, the more serious civil wrongs begin to change into criminal offences, and the most serious of these, namely homicide, begins to change from a law of pecuniary sanctions for all killings towards a law of the capital sanction for intentional homicide. In this intermediate stage the rules take a variety of forms. One characteristic sanction, only found in the Hittite Code,[3] is the handing over of a number of persons in most cases of homicide. Elsewhere the sanction for most homicides is the wergeld or a multiple of the wergeld, but towards the end of the stage it becomes in some circumstances capital. A difference in the amount of the pecuniary sanctions, based on the intention of the killer, is occasionally found. Adultery (that is, sexual intercourse by or with a married woman) becomes criminal and capital. Secondly, there is a general development and enlargement in the Central Codes of the old list of criminal offences. They are triable in the king's court and the sanctions, though usually capital or pecuniary, assume in a growing number of cases the form of mutilations – for freemen and freewomen and not, as before, merely for slaves. In marriage the institution of the bridewealth remains in full force,[4] but there are also the

---

[1] Hittite lists of holdings and title-deeds survive. For sale of land see Ed. Roth. 173, 227-8, 233-5; H.C. 48.
[2] See H.C. 48.
[3] But see *post* Chap. 24.
[4] e.g. Ed. Roth. 167, 182-3, 215; II Can. 74; H.C. 28a, 29, 30, 34-6. The L. Sax. 40 is unique in fixing the amount. The Frostathing Law provides that there is no valid marriage without bridewealth.

beginnings of the marriage settlement (a gift by the bride's father to her or to them).[1] As the amount of goods increases in the community, and rules of property in goods appear, the proprietary capacity of the wife begins to be provided for, but that capacity has nowhere yet fallen to the position reached in many of the Late Codes, where her property vests in her husband.[2] With the frequency of bailments (especially hire) comes the problem set by the claim by the owner for the return of the thing bailed, and the defence by the bailee that it has been lost or injured without his fault, and its solution by the application of the ordeal by oath to the bailee.[3] It is a further characteristic of the Central Codes that there are differences in the rules of law in different areas and between different ethnic groups.[4]

Let us look at these changes in the law in a little more detail.

The general sanction for homicide remains everywhere the wergeld,[5] subject to the following exceptions which grow and finally eat up the rule. As in the previous stage an additional payment to the king is common[6] either to represent the wrong done to him by the offence against someone in his ward or protection, or to represent the offence against the state or Crown. The amount of the wergeld is multiplied in certain cases of aggravated homicide, for example 'murder' (or secret killing). Conversely the amount is now occasionally reduced where the killing is unintentional.[7]

In the Hittite Code the general sanction is the handing over of a number of persons – 4 persons, male or female, for killing a free man or woman, and 2 for killing an unfree, 'following a quarrel' (i.e. intentionally) and half those numbers 'if his hand offends'

[1] The *faderfio* of Ed. Roth. (182-3); and see H.C. 27; Frostathing III, 7, 17 (not a true marriage portion).
[2] e.g. Frostathing XI, 5 only gives the husband the management of his wife's property during the marriage (except such moneys as were set aside at the betrothal or marriage to be under her control and accounted for by her).
[3] See *post* p. 386 and also H.C. 75, Venedotian Code II, 6, 2.
[4] e.g. L. Fris; H.C. 5.
[5] Gulathing 316 has an elaborate scale of sums payable to the various relatives of the slain.
[6] See e.g. L. Franc. Cham. 4-6, which imposes a fine of 4s. payable to the king in respect of all serious wrongs.
[7] But usually the amount is the same irrespective of intention, e.g. L. Thuring. 51; Ed. Roth. 138; L. Sax. 54-60.

(i.e. unintentionally);[1] and 1 person for killing in a fight.[2] But for killing a mere trader the sanction is pecuniary – the enormous sum of 100 minas.[3] Similarly in England, at the close of our period, 'murder' or secret killing is bootless (i.e. not emendable by compensation)[4] and a 'murderer' is to be handed over to the kinsmen.[5] In the Scandinavian world the poor strength of the central government is eked out by the institution of outlawry, whereby perpetrators of some serious offences, including some types of homicide, are made outlaws – that is to say, are deprived of the protection of the law.[6] It is a criminal offence to harbour them and if they do not leave the country they may be killed with impunity. According to the seriousness of the offence there is a distinction between common outlawry (which may be released on terms by the king) and permanent outlawry.[7] The institution is adopted in England in the Danish period[8] and remains for long afterwards. In the Russian Code, for killing by an unprovoked attack a man may be banished with his wife and children and his property confiscated.[9] In Georgian law there is a widespread and characteristic punishment whereby criminals and other serious offenders are banished from their landholding for a number of years or for ever. Where the killing is of a member of the same agnatic or natural family, so that there can be no avenging process between families to fix the wergeld, there may in places be the severe sanction of outlawry[10] or a double wergeld.[11]

Where no human killer can be found, satisfaction may still be given to the relatives of the slain. If a man has been killed by an

---

[1] H.C. 1-4.   [2] H.C. 174.
[3] H.C. 5, equivalent to the price of 100 acres of vineyard, 850 cows or 200 fine garments.
[4] II Can. 64.   [5] II Can. 56.
[6] Gulathing 142; for breaking into a man's garth and doing violence to him or his property, outlawry, or restitution of the goods and a fine of 40 marks; Frostathing I: outlawry for manslaying.
[7] Frostathing; a sentence of common outlawry for manslaying; the king could release it upon payment of a fine to him and a sum to the family. Frostathing V, 45; permanent and irrevocable outlawry for certain criminal offences (sodomy, bestiality, witchcraft, serious theft, 'murder' or killing a member of the same natural family).
[8] It is first mentioned in Alf. 4.
[9] Jaroslav's Pravda (Expanded Version), 7.
[10] See *supra* note 7.
[11] Aghbougha, 22.

inanimate object – if, for example, a tree has fallen upon him[1] – it is sometimes treated as a human slayer would have been and handed over to the next of kin to do with it as they will.[2] If a man is found dead among a strange community but no slayer can be discovered, it is sometimes held liable to compensate the relatives of the slain.[3] Both these practices survive into modern times.

For wounds, the tariffs of payment for injuries to the different parts of the body remain, and in some places they vary also according to the social class of the injured.[4] But we now hear sometimes of payments to the doctor,[5] and the provision of someone to work in the house of the injured till he recovers.[6]

There is a great change in the sanction for adultery, which is now capital for the wife and the adulterer,[7] but in practice is often treated very leniently and compensated by large or small payments.[8] In the East the husband can kill both or let off both, and if the matter comes to court, like other capital offences it is for the king's court, and the king can put both to death or pardon both.[9] But the sanctions vary from place to place. Canute[10] allows the husband to mutilate the adulterous wife by cutting off her nose and ears, and to take all her possessions. For rape of a married woman death is for the man only.[11] Rape of an unmarried woman is a serious wrong, and II Canute 52 and Aghbougha 24 provide for a payment by the man equal to his wergeld.

For theft, as in the Early Codes, the general sanction is either payment of a stated multiple of the value of the thing stolen, the multiple increasing with the more valuable kinds of property, or a sum fixed for each kind of property, increasing with the value; but theft is a serious problem and not only may a thief caught in

---

[1] e.g. Alf. 13.
[2] As in Athens as late as classical times.
[3] H.C. I, 6.
[4] L. Angl. et Werin, 2-24. In Georgia they are commonly fixed as a proportion of the victim's wergeld, according to the nature of the wound.
[5] Ed. Roth. 128; H.C. 10.
[6] H.C. 10.
[7] Frostathing I, 10; Ed. Roth. 211, 212; L. Fris. 9; H.C. 197, 198. In Gulathing 201, a man lying with another's betrothed pays the amount of her wergeld. (See also Law of Beka 5-6f.).
[8] Aghbougha, 23: full wergeld and the offender is led naked through the streets, or double wergeld; and see *ibid.*, 41.
[9] H.C. 197, 198.   [10] Can. II, 53.   [11] H.C. 197.

the act be killed, but in many places death is the sanction for the thief caught in the act,[1] at least where the property is of substantial value,[2] or for the persistent thief.[3]

Several of the codes contain a section devoted to purchase and sale[4] or the law of merchants generally,[5] but as sale is the mere exchange of goods for money there are still no practical problems except the occasional claim to return within a reasonable time a beast found to have a defect;[6] and everywhere the claim by an alleged owner to goods in another's possession, and the latter's defence that he bought them from a third party, and therefore they are not the plaintiff's, and that in any case he bought them innocently and is not a thief; the defendant is called upon to produce his seller,[7] and the latter to produce his. To check the traffic in stolen goods some English laws attempt to secure that no one shall buy goods – of substantial value, at least – except in a *port* before the port reeve or other credible witnesses, and the need for witnesses is often stressed.[8]

The expansion of the criminal offences shows itself chiefly in the following categories – treason against the king; offences against one's lord (killing him, his lady or his son, raping his daughter or killing someone in his house,[9] plotting against him[10]

---

[1] Aghbougha 167: both eyes burnt and amputation of one hand and foot, or sale of the offender and restitution of the stolen property.
[2] Ed. Roth. 253-8; II Aethelstan 1; VI Aethelstan 1; II Can. 26, 64.
[3] VI Aethelstan 4. In Norway, for lesser thefts, outlawry or flogging according to amount (Frostathing V, 45).
[4] Aghbougha 66-98; Armenian Law-Book 106-12.
[5] Gulathing 34-71; Frostathing X, XI.
[6] Already seen in Ine 56 (blemish appearing within thirty days, seller swears he knew of no blemish when he sold, or accepts return); Frostathing X, 48 (buyer may return horse within five days for latent defects, the latter being defined by examples). But these clauses are uncommon.
[7] For this confrontation of the seller and the plaintiff (English *team*, German *schub*, Russian *svod*), see P. & M. I. 59; Glanville, *Tractatus de Legibus* (ed. 1604) X, 15-17; Brunner, *Deutsche Rechtsgeschichte* (1887) II, 655, 659; Jaroslav's Pravda (Expanded Version), 34-9.
[8] I Edward 1 (early tenth century: 'No man shall buy except in a *port* and he shall have as witness the *port reeve* or other unlying man who can be trusted)'. II Aethelstan 12 (similar provision for buying goods over 20 pence); II Can. 24 ('no one shall buy anything over 4 pence in value, either livestock or other property, unless he have 4 men as trustworthy witnesses whether it be in the town or out in the country').
[9] L. Sax. 24-7; Cap. de P. Saxoniae 11-14, *M.G.H.*, Legum I, 48.
[10] II Aethelstan 4.

or deserting him on a military expedition;[1] contempt of the higher courts;[2] killing within the agnatic[3] or natural family;[4] a wife killing or scheming to kill her husband;[5] arson of a house[6] or assault upon a house;[7] some cases of serious theft;[8] false coining;[9] perjury;[10] witchcraft;[11] bestiality;[12] also a number of sacral crimes.[13] The above offences are capital or punishable by permanent outlawry or mutilations, but sometimes by payment of a multiple of the offender's wergeld.[14] There are still no sentences of imprisonment for criminal or civil offences – the community cannot afford to nourish offenders in idleness and there are no prisons of any substance; but a defendant may be put in the stocks or held in some way pending a trial.[15] We continue to hear in Christian countries of offenders taking sanctuary, usually temporarily or pending an appeal to king or bishop, and the religious codes insist on the rights of the Church in this respect,[16] but as some civil offences become capital the right of sanctuary for these and other crimes is taken away by legal codes.[17]

Although the religious matter continues to be very scanty, there is more of it in the Central Codes than earlier or later. There are no religious rules of conduct – that is to say, rules with religious and not secular sanctions, in the continental codes of Europe, but several contain a separate section on ecclesiastical law.[18]

The English codes, which are of poor quality and often of

[1] II Can. 77.   [2] H.C. 173.   [3] Ed. Roth. 163.
[4] See *supra*.   [5] L. Sax. 38; II Can. 64.   [6] II Can. 64.
[7] II Can. 64.   [8] See *supra*.
[9] III Aethelred 8, 16 (capital); IV Aethelred 5 (3) (forfeiture of hand, to be fastened up over the mint).
[10] III Edgar 4 (wergeld or forfeiture of tongue); L. Sax. 21, 22 (capital or loss of hand), II Can. 36 (loss of hand).
[11] II Aethelstan 6; H.C. 44b (capital).
[12] H.C. 187, 188, 199 (capital); Frostathing I, II (castration and outlawry).
[13] L. Sax. 21 (capital offences in a church), 23; Cap. de P. Saxoniae 1-10.
[14] Aghbougha 116-52.
[15] See II Edward 3 (2); II Aethelstan, 1 (3) and 4; II Can. 35.
[16] See II Edmund 2; I Can. 2 (3).
[17] See e.g. IV Aethelstan 6, and III Edgar 7 (3) (proved theft, i.e. manifest, or proved by ordeal or admitted); II Can. 26 (proved theft and treason against a man's lord).
[18] Aghbougha 99-115 (offences against ecclesiastics and churches); Armenian Law-Book 8-62, Gulathing 1-33 and Frostathing II and III (ecclesiastical law).

D*

doubtful authenticity, tend to divide themselves into religious codes (with which we are not concerned) and secular codes, but several contain an unsavoury mixture of both. The Assisē David I contain one clause relating to a prosecutor of an innocent man committing perjury on the gospel or other sacred object; he shall be deprived of all comfort and communion with Christians till before God he performs the penances adjudged (by the ecclesiastical court) and pays eight cows to the king, and thereafter he shall not be admitted as a witness or take an oath in any matter. The Hittite Code contains two or three provisions of a religious nature, but they are all contained in one of the two miscellaneous added groups, to which we have referred,[1] and are therefore more recent than the bulk. This is not surprising, for the earliest of our Early Codes were all secular; moreover we thought the Hittite Code began as legislation and later assumed the character of a law-book, being brought up to date under the hands of ecclesiastics, describing the state of the law.

But as the ecclesiastic influence grows and its interest in the law increases, the Church begins to inflict its own pecuniary and corporal sanctions on its flock for wrong conduct in fields of religious importance, and there is a beginning of a competition with the king for jurisdiction in certain sacral offences. For example, I Edmund 3 (one of the English religious codes) provides that 'if anyone sheds the blood of a Christian man, he shall not come anywhere near the king till he proceeds to do penance, as the bishop appoints for him or his confessor directs him'.[2] And V Aethelred 29 (another religious code) lays it down that 'if any excommunicated man, unless he be a suppliant for protection, stays anywhere near the king, before he has readily submitted to the amends required by the church, it shall be at the risk of his life or his estate'. VI Aethelred 36 (a religious code) repeats the provision for murderers, perjurers and proved homi-

---

[1] In the group 43-5, only 44b, which says that certain conduct is witchcraft and a matter for the King's Court (the sanction is not religious). In the group 162-76, only 166-70 can be called religious: 166-7, the religious offence of sowing a field twice with seed and a statement that animal sacrifice has been substituted for the death of the offender; 168-9, animal sacrifice on violating the boundary of a field; 170, witchcraft (again the sanction is not religious). But the meaning of these clauses is doubtful.

[2] Middle tenth century; repeated in II Edward 4 – two brief and poor codes.

cides.[1] We may perhaps conjecture a similar background to the Hittite Code which provides,[2] in a section added at its close concerning sacral offences, that when a man commits bestiality 'it is an abomination. He is put to death. They bring him to the king's gate. But the king can put him to death and the king can let him live. But he may not come before the king.'

Codes of primitive law have rarely much to tell us of the feudalism of the country[3] – there is, for example, hardly a word of it in the whole of the English laws – probably because this is a matter of government and public administration, which rarely sets problems between litigants for the courts to answer. In the Hittite Code, however, towards the close of the Central stage, when feudalism reaches its height, there is a substantial group of laws on this subject.[4] Their meaning is not clear, but they show that certain lands held on feudal tenures were inalienable, and that the occupier's vineyard and children[5] were equally unassignable; that persons occupying the land of others which was subject to particular feudal obligations forfeited their right to occupy for failure to discharge them; they show the right of certain persons holding on military tenures to engage others at a remuneration to perform their military service, and define their obligations in the event of the mercenary's death in action; they raise the question of who performs the services when land is the subject of a gift; they protect certain holders even from liability for some civil wrongs; they distinguish between feudal services attached to particular holdings and *corvée* (forced labour) imposed on subjects generally; they answer the question whether landholders in certain areas are liable to military service or not.

The space devoted to rules of inheritance continues to increase.[6]

[1] 51 shows how the compensation paid for religious offences should be used by the Church.
[2] 187, 188, 199, 200a.
[3] In the Armenian Law-Book, 5-7, is a short section on the relations between lords and dependants; and the Georgian, Armenian and Scottish Kingdoms were plainly feudal.
[4] Stretching from 39 to 56, but with an inset (43-5) of irrelevant miscellaneous clauses.
[5] Presumably as debt slaves or security for debt.
[6] L. Sax. 44-9, 61-4; L. Angl. et Werin, 25-34; Gulathing 103-30; Frostathing VIII, IX; Aghbougha 153-8; Armenian Law Book 94-6, 113-14.

England   1100 – 1250

CHAPTER 7

The Late Codes of the Past – the Flowering of Civilization

dates

The 'Late Codes' is the name given in this book to all codes of law of the state of material culture represented by the scanty English codes between A.D. 1100 and 1250. They therefore include the legislation of the Norman kings, the legal treatise attributed to Glanville, and the sparse continental material between A.D. 1000 and 1150,[1] but they also include the substantial codes of law of around A.D. 500, produced at the downfall of the Roman Empire by three peoples who had lived long within the Empire and been much influenced by its culture – the Edictum Theoderici (the code of the Ostrogoths) of about 500; the code of the Burgundians, issued by Gundobad about 502 and amended by his son Sigismund; and the code of the Visigoths, promulgated about 654 by Recesswinth, being that of Euric of about 475, amended by their successors. The Late Codes also include the Hebrew Code,[2] scanty Greek material (being little more than the remaining traces of Draco's legislation of about 620 B.C.) and the Roman Twelve Tables. The most valuable material, however, comes from ancient Babylonia, and dates from between the end of the third millennium B.C. and the end of the second – the fragments of a Code of about 2050 B.C. from the Sumerian third dynasty of Ur, bearing the name of its founder Ur-Nammu; the codes of the Kingdom of Eshnunna and of Lipit Ishtar of Isin, of around 1900 B.C., and one of the greatest legal instruments of all time, the code of Hammurabi, sixth king of the Amorite dynasty of Babylon (about 1752 B.C.). These Babylonian enactments,

[1] The western parts of the continent of Europe being still about a century in advance economically of England.
[2] Which may be attributed to the ninth to seventh centuries B.C.

especially during the third dynasty of Ur and that of Hammurabi, are illustrated by a vast mass of surviving tablets, the legal and commercial transactions of every day, as well as administrative records. There also survive the fragments that have been mentioned, from the Old Assyrian trading colony in Asia Minor of about 1900 B.C. and the important Assyrian Women's Code of about 1125, and a plentiful harvest of legal documents of the latter period, as well as the surviving documents from Mari, Alalakh, Nuzi and Ugarit. The early legal literature of India from 500 B.C. onwards also illustrates the law of the Late Codes, as does that of China from the dawn of history in the tenth century B.C. to A.D. 1900.[1] The Chinese economy was static for so long, the pattern of its civilization and law so permanent, and its population so large, that the penal law of its codes exemplifies, in its wealth of illustration and distinctions, as no other system does, the spirit of the law of the Late Codes. Muhammadan Law also belongs to the Late Codes, but in this book is chiefly considered among the Recent Peoples of the Late Codes, in particular the Emirates of Northern Nigeria.

Apart from criteria of date and place we define the Late Codes briefly in the following terms of material culture. This is the age of the blossoming of civilization. It gives birth to the great faiths of man in all lands and at all times – in Jerusalem,[2] in North-West India, where Brahmanism reached its full development and, amid a vast number of other sects and schools, Buddhism[3] and Jainism[4] were born, in China, which saw the great age of Confucius[5] and Lao-Tse,[6] in Western Arabia and the Fertile Crescent where Islam was born and grew.[7] In Western Europe it was the

[margin note: economic definition]

---

[1] The first half of the period of the Late Codes is represented by twelfth-century England, the Ostrogothic and Burgundian Codes and those of Ur-Nammu and Eshnunna and the Muhammadan Law; the middle of the period (late twelfth century in England) by the Code of Lipit Ishtar and the Hebrew, Roman and Visigothic Codes; the second half of the period of the Late Codes by the English law of 1200 to 1250, the Code of Hammurabi, the Middle Assyrian Laws, the law of India in the Code of Manu and after, and the traditional law of China.

[2] Culminating in Josiah's reforms about 621 B.C.

[3] Gautama the Buddha lived about 560 to 480 B.C.

[4] Chiefly attributed to Vardhamana Mahavira (lived about 540 to 468 B.C.).

[5] About 551 to 478 B.C.   [6] Born 604 B.C.

[7] Muhammad lived 570 to 632, but the following century witnessed the main development of Muhammadan Law. The legal part of the Qur'ān is small.

age of the Crusades. Never again does religion hold such sway over the mind of man. The arts burst into a brilliant maturity – in Egypt, Babylonia, Assyria and Western Europe the arts of architecture and sculpture; in Jerusalem of literature. All the world's great legal systems are born in this age – in Babylonia, Rome, and England, and also India, Jerusalem and Arabia. Feudalism, which has reached its height at the beginning of the age,[1] begins its slow decline, for while the central authority of kingship continues to strengthen as against local lords, in the great economic advance of the age a metal currency is in wide use in the towns, and from the middle of this period money rents begin to take the place of feudal dues and taxes of military service. So in England from the middle of the twelfth century the villein begins to give tallage instead of labour, the tenant holding on knight's service to pay scutage in place of the performance of military duties, and the king is provided with the means of acquiring a mercenary, professional and mobile force in place of or in addition to the enormous feudal levies that can be called out for war but not for training. With the advance in trade and credit the status of the free peasant continues to fall and the classes of the population below the king seem to be in most nations the nobles and the commoners (or patricians and plebeians),[2] the priesthood and the slaves (or serfs). The size of the kingdoms and empires and the numbers of the populations rapidly increase. The English Kingdom doubles during this age to some 3,500,000 persons and the density to some 40 persons per square mile, and in Western Europe the average village now holds some 300 persons. But the towns show a great growth and the population of London in the middle of the period is some 20,000, that of York, Lincoln and Norwich a little over 8,000 each, Northampton 7,000 and Gloucester 4,000.[3] Some 75 to 77 per cent of the population still

---

[1] See C.H. 26-41, which deals with classes of the population holding land on terms of services to the Crown.

[2] Babylonian *amilu* and *muškenu*. The Hebrew lords are the *śarim*, and the commoners are the *'am ha'ares* ('the people of the land').

[3] The combined population of Israel and Judah is of the order of a million and the density again about 40 per square mile; Jerusalem holds about 20,000 souls. The average village in Judah, India and China is also probably about 300 persons. The population of China is said to have reached 50,000,000 in A.D. 156.

earn their living on the land. The heavy ox-drawn plough is in use in Babylonia and Egypt in the third millenium B.C., and in India and Europe before our period. The farm wagon is equally old in the ancient world. Irrigation canals, terrace-cultivation and rotation of crops are in evidence and there is much more variety in the products of agriculture. But there is also a great increase in the number of artisans and craftsmen,[1] who now number some 5 per cent of the population, mainly practising hereditary skills, and apprenticeship is seen.[2] The number of traders has also increased, to perhaps 5 per cent of the population, and trade and markets grow and increase with the towns. In the markets the women are everywhere active in petty trading and have also a virtual monopoly in spinning. They form a great majority of the weavers[3] and almost monopolize the brewing.[4]

In legal terms we define our late Codes as follows, remembering, however, that the pace of advance increases and there is considerable difference between the least and most developed of these Codes. The Late Codes begin at the point where intentional homicide becomes capital, though unintentional or accidental homicide and homicide in self-defence are not free of sanctions. In the middle of the age, by analogy with the law of death for death, talion for the more serious cases of wounding – that is to say, the rule of 'eye for eye and tooth for tooth' – makes its brief appearance, but it does not by any means enjoy general acceptance. Similarly, for the more serious criminal offences appropriate mutilations are common and usual (since prisons are yet in little use) and it is indeed characteristic of the age that the law of criminal and civil offences is closer together than at any other time before or since. The more serious of the private wrongs, namely, intentional homicide, adultery, rape and substantial theft, become criminal as well as civil.

Land is generally considered to belong to the king in theory.[5]

---

[1] Including doctors everywhere.
[2] In England apprenticeship appears in the twelfth century (Clapham 133; P. & M. I, 672).
[3] cf. English 'wife' and 'webster' (fem.).
[4] c.f. English 'brewster', or ale-wife of the thirteenth century, and C.H. 108-10.
[5] In the religious literatures the land is sometimes thought of as belonging to a God (e.g. in the Old Testament).

Tenures vary vastly, but feudal tenures are much in evidence. At the end of the period, with the weakening of ties in the larger kinship groups,[1] an expansion of credit and trade, a new pressure on the land and a new need to realize land for money, there is in England and elsewhere[2] for the first time a ready market in land, which (subject to certain limitations) is sold, leased and exchanged. The other most frequent commercial transaction is the ready-money sale of cattle and slaves (or serfs), and in Babylonia and Egypt of ships. There is also barter of produce, often not con-temporaneous, and at the end of the period loan of money and suretyship are common. Bailments of goods are also common[3], deposit (especially of currency – that is to say, banking)[4] and hire of ploughs, wagons and oxen or asses (with or without drivers). With a growing landless class[5] and an increasing specialization of occupations there is much hiring of agricultural servants and artisans. The former are normally hired by the year in Israel and Judah, Babylonia and England and paid in kind, but there are extra harvesters everywhere paid for the work or the day in kind. The artisan of the towns is generally paid everywhere by the day and in money.[6] There are market courts[7] and more fixing by law of prices and hire of goods and wages of employees,[8] but the law

---

[1] But in the family, on the death of a father, brothers commonly live together and manage the estate as a whole for a considerable period before they divide, in Eshnunna (L.E. § 38), among the Hebrews (Deut. 25[5]), Romans, Assyrians (Driver & Miles 1935, 40), Babylonians (C.H. 165, 166, 178), especially India (see Manu. IX, 104f.) and China.

[2] Babylon, Rome, Hebrews, China and India. Compare L. Burg. 84-5.

[3] See further as to bailments and their importance in the history of the ordeal, *post* Chaps. 21, 27.

[4] See, for the Hebrews Ex. 22[7] (silver and cloth).

[5] See the Old Testament *passim*, e.g. 10th Commandment, Is. 5[8]; Micah 2[2]; Amos 8[5].

[6] In C.H. the artisans are paid in silver by the day (274), the hire of farm labourers and herdsmen is fixed in corn by the year (257-8, 281) and the hire of farm animals for threshing and transport and wagons and wagoners in corn for the day (268-78). See similarly L.E. 3-9, India (see C.H. I, I, 287), and China. The Hebrew agricultural worker is engaged for the year or for three years (Is. 21[16] and 16[14], Deut. 15[18], Lev. 25[53]). The artisan in the towns is engaged by the day and paid in money (Lev. 19[13], Deut. 15[18]). In England the labourer in the towns is paid by the day, usually a (silver) penny, and the agricultural worker by the year, probably in kind.

[7] Rome, England, India, China and probably everywhere else.

[8] L.E. 1-11; C.H. 215-77.

does not seem to be effective.[1] Gilds and gild courts are to be seen in England and elsewhere.

With the weakening of ties in the wider kinship group and the great economic development there is a continued fall in the status of women, and the father of the family is the despotic head of the household.[2] He tends to become the legal owner of all its property,[3] which is liable in his hands for the debts of the family. He has to a large extent power of life and death over the children and they are liable to be seized by creditors for his debts during his lifetime and after his death.[4] Similarly he may sell himself, his unmarried sister or children to the creditor as debt-slaves, by way of security for the repayment of his debts[5] (for their labour does not extinguish the debt but only the interest upon it). Consequently they might never recover their freedom, and the law commonly intervenes to restore the freedom of debt-slaves after a fixed number of years (in the Code of Hammurabi three years, among the Hebrews six)[6], and some pains are taken (with what success we cannot tell) to ensure that the law is not ignored.[7]

Further attempts are made to protect the population from succumbing to debt and losing its land, by granting releases of debt. In the Old Babylonian period, statutes are enacted from time to time with that object, commonly to celebrate the beginning of a new reign, and also at other times, but we do not know much of their terms or to what areas or transactions each applied.[8] Elsewhere, provisions of the general law give the right

[1] Hammurabi's object was in part to keep up the level of wages but according to the tablets lesser rates were in fact paid.

[2] Striking or cursing the father is punishable with death or loss of the hand, and to a large extent the same applies with the mother among the Hebrews (Ex. 21[15-17]), in Babylonia (C.H. 195) and China.

[3] Rome: Assyria (A.C. 3, 4, 6, 35). In China the wife owned no Ch'ü property and had no right to inherit from the husband (Ch'ü, 1961, 104). See *Manu* viii, 416 (the wife and son had no property).

[4] L.E. 24; Hebrews, 2 Kings 4[1].

[5] But the Visigothic Code prohibits selling wife and children, and there is less of this in Western Europe.

[6] Hebrews, Ex. 21[2], Deut. 15[12f.], Lev. 25[39f.]; C.H. 117; Rome ('Si pater filium ter venum duuit, filius a patre liber esto' – 'if a father sells his son three times, the son shall be free of the father', which suggests that there was a period fixed by law for the release of the son).

[7] Hebrews (Ex. 21[2]; Jer. 24[14]; Neh. 5[1-13]).

[8] Kraus (1965), 225f.; Finkelstein (1965), 233f. For the Hebrew religious literature see *post* p. 148.

of pre-emption or redemption to the former seller of land or his nearest of kin.[1]

The institution of the brideprice everywhere remains[2] but is waning, and there is opposition to it.[3] The sum represents a diminishing proportion of the people's wealth, and in Babylonia, India and England it is not always paid.[4] Countervailing gifts are increasingly common; a marriage-portion (often the bridewealth repaid by the father, and often with additions to it) is to be seen almost everywhere, in Israel, Babylonia and Assyria, India, China and Western Europe. Partly, perhaps, to avoid this personal and proprietary subjection to the husband, there are many looser marriages where the wife continues to live in her father's house,[5] and the law is concerned to regularize the situation. There is in most lands a marriage contract, and in Eshnunna,[6] in Hammurabi's Babylon[7] and in China if there is no marriage-deed the woman is no wife. In certain cases, however, in Eshnunna, Rome and Assyria, if the woman lives for a defined period in the man's house she comes under his control.[8]

By the religious devotion of the peoples the priesthood has increased in numbers and influence. It seems probable that in England in the thirteenth century A.D. and in Judah of the seventh and early sixth centuries B.C. (and, as we shall see, elsewhere)[9] the various religious orders now number about one-quarter of the adult male population and own about a third of the land. We cannot guess the figures in Egypt and Babylonia but they may well be as large. The religious history of early Rome has been lost. In Babylonia, Assyria, Egypt and Western Europe the finest and most developed estates are those of the great temples and churches. As great landowners and advisers of the Crown, as rulers of their orders, as the chief repositories of learning and as religious leaders

---

[1] e.g. L.E. 38, 39, and the Assyrian and Hebrew Law, and see *post* p. 373.
[2] e.g. L. Burg. 12, 66, 69; L. Vis. *passim*; Hebrews (Ex. 22[16-17]), Rome (the coemptio); Babylonia (everywhere).
[3] e.g. India: contrast Manu iii ('this would be a sale') with viii, 204; and ix, 98, with ix, 97 and viii, 366.
[4] e.g. C.H. 139.
[5] e.g. A.C. 25-38 and see *post* pp. 367, 374.
[6] L.E. 27.   [7] C.H. 128.
[8] See L.E. 27 (no marriage-deed or brideprice); A.C. 34 (no marriage-deed or brideprice); Rome, XII Tables (no ceremony or brideprice).
[9] See *post* p. 389.

of the nation, their influence is enormous. Most of the priesthood, however, have little knowledge of reading and writing, but the schools for scribes, so far as our knowledge goes, are only held at temples and churches, and the scribes, who still have a virtual monopoly of writing, are in most places a distinct calling closely allied to the priesthood.[1] Yet in spite of their ecclesiastical bias and near monopoly of writing, there is hardly a word of religious *religion* matter – of religious or ecclesiastical rules or religious sanctions – in the Hebrew and Roman codes and nothing in the rest, that is to say in the codes of the ancient East or of Mediaeval Europe after A.D. 1200. The main reason is that law and religion are, as they always have been, very different things, and we have seen little of religious matter in the codes of law at any stage. But it should be added that there is now some specialization of the scribes as of the other religious orders, and there are royal scribes, who might well be called Lord Treasurers or Secretaries of State, and there are temple scribes, and also the scribes who are the letter writers and the petition writers and the draftsmen and students of deeds and laws. There is hardly a legal profession but there are scribes with special knowledge of law. Moreover there is towards the end of our period the beginning of an extension to the layman of the art of writing, though education remains the function of church schools for long after (in England till 1870).

But this powerful influence of the religious orders brings about in this age first, a jealous rivalry between priesthood and kingship for the control of the people and secondly, a reaction and even a revolt against the Church. The ecclesiastical literature of the age, so far as it survives, contains much reproach and abuse of the kings. The historical books of the Old Testament have little to say in their favour; all the kings of Israel and most of the kings of Judah are bad kings. In the fourth chapter of Manu[2] it is declared that a king is equal in wickedness to a butcher who keeps 100,000 slaughterers: to accept presents from him is a terrible crime. In Rome echoes from this period still reverberate in classical times and in the traditions of the origin of the Twelve Tables. In England the quarrel culminates in A.D. 1170 with the murder of

[1] In Israel and Judah, Rome, Western Europe, Egypt, Babylonia and Assyria. For India, see Chap. 9.
Manu iv. 86; but it is also stated elsewhere that presents may be accepted.

Thomas Becket by henchmen of the king. In Judah the possibility
of such a result is avoided by the fall of the monarchy to the
Babylonians. In the history of Egypt such events were probably
not infrequent.

It would seem likely that under a monotheism, or other religious system creating a united church, and especially where the
devotion and subservience of the people to its god is intense, and
above all where (as in Mediaeval Europe) one international and
supra-national church faces each kingship, this ecclesiastical influence will be at its highest. In the period of the Late Codes this
power may show itself in relation to the law in the following
three respects. First, the method of trial by an appeal to a god,
that is to say, by an oath of purgation – may show an abnormal
extension. Second, in the law of homicide the sanctuary may play
an abnormally prominent part, for the fleeing slayer may rely to
an increased extent on its efficacy to stay the avenging hand of the
next of kin, and, the ethical element in religion being much
enlarged in the peoples of the Late Codes, with their devoted
interest in the law, the rules of the sanctuary may become an
important part of the procedural law of homicide. Thirdly, by
reason of the same increase in the ethical element in religion, the
priesthoods may exact from their flocks standards of conduct in
certain familiar departments where law and religion adjoin, and
for breaches of these they may impose sanctions in the form of
penances, offerings or fines.

There is less difference in these respects between the peoples of
the Late Codes than might have been supposed, and such differences as appear are partly explained by the difference in the character of the records, and the absence in some lands of legal relics and
in others of religious writings. In China, where religion in the
usual sense of that word hardly existed, the ordeal was practically
unknown;[1] but even in Isin, Eshnunna, Babylonia generally,
Mari, Alalakh, Ugarit, Assyria and India, and even among the
Hebrews, the use of the ordeal was within normal limits, namely,
confined to cases where evidence was wanting, and even in
Western Europe the abnormal extension that we saw in the Early
and Central Codes is narrowing. Again, the sanctuary is practically
unknown in China, and though sanctuaries must have existed in the

[1] Ch'ü (1961), 209f.

other lands, they play no visible part even in the literature of India, or apparently in any other of these peoples except Israel and Western Europe; but then we are told little of the law of homicide in the Codes of the Near East. And though priests were often to be found among the judges in Egypt,[1] Mesopotamia and Israel, we have no records of any ecclesiastical jurisdiction at the boundaries of law and religion except in Israel, India, Western Europe and (by inference) Rome. Here we find close resemblances between the topics of the priestly jurisdiction in the different lands. In Rome, even in the late days of the republic, the Pontifex Maximus still retained a jurisdiction in respect of wills and adoptions, burials, witchcraft and incest. In England in the twelfth century the ecclesiastical courts obtained for their exclusive province matters of ecclesiastical economy, punishment of felonious clerics, matrimonial causes and (except as to land) testamentary causes, and sexual immorality (fornication, adultery and incest). In Israel and India the priestly jurisdiction is similar and its details are well authenticated. The power of the Hebrew priesthood enabled it to claim, even before the first exile, to divide the legal jurisdiction between the priestly and the secular. In England this division between the jurisdictions, partly enacted by William, is the effect of the Constitutions of Clarendon of 1164, and it is this competition for jurisdiction, as much as anything else, that leads to the murder of the archbishop.

Among the peoples of the Late Codes wills begin to be prominent, and succession on death takes up a growing amount of space in the Codes.[2]

---

[1] See the edict of Horemheb (fourteenth century B.C.).
[2] e.g. L. Burg. 1, 14, 24, 42; Ed. Theod. 23-33; L.I. 24f.; C.H. 162-82.

CHAPTER 8

The Late Codes of the Past

(Continued)

Let us now shortly survey, in a little more detail, the characteristic developments of the civil and criminal law in the Late Codes.

The law of homicide is little mentioned in the Late Codes, but there is enough to show that the directions of change are those we witnessed in the Central Codes. There the general rule of pecuniary compensation, the amounts varying chiefly with the social class of the slain, was ceasing to satisfy, and the central authority was gaining or increasing the ability to impose sanctions by force. The new sanction for homicide was the handing over of a number of persons to the family of the slain, varying partly with the intention of the slayer. At the end of the period of the Central Codes killing by ambush was in England *bootless*, that is to say, unemendable by composition. The new law of the Late Codes is the wider rule that intentional homicide is capital.[1]

The circumstances leading up to the trial have changed little. The slayer flees, if he can, either to a frontier or abroad or to some place in the country which will give him at least temporary protection. So, for example, on the borders of England in the twelfth and thirteenth centuries the number of fleeing homicides is enormous. The chief places of refuge within the country are those whose sanctity will deter the pursuing next of kin from a violent revenge – shrines, temples or churches among the Hebrews and Athenians and in Western Europe. But intentional homicide

---

[1] L. Burg. 2, 29; Ed. Theod. clearly implied, 99, 152; L. Vis. clearly implied, VI, 5, 11-12 and *passim*; L.E. 24 and a fragment of L.I. clearly implied; Heb. Ex. 21$^{12-14}$; Rome; C.H. clearly implied, *passim*; Assyria, A.C., clearly implied. The sanction for intentional homicide is obviously too well known to need to be stated. It is also the law of China. In England so complete is the change from the pecuniary to the capital sanction for homicide, that the kin of the slain lose all right to compensation for death, and it needs the Fatal Accidents Act of 1846 to restore it: see P. & M., vol. 2, 458f.

is now considered not merely a wrong against the victim and his next of kin but also an offence against the nation and a threat to its security and if at the subsequent trial at the place of refuge the defendant is found guilty of intentional homicide he is handed over to the next of kin to put to death.[1]

But the temptation to accept an enormous sum of blood money remains and it is sometimes taken. Nevertheless there are a number of powerful factors which militate against acceptance. There is, first, the pride and solidarity of the family, and public opinion that despises those who accept, and there is the religious aspect of the same rule. Much as the religions of the Athenians and Hebrews differed, their doctrine in this was closely similar, namely, that the land is polluted by the shedding of innocent blood and no expiation can be made for the land but by the death of the offender. It is the duty of the nearest kin to obtain revenge for the slain and the presence of the slayer in the land destroys its fertility. Equally if vengeance falls on the innocent the same dire results ensue.[2] Therefore at Athens, at one of these places of refuge, namely the Areopagus, charges of intentional homicide were heard and punished by death and confiscation of goods. The court at the Palladion heard pleas of unintentional homicide, which were punished by banishment for a limited period, and that at the Delphinion heard the cases of those who pleaded that the homicide was committed in self-defence, and if that defence was made out there was no punishment but the defendant was admitted to purification. These are the rules of the classical law in the fourth century B.C. nearly three hundred years after Draco's time.[3] Similarly in holy writ: 'Thine eye shall not pity him, but thou shalt put away the innocent blood from Israel that it may go well with thee'.[4]

'Ye shall take no ransom for the life of a manslayer liable to death, for he shall surely die. . . . So ye shall not pollute the

---

[1] cf. L. Vis. VI, 5, 16.
[2] In the Pentateuch (see Deut. 19[10]) one reason given for the establishment of the sanctuaries is that 'innocent blood be not shed in the midst of the land'.
[3] e.g. Calhoun, *The Growth of Criminal Law in Ancient Greece* (Berkley, California, 1927); MacDowell, *Athenian Homicide Law in the Age of the Orators* (1963).
[4] Deut. 19[13].

land wherein ye are, for blood it polluteth the land and no expiation can be made for the land for the blood which is shed therein, but by the blood of him that shed it. And thou shalt not defile the land which ye inhabit, in the midst of which I dwell; for I the Lord dwell in the midst of the children of Israel.'[1]

There is another factor which discourages the payment and acceptance of blood money – namely, that in some lands, at least, the king's court retains jurisdiction and the death sentence may still await the slayer. Nevertheless, in the Late Codes, so far as our knowledge goes, homicide still remains, in part at least, a private wrong. In Athens, throughout the classical age, proceedings for homicide are called δικαί (civil actions) not γραφαί (prosecutions). Only the next of kin can take proceedings. It was to the slain man that vengeance was due, and if before his death he forgave the killer or waived his rights no one else could demand them and the slayer was immune from all proceedings and punishment. And in no case was the accused arrested pending the trial, but only forbidden by proclamation to enter the agora or sacred places, and even after the trial began he could escape the death sentence by voluntary exile.[2] In England neither the king nor the relative could, by pardoning the accused, save him from proceedings by the other. In Judah, if at the trial in the sanctuary he was found guilty of intentional killing, he was not stoned by the community (as for a crime) but was handed over to the next of kin to do his duty. If he was found not to have killed intentionally, he was not delivered up to the next of kin; but if he sallied forth before a defined period (after the first exile it was before the death of the High Priest[3]) he might be killed with impunity, and again the religious doctrine of the pollution of the land supported the action. 'Ye shall take no ransom', says the same passage in Numbers, 'for him that is fled to his city of refuge that he should return to dwell in the land until the death of the Priest. So ye shall not pollute the land wherein ye are, for blood, it polluteth the land.'

[1] Num. 35[31f.].
[2] In England, under the Assize of Clarendon (1166) he can abjure the realm and be escorted abroad.   [3] Num. 35[31f] See Deut. 19[8f.].

But in none of the Late Codes, if the killer did not slay intentionally, does he go scot-free. Such a rule does not meet the needs of the law, which must satisfy the family of the slain as well as the general public. Negligence is not the test: that is a new category, only just creeping into the law.[1] For some acts of homicide which we would call negligent the law imposes a death sentence – as in the Hebrew Code, where a man is gored to death by an ox known to its owner to have gored in the past;[2] or in the Code of Hammurabi, where a man is killed by the collapse of a house which the defendant built.[3] For other acts of homicide a compensatory sum is payable. In England, in the middle of the twelfth century, a man who slays unintentionally is still liable to the violence of the kin of the deceased. In the middle of the thirteenth century he receives a pardon from the Crown, but all his chattels are forfeited. As for the man who killed in self-defence, in England he deserves but needs a pardon; in Athens (as has been mentioned) he was admitted to purification.

There are two other practices, supported by the same legal and religious doctrine and also by the common feeling (still familiar in our day) that where a man is killed someone or something should be made to pay; the first concerns the deodand (the tree, animal or other object by which the deceased was killed) and the other the liability of the territory where he was slain by a person unknown. The deodand (which we have already met) is either delivered up[4] or destroyed or declared religiously unclean or, at the end of our period, devoted to religious or pious uses. In the Hebrew Code, for example, the goring ox is stoned (this indicating a criminal and public 'offence') and the flesh is not to be eaten;[5] and in England in the thirteenth century the thing is usually delivered up to the men of the township in which the deceased was killed and they must answer to the royal officers for the

---

[1] e.g. L.E. 5; C.H. 236-8 (boatmen causing a boat to sink). The conception is familiar in the West (Lex. Vis. in a dozen places) in the latter half of the period.
[2] Ex. 21[29-36].
[3] C.H. 229, 230. Cf. 209-14 (if a man strikes the daughter of a patrician and causes her death, they shall put his daughter to death), and its forerunner in a probable fragment of L.I. (Civil (1965)), Tablet U.M. 55-7, 1, iii, 7[1]-8[1].
[4] Lex. Burg. 18; Ex. 21[35, 36] (animal killing another is handed over to the owner of the latter).
[5] Ex. 21[28].

proceeds of sale. Sometimes the judges declare the charitable purpose to which the money is to be applied – it is, for example, devoted 'for God's sake' to the repair of the bridge or given to a relative in distress.[1] The forfeiture of deodands survived till 1846. Similarly among the Athenians of the fourth century B.C., the king archon and the tribal kings, sitting at the Prytaneum and exercising a kind of criminal jurisdiction, still tried for homicide both animals and inanimate objects and cast them beyond the boundaries of Attica.[2] The notion of the legal liability of the occupiers of a territory to compensate the relatives of a person slain there by an unknown hand is frequently met with. We have seen a trace of it in the Hittite Code,[3] and in the Pentateuch we find the complementary rule of the religious liability of the territory (another aspect of the doctrine of the pollution of the land by unexpiated blood) where it is provided that a heifer shall be sacrificed by the elders of the town nearest to the spot where the slain man was found.[4]

There is another practice, called in England 'benefit of clergy', which relates especially to homicide, though also to all felonies. An ordained clerk can only be convicted in an ecclesiastical court under ecclesiastical law, and is never put to death (for the court never pronounces a death sentence) but may only suffer a sentence of whipping, branding or banishment, or he may be immured. Early in the thirteenth century and thereabouts almost everyone who could read or write was still a cleric, and there was in the public mind a notion that a man who could read or write should not be lightly lost. But at the end of the century the knowledge of writing was spreading to the layman and 'benefit of clergy' becomes the privilege of everyone who can read, or pretend to read, a verse of the Bible, and if convicted he is only burnt in the hand. In the Indian literature we see the earlier stage of the practice: the Brahman is not put to death for homicide or any other capital offence except treason. He can be branded or even blinded, but more commonly he is banished, and the same rule is still found in Nepal in the nineteenth century. The later stage is to be seen in traditional China. The privilege is not that of

[1] P. & M. II, 473.
[2] They also tried and sentenced undiscovered homicides.
[3] H.C. I. 6.   [4] Deut. 21[1-9].

the priest (the Buddhist or other priest is indeed treated by the law with especial severity as one who should know better) it is the privilege of the literate. No graduate, even if he has bought his degree, suffers capital punishment, unless at least he is convicted of robbery or rape or some other offence of a disgraceful character.[1]

We have seen then that everywhere, at the beginning of the age of the Late Codes, intentional homicide ceased to be a wrong calling for compensation and became a capital offence: the law was now death for death. In the second half of the age the more serious personal injuries are also thought worthy of corporal sanctions. It is no longer tolerable that in this period of growing disparity of wealth a man of means should be permitted to wound or break a limb of his neighbour and be immune from any but a pecuniary sanction, whether it be compensation payable to the injured or a fine to the king or chief. The pride and solidarity of the family will not endure the affront and vengeance is no longer to be stayed by money. Nor does the social conscience of the people tolerate it. As yet there is no means of achieving progress except by corporal sanctions, for there are, for example, hardly any prisons. They appear now for the first time and in very small numbers,[2] but there is no question of the state providing nourishment in idleness for every malefactor in this violent age. The prisons are mere dungeons, and prisoners must be fed by their relations in thirteenth-century England, in India and China, if they are to be fed at all. Nor is there any question of a system of state-initiated prosecutions: the law exists for the head of the family to vindicate the injuries of its members.

We have already seen in the Central Codes a good deal of corporal sanctions, including horrible mutilations, for criminal offences; another aspect of the present development is that severe intentional personal injuries are undergoing a process of transformation into crimes, wrongs thought to be offences against the king or community and not merely against an individual.

But there is one difficulty in this part of the law that is not to be found in the law of homicide. A killing is a precise and distinct type of offence: a personal injury less than a killing is anything between the most serious and permanent maiming and a mere

[1] Alabaster (1899), 114-15.   [2] L. Vis. VII, 4, 3 & 4.

graze or blow. Nature knows no dividing line. Even in a modern court, pecuniary compensation is the appropriate sanction for most negligent injuries, and even at the close of the Late Codes it is always the most fitting sanction for a minor injury, whether intentional or not.

In truth, there is never at any stage of law, even in the Late Codes, a regular application of a law of 'an eye for an eye and a tooth for a tooth'. There is only a principle or maxim, which appeals to some legislators, courts and writers more than others, which to some extent is used as a deterrent or maximum penalty, but which is in practice limited to a vaguely defined class of the most serious personal injuries. The law will sometimes allow or inculcate self-help to the extent of inflicting talionic penalties, and the courts sometimes impose talionic sentences, but compensation continues in large measure to be offered and accepted between individuals and imposed by courts. Nevertheless the talion is generally found in the second half of the age of the Late Codes.

Moreover the talion is not an appropriate remedy for some of the most serious injuries. The appropriate corporal sanction for rape is not rape of the offender's wife or nearest female relative (though this rule is found)[1] but castration of the offender; for a kick inflicted on a member of a higher class or caste not a kick in return but mutilation of the foot; for stealing, loss of the hand or arm (as it was also in England in the period of the Central Codes for the crime of false coining).[2] Such 'sympathetic' punishments express the same outlook of the law in the same age.

In England the development of the law can easily be seen. At the beginning of our period, in the so-called Leis Willelme, the sanctions for wounding are still pecuniary and there is a tariff-list (briefer than before) of payments varying according to the part of the body injured and the nature of the injury, but the offender must also pay the cost of the medical attendance.[3] The twelfth century is a period of transition of which we know little in detail. The tariff-lists of wounds disappear. Wounding and *mayhem* (the

---

[1] e.g. Assyria (A.C. 55).   [2] II Aethelstan 14; II Can. 8.
[3] Chaps. 10, 11. Early twelfth century, but this is in a section of the Leis which contains many rules in force in the Conqueror's time (see Liebermann III, p. 283f.; Robertson (1925), 226f., 253f.).

latter being defined as the loss of use of a member serviceable in a fight) are becoming partly criminal, and at the same time the sanctions are becoming corporal and sometimes they involve loss of life or limb. At the end of the so-called Ten Articles of William I, commencing *Hic Intimatur* and dating from about 1125, comes a chapter reading: 'I also forbid the killing or hanging of a man for any offence, but let his eyes be gouged out and his testicles cut off.' There is also a later version of the same collection (probably dating from about 1210), known as the *Willelmi Articuli Retractati*, and reading:

> 'We also forbid that anyone be killed or hanged for any offence, but let his eyes be gouged out and his feet cut off or his testicles or hands, so that the trunk remain alive as a sign of his treachery and villainy, for according to the size of the wrong should the penalty be inflicted upon evil-doers.'

This is perhaps the first expression in England of the talion, which increases in popularity, and at the end of our period Britton (1291) advocates an out-and-out talion of member for member, wound for wound, imprisonment for imprisonment.[1] And yet it is not true that talionic sanctions were regular in England.

We can watch the same historical development in ancient Babylonia and Assyria. The oldest surviving Code of the Near East, that of Ur-Nammu, founder of the Sumerian Third Dynasty of Ur (who began his reign about 2050 B.C.) contains a number of fragments which can be read, and which provide for serious personal injuries, and in each case the sanction is pecuniary. In the Code of Eshnunna, of about 1900 B.C., the sanctions for wounding are all pecuniary. The code of Lipit Ishtar of Isin (about the same date) contains practically nothing legible on the

---

[1] Britton, ed. F. M. Nichols (Oxford, 1865) I, 123-4; see also Fleta (ed. 1685), 59. Pollock & Maitland, however (II. 489) observe 'but here he is hebraizing and introducing an element that is foreign to the law of our race', and they add in a footnote: 'When crude retaliation appears in a mediaeval code, the influence of the Bible may always be suspected. What we call characteristic punishment, e.g. castration for adultery, or loss of a hand for forgery is a very different thing.' The authors were here blinded by contemporary German racial theory, and crowd these sentences with misapprehension.

topic of wounding,[1] but raises a doubt whether theft was capital. Finally the Code of Hammurabi (*c.* 1752 B.C.) of about 282 clauses contains no less than twenty-seven clauses imposing capital sentences for a wide variety of wrongs and a number provide talionic sanctions.

> If a builder has built a house for a man and has not made his work strong, and the house he has built collapses and causes the death of the householder, that builder shall be put to death. If it causes the death of the son of the householder, they shall put to death the builder's son (229, 230).
>
> If a man puts out the eye of a free man, they shall put out his eye. If he breaks the bone of a free man they shall break his bone. If he puts out the eye of a villein[2] or breaks the bone of a villein, he shall pay 1 mina of silver (196, 197).

And yet the tablets show lighter sanctions, in fact, imposed. The process continues and the Middle Assyrian Laws (about the twelfth century) are full of cruel, brutal sanctions, especially sanctions of a sympathetic character, such as cutting off a man's lower lip for kissing a married woman, and cutting off a finger for indecent assault upon her.[3] The same picture of development can be seen in the laws of ancient India, and the sanctions of traditional China are of the same general character.

The Late Codes of the period of collapse of the Roman Empire all provide or imply the death sentence for intentional homicide, and the latest and most advanced of these, the Visigothic Code of the seventh century, lays down at great length a general rule of talionic penalties for the most serious personal injuries intentionally inflicted, including disfigurements and false imprisonment or binding, whilst providing money compensation for unintentional injuries.[4]

---

[1] Only two provisions (if they belong to this Code) imposing pecuniary sanctions for assaults on a woman causing miscarriage (Civil, 1965).
[2] Driver & Miles (1955), who translate *awilum* by 'free man', and *muškenum* by 'villein' but the meanings are the subject of much debate (see Driver & Miles (1952), 86f.; Yaron (1969), 83f).   [3] A.C. 9.
[4] L. Vis. VI, 4, 3; VI, 4, 1; contrast L. Burg. which in 11, 48 still has a tariff for wounds. Ed. Theod. 1, 13, L. Vis. and C.H. 3-4, provide a talionic penalty for witnesses falsely accusing a person, and a judge falsely convicting.

The Hebrew and Roman Codes are of special interest in this connection as representing the transitional stage at the middle of the period of the Late Codes. There is no longer a tariff of payments for wounds, but only one or two general rules providing for pecuniary sanctions and one general rule imposing talionic sanctions for the more serious injuries, and in both codes the boundary is vague. In the Twelve Tables the talion only applies 'if he does not make his peace with him' (presumably by paying an agreed compensation) and it is probable that in the Hebrew Code the talionic rule only applies in the same circumstances; and it is plainly an amendment and addition.[1] There is no surviving evidence that it was ever applied.

In the Late Codes, adultery with a married woman is generally criminal as well as civil,[2] if the man knew she was married. The husband is well entitled, if he has the opportunity, to put both his wife and the adulterer to death[3] or to mutilate them both, but not the adulterer alone, for that would savour of conspiracy between husband and wife.[4] But more usually the pair are not caught in the act and direct evidence is not available, and the charge against the wife is tried by ordeal everywhere.[5] If criminal proceedings take place, the king has the prerogative to be merciful and the sentence of the court is often lighter.[6] Adultery is in some lands also an ecclesiastical offence, and if tried in the inept ecclesiastical courts is apt to be visited with a remarkably light sanction – often mere penances redeemed by money payments to the Church.[7]

Rape of a virgin is a lesser but serious offence and almost always criminal.[8] In England the sanction is castration and blinding;[9]

[1] See *post* p. 150.   [2] A.C. 15 (triable before the king or the judges).
[3] L.E. 28 ('she shall not get away alive'); Ur-Nammu; Gurney & Kramer (1965); Hebrews (Lev. 20[16]).
[4] L. Burg. 68; Ed. Theod. 17, 38; L. Vis. III, 4, 4; C.H. 129; A.C. 15, 16 (cf. 3, 4 – wife and receiver, where she steals from her husband); England; India; Manu (VIII, 371f. – woman to be devoured by dogs, man burnt alive); China (Alabaster 253f.; Chü 110).
[5] By water in the East and in Western Europe, but also by oath (Babylonia, see C.H. 132, 131. Hebrews, Num. 5[11]f.).
[6] Ch'ü 65, 104; Alabaster (1899), 369 (usually beating or imprisonment).
[7] See P. & M. II, 484, 544. Hebrews, death (Lev. 20[10]).
[8] L. Burg. 12 (9 times the amount of the brideprice and a fine, or is handed over if he cannot pay). Ed. Theod. 59 (death, or a third of a rich noble's estate).   [9] Bracton f. 147-8b.

among the Hebrews and Assyrians a sum by way of compensation to the father, and also, at the father's option, the man must marry her and pay the usual bridewealth. But in the Assyrian Women's Code, if the man is already married, the talion applies and the girl's father is entitled to seize the offender's wife to be dishonoured. In India the normal sentence is castration; in China strangulation, but if the girl is under twelve years of age, decapitation (a severer sentence for the spirit of the mutilated criminal among the shades). Seduction of a virgin is a common prelude to marriage everywhere, but if the father or the offender objects to the marriage, the latter pays the bridewealth or a multiple of it.[1]

In the first half of the age of the Late Codes (for example, in England in the twelfth century[2]) the sanction for theft is generally payment of a multiple of the value of the thing stolen – double or more the value of the less valuable property, but death or mutilation or a higher multiple for cattle;[3] sometimes death for the thief caught in the act,[4] especially in housebreaking and especially at night[5] or for theft in special places, such as a highway, or for a persistent thief; often the thief who cannot pay is sold for his theft.[6] In the latter half of the period, theft of property of substantial value has commonly become criminal and capital, whether the thief is caught in the act or not. This is the law in England of the thirteenth century, in Babylonia and Assyria, India and China.[7] If the value is less the sentence might be only the cutting off of hand or nose, or fine or multiple restitution.

These continue to be the most frequent wrongs in an expanding list. In the middle of the age of the Late Codes, at the close of the twelfth century, the first treatise on the law of England, that attributed to Glanville, begins with the words: 'There are two kinds of pleas: one criminal and the other civil'. But by the end

---

[1] Ex. 22; L. Vis. III, 4, 7-8; A.C. 55.
[2] Double value (Glanville I, 2; XIV, 48).
[3] L. Burg. 4, 70; Ed. Theod. 56-7; Ex. 22; L. Vis VII, 2, 13.
[4] Romans (XII Tables).
[5] L. Burg. 26; L.E. 12, 13 ('He shall not get away alive'); Hebrews Ex. 22$^{1-3}$; L. Vis. VII, 2, 16.
[6] L. Vis. VII, 2, 13.
[7] See Assize of Clarendon (1166) Chaps. 1, 12; P. & M. II, 494f.; A.C. 3ff.; C.H. 6, 7, 10, 14, 15, 19, 21, 22 and 25: especially 10 ('the buyer shall be put to death as a thief'). For China, see Alabaster (1899) 394; for India, Brihaspati XXII, 2; Manu viii, 320.

of the thirteenth century in England and the close of the period of the Late Codes everywhere, it is clear that the main wrongs of the old civil law – homicide, wounding, adultery, rape and theft – have also become criminal, and the boundary between civil and criminal law is vaguer than ever before or since. Nevertheless there are also wrongs of lesser kinds which are certainly civil, and there are purely criminal offences, some tried in the king's court and some in the ecclesiastical courts, where such exist. There is, above all, treason, and there is, as ever, witchcraft, commonly tried by ordeal of water,[1] and incest, blasphemy, suicide,[2] forgery and others. Outside the ecclesiastical courts the penalty for crime is commonly the loss of life or limb and confiscation of all property to the king and for some offences even this is not enough and the savagery of the sentences long remains. In England the convicted traitor, after a semblance of a trial, is liable to be dragged by a horse to the scaffold, hanged, disembowelled, burnt, beheaded and quartered. The brutality of the Assyrian sanctions for serious offences in the Women's Code is extreme and often a period of forced labour is included. In India the sympathetic sanctions are savage, and the refined brutality of the Chinese punishments for crime is unspeakable. In these ways the criminal law develops and expands with the growth of the social conscience and the royal authority, and by its means, in England and elsewhere, the royal jurisdiction extends itself over the whole realm, gradually levelling a maze of local jurisdictions and spreading one coherent system of national law.

[1] Europe; Babylonia (C.H. 2); Assyria (A.C. 47).
[2] For China, see Alabaster (1899) 303f. Suicide of a senior member of a family is visited on the junior (Ch'ü *passim*).

E

CHAPTER 9

The Early Law of India

Amidst the considerable mass of the early literature of India there survive a few books which each contain both religious and legal rules of conduct. For this reason they have sometimes been thought to furnish evidence that law originates by a differentiation of rules of conduct which are at the same time legal, moral and religious in nature. 'We can see,' wrote Maine, 'that Brahminical India has not passed beyond a stage which occurs in the history of all the families of mankind, the stage at which a rule of law is not yet discriminated from a rule of religion.'[1] A review, therefore, of this Indian evidence is important in our study: it presents many features common or frequent in the general history of early law and it illustrates the necessity and value of distinguishing the history of law from the history of literature.

No written legislation has survived from early India, and it is probable, and Megasthenes[2] states, that there was none. It is not clear when writing was first used in India. No inscription survives from a period earlier than the rise of the Maurya dynasty at the end of the fourth century B.C., when writing came into common use for public and general as well as literary purposes. But India was probably in commercial connection with Babylonia and Western Asia for some time before the invasion of Darius in

---

[1] *A.L.* p. 23. On the other hand, he says at p. 17, not altogether fairly, speaking of 'the religious oligarchies of Asia', that 'their complete monopoly of legal knowledge appears to have enabled them to put off on the world collections, not so much of the rules actually observed as of the rules which the priestly order considered proper to be observed. The Hindu Code, called the Laws of Man, ... undoubtedly enshrines many genuine observances of the Hindu race, but ... it does not, as a whole, represent a set of rules ever actually administered in Hindustan. It is, in great part, an ideal picture of that which, in the view of the Brahmins, *ought* to be the law.'
[2] For Megasthenes see *post* p. 109.

518 B.C., and it is possible that the Brahmi script was developed from the example of a Western Asiatic alphabet as early as the seventh or even the eighth century B.C., a period of considerable material development in India.[1]

Whenever the use of writing emerged it was, according to the evidence, the exclusive possession of members of the priestly order of the brahmans, and the literature which it embodied and the thought it recorded were for many centuries and throughout our period their province and product. It told at the same time something of the history of the culture of the Aryas, a primitive people who had invaded North-West India in the middle of the second millenium B.C., destroying the civilization of the Indus Valley and spreading in the ensuing centuries slowly east and south.[2]

The various dates when the sacred books of India were produced have been the subject of a large measure of agreement between at least European scholars for many years, though it is also agreed that they have each had their history of development and their frail manuscripts were copied and altered by many hands.

The Rigveda is the oldest of the surviving Indian books, being mainly a collection of hymns addressed to the many deities of the Hindu pantheon. Though they cannot have been reduced to writing till later centuries, they are generally considered to have come down from the period 1200 to 800 B.C.[3] The home of the Aryas was now in Afghanistan and on the Indus, but they had covered much of the Punjab. The tribes were primarily pastoral but also practised much agriculture and were settled in small villages. They kept large cattle, of which the cow was their dearest possession, and also horses and other domestic animals, and they used the plough and the cart and practised irrigation and some hunting, and we hear much of artisans in wood and bronze or copper, and especially the makers of chariots, ploughs and carts. Society was divided into kings (*rajas*), nobles (*rajanyas*), the

---

[1] See summary of the evidence in Diringer (1948) Chap. VI.
[2] For an introduction to the history and law of early India, see *Cambridge History of India*, vol. 1, and (by a Hindu lawyer) N. C. Sen-Gupta, *Evolution of Ancient Indian Law* (Calcutta and London, 1953) and recent authorities there cited. For the developed law, see J. D. Mayne, *Hindu Law and Usage*.
[3] We must, therefore, doubt the possibility that they came down wholly unaltered. For translations, see *S.B.E.*, vols 32, 46.

priestly order (*brahmans*) and the commoners (*viç*) – all mainly hereditary conditions, though caste was not yet far developed – and they also kept some slaves. The brahman performs the sacrifices and is the author of these hymns, and if he should become a *purohita*, or domestic priest of the ruler, enjoys some influence. The kings lead the tribes in battle, kings and nobles fight from chariots but the horse is not yet ridden in war. The noble warrior wears a helmet and coat of mail; the common people fight on foot with bows and arrows, axes and stones. In peace the kings appear in the popular assemblies, but we hear nothing of the administration of justice, and nothing of law or legal thought, though there is frequent mention of *rita* (right), the moral order of things. We need not doubt that civil and criminal justice is done by the kings and the local nobles and elders. The father is the head of the family and owner of its property, but the position of women is not as low as it later becomes. Apart from the kings and nobles monogyny is the general practice and marriage is for life. We hear much of bridewealth and the levirate is practised. There is mention of a market and much of barter, and debt for gambling and something of debt-slaves. We hear of a man's wergeld, but the chief offences are theft and robbery and burglary and men are put in the stocks for thieving. Incest is a crime. We can infer from all this that the economy and law of the Rigveda are those of peoples at the close of our Early Codes and the beginning of the Central Codes, and that the humble brahman is little concerned with the administration of justice.

There follows the rest of the Vedic literature – the later Samhitas (or collections), the Brahmanas, the Aranyakas and the Upanishads, belonging mainly to the period 800 to 600 B.C.[1] and consisting chiefly of chants, *mantras* (or forms of prayer) ritual and commentary. There is still no evidence of the knowledge or use of writing, and most of this material, too, must have been orally handed down to a later age. The Aryan culture has now spread further east and south, and covers much of Northern India, perhaps as far south as the Vindhya. The names of tribes are new, and there are amalgamations of peoples and larger kingships. There is a

[1] See translations in *S.B.E.*

great development in the agricultural and commercial economy. The heavy plough is in use and there is a greater variety of crops. Iron and other new materials are mentioned and growing towns, and there is a greater variety of occupations in production and trade. Gold and other valuables and other articles are in use as units of weight and value though there is no currency. Astronomy has made great strides and there is a vast development in the scale and detail of ritual and in religious philosophy. Because, presumably, the communities are more settled and the available land begins to be limited by the growth of population there is much evidence of feudalism, and the *vaiçya* (commoner) cultivating his own land, like the English peasant in the late Anglo-Saxon and early Norman period, is falling in status and becoming a feudal tenant and sometimes a serf. The royal power has increased: the king is the ruler of the land of the community and the *vaiçya* holds at his will and pays tribute in goods or services for his holding, and nobles are interposed between them (either by grant from the king or as being the local rulers) receiving the food and goods which enable them to serve the king's administration. The skilled artisan is also losing status, and landless employees and slaves increase in number. Occupations are crystallizing into castes, namely the *kshatriya* (warrior), *brahman*, *vaiçya* and *çudra* (low-caste), and the number of classes of priests increases and there are many divisions of the caste of the *vaiçya*. It is a matter of doubt if a man can change his caste. There is growth and detail in the prohibitions of marriage and an increased extent of polygyny and a fall in the estimation of women. As the royal power increases less is heard of the assemblies of the people. The king administers justice with the assistance of nobles, but more we do not know. We hear something of the practices of inheritance but there is still substantially no law or legal matter in the books: the literature is still purely religious. There are priests of the villages and *purohitas* of the kings but their functions are mainly the conduct of the sacrifices and the brahman is described as 'a receiver of gifts . . . a seeker of food and liable to removal at will'. He has not yet the influence derived from the possession of writing and the law is none of his business. We can infer that the law of the day is that of peoples of our Central Codes.

In the late seventh and the sixth centuries B.C. (as in other lands

stretching east and west from Babylon as they rose to the stage of
the Late Codes) there was a vast religious ferment in India, in
north and south and east and west, giving birth to many schools
of religious philosophy as well as the communities of the Jains
and Buddhists, and stimulating the old Vedic *karanas*, or schools
of sacred traditional learning, into new activity. The period from
600 to 200 B.C. is the age of the Sutras – manuals of instruction,
'strings' of rules expressed in brief maxims, and devised to teach
the proper conduct of the brahman at every moment of his life.
The great bulk are the Çrauta Sutras, ordaining the details of
sacrificial ritual, but there are also the Grihya Sutras, the maxims
of conduct in domestic relations, mainly for villagers and looking
askance at life in the towns, and later, from 300 B.C. onwards the
Dharma Sutras,[1] maxims of behaviour in all social relations
throughout the life of the brahman, sometimes part of a whole
product (a Kalpa Sutra) of a particular local Vedic school, and
sometimes becoming a separate work. It is common in the Dharma
Sutras to devote a chapter to the duties of the king, as well as of
the other classes of the community, and as he is the head of the
system of administration of justice, still represented as administering it largely in person, amongst the maxims for his conduct
are those for his conduct of trials, criminal and civil. Putting
aside their religious merits, the legal matter of the Dharma Sutras
is poor and scanty. For example, the Gautama,[2] perhaps the oldest
of the surviving Dharma Sutras, and part of a larger mass of
sutras the product of a Gautama Vedic karana, contains only a few
sentences of legal matter, and of this a good deal is no more than
religious aspiration and condemnation, and it is doubtful if any of
it is to be regarded as law rather than religious teaching.[3] But the
authors, like the ecclesiastics of Mediaeval Europe, have many
rules of penances (the typical sanctions for religious offences) and
have already conceived a special interest in inheritance, and indeed
the last chapter (perhaps partly of later date) is a description of
almost all the methods known to social anthropology by which

---

[1] *Dharma* (commonly translated the 'sacred law') is close in meaning to the
Hebrew *Torah*, i.e. divine teaching as to conduct.
[2] *S.B.E.*, vol. 2, part I.
[3] The same wergelds are still mentioned, but seem to be archaisms which
survive as penances and not law (Gautama, XXII; Baudhayana, I, 10, 18,
20; I, 10, 19; Apastamba, I, 9, 24).

property is inherited in a patrilineal community. What is true of Gautama is largely true of the other Dharma Sutras,[1] which are similar in construction and in much of the detail, and adopt rules and even chapters from one another.

The legal matter begins to appear in the religious literature because the possession of writing and monopoly of learning have given the brahmans a new influence, and some of them become advisers to the king in matters of state, and, we may be sure, upon legislation or edicts and in trials,[2] and hence they derive a new interest in law. It is only when we look at the Dharma Sutras in the light of their day that their poverty in legal matters is truly seen. For the third century B.C., in which they appear, is that of the Maurya Empire and the reigns of Chandragupta and Açoka, when India is for the first time largely united under one paramount power and the organization of commerce and government is elaborate, and the law, as we must infer, has developed in corresponding degree. There is much information on these topics in the surviving fragments of Megasthenes, a Greek who spent much time at the court of Chandragupta as ambassador of the first Seleucid king, and if we could doubt the existence of a developed secular administration and law there survives the Artha-çastra of Kautilya,[3] discovered at the beginning of the present century and attributed to the brahman statesman who overturned the previous dynasty and ushered in the Maurya Empire – the Macchiavelli of India. This is a substantial practical treatise on the real and ideal political economy of the India of that century, and corroborates what we learn from the Greek authors, and although it is not a study of the law it enables us to infer much of its general character. Book III concerns the administration of justice, and in the first chapter, after declaring that it is royal power, when exercised with impartiality and in due proportion to guilt, that maintains the fabric of the world, the author proceeds to enumerate the four elements which are the foundations of the proper administration of justice – royal edicts (*rajasasana*), history or

---

[1] Baudhayana (*S.B.E.*, vol. 14, part II); Vasishtha (*ibid.*); Apastamba (*S.B.E.*, vol. 2, part I) from South-East India.
[2] Vasishtha, XVI, 2 ('the king or his minister'). Apastamba II, 11, 29, 5 ('men of learning and pure descent').
[3] Translated, R. Shamasastry (Mysore, 2nd edn, 1923).

precedent (*charitra*), the evidence of witnesses, (*vyavahara*)[1] and religious law (*dharma*); he affirms that this is their order of importance and that where there is a conflict between king's law or rational law (*dharmanyaya*) and religious law the former prevails. There is no religious law or teaching in the Arthaçastra from first to last, and indeed its spirit is the antithesis of religion.

The religious literary tradition continues with the age of the Dharma Çastras, dating from perhaps 200 B.C. onwards. In them the quasi-legal matter of the Dharma Sutras is expanded into metrical codes, and whereas the Dharma Sutras were strings of maxims, based upon the Vedas and good custom and devised by human teachers for the instruction of their pupils at the various schools, the Çastras are invested with divine authority and purport to be revealed truth. The earliest and most authoritative is the Code of Manu,[2] or Manava Dharma Çastra, or more properly Bhrigu's version of the Institutes proclaimed by Manu, and dates from about the first century B.C. In the opening verses the great sages approach the divine Manu, the father of man, and pray to him to declare the sacred laws of each of the castes, and he consents to do so and gives them an account of the Creation as well as of his own origin from the self-existent Brahman, and declares that having learned these Institutes of the Sacred Law from the Creator, he has brought them to the sages and assigns to Bhrigu the task of expounding them. Apart from the introductory chapter and the advance in the quality of the work the general structure of the code is that of the Dharma Sutras and clearly betokens its original in a Manava Dharma Sutra. It remains a school-book for the instruction of Aryas by brahmans, but the school now specializes in the study of law and the administration of justice, and while the volume of the whole is three times that of the Dharma Sutras, the volume of the legal section (that is, the few chapters devoted to the duties of the king, the civil and criminal law and inheritance)[3] has multiplied ten or twenty-fold. These chapters are compounded of descriptions of existing practices and practices that ought to be followed, of religious and moral apophthegms

---

[1] *Vyavahara* is also used in the literature for 'the king's administration of justice'.
[2] Translated, *S.B.E.*, vol. 25.
[3] Chaps. VII, VIII and IX, but mainly VIII.

and exhortations, of accounts of divers laws that exist in different places, of the proper administration of justice and the giving of evidence. The learned brahman is now the legal adviser of the king and his deputy in the decision of law-suits. 'Let the king, rising early in the morning, worship brahmans who are well-versed in the three-fold sacred science[1] and learned in polity, and follow their advice.'[2] 'If the King does not personally investigate the suits, then let him appoint a learned brahman to try them.'[3] 'A king, desirous of investigating law cases, must enter his court of justice, keeping a dignified demeanour, together with brahmans and experienced advisers.'[4] But there is a competition and rivalry for jurisdiction and influence between brahman and king characteristic of literatures of the Late Codes. 'A King is declared to be equal in wickedness to a butcher who keeps 100,000 slaughter-houses: to accept presents from him is terrible.'[5] The code seeks to influence the king as head of the administration of justice by rules claiming high intrinsic moral authority, and much is for the benefit of the caste of the brahmans. When a king finds treasure-trove he must give half to brahmans, but a learned brahman who finds it may take the whole 'for he is master of everything'.[6]

These chapters of legal interest comprise only one-third of the whole, and even of these only a third is law. There is much obscurity and contradiction and little legal skill, and much of the law is unstated. The legal rules of the code are to be subject to all customs and all local and special law.[7] The king is to decide all cases 'according to principles drawn from local usages and from the Institutes of the sacred law' (i.e. of Manu).[8] 'He must enquire into the laws of castes, districts, gilds and families and settle the peculiar law of each.'[9] But such rules of law as the code contains are generally characteristic of the Late Codes. The wergelds have gone; the sanction for intentional homicide is not expressly stated but must have been capital[10] except for the brahman. There is no capital punishment for a brahman, only fines, tonsure or banishment.[11] The sanctions for wounding and serious assaults upon an

[1] Government, dialectics and the knowledge of the soul. See also VIII, 20.
[2] VII, 37.   [3] VIII, 9.   [4] VIII, 1.
[5] IV, 86.   [6] VIII, 37, 38.
[7] See also the Dharma Sutras (Gautama, XI, 19, 20).
[8] VIII, 3.   [9] VIII, 41.
[10] See VIII, 350, 351.   [11] VIII, 379, 380.

equal are generally fines and the expenses of the case,[1] but the punishment for a sudra assaulting one of the higher castes is 'sympathetic' – the limb by which the wrong was done is to be cut off,[2] and much the same applies to defamation.[3] Adultery with a married woman may be capital for her and her paramour.[4] Rape of a maiden is punished by mutilation;[5] but if she consented and they are of the same caste there is only a fine.[6] Intercourse, however, of a sudra with a woman of one of the higher castes is punishable by mutilation or death.[7] The sanction for theft varies in proportion to the value of the property and the status of the offender. As regards the value of the property the sanction varies from the double value (that is to say, compensation plus a fine of equal amount) upwards to higher multiples, fetters, imprisonment, cutting off of the offending hand, or death.[8] So disgraceful is theft that the higher the status of the offender the higher the multiple of restitution. 'Where a common man would be fined one karshapana the king shall be fined a thousand; that is the settled rule.'[9] 'The guilt of a brahman is sixty-four-fold or quite a hundred-fold or even four times sixty-fold if he knows the nature of the offence.'[10] Such unenforceable rules show the unreality of the sanctions. For damage to property the sanction is compensation and a fine.[11] There is a beginning of the concept of negligence.[12] As regards procedure, evidence is generally unsworn, but in cases of deposit or other instances where witnesses are not available there are rules relating to the oaths or other ordeals to be undergone by the party.[13] As to the law of property, 'A wife, a son and a slave, these three are declared to have no property: the wealth they earn is acquired for him to whom they belong.'[14] There is perpetual guardianship of women.[15] The payment of bridewealth begins to be discountenanced.[16]

As these are the characteristic rules of the Late Codes the bulk of them must have been the law of the land for some two or three centuries before the date of the Code of Manu. But its influence

---

[1] VIII, 287.   [2] VIII, 279-83.   [3] VIII, 270.
[4] VIII, 359, 371, 372; but see 352, 375. There is much contradiction in the sanctions.
[5] VIII, 364, 367.   [6] VIII, 368.   [7] VIII, 374.
[8] VIII, 319f.   [9] VIII, 336.   [10] VIII, 338.
[11] VIII, 288-98.   [12] VIII, 229f., 293, 409. [13] VIII, 190, 109f.
[14] VIII, 416.   [15] V, 148; IX, 3.   [16] IX, 98.

steadily spread and strengthened, mainly perhaps because of its completeness as a code of conduct and its attribution to Manu. We can see this influence, and a progressive improvement in the drafting and content of the legal sections and at the same time the normal development and changes of the rules of law, in the subsequent Institutes of Vishnu,[1] the Yaynavalkya[2] and finally the Narada,[3] which is free of religious matter and is a skilled and valuable treatise upon a system of law that has advanced far beyond our period.

The above summary may suffice to show how far from reality is the passage quoted from Maine at the head of this chapter. The literature of India at its beginning is purely religious, and then religious and moral. Law properly so-called, that is to say, the law of the courts, only enters into it towards the close of our period when the brahmans have begun to take a practical part in its administration. At first the legal passages are unskilful and contradictory and an inadequate reflection of the law as it must have been, but over the centuries they improve with the knowledge and experience of the authors, and the Narada consists of law alone, though the religious influence of the brahmanical authors of the earlier literature has left a lasting quality in the law of India.

[1] Translated, *S.B.E.,* vol. 7. Capital sentences for most serious offences (V, 1), but only branding and banishment for a brahman (V, 2f.); more prisons (V, 71); talion of eyes for eyes (V. 72); much of writing, written evidence and written contracts (VI, 23f., and VII); an increase of rules as to ordeals (the whole of Chaps. IX to XIV).
[2] Translated by Mandlik (fourth century A.D.).
[3] Translated by Jolly, *S.B.E.,* vol. 33, part I (fifth century A.D.).

CHAPTER 10

The Roman Twelve Tables

Among the early Roman texts containing rules of conduct are a
number of clauses known as the Leges Regiae, or Laws of the
Rex.[1] This title may signify that later Romans attributed them to
a legendary king or, as is more likely, that they, or some of them,
were issued by the Rex Sacrorum, an ecclesiastical official of the
Republic. However that may be, some are palpably spurious, and
the rest (recorded mainly by Dionysius and Plutarch in the first
century B.C. and the first century A.D.) are religious in character:
their sanctions, where they contain sanctions, are religious.[2] Some
may have been issued as ordinances relating to public worship
and ritual, but others seem to represent customary ecclesiastical
rules and maxims. Though some may embody old traditions in
modernized language, their historical value is little and they
shed no light on the early civil law.

Of the earliest Roman law nothing is known except what we
hear of the contents of a code which is called the 'Twelve Tables'
and according to tradition was compiled in the years 450 and 449
B.C. One Sextus Aelius, who was Consul in 198 B.C., published a
collection of rules called the Tripertita, which contained what
was known of the contents of the Twelve Tables (destroyed, we
are told, two centuries before), the *interpretatio* (or subsequent
development of the law) and something of procedure. All later
writers derived their knowledge of the Twelve Tables directly or

[1] For a summary of references, see Jolowicz, *Historical Introduction to Roman
Law* (2nd edn, Cambridge, 1952), 83; Westrup, *Introduction to Early Roman
Law* (1950), vol. IV, 47f.
[2] The sanction is commonly of the form *sacer esto*, which may be translated
'he shall be accursed'. According to Festus, s.v. *Sacer Mons,* the effect was that
anyone killing him would not be accounted a murderer, but this is very
late evidence.

indirectly from copies of the Tripertita,[1] and our own information consists of passages attributed to the Tables and scattered about their works.[2] Some purport to quote verbatim from the code, most merely to give the drift. Our earliest evidence comes from the works of Cicero[3] (four centuries after the traditional date of the code) and Festus, Gellius and Gaius (all two centuries later than Cicero) are our main authorities. The quotations that purport to give the words of the Tables are couched in language which seems more characteristic of the time of Sextus Aelius than of 450 B.C., though it contains some archaisms and may have been gradually modernized by a succession of copyists.

What, then, is the evidence that there was a code of 450 B.C.; what were Sextus Aelius' sources of information as to its contents; and what light is afforded by surviving quotations?

Our story of the compilation of the Twelve Tables comes from the middle of the first century B.C. and later, some four hundred years after the traditional date.[4] The outlines of Livy's account are familiar. The law was unwritten, and there was much discontent with it among the plebeians – a class, perhaps, descended from immigrant families of lesser means and devoid of many of the rights of the patricians. In particular they complained of the high-handed actions of the consuls, an office from which they were by law excluded. In the year 462 B.C. one of the Tribunes, C. Terentilius Arsa, demanded on their behalf 'the appointment of a commission of five to draw up laws defining the powers of the consuls'.[5] For some years the patricians successfully resisted the proposal, but in the end it was expanded (why, does not appear) to an agreement that measures should be proposed 'which would be of advantage to patrician and plebeian alike and would secure equal liberty for both'. A Commission of three patricians was 'dispatched to Athens to copy the famous laws of Solon and

---

[1] It still survived in the second century A.D. when it was called (according to Pomponius) 'the cradle of the law'.
[2] These passages have for the last century and a half been arranged in a more or less arbitrary order, following Dirksen. For the collected passages, see Girard, *Textes de Droit Romain* (Paris, 1913), 9f.; Muirhead, *Historical Introduction to the Private Law of Rome* (1916), 420f.; Westrup (1950), vol. IV, 129f.
[3] Chiefly his *De Leg.*, which contains some spurious versions of old laws.
[4] Livy, 3, 9-57 and Cicero, *De Rep.* II, 36, 37 are our earliest authorities.
[5] Livy, 3, 9.

learn the institutions, customs and laws of other Greek states',[1] and on their return 'with the laws of Athens'[2] it was resolved to change the form of government by substituting for the supreme authority of the Consuls a Commission of Ten from whose decision there should be no appeal. The Ten elected were all patricians and included one Appius Claudius and the three envoys, the latter appointed as a reward for their distant mission and also because it was thought that their knowledge of foreign laws would be of use in the enacting of new laws.[3] The Commission of Ten drafted the laws of the Ten Tables, 'which even now', says Livy, 'in this immense accumulation of statutes, are the fountain of all law private and public'. Then 'it was generally mooted that there lacked two tables, by the addition of which, as it were, a corpus of all Roman law might be finished off'.[4] A new Commission was appointed, consisting of Appius Claudius and nine new members. They proved themselves tyrants and Appius Claudius now displayed himself in his true colours. Among his other misdeeds he sought to bring about the disgraceful seduction of the virgin Verginia by the abuse of his authority and power, and her shame was only prevented by her death at her father's hands. Two further tables of law, tyrannical in their terms, were added to the ten. The Assembly carried the Code and it was inscribed on tablets set up in the Forum. In 390 B.C. Rome was sacked by the Gauls and the Tables destroyed, but later a collection was made of treaties and laws,[5] including the Twelve Tables and some Leges Regiae, and part of it was published to the people.

This story of the events of the fifth century B.C. can hardly be considered satisfactory in view of its inconsistencies and improbabilities, and part is legendary and incredible. At the commencement of his sixth book Livy, uncritical historian though he

---

[1] Livy, 3, 31.
[2] Livy, 3, 32. According to Pomponius, however (Dig. 1, 2, 2, 4) Hermodorus of Ephesus was the author of some of the laws. See also Pliny, H.N. 34, 11, 5.
[3] 'Condenda nova jura.'
[4] Livy, 3, 34, 'absolvi posset corpus omnis Romani juris'.
[5] 'They gave instructions', says Livy in the vaguest terms, 'for treaties and laws – and these were the Twelve Tables and certain *leges regiae* – so far as they could be found, to be searched out. Some of these were even made available to the common people, but those dealing with sacred rights were kept private by the pontiffs.'

is, apologizes for the character of his narrative of the early days of Rome. Down to its capture by the Gauls in 390, he says (and we can well believe him) there was but slight and scanty use of writing, the sole trustworthy guardian of the memory of past events, and even such records as existed perished almost entirely in the conflagration of the city.[1] In truth, history does not dawn at Rome before the war with Pyrrhus (280 B.C.) and it is unlikely that till then any great number of persons outside the ecclesiastical orders could read or write, or that before 250 B.C. writing was in use by the general population. The early Romans were remarkably illiterate, for whereas the earlier peoples of the Near East of a comparable degree of economic development – the Babylonians, Assyrians and Hebrews – as well as the English of the twelfth century, were mostly unable to write or read, they used the services of scribes to draw up their legal and commercial documents on which parties and witnesses made their marks, or put their seals or signatures, and this practice fixed the form of the deed among these peoples. But the early Romans made no use of writing for these purposes, as is well shown by the fact that a formal oral delivery, namely the *mancipium* – originally the simple procedure of a cash sale of valuable classes of property – survived into the classical law as the usual and proper method of conveyance of valuables of the same classes.

But there was indeed an order of persons in Rome who for some time before the fifth century had been able to read and write. They were few in number – they were later called a 'college' – and they did not apparently draw up the transactions of the illiterate layman, but in most other respects they corresponded closely to the scribes of the peoples named. They were not priests (for the priests of Rome were charged with the conduct of the worship of their particular deities) but they were one of the ecclesiastical orders entrusted with the duty to preserve and hand on the traditional rules respecting general religious observances. They had a monopoly of the learning of the age. They added arithmetic to the other two R's: they were the engineers of the time and their name went down to posterity as that of the *pontifices* (road and bridge builders).[2] They possessed what primitive

---

[1] And even the fact of a conflagration is not supported by archaeology.
[2] The early meaning of 'pons' was probably 'path' and 'bridge'.

knowledge of astronomy the Romans had acquired. From at least the middle of the fifth century B.C. they kept whatever annals were maintained, chronicling the important events of the year, and such state archives as existed. Whenever legislation and law were reduced to writing it was only they who could write and read it and there is a clear and unanimous tradition that the *interpretatio* (the development of the law) was in their hands. By reason of their reputation for learning they were appealed to for their opinions on questions of law, and they became the first Roman jurists. As the system of government of republican Rome developed, the college of the pontiffs became a department of state and their head, the Pontifex Maximus, still usually a lawyer even in Cicero's time, was a magistrate with a magistrate's power of issuing regulations within the field of his duties. In the course of time they declared and built up a body of written rules of ecclesiastical law and practice, which they had power to enforce. So, for example, they punished offences such as incest and witchcraft, and burials, wills and adoptions, and some matters relating to marriage,[1] fell within their province: in short, they came to exercise under this polytheistic regime much of the jurisdiction of the ecclesiastical courts of Mediaeval Europe. We are also told, though the importance of the matter has perhaps been exaggerated and is one of doubt, that, because they were the repository of astronomical and legal and religious knowledge, they had absolute control over the calendar and could say whether for religious reasons it was permissible (*fas*) for courts to be held on a particular day;[2] so that an unscrupulous pontiff could veto or postpone a trial. For this reason and because the illiterate population suspected the pontiffs of adducing from their custody such laws as suited their interest, their privileges were attacked. There was a tradition that one Appius Claudius (Censor in 312 B.C.) and his clerk Cn. Flavius published to the people the calendar and a list of legal procedural rules hitherto kept secret by the pontiffs, and that this was the beginning of the end of their power, though it should be added that it must have begun if and when Appius Claudius and his decemvirs of 450 B.C. published the Twelve Tables, and

---

[1] At least the patrician religious marriage by *confarreatio* continued to take place before the Pontifex Maximus.
[2] cf. in the earliest Norwegian Laws, Frostathing III, 20.

continued when Sextus Aelius published his Tripertita; in about 190 B.C. and yet it is probable that not until 191 B.C. was a law passed giving the pontiffs the complete control over the calendar.[1]

From the earliest times the transfer to their successors of all these functions necessitated the maintenance of a school where writing and reading and all this learning could be taught to the pupil, and until the third century the pontifical were probably the chief or only schools.[2]

But the authenticity of the events of 450 B.C. has not escaped criticism. About the beginning of the present century it was attacked by the vigorous arguments of Pais[3] and Lambert.[4] Pais, in a detailed examination of the story, arrives at the view that it is a myth, that Appius Claudius, the Decemvir of 450 B.C., and Appius Claudius, the Censor of 312 B.C., double the same traditional figure and that though some legislation is contained in them the so-called Twelve Tables grew up piecemeal and were not completed till the time of the Censor at the beginning of the fourth century. Lambert goes further and regards the Tables as a collection of rules, some very old, made in the early part of the second century, probably by Sextus Aelius. On the whole, however, scholars have not been convinced by the views of Lambert or Pais, for though it is generally agreed that the story contains some legendary matter and the quotations from the Tables some interpolations, the tradition is accepted as probable in its outline.

It is no necessary part of the theme of this book to attribute a date to the Tables. It might suffice for our purposes to point out, first, that literature begins at Rome, as in so many other countries, with law, and, second, that the Tables are (secular) law even though recorded by the hand of ecclesiastics, and afford no evidence of an origin of law in a confusion with rules of religion and morality. When Rome became mistress of the western world her legends and traditional events were ordered, spaced out,

---

[1] Censorinus, 20, 6; Solinus, 1, 43; Macrobius, 1, 13, 31.
[2] According to Plutarch (Quest. Rom. 59) the first school in Rome was opened, about 250 B.C., by one Spurius Carvilius.
[3] *Storia di Roma*, I, 1 (Rome, 1898), 530f.; 2 (1899), 546f., 631f.; II, 217f. *Ricerche* I, paras. I-VII.
[4] *Nouvelle Revue Historique*, XXVI (Paris, 1902), 149-200; *Revue Générale de Droit*, XXVI (Paris, 1902), 385f., 480; XXVII, 15f.; *Mélanges*, Appleton, 1 (Paris, 1903), 398.

reconciled, expanded and improved by the labours of imaginative and industrious historians, first Greek and then Roman, to give her people a pedigree and her institutions a development; and unless and until archaeology makes possible a new start it is far too late to test the authenticity of the story and the contents of the Tables by reference to the rest of early Roman history. But a comparison of the contents with other Late Codes enables us to draw some justifiable inferences.

There is no sufficient reason to doubt that the bulk has survived of the more important provisions of the document which the Romans called the Twelve Tables – about forty in quotations, complete or incomplete, and a further eighty or so merely in their drift. The code, therefore, was short but not abnormally so by the standards of the Late Codes. Some of the quotations are in the familiar form of early legislation, that is to say brief conditional sentences, the apodosis here being in the imperative, which in Latin can equally denote the second or third person.

But by the standard of the Late Codes it is difficult to suppose that it consisted, as a whole, of legislation, whether laying down existing or new law. Genuine legislation of these codes – that is to say, legislation that survives on the stone on which it was published or in documents that pass any test of authenticity – consists of a series of decisions upon isolated facts or groups of facts of common occurrence. They, therefore, almost always specify the facts supposed and the appropriate sanctions. We must make all due allowance for the unique Roman genius for law, but the bulk of the Twelve Tables consists of short maxims or rules of legal practice, with few or no expressed sanctions, thus indicating the contents of a school-book, the maxims or rules being intended to be copied out by the pupil taught to write and read, and in suitable form to be memorized and learned as the foundations of a knowledge of legal practice. It is, therefore, comparable with such a school law-book as the surviving Neo-Assyrian copies of the old Babylonian 'ana ittišu', long in use in the scribal schools to teach legal terminology and practice.[1]

It probably began with a number of short rules in simple language indicating how to start and pursue legal proceedings.

[1] See *ante* p. 15. Like the Twelve Tables it also contained a few old laws (see Driver & Miles (1952), 25; (1955), 308).

'(1) If he summon him to law, let him go. (2) If he does not go, let him call witnesses, then seize him. (3) If he evades him or takes to flight, let him lay hands upon him.' These passages continue to judgment in the action, execution by seizure of the defendant's person and division of his goods among the creditors. These rules, which mostly survive in quotation, number some seventeen (two-fifths of all quotations from the Code) and cover most of the first three tables as commonly arranged.

A second large group, embracing most of the tables 4 to 6, five in quotation and the drift of several others, are fundamental maxims or principles of conveyancing and property law. 'When he makes a *nexum* and *mancipium*, as he declares by word of mouth so shall be law.' 'As he wills concerning his money and tutelage it shall be law.' 'If he dies intestate without a house-heir, the nearest agnate shall have the household.' 'If there is no agnate, the clan-members shall have the household.' A patron inherits from his intestate freedman. 'If a father sells his son three times, the son shall be free of the father.'[1] Two years was the period in respect of land, and one year in respect of other property, for perfecting title against third parties and for the vendor's guarantee against dispossession.[1] A married woman, absent for three nights in a year, does not come under her husband's *manus* (power). Three rules relate to the tutelage of women and children – Vestal Virgins are free – and the curatorship of madmen and prodigals. One rule relates to the procedure of divorce, and another to the procedure of the division of the household between joint heirs.

But next we must notice a substantial section of maxims, mostly only in their drift, and now in table 8, of what we would call in England the law of torts or civil wrongs, but approaching closely, in the manner characteristic of the stage of the Late Codes, to the criminal law, and generally typical of the Late Codes. Intentional homicide is capital. In the law of wounding there is a contradiction, characteristic of this stage, between two rules, one (of a nature surviving from earlier stages) imposing pecuniary sanctions for wounding, and another (recent, temporary and not generally accepted) imposing the talionic penalty of like for like in cases of serious wounding.[2] There is, again,

---

[1] This rule may well have originally been laid down in legislation.
[2] See the parallel in the Hebrew Code, *post* p. 150.

characteristically, a large number of rules of theft, the sanctions varying much in severity between the double value for theft which is not 'manifest', and the capital sentence for the thief caught in the act and for most other substantial thefts, and also for intentionally setting fire to a dwelling-house or harvested crops. There are a few rules relating to damage to property – cutting down a neighbour's trees, depasturing his fields. There is also the offence of the judge or arbitrator caught taking a bribe or the witness giving false evidence, probably capital where the charge was capital.

There are also to be noticed two or three rules which go to support one of the traditional objects of the work of the Commission of Ten, in that they make for the equality of the citizen before the law. *Privilegia ne irroganto* ('no law to be proposed in regard to an individual'). No citizen to be condemned capitally except by the whole assembly of citizens. The legislature cannot be bound by its previous decision. Gilds and other associations may agree upon laws for themselves, provided they are not inconsistent with the general law.

Lastly there is a group of maxims which we would expect to find in a pontifical school-book. A whole table – ten rules in table 10, much of which survives in quotations and consists of prohibitions without sanctions – regarding the conduct of funerals;[1] two legal regulations relating to the purchase of victims for sacrifice; one perhaps to the making of roads; and two relating to the offence of witchcraft.

We may sum up, then, as follows. The tradition that there was some legislation in or about the fifth century need not be gainsaid and the origin of the Tables in a few rules of the fifth or fourth century (now contained in the passages relating to homicide, wounding, theft and damage to property) is not unlikely. The story, however, of the compilation of the Tables cannot be accepted and has been built up largely by inference from their contents. What we have is a school-book of the pontifical schools chiefly containing legal maxims handed down and developed

---

[1] e.g. *Hominem mortuum in urbe ne sepelito neve urito* ('Do not bury or cremate a man in the city'); *Hoc plus ne facito, rogum ascea ne polito* ('Do not do this either – do not smooth a funeral pyre with an axe'). These are two prohibitions, without sanctions, in almost classical latinity.

by successive copyists, and dating from an age when there were few other documents by which to test and correct it. Its contents would tend to become fixed about 280 B.C. in the days of Appius Claudius the Censor, when history began, and especially by 250 B.C. when the general population began to use writing, and it was out of such materials that Sextus Aelius about 190 B.C. selected and published his Tripertita, though to what extent he distinguished between the Twelve Tables and the *interpretatio* we do not know.[1] By then its reputation had begun to grow as the fountain-head of the law of Rome. The surviving references, however, to that compilation in succeeding centuries include some spurious passages, but when they came into existence we do not know. It is, in sum, largely a creation of the early third century, mainly embodying law of that period.

In the latter half of the third century, law still formed an important place in the curriculum of the patrician schoolboy. Plautus[2] says of parental education 'Expoliunt, docent litteras, jura, leges'[3] and law in Cato's view[4] formed one of the essential means of the training of a Roman. At the beginning of the first century B.C. the Tables were still a school-book, for Cicero[5] tells us that when he was a boy at school they learned the 'Si in jus vocat' (presumably the initial words) 'as a compulsory chant' but that no one now studied them.[6] We can thus understand the presence in this collection of one of the few quoted rules which has a religious or moral sanction. In time to come the boy would be called upon to advise his *clientes* (dependants), however undistinguished his knowledge of the law might be, and he must be told that a man who deceived his *clientes* was 'taboo'.[7]

[1] So that it is not clear that some of the quotations from the Code might not be from the *interpretatio*.
[2] About 254-184 B.C.
[3] *Most.* 126. [4] 234-149 B.C. [5] 106-43 B.C.
[6] *De Leg.* II, 4, 9, 23, 59. He says they learned the XII Tables *and other laws of that kind* (!).
[7] 'Patronus si clienti fraudem faxit, sacer esto.'

CHAPTER II

The Law of the Hebrews

The Pentateuch is not specifically referred to by Maine as one of the ancient bodies of rules thought by him to yield evidence in support of the view that law originates as a mixture of legal, religious and ethical rules. No doubt in his day the revelation recorded in the Bible would have been generally regarded as standing outside the ordinary processes of legal history, yet legal historians and others have been predisposed in favour of such a theory by the confusion of law and religion which the Bible appears to them to disclose. In fact there is no sufficient reason to believe that there was any such confusion in the mind of the Hebrew, and nothing in the Bible shows it.

The book of Genesis and that of the Exodus to the end of the nineteenth chapter contain a redaction of Hebrew traditions of events from the creation of the world to the giving of the law at Sinai, and serve as an historical introduction to that climax. There follow a great body of rules of conduct of various kinds, which are expressed as having been issued by Moses to the children of Israel at the command of God and they occupy the rest of the Pentateuch. The name by which these rules are generally called in the Old Testament – namely the *toráh* – is translated in the English Bibles by the word 'law', and the ubiquitous use of this word has no doubt done much to create the existing impression of the function and purpose of these rules and the light in which they were regarded by the Hebrews, but the word *toráh* is a noun of the verb *yarah*, which means 'to point'[1] or 'show the way' and is the common Hebrew word for 'to teach'[2] and *toráh* signifies 'the teaching', and always religious or divine teaching.

---

[1] Closely akin is its frequent use with the meaning of 'throw' or 'shoot', for the hand or missile is 'pointed' towards its object.

[2] The present participle '*moreh*' is the common Hebrew word for 'teacher'.

The part of the Pentateuch which contains the *toráh* begins in Exodus, Chap. 20, with what are known as the Ten Commandments, but are referred to in the Hebrew as the Ten Words, an expression implying perhaps a command but certainly the brevity of a 'maxim'. Some of these now include an added commentary.[1] They are couched in the second person singular, language in which law never appears, and their only sanction is that to be implied from the words which introduce them: 'I am the Lord thy God who brought thee out of the land of Egypt'. It consists therefore in the displeasure of God that will attend on disobedience and no secular sanction is stated. The first four Words are rules for the conduct of man towards God, the 5th to the 10th for the conduct of man towards man, and the 5th and 10th prohibit not so much conduct as a state of mind. The Ten Words are, then, a religious code, the essential rules or maxims of a good and pious life. After them follows a short narrative and a restatement and amplification of the first commandment.[2]

---

[1] The original form presumably was: (1) Thou shalt have no other gods before me. (2) Thou shalt not make unto thee a graven image. (3) Thou shalt not take the name of the Lord thy God in vain. (4) Remember the Sabbath day to keep it holy. (5) Honour thy father and thy mother. (6) Thou shalt not murder. (7) Thou shalt not commit adultery. (8) Thou shalt not steal. (9) Thou shalt not bear false witness against thy neighbour. (10) Thou shalt not covet thy neighbour's house. The 6th to the 9th Words contain no commentary, perhaps because, being also serious legal offences, they need no reason for obedience.

[2] There are two sets of Ten Words in the Pentateuch. The first is that in Ex. 20$^{2\text{-}17}$ (*supra*), repeated in Deut. 5$^{6\text{-}21}$. The second is that in Ex. 20$^{23\text{-}26}$, continued at Ex. 23$^{12\text{-}19}$, and repeated in Ex. 34$^{14\text{-}26}$, in much the same order, but much overlaid by different commentaries. The first is an ethical or prophetic version. The second is a ritualistic version; the rules are different in content and probably much older and therefore more overlaid with commentaries. It is the second set which is called the Ten Words (see Ex. 34^{28}). These Ten Words are : (1) Ye shall not make other gods with me (Ex. 20^{23} and 34^{14}). (2) Six days shalt thou labour but on the 7th day thou shalt rest (Ex. 23^{12} and 34^{21}). (3) Three times in the year all thy males shall appear before the Lord God (Ex. 23^{17}, 34^{23}). (4) The Feast of Unleavened Bread shalt thou keep (Ex. 23^{15}, 34^{18}). (5) Thou shalt keep the Feast of Weeks, the first-fruits of thy labours (Ex. 23^{16}, 34^{22}). (6) Thou shalt keep the Feast of Ingathering at the end of the year (Ex. 23^{16}, 34^{22}). (7) Thou shalt not offer the blood of my sacrifice with leavened bread (Ex. 23^{18}, 34^{25}). (8) The fat of my feast shall not remain all night until the morning (Ex. 23^{18}, 34^{25}). (9) The first-fruits of thy ground thou shalt bring into the house of the Lord thy God (Ex. 23^{19}, 34^{26}). (10) Thou shalt not seethe a kid in its mother's milk (Ex. 23^{19}, 34^{26}).

There ensues a sudden change in the language and the matter, for Exodus 21² to 22¹⁷ is nothing less than a characteristic code of primitive law of the age of the Late Codes. Its rules are terse and simple and expressed in precise and skilful language. They are couched in conditional sentences in the third person singular.¹ The sanctions are expressed and are definite and secular. The topics are those of the Late Codes systematically arranged in the manner of the codes, indeed this is one of the best extant specimens of a primitive code.

Not only is this a code of law, but it was plainly so regarded by the editors who placed it in its present position. The words by which it is introduced are: 'Now these are the *mishpatím* (plural of *mishpát*) which thou [Moses] shalt set before them.' No other group of rules of the Pentateuch is so introduced. The word *mishpát*, which is here translated in the English Bibles as 'judgement', was the Hebrew word in ordinary use with the meaning of 'law' or 'a law' in the modern lawyer's sense of the term. Its meaning, like that of most words, is an area of human experience, not a point; or, to express the same matter differently, it has a number of associated meanings. Like many words signifying 'law' in languages of simpler and maturer cultures, it denotes, *inter alia*, a judgment² – for law is, or was till recently, chiefly expressed in judgments of courts. Secondly, it signifies a decision of a ruler (modern English 'law' or 'statute'³), for the root-verb *shaphát* was to 'rule' or 'govern', and so to be a lawgiver as well as to judge; and also to execute a judgment; and *mishpát* also signified the execution of a judgment. Thirdly, *mishpát* widely signified 'right' and 'a right' and 'custom' and 'justice' and 'fitness'.⁴ Lastly, it denoted also a law-suit and the place of the hearing and the act of giving judgment. Its meaning, therefore, was 'law' in the modern sense of the term, though in the religious literature of the Bible it is sometimes used figuratively, in such expressions as 'my *mishpatím*',⁵ of the law (or decisions) of God.

So that the words introducing the Hebrew Code signify that

¹ See *post* p. 139, for the late additions to the code.
² cf. the Old English *dom* and its equivalent in the Leges Barbarorum *judicium*; the Assyrian *dinu* (*diānu*, to judge; *dayānu*, a judge); Babylonian *dinu* (*dānu, daiyanu*); Hebrew *din* (*dayan*).
³ Old Norse *lagu*; cf. Roman *lex*.
⁴ cf. Old English *riht*.   ⁵ *Mishpatai* – cf. Deut. 33¹⁰.

these are the rules of law, as distinct from the religious and moral rules, which Moses is called upon to lay before Israel, and in a subsequent passage, referring to the Ten Words and the Code, it is related that Moses came and told the people all the Words of the Lord and all the *mishpatîm*. In the Code itself the word is used in the same sense.[1] The provisions of the Code are plainly not judgments but propositions of law.

In this proper sense of secular law there is nothing of law in the rest of the Pentateuch. There are ecclesiastical enunciations of sacral offences – that is to say, criminal offences of religious purport. There are sometimes repetitions of the subject-matter of a few clauses of the Code of interest to ecclesiastics, but in vaguer language and sometimes in conflict with the Code. There are rules of ecclesiastical law – special rules for the conduct of the clergy, including rules for the conduct of cases in the ecclesiastical courts, for the procedure of the ordeal in secular trials and for the administration of the sanctuaries and trial of homicides taking sanctuary. There are scattered passages that help to provide a background and thereby supplement rules of the Code, especially those related to religious doctrine, such as rules of inheritance and the prohibited degrees of marriage. There are statements of what ought to be law; there are rules of religious ritual and much moral teaching upon the conduct of man towards man. But there is no true, secular law.

The Ten Words and the Code are contained in a part of Exodus which is often referred to as the Book of the Covenant (a name by which it is called in Exodus 24[7]) and is generally regarded as one of the earliest parts of the Pentateuch. To the fundamentalist this is part of the law issued by God to Moses. By others it is widely recognized as a separate document because of its distinct subject-matter and language. One view, which goes back to W. Caspari and Albrecht Alt,[2] regards as native to Israel the formulation of rules of conduct as prohibitions or injunctions in the second person, and considers the formulation (in the Code) as sets of facts in the third person to have been adopted from the Canaanites

---

[1] Ex. 21[31] 'according to this law'. Cf. Deut. 19[6] 'There is no law of death for him'; Jer. 26[16].
[2] See some references in Martin Noth, *The Laws in the Pentateuch and other Studies* (1966), 19.

in the period of the Judges. This would run counter to all we know of law. All codes of law are couched in conditional sentences in the third person and set out the sanction applicable to specified sets of facts. The prohibitions and injunctions of the Ten Words state no sanctions. To the present author this is the Hebrew Code of law – the rest is the religious literature. As for the fundamentalist's view, this is no code for nomads or desert dwellers, but a people of a simple civilization, living in permanent houses, enjoying a developed agriculture which includes the tilling of cornland and the cultivation of vineyards and olive groves, with extensive keeping of large cattle (oxen as well as sheep) and asses for draught animals. There is a developed mercantile economy involving sale, hire and deposit and a beginning of banking in the form of deposit of silver, and also the attendant evil of a landless class with debt and Hebrew debt-slaves. Moreover the Code shows on its face evident signs of development and amendment.[1]

Before we examine the contents of the Code, let us look at the Pentateuch and the historical and prophetic writings, and having considered what class of the population wrote and edited these books, decide whether they show that the functions of the administration of justice and of the direction of the religious life of the community belonged to the same or separate classes, and whether they indicate that law and religion, *mishpát* and *toráh*, were separate conceptions in the minds of the Hebrew. We shall see a picture resembling in many respects that of England about the A.D. 1160s.

The hands that wrote and handed down and edited these books were the hands of the scribes, the *sopherím*, a class closely connected with the priesthood but separate from it. There is no mention of the *sopher* before the settlement in Canaan, but thereafter this class comprised almost all who could read or write. The use and number of the scribes apparently increased up to the eve of the First Exile, by which time a considerable number of other persons seem also to have possessed that knowledge,[2] but the connection of the scribes with the priesthood is shown by the

[1] See *post* p. 139f.
[2] Jezebel (1 Kings 21[8]), Isaiah (Is. 8[1]), Josiah (2 Kings 23[2]), and see Judges 8[14]. Jeremiah and the witnesses to his deed of purchase of land could subscribe their names in some form (Jer. 32[10, 12]) and such texts as Deut. 6[9] and 11[20] indicate a spread of literacy.

fact that they are commonly mentioned along with the priests,[1] and indeed the post-exilic book of Chronicles includes some, at least, of the scribes among the Levites.[2] One of their chief functions from earliest times seems to have been to keep accounts,[3] but many specialized in different posts and functions. The earliest mention in the Old Testament is of the military scribe,[4] who was, as in Egypt, a high administrative officer charged till the end of the Kingdom, with matters concerning enlistment.[5] There were royal scribes, the most eminent of whom might be called the Secretary of State or Lord Treasurer, who was a member of David's and Solomon's council of ministers,[6] and there were temple scribes,[7] and there were the letter-writers, called in for everyday drafting of messages on potsherds,[8] limestone sheets or papyrus, and they also wrote out the legal documents, for example on a sale and purchase of land.[9] Like the possessors of other skills they carried on for the most part a hereditary calling,[10] and probably at all times, except where a father taught his son or a master his apprentice, writing was only learned in schools attached to temple or shrine, and there was a close professional sympathy and solidarity with the rest of the clergy.

Moreover the Pentateuch, the historical and prophetic books are a purely religious history of the Hebrew and such secular literature as existed has almost wholly disappeared. The book of Kings, our chief authority, shows this most clearly. For example, of an important and comparatively prosperous century stretching from about 835 to 739 B.C., a third of the total span of the Kingdom of Judah, almost all that it tells us is contained in a few verses of the Second Book of Kings.[11] Joash, we are told, was seven

---

[1] e.g. 2 Sam. 8^{17}; 1 Kings 4^2, 2 Kings 12^{10}, 18, 19, 22; Is. 36, 37.
[2] 1 Chron. 24^6; 2 Chron. 34^{13}.
[3] *Sopher* also signifies 'one who numbers', and there is a close connection here and in many other languages between accounts in the numerical sense and accounts in the sense of narration.   [4] Judges 5^{14}.
[5] See 2 Kings 25^{19}; Jer. 52^{25}; 2 Chron. 26^{11}.
[6] 2 Sam. 8^{16}; 2 Sam. 20^{25}; 1 Kings 4^2; and see Jer. 36^{12} (Jehoiakim's time).
[7] e.g. Gemariah (Jer. 36^{10}).
[8] e.g. the Lachish letters.
[9] e.g. Baruch (Jer. 32^{6}f.) who was also Jeremiah's scribe, and recorded much of the book of Jeremiah.
[10] See e.g. 1 Kings 4^3. 1 Chron. 2^{55} refers to 'families of scribes'.
[11] 2 Kings 12; 14$^{1-22}$, 15$^{1-7}$.

years old when he began to reign as King of Judah, and he reigned
forty years. We are given his mother's name and told that he did
what was right in the eyes of the Lord all his days wherein Johoiada
the Priest instructed him, though the high places were not taken
away. He arranged that the money dues brought in to the Temple
should be placed by the priests in a chest and used for its repair.
He bought off the invading King of Syria by giving him all the
holy vessels dedicated by his family to the Temple and all the
treasures of the palace. The passage ends: 'Now the rest of the acts
of Joash, and all that he did, are they not written in the book of the
Chronicles of the Kings of Judah?'; and it gives the names of his
servants who murdered him. His son Amaziah succeeded him at
twenty-five and reigned twenty-nine years. His mother's name is
given and we are told that he did what was right in the eyes of
the Lord save that the high places were not taken away. He slew
his father's murderers and won a victory over Edom. There was
a war between Judah and Israel, of which we are only told there
was a battle in which Amaziah was taken captive and the King
of Israel carried off all the treasures of the Temple and the palace.
And for the rest of the acts of Amaziah, observes the author, are
they not written in the book of the Chronicles of the Kings of
Judah? There was a conspiracy against him, and he fled to Lachish
and there was murdered. He was succeeded by his son Azariah,
who was sixteen years old and reigned fifty-two years. His mother's
name is given, and the fact that he did what was right in the eyes
of the Lord, although the high places were not taken away. He
built Elath. The Lord smote him with leprosy and his son Jotham
acted as regent for him. And the rest of his acts, are they not
written in the book of the Chronicles of the Kings of Judah? The
later book of Chronicles has the same account of these three
reigns, largely in the same words, but with a few more statements
of fact and these highly improbable.[1]

Even the few statements in these verses of Kings are not wholly
correct: for example, the total of the reigns is too long; and as
against these few verses there are nine preceding chapters mainly
filled with traditions of the life of the prophet Elisha.[2] Of the
contemporary history of the Kingdom of Israel we are told even
less. To attempt to learn something of the political economy and

[1] 2 Chron. 24-26.   [2] 2 Kings, 2-9, 13.

law of the Hebrews we must piece together all the hints afforded us and look behind these dim outlines of the religious face of the country.

The economy of the Hebrew state was a type of feudalism. A system is recorded in the Old Testament as going back to Moses, under which the tribe (*shebet*) is divided into patrilineal clans, and each clan (*mishpaḥah*) consists (in theory at any rate) of 1,000 adult males[1] subdivided into units of 100, 50 and 10; and the chiefs (*roshim*) or lords (*śarim*), and under them the heads of the smaller units, are both the civil rulers, military commanders and judges of their units.[2] Upon the settlement in Canaan the tribes and clans must have held their lands under the same *śarim* and though the tribe and clan faded, the military units of the 1,000 and 100 continued till the First Exile and after, at least in theory.[3] Under the Hebrew monarchy the King gained a centralized authority at the expense of feudal nobles, and the tenant occupier inherited his landholding and could dispose of it subject to a right of pre-emption and redemption vested in the nearest members of the clan in succession, if he desired to sell or pledged it.[4]

The Hebrew king rules over the civil, military, judicial and religious organization. He is not a priest-king and does not normally perform the sacrificial services at Temple or shrine, but he is entitled to do so[5] and on great occasions often does so. He builds the Temple[6] and the sanctuary in Bethel and largely equips them,[7] and in cases of need he might seize the treasures of the Temple to buy off an enemy.[8] He nominates[9] and dismisses the chief priests[10] and he initiates and carries through important changes of ritual and great reforms in the organized religious life of the state.[11] He enjoys a great measure of control over the revenues of the state,

[1] So that the clans are also called the 'thousands', see e.g. 1 Sam. 10[19, 21].
[2] Ex. 18[13f.], Deut. 1[15].
[3] In Numbers 31[14, 54] (post-exilic) the organization is only military.
[4] e.g. Ruth 4, Jer. 32[6f.].
[5] Not till Chronicles is there a suggestion to the contrary (e.g. 2 Chron. 26[16-20]; 1 Chron. 23[13]).
[6] 2 Sam. 7[2-3]; 1 Kings 5-8.
[7] 2 Sam. 8[11]; 1 Kings 7[51]; 1 Kings 15[15]; 2 Kings 12[18].
[8] See 1 Kings 15[18]; 2 Kings 12[18]; 16[8], 18[15].
[9] See below.   [10] 1 Kings 2[27, 28].
[11] e.g. Jeroboam (1 Kings 12[26-33]); Jehoash (2 Kings 12[5-9]); Ahaz (2 Kings 16[10-18]); Josiah (2 Kings 22[3-7], 23).

which are largely his own. He conducts direct trading operations with foreign lands on a large scale[1] and receives the profits as well as transit and import taxes, and in times of prosperity the gifts and tribute of foreign ambassadors and vassals as well as of his own subjects. He is a great landowner in his own legal right and enjoys the produce of the royal demesne. But the main source of his revenue must be the dues received from the whole territory of the state, paid by the occupiers to their immediate lord and by him directly or indirectly to the king, coming from the produce of the occupier's land and cattle and rendered according to the terms of his holding.[2] There are also special imposts[3] and perhaps forced labour in times of national emergency or for great public purposes.[4] He has large powers over his tenants and might deprive a subject of his land and award it to another[5] but such conduct would be rare and high-handed.

The king is commander-in-chief of the armed forces consisting mainly of the ill-armed adult population, which can be called up for war but not for training and serving mainly under their local and clan leaders. In addition, however, the king has the nucleus of a professional army under its commander and officers, consisting chiefly of his bodyguard of foreign mercenaries[6] but also of Hebrew soldiers, who hold their lands on military tenure; and in the Northern Kingdom, as in the neighbouring countries, the chief arm is the heavy horsed chariots,[7] kept in a number of suitable centres bordering on the plains, and some are provided by the king but others by local nobles[8] holding their lands on terms of supplying equipment or retainers.

The civil administration in the country generally is based on the local lords (śarim), the chief landowners. Though the tribal organization is fading the śar is often the head of his tribe or clan

---

[1] 1 Kings 9²⁶, 10¹⁵, ²², ²⁸; 20³⁴.
[2] 1 Sam. 8¹⁵ᶠ·; and especially 1 Kings 4⁷ᶠ· (generally considered to be based on a contemporary document).
[3] 2 Kings 15²⁰; 23³⁵.
[4] 1 Sam. 8¹²; 1 Kings 5¹³, 9, 15²².
[5] 1 Sam. 8¹⁴; 1 Kings 21.
[6] In David's time they consisted of Keréthim and Peléthim (Cretan and Philistine groups) chosen, perhaps, partly because they would be free of Hebrew clan ties and loyalties.
[7] See Yadin, The Art of Warfare in Biblical Times (1963).
[8] Śarim.

and the king would normally use such a man as his officer. The
śar is in any case a nobleman and vassal of the king as well as a
local military commander, and a royal official and adviser in all
civil matters, as well as judge over a district.[1] Some of the greatest
śarim are the king's relatives by blood or marriage. He has his
advisers in the capital, either permanently there or visiting from
time to time to do homage, to advise on local conditions or ask
favours. In Jerusalem and Samaria there is a śar haʿir (governor of
the city) and in the provinces a śar hammedinah (governor of the
district). The towns do not quite fit into this pattern, and we hear
more of them than of the countryside. The local administration
is for the most part in the hands of the leaders influential by birth
and wealth, the elders (ẓeqēním) meeting for business at the town
gate,[2] where the markets are also held.[3] In the countryside the
ẓeqēním are the councillors of the śar. They are the chief administrators of the country in its local day-to-day affairs. At the head
of the whole administration is the king's council of advisers,[4]
consisting commonly of the head of the tribute or levy, the head
of the armed forces, the commander of the royal bodyguard, an
eminent priest or two, the royal scribe and the maẓkir (Remem-
brancer or Herald)[5] and might include an expert who is a freedman
or other foreigner.

Above all, the king's function is, in the public mind, to administer justice with impartiality, humanity and vigour.[6] By his
conduct in this respect he is ever tested.[7] The Israelites, it is
recorded,[8] said to Samuel: 'Make us a King to judge us, like the
other nations', and the same word (shaphát) denotes to rule and
to judge. The ideal king of Isaiah is an impartial and incorruptible
judge.[9] The king is the ultimate court of appeal from other courts,
and in addition certain matters, chiefly capital cases and serious
criminal charges, are reserved to him,[10] though he does not
usually sit in person but appoints a son or other adviser to preside

[1] All these uses of the word śar occur in the Bible.
[2] Ruth 4.   [3] 2 Kings 7[1].
[4] Referred to in 1 Kings 4[2] (Solomon) as the 'śarim of the King'.
[5] For David's chief ministers, see 2 Sam. 8[16-18]; 1 Chron. 18[14-17]; 2 Sam.
20[23-26]; for Solomon's, 1 Kings 4[1-6].
[6] See the messianic dream in Is. 11.
[7] See 2 Sam. 15[1-6] (Absalom using this situation in order to oust the King)
and passim.
[8] 1 Sam. 8[5].   [9] Is. 11[3-4].   [10] Jer. 26[19, 21].

in his place,[1] and the cases are heard by the leading men of the realm and his justices. The system of administration of justice is very close to that of England in the 1160s. First, the old customary courts continue to try disputes everywhere, in the context of this feudal-monarchical system, and here the judges are the civil rulers: that is to say, the local lord (śar) sitting with other leading local men who tend to be the elderly heads of families, the *zeqēním*, and in the towns, in the ordinary disputes of everyday, it is the local elders (leading citizens of the town and leaders of the families) together with heads of the local noble families and sometimes the governor of the town or district with them, who hear the law-suits. Secondly, the King appoints professional justices and their officers and clerks,[2] and some travel in circuit around their district.[3]

Of the religious order, the priest, in the early days of the settlement in Canaan, was such by appointment, to be guardian and to officiate at a public or private shrine; but during the monarchy the heads of the priesthood in Jerusalem and Samaria had great influence. The Levites were a community of scattered, mendicant and travelling men, devoted to the worship of Jehovah, and being such mainly by heredity, like those of other callings, but perhaps never a tribe. Priests were not necessarily,[4] though they were usually, Levites. The rise in the status and influence of the clergy is well seen in the historical books. In the book of Kings there is hardly a mention of the Levites,[5] and in the books of Deuteronomy and Ezekiel, on the eve of the First Exile, the Levite is still a class set aside for the worship of Jehovah but relying on charity for its support. As the Levite has been chosen to stand before the Lord and minister to him,

'Levi hath no share nor allotment[6] with his brethren: the Lord is his allotment.'[7]

'The priests, the Levites, and all the tribe of Levi, shall have

[1] 2 Sam. 15[1-6], 2 Kings 15[5].   [2] 2 Chron. 19[5] (Jehoshaphat).
[3] Like Samuel (1 Sam. 7[16]).   [4] See e.g. Judges 17[5, 13], 1 Sam. 7.
[5] But see 1 Kings 8[4]; and the passages where Jereboam is accused of appointing priests for his high places who were not Levites (1 Kings 12[31], 13[33]).
[6] i.e., on the partitioning of Canaan among the tribes; not 'inheritance'. (cf. Deut. 18[8]).   [7] Deut. 10[9], repeated in 12[12].

no share nor allotment with Israel; they shall eat the fire-
offerings of the Lord and his allotment. They shall have no
allotment among their brethren: the Lord is their allotment,
as he spake to him.'[1]

'Take heed that thou forsake not the Levite all the days of
thy life upon thy land.'[2]

In the later, post-exilic, chapters of the Pentateuch and Joshua,
first a tithe is ordered to be paid to them,[3] and finally forty-eight
cities and their suburbs (including the cities of refuge, which were
three in number[4] and are now six[5]) are to be taken from their
owners and allotted to the Levites to dwell in.[6] It is even com-
manded here that land in the cities of the Levites, sold by a Levite,
is to be perpetually redeemable,[7] and that their fields in the
suburbs of their cities are to be unassignable.[8]

Up to the first exile, the priestly order had little part in the
secular system of administration of justice referred to above. No
doubt to the extent that a code of laws was recorded or a new law
was promulgated, it was the hand of a scribe that wrote, but we
do not know, apart from the Hebrew Code, how much was the
legislative activity or to what extent it was in writing. The priests,
however, took one important part in the decisions of the secular
courts: when, chiefly owing to the absence of evidence on one side,
recourse was had to the ordeal by oath, it was administered by the
priest with solemn religious ritual in the Temple or other shrine.
Several biblical texts make this clear. For example, in Solomon's
dedication of the Temple:[9]

'When a man wrongs his neighbour and he requires of him
an oath,[10] to cause him to swear, and the oath comes before
Thine altar in this house, then hear Thou in heaven and do and
judge Thy servants, condemning the guilty and bringing his

---

[1] Deut. 18[1f]. Repeated 14[27].   [2] Deut. 12[19].
[3] Deut. 26[12] (here the Levites share it with the stranger, the orphan and
the widow); Numbers 18[21] (for the Levites alone, for their service of the
tabernacle of Israel).
[4] Deut. 4[41], 19[2].   [5] Numbers 35[6, 13].
[6] Numbers 35[1-8]; cf. Josh. 21[8]; I Chron. 6[64]; 2 Chron. 11[14].
[7] Lev. 25[32].   [8] Lev. 25[34].   [9] I Kings 8[31]; 2 Chron. 6[22].
[10] Or imprecation.

F

conduct upon his head and justifying the righteous[1] and giving him according to his righteousness.'[2]

Or, in Deuteronomy 17[8f.]:

'If there be a matter too difficult for thee to decide, between blood and blood, between plea and plea and between blow and blow, being matters in suit at thy gate, then thou shalt arise and go up to the place which the Lord thy God shall choose.[3] And thou shalt come to the priests, the Levites, and to the judge who shall be in those days, and thou shalt ask and they shall tell thee the sentence of the law. And thou shalt do according to the law which they shall tell thee from that place which the Lord shall choose, and thou shalt observe to do according to all that they shall teach thee, according to the toráh which they shall teach thee and according to the law which they shall tell thee . . . and the man that shall presume not to hearken to the priest that standeth to minister there to the Lord thy God or to the judge, that man shall die.'[4]

And again in Deuteronomy 19[16f.]:

'If a false witness shall rise up against a man, to give corrupt evidence against him, then the two men, between whom the suit is, shall stand before the Lord, before the priests and judges which shall be in those days. And the judges shall thoroughly examine, and if the witness is a lying witness, and has lied in his evidence against his brother then ye shall do to him as he schemed to do to his brother.'[5]

The post-exilic author of 2 Chron. 19[5f.] records a tradition that King Jehoshaphat[6] (some 450 years earlier) had set judges in each of the walled towns of Judah,

'and also in Jerusalem did Jehoshaphat set of the Levites and

---

[1] Or 'him who is in the right'.   [2] Or 'rightness'.   [3] i.e. the future Temple.
[4] Note the ecclesiastical bias of the author – 'priests' come before 'judge' and 'the toráh' before 'the law', and it is thought necessary to bolster up the priestly authority with the threat of death.
[5] The threat is of the talion.   [6] 'Jehovah is judge.'

priests and of the heads of the fathers of Israel, for the judgement of the Lord and for suits . . . And he charged them
saying . . . Behold Amariah, the chief priest, is over you in
every matter of the Lord and Zebadiah son of Ishmael the
ruler of the house of Judah in every matter of the King and
the Levites shall be officers before you. Be strong and act and
may the Lord be with the good.'

There was, in addition, a separate ecclesiastical jurisdiction over
homicides who had taken refuge in one of the sanctuaries, the
'cities of refuge', belonging to the Levites. The local community
decided on the refugee's right to stay, and for this purpose was
compelled to try the question whether the defendant had killed
with intention to kill.[1] But the priests were building up a separate
and wider ecclesiastical jurisdiction through their influence over
their flocks.[2] In all cases where a sin had been committed, the
toráh required the offender to make a sin-offering as a condition of
atonement and divine forgiveness, and while some such sins had
no relation to law,[3] others were sins committed in circumstances
which also constituted a legal wrong.[4] In the latter cases, in the
developed doctrine, which is only post-exilic and represented the
practice of the Second Temple, the defendant found guilty of
such a sin restored the article or money of which the owner had
been deprived together with an additional one-fifth of its value,
as well as the ram of reparation which went to the priest, who
thereupon made atonement for the sinner. And if there was no
kinsman of the owner, to whom to pay the fifth, that also went
to the priest.[5] In all these cases, any question as to whether a sin
had in fact been committed would necessarily be decided by the
priests alone.

And yet throughout Hebrew history, the Pentateuch,[6] the

---

[1] Numbers 35 (post exilic) and see below.
[2] See the passages quoted above from Deut. 17[8f.], 19[16f.], 19[1f.]; 2 Chron. 19[5f.].
[3] e.g. eating a holy thing unwittingly (Lev. 22[14]) and see Lev. 5[15]. See also
Deut. 21[5] (where a man is found slain by someone unknown, the elders of
the nearest town are to bring a sacrifice and undergo an ordeal, as to their
innocence and ignorance of the matter, before the priests, the Levites, for
'according to their words shall every suit and every blow be'.)
[4] For example, in the matter of the deposit of an article for safe keeping, or
violence practised upon a neighbour (Lev. 6[1f.]).   [5] Numbers 5[7].
[6] For the elders in Deut. see also 19[12], 21[2], [19], 22[15], 25[8].

historical and the prophetic books are unanimous in showing
that in the Hebrew mind law was one thing and *toráh* was another,
and while the *toráh* was the province of the priest, the law and its
administration belonged to the civil rulers. 'Where now is thy
King', asks God by the mouth of Hosea[1] 'that he may save thee
in all thy cities, and thy judges of whom thou didst say "Give me
a King and śarim"?' 'Thy śarim are transgressors[2] and associates
of thieves,' says Isaiah,[3] 'every one loveth a bribe and runneth
after rewards. They judge not the orphan and the suit of the
widow doth not come before them.' 'Hear, I pray, ye heads of
Jacob', cries Micah,[4] 'and rulers of the house of Israel, is it not
for you to know the law?'[5] 'Hear this, I pray, ye heads of the
house of Jacob and rulers of the house of Israel, that abhor law[6]
and twist all straight conduct, building Zion with blood and
Jerusalem with injustice. Her heads judge for a bribe and her
priests teach[7] for a price and her prophets divine for money.'[8]
And again 'The śar asketh, and the judge, for a payment and the
great man speaketh the desire of his mind, and they wind it
about.'[9] 'Come', say the enemies of Jeremiah, 'let us devise
devices against Jeremiah, for toráh shall not perish from the
priest nor counsel from the wise nor the word from the prophet:
come let us smite him with the tongue.'[10] 'They shall seek in vain
a vision from the prophet', prophesies Exekiel, 'and toráh shall
perish from the priest and counsel from the elders.'[11, 12].

---

[1] Hos. 13[10].
[2] *Sorerim* (a play on the word Śarim).
[3] Is. 1[23].   [4] Mic. 3[1].
[5] *et-hammishpát* (note the definite article).
[6] Or 'justice' (*mishpát*).   [7] Root of *toráh*.
[8] Mic. 3[9f].   [9] Mic. 7[3].   [10] Jer. 18[18].
[11] Zeqēním.   [12] Ez. 7[26].

CHAPTER 12

The Hebrew Code

Here then is the Hebrew Code. It is printed in two columns to separate the main body of the Code from later additions and amendments. The reasons for regarding some of its provisions as later than the rest will presently appear. Meanwhile the precision and aptness of the language of the Code as a whole is to be noted: it is the work of scribal specialists in law, and with this lawyer-like precision and practical outlook may be contrasted the inapt language and impracticable provisions of the religious writings of the Bible where they concern themselves with what is, or should be, law or good conduct, and the repeated contradictions between a rule as expressed in both places.

Among other precise usages may be noted the employment of one conjunction (*Ki*, translated as 'when') to introduce a main rule, and another (*im*, translated as 'if') to introduce a sub-rule.

THE HEBREW CODE
Exodus xxi[1]-xxii[17]

Ex. xxi

1. Now these are the laws which thou[1] shalt set before them.

[*Main Code*]   [*Additions and amendments*]

Ex. xxi 2 When thou[2] acquirest a male Hebrew slave,[3] he shall serve six years and in the seventh shall go out free for nothing.

---

[1] Moses.   [2] Note the second person.   [3] i.e. a debt-slave.

[*Main Code*]   [*Additions and amendments*]

3 If he comes in by himself he shall go out by himself: if he has a wife, his wife shall go out with him.

4 If his master[1] gives him a wife and she bears him sons or daughters, the wife and her children shall be her master's and he shall go out by himself.

5 But if the slave plainly says: 'I love my master, my wife and my children; I will not go out free,'

6 then his master shall bring him to God[2] and shall bring him to the door or to the door-post, and his master shall bore his ear[3] with an awl and he shall serve him for ever.

7 But when a man sells his daughter to be a handmaid, she shall not go out as the male slaves go out.

8 If she is unpleasing to her master who has espoused her to himself then he shall cause her to be redeemed: he shall not be entitled to sell her to a foreign people, because he has betrayed her.

[1] Or 'owner'.
[2] Used quasi-technically (as e.g. in the Code of Hammurabi) to indicate a sacred place where an ordeal is undergone.
[3] A common place for the branding of a slave (as in the Leges Barbarorum).

[*Main Code*]   [*Additions and amendments*]

9 And if he has espoused her to his son, he shall treat her according to the custom[1] relating to daughters.

10 If he takes to himself another woman,[2] he shall not withhold her food, her clothing and her marital rights.[3]

11 If he does not give her these three things, then she shall go out for nothing, without money.

12 [A man] striking a man, if[4] he dies, shall surely die.

13 But if he lay not in wait, but God brought it to his hand, then I[5] shall appoint thee a place whither he shall flee.

14 But when a man comes intentionally[6] against another to slay him with malice,[7] thou shalt take him from my altar to die.

15 And [a man] striking his father or[4] his mother shall surely die.

16 And [a man] stealing a man and selling him, or[4] [if] he is found in his hand, shall surely die.

---

[1] Or 'law' (*mishpát*). The reference is to the gift of a marriage-portion.
[2] Or 'wife'.
[3] It is a commonly understood obligation of a husband, in a polygynous society, to be fair and equal in his attentions to his wives.
[4] Heb. 'and'.
[5] Note the repeated use in these two clauses of the first and second persons.
[6] Or 'presumptuously'.   [7] Or 'guile'.

[*Main Code*]   [*Additions and amendments*]

17 And [a man] cursing his
father or[1] his mother shall
surely die.

18 And when men quarrel and
one strikes the other with a
stone or his fist, and he does
not die but falls to his bed,

19 if he rises and walks
abroad on his staff, then
the striker shall be clear,[2]
only he shall provide for
his time of resting and
shall cause him to be
thoroughly healed.

20 But when a man strikes his
male slave or his handmaid
with the rod, and he dies
under his hand, he shall surely
be avenged.[3]

21 But if he survives for a
day or two[4] he shall not
be avenged, for he is his
money.

22 And when men fight and strike
against a pregnant woman,
and she loses her child

and there is no harm

he shall surely be mulcted as
the husband lays upon him,

and he shall pay according to
[the decision of] judges.[5]

23 But if there is harm, then
thou[6] shalt give life for
life,

---

[1] Heb. 'and'.
[2] i.e. free of liability – even, apparently, if the injured man later dies.
[3] Note the vagueness of the sanction.
[4] Note the vagueness.
[5] Or 'arbitrators'.   [6] Note the second person.

[*Main Code*]   [*Additions and amendments*]

24 eye for eye, tooth for tooth, hand for hand, foot for foot,

25 burn for burn, bruise for bruise.

26 And when a man strikes the eye of his male slave or the eye of his handmaid and ruins it, he shall set him free for his eye,

27 and if a man knocks out the tooth of his male slave or the tooth of his handmaid, he shall set him free for his tooth.

28 And when an ox gores a man or woman and he dies, the ox shall surely be stoned

and its flesh shall not be eaten

but the owner of the ox shall be clear.

29 But if the ox has gored in time past and notice has been given to its owner and he has not guarded it but it has killed a man or woman, the ox shall be stoned and its owner also shall die.

30 If reparation money is laid upon him, he shall give for the redemption of his life whatever is laid upon him.

31 Or if it gores a son or gores a daughter, according to this same law[1] shall he be treated.

[1] i.e. clauses 29 and 30.

F*

[*Main Code*]   [*Additions and amendments*]

32 If the ox gores a male slave or a handmaid, he shall give to his master thirty shekels and the ox shall be stoned.

33 And when a man uncovers a pit or when a man digs a pit and does not cover it, and an ox or ass falls therein

34 the owner of the pit shall restore its value in money to its owner and the dead shall be his.

35 And when a man's ox strikes another's ox and it dies, then they shall sell the live ox and divide its price and they shall divide the dead also.

36 Or if it was known that the ox had gored in time past, and its owner did not guard it, he shall surely pay ox for ox and the dead shall be his.

Exodus xxii

1 When a man steals an ox or a sheep and slaughters it or sells it, he shall pay five oxen for the ox and four sheep for the sheep.

2 If the thief is caught breaking in[1] and is struck and dies, there shall be no blood-revenge for him.

[1] Lit. 'digging through': a term applicable to houses of earth or clay (cf. C.H. 21).

[Main Code]   *[Additions and amendments]*

3 If the sun has shone upon
him there shall be blood-
revenge for him. He shall
surely pay. If he has not
[the means] then he shall
be sold for his theft.

4 If the theft is surely
found in his hand alive,
whether ox, ass or sheep,
he shall pay double.

5 When a man causes a field or
vineyard to be consumed, or
lets loose his cattle and it
consumes another man's field,
he shall make it good from the
best of his field and from the
best of his vineyard.

6 When a fire spreads and gets
a hold on thorns, and a stack
of corn or the standing corn
or the field is consumed, he
who kindled the fire shall
surely make it good.

7 When a man gives to another
money or goods[1] to keep [for
him] and it is stolen from the
man's house, if the thief is
found he shall pay double.

8 If the thief is not found
then the owner of the
house shall be brought to
God [to see] if he has
not laid his hand on the
other's property.

9 In every case of wrongdoing,
in case of ox, of ass, of sheep,
of garment, [and] in every

[1] Lit. 'utensils' or 'implements', the only other common moveable article of
property.

[*Main Code*]   [*Additions and amendments*]

case of a lost thing where a man says 'This is it',[1] the case of the two of them shall come before God: he whom God finds guilty shall pay double to the other.

10 When a man gives to another an ass or ox or sheep or any other beast to keep [for him], and it dies or is maimed or carried off, no man seeing,

11 the oath of Yahweh shall be between the two of them, whether he have not laid his hand upon the property of the other, and its owner shall accept it and he shall not make it good.

12 But if it was surely stolen from him he shall make it good to its owner.

13 If it was surely torn[2] he shall bring it as witness: he shall not make good what is torn.

14 And when a man borrows anything from another and it is maimed or dies, its owner not being with it, he shall surely make it good.

15 If its owner was with it he shall not make it good. If it is a hired thing it came for the price of its hire.

16 And when a man seduces a maiden who is not betrothed, and lies with her, he shall

---

[1] i.e. 'This is my property'.   [2] i.e. by a wild beast.

[*Main Code*]   [*Additions and amendments*]

surely pay bridewealth[1] for her
to be his wife.

17 If her father surely refuses
to give her to him he
shall surely weigh out
money[2] according to the
bridewealth of maidens.[3]

*   *   *

18 A sorceress thou shalt not
suffer to live.

19 Everyone that lieth with a
beast shall surely die.

20 He that sacrifices to any god
save the Lord alone shall be
destroyed.

21 A stranger thou shalt not vex
or oppress, for ye were strangers in the land of Egypt.

22 A widow or orphan ye shall
not afflict . . .

It will be noticed that all the rules in the right-hand column
are concerned with topics that figure in the religious writings of
the rest of the Pentateuch: the lot of the slave,[4] which is the
chief subject, and especially the release of debt-slaves in the
seventh year,[5] the rules of the sanctuaries in regard to homicide,
the rule of 'an eye for an eye and a tooth for a tooth',[6] the use of
the ordeal by oath,[7] forbidden food[8] and a sexual wrong.[9] The
other topics of the Code are not mentioned in the religious writings
of the Pentateuch.[10] It will also be observed that, omitting these

[1] The brideprice.
[2] The father will not obtain the brideprice, or at least the full brideprice,
from a subsequent suitor, for she is not a virgin.
[3] Here ends the Code, including the additions and amendments. A number
of sacral crimes follow, and some ethical teaching.
[4] Ex. 21 $^{2\text{-}11, 20, 21, 26, 27}$.   [5] Ex. 21$^{2\text{-}11}$.   [6] Ex. 21$^{23\text{-}27}$.
[7] Ex. 22^9.   [8] Ex. 21^{28}.   [9] Ex. 22$^{16\text{-}17}$.
[10] Except the offence of cursing father or mother (Lev. 20^9).

additions, the rules of the Code follow a clear order of arrangement, of a kind typical of the Codes. First is a group of capital offences: homicide, assault on a parent, theft of a man to sell him into slavery, cursing a parent. Next comes a series of provisions[1] relating to personal injuries which are not capital: manslaughter or personal injury caused in a fight, miscarriage caused to a pregnant woman in a fight, manslaughter caused by goring oxen. The topic of goring oxen introduces a group of clauses[2] providing for the wrong of the killing of oxen by goring oxen and by uncovered pits. The killing of farm animals leads to other wrongs in relation to farm animals (theft of animals, and the consumption of a man's field by animals[3]) and this leads to the consumption of a man's field by a fire.[4] There follows a group of clauses concerned with bailments of animals and other property, in which ordeal and oath are first mentioned, beginning with deposit and followed by loan and hire.[5] Into this orderly arrangement these additions and amendments have been inserted, so that, for example, the Code now oddly begins with ten clauses relating to the release of debt-slaves in the seventh year and occupying nearly one-fifth of the total Code. At the end are two clauses relating to seduction.

Let us look at the Code in a little more detail.

The rules providing for the release of debt-slaves in the seventh year deal with a topic familiar to the other peoples of the Late Codes,[6] but at much greater length; they are more precise, lawyerlike and wise than the corresponding passages of the Hebrew religious writings, and their terms are different.[7] Moreover, in the religious literature they are part and parcel of a system, impracticable and difficult to understand and not found elsewhere, in which the notion of the sanctity of the Sabbath is extended to fulfil various social purposes – the release of debt-

---

[1] Ex. 21[18-32].   [2] Ex. 21[33-6].   [3] Ex. 22[1-5].
[4] Ex. 22[6].   [5] Ex. 22[7-15].
[6] In C.H. 117, male and female debt-slaves go out in the fourth year.
[7] Deut. 15[12f.] (both male and female debt-slaves alike go out in the seventh year, with their hands full; but may both choose to remain permanently their masters' slaves, and they are not brought to God before their ears are bored); Lev. 25[39f.] (male debt-slaves, and by implication female debt-slaves, go out with their hands full in the year of jubilee); Jer. 34[8f.] (male debt-slaves and handmaids go out in the seventh year).

slaves in the seventh year, the release of debts every seven years,[1] the seventh year of fallow,[2] and lastly the jubilee year after seven times seven years, when all land and persons shall be redeemed[3] – but only the release of debt-slaves is provided for in the Code.

These provisions enabling the debt-slave to be branded, with his consent, as a permanent slave are probably not found in other systems. To avoid evasion (which was frequent)[4] the master and slave are to go to a temple or shrine, and the oath is here extended to a new use: apparently the slave (or perhaps the master) is to state on oath that he does not wish to be free.

The female is sold to be a concubine, that is, a wife of lower degree, of the creditor or buyer or his son. Consequently although, like other Hebrew wives, she could be divorced without grounds (if the husband could afford it), in which case she would be free, she cannot be re-sold as a slave, and the husband cannot evade his obligations (which the rule defines) by selling her abroad.

There follows the main Code, which, it seems, originally began with four capital offences[5] stated in crude, simple and archaic language, there are no subordinate sentences and no conjunction but 'and'. The first states in the most precise terms the law that homicide is capital, that is to say that, in general, if you strike a man and he dies you have committed a capital offence. Two laws of the sanctuary have been added with equal precision, the first, corresponding to the English law at the Conquest,[6] that he may take sanctuary unless he slew in ambush. The second, later and wider rule, corresponding to the law of England from the middle of the twelfth century, provides that if he is found to have slain with malice aforethought, he is to be extruded from the sanctuary to his death. These are laws of the sanctuary because men often take refuge in a sacred place when they have killed, and the question of guilt is the question whether they are entitled to take sanctuary, and it is tried at the sanctuary; and if the slayer does not take sanctuary he may be killed with impunity by the next of kin, and, it may be added, the latter is forbidden by the religious writings to accept blood money.[7] The ecclesiastical

---

[1] Deut. 15[1f.], 31[9f.]. [2] Ex. 23[11], Lev. 25[4]. [3] Lev. 25[8], 27[17f.], Numbers 36[4].
[4] See Jer. 34[8f.]. [5] In Ex. 21[12, 15, 16, 17].
[6] Namely that slaying in ambush is bootless (i.e. unemendable by money).
[7] See *ante* p. 93.

authorship of these two laws is shown by the priestly interest in the administration of the sanctuary and by the language, with its repeated use of the first and second persons. If the killer does not take sanctuary, any trial will be in the king's court. There is apparently no right to take sanctuary for the other three capital charges: at any rate, it would not often occur,[1] and the questions at issue would be different.

After the capital offences comes the case of personal injuries caused in a fight. The sanction is that familiar at the end of the Central Codes and the beginning of the Late, namely support during incapacity and the doctor's fees. It is to be noted that this law is quite inconsistent with the talion. The next rule, which is also an exception from the law of homicide, and also provides for an injury done in a fight, applies to the case, commonly dealt with in the Codes, of a miscarriage caused to a woman who is jostled by the contestants. As the loss is of a foetus, not a living person, the injured husband is to accept a compensation, in such sum as he shall demand,[2] but the clause has been later varied by an addition which entrusts the assessment of the amount to judges or arbitrators. A further amendment introduces, in the second person, the rule of the talion, and to reconcile this with the previous rule it is stated that this only applies where 'no harm' has been done – an absurd expression where the monetary sanction is so heavy. But the talionic rule, as here stated, with its phraseology of 'hand for hand, foot for foot, burn for burn' is quite inappropriate to a miscarriage. The same talionic rule is extended to the slave, in the sense that he obtains his freedom for loss of eye or loss of tooth. The diffuseness of the language of these clauses is noticeable. It is also to be noticed that in each case where the rule of the talion occurs in the religious literature of the Pentateuch it is also a late addition to the context.[3] But the vogue of the talionic idea is short-lived: it was in practice unknown in the later Jewish law, and there was much debate as

---

[1] We do not hear much in other lands of defendants taking asylum for other capital charges.
[2] As in the case in verse 30.
[3] Deut. 19^{21}; Lev. 24^{20} (the passage, beginning at v. 10, is concerned with a certain case of blasphemy. The talion is irrelevantly inserted in vv. 17-22, and there is a return to the blasphemers in v. 23).

to the meaning of the rule and as to whether it had ever been literally applied.[1]

The Code next deals with yet another case of killing, that by goring oxen. The liability of the owner, in a rule reminiscent of English law, depends on the owner's knowledge of the vicious propensity of the beast. In the only ritual rule found in this connection it is provided that the flesh of the goring ox shall not be eaten – because it has been stoned and not ritually killed.[2] These words read as an addition to the Code, but this cannot be considered certain.

The next group of clauses of the Code is concerned entirely with bailments, and apart from an occasional clause in the Central Codes[3] it is in the Late Codes that this topic first appears, and in these clauses the ordeal by oath is first mentioned and always mentioned. The first of these clauses of the Hebrew Code deals with the deposit of money or goods (implements) for safekeeping and merely provides that if the property is stolen from the bailee's house the thief, if found, shall pay double. If he is not found the question whether the bailee has 'laid his hand on the other's property' is to be decided by ordeal undergone by him. In the nature of the case supposed there is no evidence except his, hence the ordeal is applied to him. Next (omitting verse 9) the Code deals with the deposit of animals, and similarly provides that if the beast is lost – by death or theft – or is maimed, and there is no evidence but the bailee's, he is to take the same oath and the owner must accept it. But now[4] the contractual element enters into the decision of the matter, which was previously a question of wrongdoing: if the beast was stolen, the depositee is liable,[5] but not if it was torn by a wild animal and the carcass is produced to prove it; this is a risk which he did not undertake and a loss for

---

[1] See Josephus Antiquities IV, 8, 35, who interprets the passage in the Code as follows: 'He that maimed a man shall suffer the like, being deprived of what the other was deprived of, unless he that was maimed was willing to accept money, for there the sufferer is empowered by law himself to assess the injury that has happened to him, and is allowed to do so unless he decides to be too severe.' This is substantially the interpretation of the Pharisees; the Sadducees, however, considered that the effect of the rule was only to award damages, to be fixed not by the individual but the competent tribunal (Baba Kamma 83b).
[2] See Lev. 17.
[3] See H.C. I, 75.
[4] Clauses 12 and 13.
[5] C.H. 262, 263.

which he does not pay.[1] The contractual obligation continues to shape the decisions: if the transaction is a mere gratuitous borrowing of a beast, the owner not being with it, the borrower is liable if it dies or is maimed. If it was hired, he is not liable: the owner was paid for the risk.

In between these clauses has been inserted (verse 9) a new general principle, extending to all property and all wrongs (including the case of a claim by the plaintiff that a thing found in the defendant's possession is his, having been lost or stolen from him), and it provides that the trial shall be on oath in the temple or shrine, and God shall decide. This is not language of a primitive code, which never provides for wrongdoing in general but groups of facts, and it is plainly an insertion, or attempted insertion, into the law, of the ideal of the priesthood and practice of the ecclesiastical courts, that all trials shall be in a sacred place by ordeal of oath, applied to all appropriate parties,[2] whether there is other evidence or not. In regard to this insertion into the Code we are fortunate enough to see the origin from which it comes, for it is taken either from Leviticus 6[1f.] or from the practice there set out. It is also interesting to see the changes that have been made in introducing it into the law. The ecclesiastical practice refers to any 'sin' against the Lord:[3] the new rule refers to 'wrongdoing'[4] – a term which is secular as well as religious in its meaning. In place of a miscellaneous collection of named situations of vague meaning, the new rule is made to apply to all wrongdoing. In place of the ecclesiastical sanction of restitution plus an additional fifth and a sin offering, it substitutes the common secular sanction of payment of the double value; the language is pruned and the drafting improved.

At the end of the main Code – a favourite place for additions – come two clauses regarding seduction. They are probably (but not certainly) late provisions from an ecclesiastical jurisdiction which claimed to share with the secular courts questions of sexual

---

[1] As generally in the ancient Near East, H.C. I, 75; C.H. 266.
[2] Where the plaintiff claims that property in the defendant's possession is his, and the latter says he acquired it innocently, the oath is to be applied to both, but such a rule is not uncommon.
[3] 'If a soul errs (or sins) and acts treacherously against the Lord', Lev. 6[1].
[4] *pesha‘* – used of a wrong against an individual or a people, e.g. a rebellion against a nation, as well as against God.

misconduct and offences against the marriage-tie (i.e. they are a legal and improved version of Deut.28[29]).[1]

The last question that remains is how and when these additions came into the main Code: was it clause by clause, in the course of development of the Hebrew law, or was it mainly on one occasion under an editor's hands? The latter alternative seems to be true. The main body of the Code is a unity, and is one of the earliest documents of the Bible. The rules for the release of debt-slaves are so different and so much an improvement over those in the religious literature that we must infer them to be later. The rules of the sanctuary as to homicide are represented in one of the latest chapters of the religious writings.[2] The rule of the talion is an interpolation and addition wherever it occurs in the Pentateuch. Exodus 22[9], which purports to extend the procedure of trial by ordeal of oath to all cases, is drawn from the ecclesiastical practice of the Second Temple.

By the beginning of the fourth century B.C. the country was ruled by the leading priestly families, and the high priest was the Head of State subject to the suzerainty of the Persian monarch. It was an object of the editors of the Pentateuch to issue a grand compilation of rules to govern the conduct of the Jew in all its aspects. For this purpose it was necessary that the *toráh* should include laws for the government of the secular life of the citizen as well as the religious. Therefore among the documents embodied in the new Pentateuch was the ancient Code of the Hebrew Kingdom, or the Kingdom of Judah, that may even in some form be as old as Solomon, and had been handed down and developed over several centuries – so old that in 400 B.C. tradition ascribed it to Moses. But, to be enforceable, it was necessary to bring it up to date by amendments embodying the substance of the post-exilic religious literature and the practice of the Second Temple, in so far as it could be applied as law. In this form the Code was promulgated in the Pentateuch and, as interpreted by the Rabbis of mishnaic and talmudic times, provided the bulk of the Jewish civil law. It might hastily be inferred that here is an example of

---

[1] Compare Lev. 19[20]. Ex. 22[16-17] corresponds closely with A.C. 55. Hebrew Law made adultery with a married woman capital. For the ritual of the ordeal of jealousy, see Numbers 5[12f.].

[2] Numbers 35.

religious doctrine bringing about the development of secular law, but this is not so. On the whole, these additions to the Code are common form and substance of the Late Codes, and point the contrast between the heights of the religious and ethical doctrine of the Hebrew prophets, perhaps never scaled before, and the normal cruelties of the secular law of that stage of economic development.

PART II

CHAPTER 13

The Food Gatherers

The Food Gatherers we define as comprising those peoples who live more by gathering their food than by the hunt, and do not plant or sow crops or domesticate animals except an occasional pet. They are the modern representatives of the Palaeolithic Age: their stone-work is of the crudest and their tools are mainly of wood or bone. They have no spinning, pottery or metal, and no weaving except basketry and other plaiting and some simple woodwork and leatherwork.[1] Those who live by the sea have bark canoes, dug-outs or rafts. Food Gatherers have no permanent dwellings and sleep on the open ground or in caves or rock shelters and protect themselves only by the erection of a lean-to or windbreak, or a rude shelter of branches or poles covered by grass or skins. They know how to make fire by drill or percussion,[2] but many carry it around rather than make it. Apart from the medicine-men or *shamans* there is no economic specialization except as between the sexes. They have no weapons of war except the weapons of the hunt, of which the chief is the bow and arrow, and they have no shields. There is no trade and no markets.[3]

This is the type of the Food Gatherer, but some are in some respects more advanced and some more backward. Some peoples, for example, have no, or practically no, stone-work;[4] some have,

[1] Their other arts consist mainly of music and the dance (the bulk have musical instruments) and painting; there are rock paintings here and there. The beating-out of bark cloth is widespread.
[2] Percussion among the Yahgan, Alacaluf, Ona and Guayakí.
[3] Except where Food Gatherers live in close association with more civilized man.
[4] Andamanese, none: Radcliffe-Brown (1922), 492. Semang, none: Schebesta (1929), 158. Alacaluf, none now (knowledge of pressure-flaking of arrow points came late): Bird (1946), 67.

now at least, no bow and arrow;[1] some have no method of making fire but carry it with them;[2] some, on the other hand, make a crude clay vessel;[3] several have acquired pieces of iron or tin from surrounding peoples and beat it cold for spear or arrow points;[4] all have the dog, which they have acquired from more civilized man.

Several of the food-gathering peoples are of the dwarf races of mankind, among whom the average height of the adult male is a little below five feet and of the female about four feet nine or ten inches. These are such forest dwellers as the Negritos (the Andaman Islanders, the Semang tribes of Malaya, and Aëtas of the Philippines), theMbuti (Pygmies) of the Ituri forest of Central Africa, and also the Bushmen of the Kalahari Desert and South-West Africa and adjoining areas. The Food Gatherers also include some Punans of Borneo and Kubu of Sumatra, and the peoples of the extremity of South America – namely, the Ona of Tierra del Fuego and the Yahgan and Alacaluf of the Magellan Archipelago – and the Guayakí of Eastern Paraguay, the Botocudo and Puri of Eastern Brazil and the Western Shoshoni of the Basin-Plateau area in Western North America.[5] They also include the Tasmanians[6] and some Sakai of Malaya and some Veddahs of Ceylon. The populations of nearly all these tribes are sadly reduced and several have become extinct in recent times or recent years, but while we must rely on the accounts of contemporary observers, past and

---

[1] Tasmanians, no bow and arrow or blowpipe: Roth (1899), 68f. Alacaluf obsolete and never important, a late introduction from the south: Bird (1946), 70. Semang have now mainly abandoned bow and arrow for blow pipe, acquired from the Sakai.

[2] Andamanese: Radcliffe-Brown (1922), 472. Mbuti: Turnbull (1966), 35.

[3] Andamanese have been making a crude pot of one shape for a long time; the other Negritos have no pottery; Botocudo had no pottery until recent times (Métraux (1946), 535); Puri make a few crude globular pots; formerly the Cape Bushmen made some crude clay pots (Schapera (1930), 144, Dornan (1925), 92).

[4] Andamanese from at least the eighteenth century: Radcliffe-Brown (1922), 444. Semang in the last two or three generations have taken to smelting iron to make arrows: Schebesta (1929), 76. The Mbuti acquire iron blades and spear and arrow points from the Bantu but do not work metal, cold or hot.

[5] Mainly of Nevada and adjoining areas of California; see the following chapter.

[6] For bibliography see Plomly (1968).

present (in many cases all too brief) we refer to them generally in this chapter in the present tense. Some of the tribes now survive only in dependence on, or close association with, neighbouring peoples of higher material status – some Bushmen and most Pygmies[1] with Bantu, and most Semang with the Malay – and others have recently acquired social and economic practices from surrounding communities. Many of these peoples are inhabitants of forest or desert, and it might have been thought that their way of life is that of peoples driven into unfavourable environments and therefore reduced in economic status to that of Food Gatherers; but there is irresistible evidence that they are societies of forest and desert, remote islands, isolated mountain valleys and distant wastes, surviving from the cultures and even races of the Old Stone Age.

Food Gatherers require a vast territory for their sustenance. In Tierra del Fuego the density of population among the Ona is about one person per eight square miles, the population of the whole South Chilean Archipelago is about one person per four square miles, and among the Botocudo about one per three square miles. In Tasmania at the coming of the European it was one per seven square miles.[2] At the other extreme, in the favoured conditions of the Andaman Islands, where no place is more than ten miles from the sea, with its rich resources of dugong, turtle and fish, the density in 1858 was two persons per square mile. The populations of all these tribes are least sparse along river and coast, and therefore they need not travel so wide an area and their houses are more permanent and substantial.[3] An average figure of the order of one person to every five or seven square miles may be taken to be characteristic of all these peoples.

The general sparseness of food cannot support a stationary population nor even a substantial roving group.[4] The normal and effective unit of population is the band, or local group, consisting commonly of one or two or more extended families

[1] For a recent study of the symbiosis of Mbuti and Bantu, in which the culture of the former remains almost unchanged, see Turnbull (1966).
[2] For the Shoshoni see *post* p. 175.
[3] Radcliffe-Brown (1922), 409f.; Cooper (Yahgan), 84-7; Steward (1938).
[4] In times of hunger they scatter into smaller groups; e.g. Schebesta (1929), 53.

related by blood or marriage[1] and embracing an average of some fifteen to twenty persons.[2] Such a group moves in search of food over a well-defined territory of, say, 100 to 150 square miles, normally not staying more than two or three nights in the same place and frequently breaking up into smaller family groups and more rarely combining with other bands in the vicinity. The chief occasion for such a combination is a seasonal glut at one place of game or fish or fruits, or a stranded whale or other temporary abundance of food, which sometimes affords an opportunity for ceremonies of initiation,[3] and large numbers may then congregate together. These combinations are easily witnessed, whereas the normal band of some fifteen or twenty persons melts invisible into the surrounding bushes, hollows or rocks at the approach of the observer. Accordingly the figures of the populations of the Food Gatherers have often been exaggerated and the estimates show startling variation.[4]

The sum of these bands is the tribe, totalling a population of the order of 500 persons and covering an area of some 3,000 square miles, a more shadowy and mainly a linguistic unit, for it speaks a language distinct from that of the next tribe and often unrelated to it,[5] while the tribe's own language is commonly divided into some three or four dialects, each spoken by some 100 persons. The tribe bears an uncertain name, often the native

[1] Schapera (1930), 83; Bird (1946), 58, 71; Turnbull (1966), 26, 93.
[2] For example, an old man and his wife, their daughters and daughters' husbands, an unmarried son or two and the daughters' children (Thomas (1959), 10); a band of eighteen consisting of an old woman, two sons and three daughters, their wives and husbands and their children, and one other boy (*ibid*. 64); an old woman, her three sons and her daughters and their spouses and children – here the old lady had a strong hold on her family and kept them together (*ibid*. 230); a band of six, an old man, two daughters, son, grandson and son-in-law (*ibid*. 167). Evidence as to other Bushman bands is summarized in Schapera (1930), 78f. The size of the Mbuti bands is considerably larger and of the order of fifty persons or more. For details of the constitution of such a band see Turnbull (1966).
[3] For the Yahgan: Gusinde (1937), 62. Some simple ceremony of initiation at puberty for both sexes, with some simple scarification, is generally to be found among the Food Gatherers.
[4] The estimates for the number of Tasmanians in 1803 varied between 500 and 20,000: Roth (1899), 164. See generally for figures of Food Gatherers, Krzywicki (1934).
[5] The Alacaluf, Yahgan and Ona spoke unrelated languages. The Mbuti, however, have adopted languages of Bantu origin.

word for 'the fellows', 'the people' (which a neighbour or observer took to be its name) or a term of derision bestowed on it by its neighbours; often there is more than one name for the people, and the population it covers is uncertain. But the tribe, as well as the band, is a territorial unit, for the intrusion of foraging members of another tribe without permission rouses violent resentment. The tribe rarely meets as a whole. In Australia Howitt[1] defines the tribe as

> 'a larger or smaller aggregate of people who occupy a certain tract of hunting and food ground in common, who speak the same language with dialectical differences, who acknowledge a common relatedness and who deny that relatedness to other surrounding tribes',

and this definition is also applicable generally to the Food Gatherers. But in some places, especially where food is more plentiful, the bands are larger and less mobile and partake more of the nature of tribes[2] and it is difficult for observers to know whether to call the local group a tribe, a sub-tribe or a band.[3]

All these circumstances betoken the isolation of mankind at the economic grade of the Food Gatherers. Communications are scant and generally no one has knowledge of a tribe or band thirty miles away;[4] The result is most marked differences in the culture of peoples only a few miles apart. Here is an extreme example of a situation characteristic of the whole primitive age, which indicates that changes occur everywhere in culture, largely influenced by the reciprocal impact of material conditions and human propensities, and the behaviour of adaptation to environment, but slowly and often uncommunicated to neighbours. As we progress we shall see this isolation and slowness of change ever diminishing.

[1] A. W. Howitt, 'Australian Group Relations', *B.A.E.R.* (Washington D.C., 1883), 799.
[2] *e.g.* among the Mbuti net-hunters.
[3] The Ona population at its highest totalled 3,500 to 4,000 consisting of thirty-nine independent territorial hordes: Gusinde (1946), 97. The Botocudo tribes were in some cases divided into bands of between 50 and 200 persons: Nimuendajú (1946), 97f.; Métraux (1946), 536.
[4] Twenty miles in the Andamans: Radcliffe-Brown (1922), 87. With the larger Mbuti bands, whose territories may extend to three days' march, these distances are larger.

Subject to these temporary combinations and the existence here and there of favourite, traditional camping-places where a band may lodge at different seasons to scour the countryside, everywhere the sexes may be seen at their appointed tasks; the women and girls at work near the camp with the digging-stick (the woman's implement)[1] grubbing up plants, roots or bulbs, reptiles or other small animals, or collecting fruits or insects, or in coastal communities swimming and diving for shellfish and small marine animals;[2] the men are fashioning the weapons of the hunt or are further afield pursuing the larger animals,[3] climbing trees for the wild honey and sometimes collecting distant roots and plants. Each band knows the bounds of its territory and has a name for every significant hollow or rise or clump of bushes or trees and every place where a particular kind of food can be found.

The Food Gatherers have no rulers or chiefs of the bands or tribes.[4] The elder males,[5] and sometimes females, enjoy respect and influence, for example, in advice whither and when to move, and especially persons possessing exceptional prowess in the hunt or fight[6] or a reputation for supernatural powers,[7] or such personal qualities as freedom from ill-temper and, above all, generosity.[8] There is in some bands a man of such influence as to be appropriately called a headman, and his position often descends to his son or even (during his life) to a daughter's husband,[9] but his status differs little from that of the rest. Few desire prominence and leaders have no more possessions than anyone else: indeed the reputation for generosity commonly

---

[1] About three feet long.

[2] Among the Yahgan a man makes the canoe, which is propelled by the woman while he harpoons the quarry: Gusinde (1937).

[3] With bow and arrow, blowpipe, spear, throwing-stick or cudgel, pitfall or snare; or fishing with bow and arrow, spear, harpoon and line, dam of stones or poisonous branches. Among Mbuti net-hunters the whole band takes part in the hunt (see Turnbull (1966), 28) and contrast the archers (*ibid*. 107); for the division of labour between the sexes see *ibid*. 123, 151.

[4] Schapera (1930), 149; Cooper (Yahgan), 92; Bird (1946), 58, 70; Turnbull (1966), 14.

[5] Thomas (1959), 167; Radcliffe-Brown (1922), 45, Yahgan.

[6] Roth (1899), 57f.

[7] Radcliffe-Brown (1922), 175; Botocudo.

[8] Radcliffe-Brown (1922), 45f.

[9] See a description of a headman: Thomas (1959), 182f.

requires a self-imposed poverty. Only in a few of the most developed of these economies is there a headman of the tribe.

There are no clans, either patrilineal or matrilineal[1]; that is to say, no organized or recognized groups, beyond the family, consisting of persons related exclusively through the male line or female line. Nor are there any totems or totemic groups, moieties, social or marriage classes[2] and few or no classificatory kinship terms.[3] This absence of clans is an aspect not only of the mobility of these peoples but also of their marriage customs: there is no custom which obliges the married couple to live exclusively with the husband's family or the wife's. A man may marry any girl who is not a near relative,[4] usually someone outside his band[5] but within the tribe,[6] and except in cases of bride-stealing or capture[7] he usually secures her family's consent by gifts to her parents of game which he has hunted, or other presents which show that he can and will provide for them or their daughter. If they consent he comes to live with her there or close by and the marriage has taken place.[8] There is never a religious ceremony but there is sometimes (at least on a first marriage)[9] some social display.[10] They continue to live with her family and he to hunt and provide food for them for about two years, after which the couple take up their more permanent residence with her parents or his, as they prefer.[11] Marriage is

[1] Schapera (1930), 83, 85; Bird (1946), 58, 71; Cooper (Yahgan), 92.
[2] But among the Ona it is said that their thirty-nine territorial groups are patrilineal bands which do not intermarry; see R. H. Lowie, *H.S.A.*, vol. 5, 326.
[3] But see Turnbull (1966), 268f.
[4] Schapera (1930), 83; Cooper (Yahgan), 92; Radcliffe-Brown (1922), 71. Marriage with first cousins takes place but is not liked; Schebesta (1929), 114; and see Turnbull (1966), 10 (not allowed).
[5] Or inside: Radcliffe-Brown (1922), 71.
[6] Or outside: Schebesta (1929), 114. Among the Mbuti there is some exchange of sisters: Turnbull (1966), 219.
[7] Schapera (1930), 107; Roth (1899), 112.
[8] Bird (1946), 76; Schapera (1930), 105; Turnbull (1966), 61, 140; Steward (1938), Shoshoni.
[9] Turnbull (1966), 85.
[10] Schapera (1930), 105f.; Cooper (Ona), 115 (wedding feast); Schebesta (1929), 233.
[11] Thomas (1959), 88; Dornan (1925), 127; Schebesta (1929), 97; Cooper (Yahgan), 92 and Cooper (Ona), 115 (where usually they then go and live with his group).

mainly monogamous everywhere, but everywhere there are some men with two wives, being good enough hunters to afford it, and rarely with more.[1] In most places marriage breaks up easily by consent,[2] but there is much difference between tribes in the latter respect[3] and in standards of sexual morality and the status of the woman.[4] Adoption is common among some peoples.[5]

It is premature to say there is 'ownership' of land or goods. The question is, who has the right to hunt or gather food upon a tract of land, who has the right to share in the hunted prey or gathered plant or to take the fruit of a tree or to pull it up, and who can exclusively take or use without permission the few available goods. The answer is governed by the situation that whatever is regularly or generally done is considered rightly done, whether it is prompted by natural human emotion or social interests – or, as is usual, both – and the right of one person is limited by the rights of others.

In regard to land there are some differences between one tribe and another. In all, everyone can hunt and collect without permission who is born in the territory[6] or is a member of the band whose territory it is;[7] in some, the right extends to some other members of the tribe;[8] but a member of a foreign tribe, or even another band,[9] who comes without right or permission,

---

[1] Cooper (Ona), 116; Cooper (Yahgan), 92; Roth (1899), 112; Schebesta (1929), 280; Skeat and Blagden (1906), 55; Bird (1946), 77.
[2] Thomas (1959), 87; Schapera (1930), 110f.; Roth (1899), 112; Schebesta (1929), 98f., 280; at any rate till a child is born, Turnbull (1966), 73.
[3] Schapera (1930), 111.
[4] The young people's choice of spouse is usually free; Cooper (Yahgan), 92; Cooper (Ona), 115; but among Bushmen tribes a man may be found rearing a female child as his wife, to live with her after puberty. Among the Semang and Mbuti there is considerable equality of the sexes; Schebesta (1929), 279, Turnbull (1966), 271. The position of women is low in Tasmania: Roth (1899), 113.
[5] e.g. Andamese and Mbuti.
[6] Turnbull (1966), 131.
[7] e.g. Thomas (1959), 10; Radcliffe-Brown (1922), 41; Schapera (1930), 127; Turnbull (1966), 276.
[8] Bird (1946), 71; Thomas (1959), 84 (Gikwe: a man can eat the veld food if born in the area, or wherever his wife can or his father or mother could, e.g. where his wife's mother was born). The Semang seem entitled to wander over the whole territory of a tribe, but the bands have their own territories. The Shoshoni do not exclude other bands.
[9] Turnbull (1966), 174.

will commonly be attacked or even killed.[1] A man who has
killed or wounded an animal is entitled to have it, even if the
wounded prey has to be stalked for days or its body left till the
hunter can bring his group from miles away to cut it up and
transport it.[2] Elsewhere a pig belongs to the man whose arrow
first strikes it (unless it glances off), a fish or turtle to the man
who has speared or harpooned it,[3] an animal caught in a snare
to the man who set it. But all this only means that, in the case of a
large animal, it is his right to supervise the cutting-up and distribution.[4] Gifts of portions (sometimes more or less defined)[5]
have to be made to others, including the man who gave or lent
the arrow by which it was shot;[6] the others subdivide theirs to
others, and the older men may have to be given the best part by
a bachelor,[7] so that although the hunter may be entitled in the
first place to the best portion he may have to share that and in
the end get less than the rest.[8] His generosity in this respect,
especially if he is a good hunter, is the foundation of his popularity
and influence, and meanness would be calamitous and lay him
open to jealousy.[9] But an equal return is expected at some
appropriate time and must be given.[10] Presents are for ever being
given and exchanged and a request to give a particular thing, if
sufficiently persisted in, is acceded to.[11] These practices, which
apply everywhere with modifications in regard to an isolated
root[12] or a local harvest of nuts or fruits,[13] are an important aid
to survival, for there is hardly any possibility of storage and
thereby the band makes the best use of the scant gifts of
nature.

   The right to use or cut down a tree of a useful species or take its
fruit belongs commonly to the person who first declares he has

[1] Schapera (1930), 157.   [2] Thomas (1959), 22.
[3] Radcliffe-Brown, (1922), 4.   [4] Schapera (1930), 148.
[5] Turnbull (1966), 159.   [6] Thomas (1959), 167.
[7] Radcliffe-Brown (1922), 43.
[8] e.g. Thomas (1959), 49f.; Schmidt (1937), I, 190ff., Yahgan.
[9] Thomas (1959), 22.
[10] Radcliffe-Brown (1922), 42; Gusinde (1937), 980f.
[11] Gusinde (1937), 980f.; Thomas (1959), 22f.
[12] Among the Bushmen a root belongs to its digger and is shared only at
his wish. Thomas (1959), 183.
[13] The owner of the skin or bag in which they are collected may be entitled
to the contents: Thomas (1959), 214.

seen it or first selects it,[1] but fruit which has once fallen is generally free for all to take.[2] The few available goods are everywhere considered to belong to the person who made them or normally uses them.

All this applies to a woman as well as a man. Women as well as men have their trees and the things they make, and their necessities of every day.[3] A woman keeps her property on marriage as well as the things her husband gives her,[4] but like others she must share her possessions (except her few personal necessities) with the rest of the family.[5]

So few are the available goods – bows and arrows or blowpipes, canoes, nets, lines, skins, poles and sticks, bones, beads and fragments of leather and ornament – that rules of inheritance are hardly to be seen. A man before his death may divide goods between his son and daughter,[6] and a woman may give ornaments to her daughter. The little that is not given in life or destroyed at a man's death[7] usually goes to his eldest son, or his sons[8] (or if there are no sons, to brothers or sisters) who support the widow.[9] Nothing goes to a spouse.

There is also very little to be seen of rules as to sanctions for wrongful acts, that is to say, acts contrary to good order. This is partly because the communities are so small that serious wrongful acts are not frequent enough to create rules or standards. Nor are there persons with authority to fix sanctions nor to inflict them (except to punish children), nor to decide whether a wrongful act has been done or by whom,[10] nor does the need exist to decide what is known to all. If it is necessary, before the existence of law can be acknowledged, that there should be a specialized

---

[1] Radcliffe-Brown (1922), 41; Roth (1899), 60; Turnbull (1966), 93.
[2] Even fruit which has fallen within an enclosure: Schebesta (1929), 83.
[3] Radcliffe-Brown (1922), 41; Schebesta (1929), 83, 234; Bird (1946), 71.
[4] Schapera (1930), 148.   [5] Bird (1946), 71.
[6] Schebesta (1929), 234.
[7] e.g. Yahgan, Alacaluf (all of the deceased's goods are burnt except his canoe and equipment and skins for covering a hut); Auen Bushmen (most buried with him except utensils and skins); Shoshoni (most destroyed at death).
[8] Turnbull (1966), 116.   [9] Schapera (1930), 148.
[10] The contrary is reported of the Namib Bushmen by Seydel, *Aus der Namib*, 505f., but this is unique and if correct shows adoption from a neighbouring people; see Schapera (1930), 155.

organ of the society for these purposes, none exists; and if it can be recognized where a whole community acts to punish a wrongful deed committed within it, this is hardly reported to occur.[1]

Yet because human habits and social interests operate, there can already be recognized a fundamental situation which we shall witness in more developed economies in the areas of behaviour where rules of law emerge.

There are already to be seen signs of a coming distinction between the fields of the criminal and civil, that is to say, between conduct which is an offence to all, and conduct which is an offence only to individuals. The former are chiefly the cases of incest, homosexuality and adultery, which are strongly condemned, and of which adultery is already on the borderland between 'crime' and 'civil injury' and belongs to both; the latter consists of homicide, wounding, adultery and theft.[2] The boundary is perhaps more vague than it is in practice with modern man, in that both 'crime' and 'civil wrong' are punished by the individual immediately injured or other members of the offended kinship group. The parties to an incestuous marriage, for example, may be ostracized by the band[3] but are more likely to be punished by some offended relative or relatives who may kill the offender if they have the chance.[4] The husband, if he can, will kill the adulterer or wife-stealer and thrash his wife.[5] Again 'crime' already touches on the domain of religion at the same points as the complete crime of later ages: adultery is already in part a religious offence,[6] though like other 'crimes' it is common among some peoples, and there are a few other sacral offences.[7] Witchcraft is hardly found as yet, nor even magic.[8]

It is difficult to say if homicide and the other civil wrongs are

---

[1] See a rare case in Turnbull (1966), 197-8, where the hut of a man who (a) stole from the band (b) denied his mother was his mother (c) was unpopular, was stripped by hunters – that is to say that crime was punished on behalf of the band.
[2] Radcliffe-Brown (1922), 48; Thomas (1959), 85, 89; Dornan (1925), 128; Schebesta (1929), 234. As in some more advanced peoples, adultery is regarded as a kind of theft (ibid.).
[3] Turnbull (1966), 190.
[4] Thomas (1959), 85; Dornan (1925), 128.
[5] e.g. Schapera (1930), 108; Bird (1946), 71.
[6] See p. 171, and Schebesta (1929), 222.
[7] e.g. Turnbull (1966), 190.   [8] Turnbull (1966), 14, 54f.

G

more or less frequent per head of the population than in developed economies. In one people homicide is said to be unheard of, in another frequent,[1] and the advent of the European, depriving a tribe of part of its wide domain and forcing it to invade another's, has brought disorder and murder on a scale not previously known, just as the introduction of the white man's cattle, shot by the savage as game, has led to reciprocal murder between them.

There are few or no goods wherewith an offender may purchase peace, but the aggrieved person does not necessarily inflict retaliatory violence upon him. He may do nothing or vent his anger on anyone or anything in his vicinity,[2] and at his display of rage women and children and even men are likely to flee into the jungle or elsewhere. The rare killer, unless he is a powerful man, would usually take refuge in the forest or some remote place or a neighbouring band, where he might be joined by sympathizers. The relatives and friends of the deceased would be likely to kill him if they had the chance, but anger is short and if he lay low for a few months or was a man of strength he would be likely to escape retaliation.[3] The same applies to a case of wounding or adultery. Theft is said to be unknown in some places,[4] in others to be visited by violent retaliation or killing. All cases of killing by a member of another band – and these are probably the bulk – are liable to bring about a feud between the bands. But to say that the sanction for any of these offences is the law of retaliation or the feud is to use exaggerated and inaccurate language, and moreover the feud between bands[5] belongs more to the future domain of international than national law.

Of the future legal procedure there are equally few signs. A function of the headman or elders or other men of influence is to separate combatants and make peace between them, to offer an opinion, not a judgment.[6] There are the beginnings of regularized

[1] Among the Yahgan there are said to have been twenty-two homicides between 1871 and 1884 in a population of under 2,000.
[2] Roth (1899), 59.
[3] Radcliffe-Brown (1922), 48-9. So that a man can even be friendly with his father's murderer: Thomas (1959), 183.
[4] Schebesta (1929), 97; Thomas (1959), 209.
[5] See Radcliffe-Brown (1922), 85.
[6] See Métraux (1946), 536; Turnbull (1966), 127. The same function may be exercised by the 'camp clown': Turnbull (1966), 182.

and controlled modes of giving relief to the wounded feelings of persons aggrieved, whether they are individuals or the community at large. These are particularly visible in Tasmania.

'If an offence be committed against the tribe, the delinquent has to stand while a certain number of spears are, at the same time, thrown at him; these, from the unerring aim with which they are thrown, he can seldom avoid: although from the quickness of his sight, he will frequently escape unhurt; he moves not from his place, avoiding the spears merely by the contortions of his body.'[1]

In similar circumstances the community 'may place the offender upon the low branch of a tree, point at and jeer at him'.[2] In a quarrel between individuals, the parties may approach one another face to face, and folding their arms across their breasts, shake their heads (which occasionally come in contact) in each other's faces, uttering loud and angry words until one or other is exhausted or his anger subsides.[3] This, like similar procedures in Australia,[4] is known as 'growling'. With these may be compared a practice of the Botocudo where conflicts between bands are typically settled by duels between pairs of opponents who alternately strike each other with long sticks.[5] But more commonly the person aggrieved will snatch a stick or firebrand and brandish it about or strike those in the vicinity, including the offender.[6]

As for processes to ascertain facts, there is no trace of the ordeal. There are already in use in some peoples methods of divination to ascertain unknown or future circumstances[7] (for

---

[1] R. H. Davies, 'On the Aborigines of Van Diemen's Land', *Tasmanian Journal of Science*, II, 409-20 (1846).
[2] R. H. Davies, *ibid*.
[3] *The Life and Labours of G. W. Walker*, 1862, 101: cited Roth (1899), 59.
[4] e.g. Spencer and Gillen (1927), 468-9 (Arunta).
[5] Métraux (1946), 536: the Ona use arrows, first rendered harmless (L. Bridges, *Man*, vol. 38, 1938, 4-7).
[6] Roth (1899), 59f. A married woman who had selected a tree was aggrieved by the fact that by some accident it had been pulled down or mutilated by a party of persons, and struck blows right and left among them with a firebrand. A man, aggrieved by some conduct of his wife, cut the feet of seven women lying near him asleep.
[7] Not e.g. among Mbuti: Turnbull (1966), 74.

example, throwing oracle discs and drawing inferences from the positions in which they fall),[1] but these are not used to find the identity of a wrongdoer. There are medicine-men or *shamans* in many peoples[2] but they do not smell out offenders;[3] death is regarded as a natural event rather than an occasion for seeking malevolent causes and agents.[4]

In substance the existence of law is not to be recognized: it is not one of the forces which maintain order. Social control in a community which consists of the biological family extended to a band of some twenty persons closely interdependent for survival, is effected by public opinion and the disapproval, ridicule or violent reactions which may follow conduct that flouts it, by reciprocity and conservatism, by the power of habit and of ritualization of conduct, and the fact that peoples and individuals who act differently do not survive in this way of life; even more by family affection, friendships and good sense. Religion also sustains the obedience to existing standards of good conduct and reinforces devotion to them, but we can already see that it is in most respects far removed from the fields of conduct to which we have referred as those where law will appear. There is widespread and convincing evidence among the Food Gatherers, notwithstanding the incredulity of many scholars, of belief in a supreme being[5] as well as in spirits and the souls of the dead, but the list of acts disapproved by him does not touch on those fields of conduct except at the points where we shall later see law and religion adjoining. For example, among the Semang generally there is a belief in Karei or Kaei, the god of thunder, who strikes with lightning or sends a tiger or disease to destroy the person who commits a sin against him (*lawaid karei*). But murder and theft are not sins.[6] The following are widely recognized as sins: to mock at certain species of animals; to kill

[1] Thomas (1959), 228; Dornan (1925), 155.
[2] Not e.g. among Mbuti: Turnbull (1966), 14.
[3] Dornan (1925), 162.   [4] Turnbull (1966), 234, 262.
[5] Bird (1946), 78f.; Schebesta (1929), 189f., 222 and *passim*; Cooper (Yahgan), 102f.; Roth (1899), 53f.; Thomas (1959), 126-8; Turnbull (1966), 19, 191, 252, 279 (the forest is personalized as an affectionate godhead, father and mother).
[6] Schebesta (1929), 190; among the Sabubn (Negritos, but Sakai-speaking) he says, p. 191, that murder is also a sin.

one of certain sacred animals; to throw a spear before noonday; to watch dogs mating; to draw water in a vessel blackened by fire; to have sexual intercourse in the camp by day; to sleep near a close relative. The sin is expiated by blood sacrifice during a thunderstorm, usually by gashing one's own shin. Yet adultery is also a sin,[1] and by a rule which we shall find later among many primitive peoples a man who kills, whatever the merits or demerits of his conduct, is in some tribes considered unclean and requires some ritual of purification.[2]

[1] Schebesta (1929), 280. [2] Radcliffe-Brown (1922), 133.

CHAPTER 14

Early Hunters, Agriculturists and Pastoralists

As man gains control over his environment, his material culture expands and develops and becomes more diversified, specialized and complex and his methods of subsistence now change in three directions. First, whereas the Food Gatherers subsisted by gathering rather than hunting their food, there is in some peoples a large development of hunting as against gathering, and we call such peoples the Early Hunters (H.1). The second change is that, among other communities, to food gathering is added the rudiments of agriculture, and we call these the Early Agriculturists (A.1). Thirdly, among a few peoples some keeping of domestic animals for food (other than horses and dogs) is added to gathering and we call such peoples the Early Pastoralists (P.1). But of all these societies many or most still acquire more than half of their food by gathering[1] and almost all hunt. With a certain growth in specialization we find a few peoples among whom some families are agricultural and some not, the proportion of agriculturists varying from season to season.[2] Where material culture is least developed we are on the borders of the Food Gatherers and have sometimes difficulty in distinguishing the Hunters from them.[3] There is sometimes difficulty in distinguishing Hunters from Early Agriculturists where the cultivation is minimal and liable to be abandoned,[4] and sometimes from the Early Pastoralists where hunters have acquired a few sheep and cattle from the European. There is excluded from these categories, and reserved

[1] Australia: Berndt (1964), 104f. California: Kroeber (1925), 814.
[2] Hidatsa: Bowers (1965), 18.
[3] Among Australians and Basin-Plateau tribes.
[4] e.g. on the acquisition of the horse in America.

for description in the following chapters, the societies practising agriculture (or rather horticulture) as their main occupation (A.2), the rich fishing cultures of the North-West American coast (H.2) and the pure Pastoralists (P.2). The tribes of the Early Hunters and Agriculturists are numerous and we shall content ourselves with referring to them and omitting the Early Pastoralists, who are few.

The Early Hunters are chiefly to be found in Australia and North and South America, but they include a few Asiatic peoples. They embrace, for example, all the Australian aborigines and Eskimo, the Indians of the Basin-Plateau area of North America[1] (all of which are close to the Food Gatherers) and the peoples of California except in the north-west, and also such Indian tribes of North America as the Apache, Kiowa, Comanches, Blackfeet, Crees, Teton, Assiniboin and Omaha; and such Northern Athapascans as the Upper Tanana Indians of Alaska; in South America they include the Tehuelche and Puelche of the Argentine. The known Early Agriculturists are chiefly to be found in North and South America and Asia and include, in South America, most of the tribes of the Chaco and the Akwẽ-Shavante and Akwẽ-Sherente of East Brazil, and in North America many Indian peoples not already mentioned, such as the Iroquois, the Hidatsa group and Mandan, Dakota, Ponca, Cheyenne, Iowa, Oto, Missouri, Osage, Winnebago and Chippewa. The Early Pastoralists are to be found in Africa and Asia and include the Hottentots.

These peoples are mainly representatives of the Mesolithic Age. Apart from a little copper among the Eskimo and Northern Athapascans they have no metals till they acquire them from the European,[2] and they make their tools of wood, bone or stone. They have good basketry[3] and canoes and weave various materials and have some crude pottery.[4] At their more permanent camps and settlements they have some substantial houses[5] of branches

---

[1] Mainly of Utah and Nevada and adjoining areas of California, Oregon and Wyoming.
[2] For a general account of the Eskimo, see Birket-Smith (1959), 133f.
[3] Not the Puelche, Tehuelche nor the Upper Tanana Indians, who make birch-bark utensils.
[4] Not the Australians or Comanches.
[5] Not in Australia where the technology is poor: Berndt (1964), 92.

or logs or earth, covered with skins, hides or thatch, or have *tipis* (tents) or igloos. Save for the *shamans* and sorcerers there is still little specialization except between the sexes,[1] and the bulk of the gathering is done, and among most peoples the majority of the food is still acquired, by the women with the assistance of their digging-sticks. The chief hunting weapon of the men remains the bow and arrow[2] but the implements and methods of hunting and fishing are more varied. There is a general increase in the amount of animals and goods possessed, and in the more developed economies a surplus beyond the immediate needs of subsistence[3] and some trade in this, almost everywhere. Partly because much of this wealth, and especially the horse, is easily taken by raids, and chiefly because there is now more contact between peoples, most of them are much given to warfare, a pursuit hardly known before.[4] The raids are mostly conducted by small war-parties, often with general approval. There are now some warlike implements other than implements of the hunt, and especially the shield in most parts of Australia[5] and in areas of North America,[6] and in North America the acquisition of the horse from the European has transformed the life of these peoples in varying degree, enabling them in the plains to cover great distances in pursuit of enemies and – their other absorbing interest – the hunting of the buffalo. Agriculture begins in various ways, replacing the crowns of yams in the earth after removal of the tubers for eating; camping by the wild rice on the margins of lakes and marshes and tending and gathering it; irrigating wild seed patches; sowing wild seed.[7] But in the more developed

[1] There is however a degree of specialization here and there in the sense that there are people with special skill in making, for example, saddles, *tipis*. Comanches: Wallace and Hoebel (1952), 243.
[2] Not known in Australia where the chief weapons are the spear and the spear-thrower and in some areas the boomerang.
[3] If only for providing food for guests at ceremonies (Australia). Basin-Plateau: Steward (1938), 237. The Upper Tanana and other Athapascans have taken the *potlach* from the coastal peoples (see the following chapter).
[4] Steward (1938), 235, 238; McKennan (1959), 95f.
[5] For this reason the Australians are placed here and not among the Food Gatherers.
[6] Not among the Upper Tanana or most Northern Athapascans, but important in the American plains: also in parts of California where armour (not of metal) is also in use, a custom imported from the north-west.
[7] e.g. Basin-Plateau: Steward (1938), 122, 128, 183, 231.

EARLY HUNTERS AND AGRICULTURISTS 175

agriculture, fields are cultivated with digging-sticks, sometimes as much as a day's journey from the settlements.[1] The men usually do the heavy work of burning the undergrowth and breaking the ground, and the women cultivate.[2] There is a great development of magic and religion:[3] elaborate religious systems sometimes develop and spread, and in most peoples (where almost any death or illness is liable to be attributed to witchcraft) death by witchcraft is one of the chief causes of unrest and gives rise to raids of war-parties on neighbours and internal disorder and murder.

Though the groups cover wider areas, the density of population remains much as before, varying chiefly for reasons of ecology, greatest on rivers and coasts[4] and least in the arid and desert areas. In Australia, for example, though E. J. Eyre found three or four persons to every mile of the Murray River, E. M. Carr found one native to every 250 square miles among the Yanda, and Elkin[5] estimates the population of the continent in 1788 at 300,000, an average density of one person per 10 square miles. In North America in the Basin-Plateau area, Kroeber estimated an average of one person to 15·6 square miles, much greater in the less arid regions[6] and smaller among the mounted bands,[7] and in California, at the coming of the European a population of 133,000 representing a density of one person per square mile.[8] The population of native America north of Mexico (mainly consisting of Hunters and Early Agriculturists) is generally thought to have been about one million persons, that is, one person to 4 square miles,[9] and the population of Brazil about 1 million to

[1] e.g. Akwě-Shavante: Maybury-Lewis (1967), 50. Chippewa: Densmore (1929), 122.
[2] Throughout Eastern North America the bulk of the gardening is done by women.
[3] Australia: Berndt (1964), 185f., Elkin: (1964). California: Kroeber (1925), 851f. Among the Western Shoshoni and Comanches there is little.
[4] Elkin (1964), 56f.
[5] Elkin (1964), 24; Berndt (1964), 26f.
[6] In Owen's Valley, one person to 2 square miles.
[7] For estimates of populations and density in the Basin-Plateau area, see Steward (1938), 46f.
[8] Kroeber (1925), 880f.
[9] In one large area in 1786 the Comanches numbered one person to about 1½ square miles according to Ortiz: Wallace and Hoebel (1952), 31.

G*

1,500,000 – that is, one person to 2 square miles.[1] Yet it is probable that among the Early Agriculturists the density of populations has somewhat increased.

On the other hand, while these peoples scour wider territories and have wider contacts, the size of the largest tribes, where there are tribes, shows an increase. While the average size of an Australian tribe was about 500 persons,[2] in North America the figure seems to have been 1,000 to 1,500[3] though there were many small tribes no larger than 100 persons.[4] There is closer contact between communities for cultural as well as warlike purposes and many form 'communities' or 'confederacies' of tribes stretching over wide territories. Such were, in Australia, the Kamilaroi, the Wiradjuri and the Narrinyeri, which were among the largest, each numbering some 3,000 to 5,000 persons, and in recent years others in Eastern and Western Arnhemland, linked together through linguistic relationship and a notion of kinship, intermarriage, some common features of social organization and the possession of common myths or ritual.[5] In North America similar ties bind the Abnaki, Tuscarora, Iroquois, Delaware and Dakota confederacies.[6] While the tribal limits often mark the boundary of a language, itself sometimes divided into several dialects,[7] groups are found of kindred languages covering great

[1] See Rosenblat and Steward's estimates of South American populations: Steward (1949). The density of population of the Puelche and Tehuelche seems to have been similar.
[2] Elkin (1964), 25. There were about 500 tribes and subtribes in 1788: Berndt (1964), 35.
[3] The Akwě-Shavante number about 2,000 divided into about ten independent bands (or villages) about thirty miles apart, with little communication between them. The Hidatsa numbered about 1,500 in 1800. The Mandan were a little larger. See figures for North and South America in Krzywicki (1934), 71-6. The Comanches numbered about 7,000 in 1690 and about 20,000 in 1845; see Wallace and Hoebel (1952), 31f.
[4] The Caribou Eskimo do not exceed 500, and the largest settlements have a population of 50: Birket-Smith (1929), 65f., 200. The Upper Tanana population is 152 in 1929, the number in the largest band 59: McKennan (1959).
[5] Elkin (1964), 74f.; Berndt (1964), 36f.
[6] Numbering respectively in the seventeenth century, 3,000, 5,000, 15,000, 8,000 and 25,000; for figures see Mooney (1928) and Swanton (1952). See also Krzywicki (1934), Appendix II. The Iroquois were five independent warring tribes, induced in the early seventeenth century by two remarkable men, Dekanwida and Hiawatha, to form a confederacy.
[7] Australia: Elkin (1964), 57f.

areas. So, for example, the Eskimo over the vast expanse from the Aleutians to Greenland speak one community of languages, and so even do the peoples of the Australian continent,[1] though at the coming of the European they numbered some 500 tribes or sub-tribes speaking the like number of languages. Over the whole Basin-Plateau area there is little linguistic variation. The Algonkian family of languages was spoken by many peoples of the Eastern Woodlands regions of North America including such confederacies as the Abnaki, Delaware and Chippewa.[2] The Iroquois confederacy, together with the Tuscarora and Hurons, spoke languages of one family; and the Siouan family of languages was spoken by peoples of the great plains, including the Dakota confederacy as well as the Winnebago, Iowa, Hidatsa and Mandan, Ponca, Omaha and Osage. The isolation of mankind is diminishing.

Trade takes many forms among these peoples, sometimes it is barter between individuals, sometimes on a larger scale between social groups. Sometimes it takes place between permanent individual 'partners' belonging to different tribes or other social groups; sometimes at festivals and fairs; and sometimes it is enveloped in ritual. In some areas, for example among the Eskimo and Australians, certain types of goods and return goods go from hand to hand over thousands of miles on permanent routes. Much of this activity exemplifies gift-exchange, that is to say, gifts for which a return of similar value is expected and must be given, for gifts, especially between kin, are everywhere to be seen.[3] Currencies are in use in California and the Basin-Plateau area.[4]

This improvement in communications facilitates the influence of one tribe upon another or the European upon the native, and the adoption of new customs and ways of life.[5] Examples are to

---

[1] A. Cappell, *A New Approach to Australian Linguistics* (1956, 1962), 2f., 114f.
[2] The latter about 30,000 in 1650.
[3] For gift-exchange and trade in Australia: Berndt (1964), 107f.; D. F. Thomson, *Economic Structure and the Ceremonial Exchange Cycle in Arnhem Land* (1949); F. D. McCarthy, *Trade in Aboriginal Australia* etc. (Sydney, 1939). For the Eskimo see Birket-Smith (1959), 147f.
[4] Dentalium shell and the clamshell disc bead: Kroeber (1925), 824.
[5] See the recent historical spread of religious ceremonies, dances and songs, from tribe to tribe in Australia, the introduction of new customs as to burial, initiation and marriage, and the changes in social structure: Elkin (1964), 62f. 73f, 299f.

be seen everywhere, some of which will be referred to below. So, while variations in material culture are found even between neighbouring and kindred tribes, so that one may have adopted agriculture and the other not, and in the North American plains archaeology may show that a village has existed in one place with little apparent change for centuries,[1] elsewhere within a century, and especially through changes set in motion by the European, whole tribes have migrated hundreds of miles, methods of subsistence have altered, a tribe has divided into two[2] and there have been far-reaching changes in social organization.[3] In the Basin-Plateau area the acquisition of the horse by the Northern Shoshoni and the Comanches has helped to bring many of the developments described in the present chapter while the food-gathering culture of the Western Shoshoni remains unchanged.[4]

Among the simplest of these economies the biological or extended family or household is the only social-economic unit,[5] and in all these peoples it is the main such unit.[6] Almost everywhere the tribe remains a shadowy and even transient entity, mainly linguistic and bearing a name (if it has a name) more convenient for the use of the neighbour or anthropologist than significant to the people.[7] Among communities whose social structure is of the simplest there are no intermediate social, economic or political organisms. These emerge as the provision of nature grows less sparse, or, for ecological or other reasons,[8]

---

[1] For a recent archaeological study of the Mandan, see W. R. Wood, *An Interpretation of Mandan Culture History* (B.A.E.B. 198, 1967, Washington D.C.)
[2] e.g. Hidatsa and River Crow.
[3] e.g. the amalgamation of the three Hidatsa villages after 1782, and finally in 1847: Bowers (1965), 73f.
[4] Steward (1938), 236, 239. The Comanches, masters of the Southern Plains, continued to show their Shoshonean origin by the lack of many of the features of social organization characteristic of the culture of the plains.
[5] Australia: Elkin (1964), 75, 82. Western Shoshoni: Steward (1938), 230, 240. Some of these households are very small, e.g. Western Shoshoni average 6-10 persons.
[6] Comanches, family groups and bands only: Wallace and Hoebel (1952), 22. Among the Hidatsa the household (an extended family based on matrilocal residence) is the basic unit: Bowers (1965), 59.
[7] Australia: Berndt (1964), 84f. California: Kroeber (1925), 830f.
[8] For a valuable study of the effects of ecology in the Basin-Plateau area, see Steward (1938).

the family groups become less nomadic for part of the year[1] and combine or associate for subsistence or social or ritual purposes. For example, among the Eskimo the only economic or political unit is the family: there are no clans or totemic groups[2] and the tribe is a geographical entity, bearing a place-name given to it by outsiders and consisting merely of persons particularly close to one another in language and culture.[3] Similarly, among the food-gathering Western Shoshoni and in the adjoining regions of California the bilateral family was the most stable socio-economic group, politically almost independent and economically almost self-sufficient, and spent most of the year searching for food in practical isolation, without moieties, clans, totems or societies;[4] among the Comanches there was the same lack of intermediate social organisms (except that in some cases family groups became enlarged into bands);[5] among the Northern Shoshoni generally, the possession of the horse enabled large groups to live and travel and hunt together, and still larger groups emerged during parts of the year, providing the conditions for the development of permanent kinship relations;[6] however, in the remainder of California, moieties, and even sections, and totemic and local clans appear.[7] These also emerge in Australia, though the local

[1] *Omaha:* the large permanent village is not occupied for more than five months of the year. In April they come from hunting excursions, in May they plant while the young men are hunting seventy to eighty miles around. About June, chiefs assemble a council and decide when and where the next hunt of buffalo is to be, and all leave the village, returning in August. They stay till October and then go trading and trapping. Bushnell (1922), 77.

Chippewa: they make summer camp near the gardens, and in winter a permanent habitation. In between cultivation, they camp near wild rice to gather it; in the fall, men trap and women fish and harvest potatoes etc. Some peoples winter in an encampment of long houses or wigwams, containing two or three generations and at that time all are at home: Densmore (1929), 28. Contrast Hidatsa where there are few but permanent summer camps and a larger number of temporary winter camps: Bowers (1965), 50. For the Upper Tanana Indians, see McKennan (1959).
[2] Birket-Smith (1959), 141-3.
[3] Birket-Smith (1959), 144. For Australia: Elkin (1964), 71f.
[4] Steward (1938), 2f., 56.
[5] Wallace and Hoebel (1952), 22f. There were no organized societies: *ibid.* 224.
[6] Steward (1938), 232f. Among the Comanches the kinship principle was still weak: Wallace and Hoebel (1952), 23.
[7] Kroeber (1925), 830f. The Upper Tanana Indians consist of two exogamous phratries divided into impermanent clans: McKennan (1959), 123.

subdivision of the tribe, ideally an enlarged family of about twenty persons, and never perhaps more than fifty, remains fundamental to society.[1] These changes can be seen emerging historically in many places. The tribe remains an entity of little significance and both among hunters and agricultural peoples, where camps or settlements are now appropriately called villages, it is often little more than a village[2] or a small number of villages,[3] and even between these there is often little contact.

There is great variation in the shape of social organisms between one people and another.[4] Whereas in the simpler economies the family was usually bilateral, now the clans are patrilineal here and matrilineal there, that is to say descent is traced here in the male and there in the female line, and in their kinship terms relationships are classified by different peoples in sundry different ways, all strange to the modern European mind.[5] Probably nowhere is unilineal descent alone recognized, and where the clans are patrilineal the maternal relationship, though of less importance, is counted and relied upon.[6] In Australia, for example, more commonly than not, the local descent groups are patrilineal but there are also in many tribes totemic social clans consisting of persons specially associated with a particular totem[7] or myth, and these seem always to be matrilineal.[8] In many peoples the clan is an exogamous unit, that is to say, that marriage between its members is forbidden, in others (sometimes closely associated tribes) it is not. This rule of marriage outside the clan or totemic group binds together the different clans or other social groups

[1] Elkin (1964), 76.
[2] In most of California there are no tribes except in this sense: Kroeber (1925), 831.
[3] e.g. Hidatsa (three villages), Upper Tanana (two or three villages).
[4] Australia: Berndt (1964), 42f.
[5] Australia: Elkin (1964), 84f., 142f.; Berndt (1964), 69f., 86. Eskimo: Birket-Smith (1959), 142. Hidatsa: Bowers (1965), 81. For an elaborate cross-cultural survey of classificatory kinship systems, see G. P. Murdock, *Social Structure* (1949). The study of these systems has for a century been basic to Social Anthropology and has given rise to a large literature in England and America, especially in reference to the peoples considered in the present chapter.   [6] Australia: Elkin (1964), 83.
[7] For totemism in Australia: Elkin (1964), 164f.; Berndt (1964), 189f.
[8] Elkin (1964), 117f. Among the Upper Tanana Indians the distinction between the maternal and paternal lines is only carried through the first ascending generation.

and even tribes, for intermarriage with different groups may be correspondingly common. In other places the grouping into clans may serve to divide the people into jealous and violent factions.

Again in many of these peoples there is a division of the tribe into two named 'moieties',[1] which will each consist of one or more clans, and in some or most peoples the moieties are exogamous and in others not.[2] In a large and growing number of Australian tribes there is a division into four named kinship groups or sections, and in a growing number the sections are divided into subsections,[3] so that a person's relatives are divided into eight groups, and a man of a certain subsection should marry a woman of a certain other subsection and her child will always belong to a third,[4] and so on. In other peoples the notion of moiety, section or subsection is entirely foreign.[5] Where these divisions exist, with all their apparent complications they do not merely divide the community. As they cut across each other each division serves to modify the separation effected by the others. They also serve to indicate the conduct which is due from one person to another,[6] and they may bring together other villages or tribes where the structure is similar, for the same clans can be seen in different villages or tribes or, if their names differ, a people may be taught by its neighbours to regard two clans as the same.

The rules and practices of marriage[7] change correspondingly. There still remain some peoples among whom, as among the bulk of the Food Gatherers, a boy may marry any girl who is not closely related to him on either side[8] if he is accepted as a good hunter: he comes to live with her family group for a year or two or until a child is born, providing during that time for her parents,

---

[1] Australia: Elkin (1964), 121f. A few traces among the Eskimos of Bering Sea: Birket-Smith (1959), 143. Akwĕ-Shavante: 2 exogamous moieties, 2 clans in one, 1 clan in the other: Maybury-Lewis (1976), 73. Winnebago: 2 moieties, 4 clans in one, 8 in the other: Radin (1923), 187. For differences among the Hidatsa and Mandan, see Bowers (1964), 69, 78f.
[2] Hidatsa: Bowers (1965), 69, 92.   [3] Elkin (1964), 62, 125f.
[4] Berndt (1964), 47f.   [5] e.g. Ponca.
[6] Elkin (1964), 85; Berndt (1964), 81.
[7] For methods of obtaining a wife in Australia, see Elkin (1964), 155; Berndt (1964), 158f., 166f.
[8] Eskimo: Birket-Smith (1959), 139. Shoshoni: Steward (1938), 56. Comanches.

and then the young couple take up their residence where they will, according to practical and personal circumstances.[1] But now the choice is more limited[2] and the couple usually reside with his parents or hers according as the clans are patrilineal or matrilineal; but in some communities marriage is patrilocal (or rather virilocal) though the clans are matrilineal, and vice versa. In the less developed economies (e.g. Australia and Western Shoshoni) exchange marriages are common, for example, brothers marry sisters or a man who receives a bride is obliged to find one in return. The emergence of surplus wealth makes for a growing practice of the exchange of gifts on marriage,[3] the larger usually being those from the bridegroom's side,[4] and thus a beginning of marriage with bridewealth – the so-called brideprice marriage – associated mainly with patrilocal or virilocal marriage, where the gift takes into account the fact that her family have raised her and lost her.[5] On the whole, woman's status has fallen among the Hunters,[6] and this marriage in a few cases even takes on the appearance of a sale. There are various types of preferred marriage among different peoples;[7] in some the marriage with a cross-cousin or pseudo cross-cousin[8] is preferred, and the practices of the levirate and sororate[9] and (where more than one wife is taken) marriage with a sister of the wife,[10] are much in evidence among

---

[1] Western Shoshoni: Steward (1938), 240-3. Eskimo: Chippewa: Densmore (1929), 172. Hidatsa: Bowers (1965), 160. Eastern and Northern Canada: Jenness (1934), 155. Upper Tanana Indians: McKennan (1959), 119.
[2] For the difficulty in Australia of finding a wife one can properly marry, see Elkin (1964), 155f.
[3] Hidatsa: Bowers (1965), 138 – apparently from near matrilineal relatives; Chippewa and Eastern Woodlands generally; Basin-Plateau area; Puelche and Tehuelche.
[4] Gifts from the bridegroom's side are in California (except the N.W.) a mere observance: Kroeber (1925), 839
[5] Comanches: Wallace and Hoebel (1952), 135.
[6] Steward (1938), 242. See e.g. the cases of mass rape among the Northern Shoshoni and elsewhere in North America.
[7] Hidatsa: Bowers (1965), 158f.
[8] Basin-Plateau: Steward (1938), 242f., 245. A pseudo cross-cousin is a stepson or stepdaughter of the mother's brother or the father's sister.
[9] Australia, Basin-Plateau, Comanches, California, Upper Tanana. See Hidatsa: Bowers (1965), 159.
[10] Australia: Elkin (1964), 156f. Eskimo: Birket-Smith (1959), 139. Basin-Plateau: Steward (1938), 244. Comanches. Also see Akwē-Shavante, where ideal marriages are between a group of brothers and a group of sisters: Maybury-Lewis (1967), 87f.

the majority of these peoples. For some reason polyandry is more frequent than we shall later find it,[1] and wife-lending is common and required on occasion by good manners,[2] and temporary wife exchange is not unknown.[3] Marriage by capture is rare.[4] The amount of polygyny increases and it is found everywhere. As in primitive life generally, there are no unmarried women though there are a few bachelors. Marriages are easily terminable by consent[5] or desertion.[6] Adoption is frequent.[7]

Only less important than these groupings is the grouping by age. The natural association between persons of the same age begins to be organized into groupings according to age-grades, each with its particular functions and responsibilities in the community,[8] such as that of the bachelors, warriors, elders, with initiatory rites of passage[9] from one grade to the next after a more or less defined number of years.[10] There is also the grouping according to sex for social, economic and religious purposes, with different age-grades.[11] Some groups find their bonds also in the

---

[1] Not always fraternal. Basin-Plateau: Steward (1938), 116, 243f. Comanches: Wallace and Hoebel (1952). Among the Eskimo it is only general among the Netsilik though found elsewhere: Birket-Smith (1959), 139.

[2] Australia: Elkin (1964), 159f. Eskimo: Birket-Smith (1959), 139.

[3] Basin-Plateau: Steward (1938), 242. Comanches: Wallace and Hoebel (1952), 13. California: Kroeber (1925), 839.

[4] Australia: Berndt (1964), 17. Eskimo. Frequent however in Basin-Plateau: Steward (1938), 243.

[5] Eskimo: Birket-Smith (1959), 140. Chippewa: Densmore (1929), 72.

[6] e.g. Basin-Plateau: Steward (1938), 239. Among Akwẽ-Shavante, however, marriage is remarkably stable and adultery rare: Maybury-Lewis (1977), 87.

[7] Eskimo: Birket-Smith (1959), 140. Fox: S. Tax (ed.) *Horizons in Anthropology*, (Chicago, Aldine Press, 1934), 260, 276. Hidatsa: Bowers (1965), 90f.

[8] Australia: Elkin (1964), 114f. Hidatsa: Bowers (1965), 74f., 207f. No age-sets among Western Shoshoni or Comanches.

[9] Australia: Elkin (1964), 188f.; Berndt (1964), 136f. There are puberty rites for both sexes but, in North and South America, often for girls alone.

[10] See e.g. Akwẽ-Shavante: Maybury-Lewis (1967), 108, 105f. Eight age-sets in all, changing about every five years. All those initiated on leaving the bachelor's hut (at 12 to 17) are married at a joint ceremony and enter the young men's age-set. There is a certain hostile relation between proximate age-sets and a close relation between alternate age-sets (as in the generations and as among many other peoples). Finally the most senior age-set reverts to the beginning of the progression and is re-incarnated in the boys entering the bachelor's hut. There are similar age-sets of women but they are comparatively meaningless.

[11] Maybury-Lewis (1967), 149f. Australia: Elkin (1964), 115f. Hidatsa: Bowers (1965), 93.

religious life of the community[1] and have their sacred possessions, and some function as secret societies.[2] In many peoples the responsibilities laid upon the individual could hardly be discharged without the assistance of the clan and age-grade mates.[3]

When we turn to government and administration we find again variation from tribe to tribe but a degree of development from the Food Gatherers and from the simpler to the more complex economies. In the less organized social structures, for example among the Eskimo, there is no government: there are no chiefs though there is at most settlements an especially prominent person whom the rest tacitly and almost unconsciously acknowledge as the first among equals.[4] Among the Western Shoshoni, where the extended family is the only politico-economic unit, there is the influence of the head or elder of the family but little mention of chiefs. In the more developed economies, as the families spend an increasing portion of the year in association at a winter or summer settlement, the conditions favour the appointment of a chief as well as family heads, but his authority is often difficult to estimate and its extent varies from place to place. Chiefs are appointed for the reputed possession of the same qualities as among the Food Gatherers,[5] but as often as not for reasons of heredity, as being heads of leading clans or lineages or sons of chiefs.[6] As the social order widens there will commonly be a chief

---

[1] Maybury-Lewis (1967), 149f. Australia: Elkin (1964), 115f. Hidatsa: Bowers (1965), 93.
[2] Australia: Elkin (1964), 189f.; Berndt (1964), 136f. Eskimo: Birket-Smith (1959), 154. Widespread in North America.
[3] Hidatsa: Bowers (1965), 174.
[4] Called, in different areas, 'he who thinks', 'he who knows best', 'the one to whom all listen'; see Birket-Smith (1959), 144f., Hoebel (1954), 82. Only in the Aleuts and among the Chugach (Pacific Eskimos) in contact with the superior Indian cultures of the north-west coast of North America (see the following chapter) are there chiefs with power; Birket-Smith (1959), 145f. In small villages of the Basin-Plateau area there are no headmen; in the larger villages commonly a headman or 'talker'. The Tehuelche and Puelche bands of five to thirty families have each their headman. Among the Chiricahua Apache, there are only 'leaders' or 'advisers'. See a description of them and their authority; Opler (1955), 233. Similarly among the Upper Tanana: McKennan (1959), 131.
[5] See *ante* p. 162, and Lowie (1948); for the Comanches: Wallace and Hoebel (1952), 211. But they in fact attain the position by means of the very opposite qualities – ambition and ruthlessness: Maybury-Lewis (1967), 193.
[6] e.g. Winnebago, Comanches, Ponca.

and family heads, or even a chief of the tribe[1] and local headmen or chiefs. It becomes the daily delight of the elders to meet in the tent or lodge of the chief to talk of topical matters, and now an informal council is met with as frequently as chiefs.[2] Throughout these peoples, however, with the exceptions to be mentioned, the chief's authority in normal circumstances is little and his functions narrow. His task is to keep informed as to the whereabouts of the available ripening plants and animal food, to suggest the movements of the day – to the hunt, to the fields or to gather – and he should harangue the community daily and urge good and proper conduct[3] and give munificently to his followers. Action is impossible unless there is almost unanimous agreement in the community;[4] the chief announces what the council or the community agrees and a family who desires to do so may disregard his wishes and take independent action.[5] In regard to disputes and disorder arising from alleged wrongs, the chief's function and efforts are to preserve or restore peace: he may offer advice or moral suasion but not a judgment. To take an extreme case, the tribal chief of the Winnebago, whose functions were solely connected with peace and not war, and whose lodge contained a sacred fireplace, a safe asylum for all wrongdoers, always attempted a reconciliation between the offender and the avengers. 'If necessary the chief would mortify himself and with skewers inserted in his back have himself led through the village to the home of the nearest kinspeople of the murdered person.'[6] In this way he sought

---

[1] There are no chiefs of tribes in Australia: see e.g. Spencer and Gillen (1927), 1, 9. There is a headman in most or all Australian local groups and the headmen of various groups form the council: see Berndt (1964), 290f. No chiefs of the tribe among the Comanches, only of the bands.

[2] Australia: Berndt (1964), 290f.; Elkin (1964), 77, 114. Comanches: Wallace and Hoebel (1952), 213. Ponca: Howard (1965), 91. Hidatsa: Bowers (1965), 27, 33. For constitution of a council see Akwĕ-Shavante: Maybury-Lewis (1967), 145, where there is a formal order and manner for addressing the meeting.

[3] e.g. Shoshoni: Steward (1938), 438, 247. Tehuelche: Cooper (1946), 152. Comanches: Wallace and Hoebel (1952); Lowie (1948).

[4] Lowie (1948). For the Teton Dakota: Tabeau 105f. Ponca: Howard (1965), 91. Hidatsa: Bowers (1965), 33.

[5] And may join another chief: for Chippewa, see Densmore (1929), 131. The authority of the Ojibway chiefs was vague and unstable; see Tanner (1789), 151, speaking of the period 1789 to 1822. Also see references in regard to peoples considered in this chapter in Lowie (1948).

[6] Radin (1923), 209.

to show sympathy, give satisfaction to outraged feelings, arouse pity and enlist support and prevent the spread of violence.

In times of war the chiefly authority is greater[1] and in the more developed economies of the Plains Indians there is often a war leader or chief as well as a peace chief,[2] with greater if temporary powers, and there is commonly a society,[3] age-group or camp crier[4] with the function of announcing decisions of chief and council. Among the Plains Indians governmental authority is at its height. 'Police' or 'soldiers'[5] are appointed at the spring re-union of the bands of the tribe by the chief tribal authority, the tribal chief or group of chiefs or council.[6] In some peoples they are chosen for their ability and military record, in others from one of the military societies, and in others they consist of a military society.[7] In most peoples they are elected for the summer period of activity, in some for a year or even for life, but among the Dakota there is a set of police appointed for special occasions taking the place to that extent of the regular police officers. Everywhere their main activity is for the period and the purposes of the buffalo hunt (possibly the origin of this institution) but in some places also for the tribal gatherings, warlike expeditions or the Sun Dance. Mainly they are there to maintain the success of the hunt or raid against the premature activity of individuals or to protect the public peace of tribal gatherings against wrongdoers. In this activity they settle disputes and the claims for homicide, wounding and theft, which at other times and places would be private wrongs. Their power to administer punishment rather than persuasion varies from tribe to tribe, but everywhere they exist to enforce conformity rather than revenge, and though they have power in the last resort even to kill, and their chief sanctions are to whip the offender or destroy his property, upon conformity they often reinstate him with new tipi, horses and goods.[8] There

[1] See cases cited Lowie (1948), 8.
[2] Lowie (1948), 8. See also California: Kroeber (1925), 833. Comanches: Wallace and Hoebel (1952), 209f. Hidatsa: Bowers (1965), 58.
[3] Hidatsa: Bowers (1965), 185 (the Black Mouth Society: concerned only with public matters involving the entire village).
[4] Comanches.   [5] Usually called the *akicita*.
[6] But the authority is that of the police or soldiers; it does not belong to the chief or council.
[7] See note 3, *supra*.
[8] See summary of the authorities in Provinse (1937), 344f.

is also a handful of Australian cases[1] in which we hear of areas
where the chief and council meet to hear a complaint of wrongful
conduct, apparently always of a public or 'criminal' nature[2], and
sometimes adjudicate upon it and impose a punishment. In
several of these instances an armed party[3] is dispatched to carry
out the sentence – usually a sentence of death.

Among these peoples, in these instances, the chiefly authority is
at its height, although it is sometimes difficult to see who is a
chief, for in the plains some such title may be given to several
persons who are recognized as leaders of groups of any kind.[4]
Among those exercising influence are the *shamans*, but they are not
chiefs[5] and indeed a reputation for the possession of supernatural
powers is the least of the qualifications for chieftainship.[6]

The existence of chiefs and the nature of their authority may
perhaps be tested by the answers to three questions. Is there an
office or post of chief (rather than mere headship of a group of
kindred or leadership of a faction)? Has anyone a right to give an
order that must be obeyed (rather than to announce a decision or
agreement that is more or less unanimous)? Has anyone a right to
decide a dispute and punish an offender (rather than attempt to
maintain or restore order)? The answer to the first question is No,
except in the more developed economies. On the whole, the
answer to the second question is No; and the answer to the third
question is No, except in a handful of cases, mainly among the
Plains Indians, where the power only exists at certain times and
places and in regard to criminal offences, and often is not vested in
the chiefs.

Notions of property rights show modest progress from the Food

[1] Lower River Murray people where, according to Taplin (in Woods, *The
Native Tribes of South Australia*, Adelaide, 1879, 34f.), *rupulle* (spokesmen for
the tribe) or heads of clans settle disputes with men of adjoining tribes, and
elders preside over the *tendi* (court or council), hear the parties and witnesses
and sometimes give judgment and impose a penalty. For cases in East
Australia, see A. W. Howitt, *The Native Tribes of South East Australia* (1904),
295f. See also other cases in Berndt (1964), 291f. The procedure is usually
very informal.
[2] Killing by witchcraft, abduction of women, adultery, incest, sacral offences
(such as the disclosure of secrets), disputes between neighbouring tribes and
raids.
[3] Called *pinya* among the Dieri; *ininja* in Central Australia.
[4] e.g. Hidatsa: Bowers (1965), 198.
[5] California: Kroeber (1925), 833.   [6] Maybury-Lewis (1967), 198.

Gatherers. As before, the individual's right to articles made or exclusively used by him is well understood,[1] and there are more goods. Women, married or unmarried[2] and male and female children are considered entitled to such things. A woman's articles of attire or everyday use are exclusively hers and no parent sells or gives away a child's toy without its permission. Many persons have rights to share in food that has been obtained, especially among the Early Hunters,[3] or to use equipment not in use by its possessor, and the right to possession of more things than can be used is often not recognized.[4] There is a well-developed notion of the individual's exclusive right to perform or use such incorporal things as a song or dance,[5] and a name is sometimes considered to belong to a kinship group though held by an individual.[6]

In the more developed economies there is often a large-scale transfer of corporeal and incorporeal things from one group to another within the local community. Where age-groups or societies based on age are considered to possess ritual objects[7] there is a transfer for payment from one group to its immediate junior as the members pass on. This process can also be seen between a man and his son or a woman and her daughter, so that in early life a person is mainly a buyer and later a seller.[8] But these transactions are not commercial, and as a rule the transfer can only be made to one group or person, though it must be compensated by a payment. Similar considerations apply to all property: we do not speak of 'ownership' in a modern or technical sense. A man's

[1] Australia: Berndt (1964), 107, 119. Eskimo: Birket-Smith (1959), 145. Western Shoshoni: Steward (1938), 253. Comanches: Wallace and Hoebel (1952), 241f. (especially horses).
[2] Chiricahua Apache: Opler (1955), 210-11.
[3] Australia: Berndt (1964), 105. Eskimo: Birket-Smith (1959), 145. Basin-Plateau: Steward (1938). Akwē-Shavante: Maybury-Lewis (1967), 179f.
[4] Eskimo: Birket-Smith (1959), 145.
[5] Comanches: Wallace and Hoebel (1952), 242f., medicine formulae and powers. Ponca: Howard (1965), 97, 100, 102, war honours which can be transferred. Australia: Berndt (1964), 114, 119, dances and ceremonies belonging to societies or a design or pattern, which may occasionally be sold.
[6] Ponca: Howard (1965), 97f.
[7] In Australia, they usually belong to a local group or clan.
[8] e.g. among Hidatsa, sale by mother to daughter of right to build chimneys and fireplaces or make pottery: members of clan and society of daughter and her husband expected to contribute. Bowers (1965), 161, 165f.

rights may be recognized to be exclusive, but it does not follow that he can transfer them to whomsoever he will. It is better to speak of a thing as 'belonging' to someone, or being 'his', rather than as 'owned' by him.[1] Nor do we usually speak of 'payment' in a commercial sense: it might be called a necessary gift.

Turning to corporeal things other than goods, we find notions of property vague and unformed. The recognition of an area of land as a separate or distinct thing capable of ownership is more difficult than such a notion of a movable. Commonly individuals and families are found using exclusively a variety of goods, but not an area of land. The Early Hunters, indeed, have less notion than the Food Gatherers that a defined hunting territory belongs solely to a family, a band or a tribe,[2] and no notion that it belongs to an individual.[3] They roam over wider territories than the Food Gatherers, and others must be permitted to do the same:[4] but sometimes trapping sites are considered to belong to a clan or other group, and structures for hunting or fishing (such as stone weirs for salmon fishing) erected and used by the group to belong to it. Eskimo hunting territories are considered to belong to families only among the Aleut, and places where seal or fish-nets are set only in Alaska and West Greenland.[5] Some houses elsewhere used communally may belong to the community. These are vague terms: observers do not tell us what they mean by family or clan ownership, for example, what are the rights or duties of heads of family and clan, but provided these terms are allowed to be vague no great damage will be done to the facts. We may sum up by saying that there is scattered evidence of ideas of clan or family rights to some places among Early Hunters, and

---

[1] See *post* p. 368.
[2] Among Eskimo generally everyone may hunt where he pleases: Birket-Smith (1959), 145. For Basin-Plateau area, see Steward (1938), 253, and contrast there the position in the more settled conditions of Owens Valley. The Comanches had no concept of land value and land was not held individually, jointly or communally: Wallace and Hoebel (1952), 241. Similarly among the Northern Athapascans: McKennan (1959), 129. On the other hand, among the Tehuelche each band had a separate though ill-defined territory, and trespass was a frequent cause of war: Cooper (1946), 146, 151f.
[3] Australia: Berndt (1964), 119.
[4] Steward (1938), 233, 254.
[5] Birket-Smith (1959), 145.

individual and tribal rights among Early Agriculturists, but here the tribe is commonly a village.

There is little development in inheritance though an increase in goods. Goods belonging to an individual are in most places destroyed,[1] burnt or buried with him or given away to those considered to have a claim upon him for a service rendered or entitled to a gift,[2] or to some distinguished member of the village or clan.[3] Other articles may be given away at or before his death to a particular child or divided by him among his children. The little that is left will usually be inherited in the male or female line or both according to the local system of ideas.[4] But in regard to corporeal and incorporeal property we must notice the vague frontier between notions of transfer and inheritance. Some rights are always assigned to a child during life but must be paid for by a counter-gift.[5] It is common in a people for different species of rights and property to descend differently.[6] Chieftainship, to the extent that it is inherited, commonly descends in the male line even in a people where descent is generally matrilineal.

So far, then, with few exceptions, the law does not amount to much, if anything, and we shall see presently what it does amount to. It plays a small part in the mechanism of social control. The forces that effect social control are mainly provided, as among the Food Gatherers, by mutual independence for food and survival, and by reciprocity; by human habits and traditions, propensities and affections; by public approval of uniformity with existing standards[7] and fear of ridicule,[8] and now fear of charges of witchcraft, for nonconformity; and, above all, by kinship, and now increasingly by the ties not merely between

---

[1] e.g. Australia. Tuelche and Puelche. Comanches: Wallace and Hoebel (1952), 152. Upper Yanana: McKennan (1959), 130.
[2] Comanches: Wallace and Hoebel (1952), 152.
[3] Hidatsa: Bowers (1965), 171. Ponca: Howard (1965), 96.
[4] Among the Eskimo, there is no matriliny or patriliny: Birket-Smith (1959), 141f.
[5] Hidatsa: Bowers (1965), 160f., and see above.
[6] e.g. among the Hidatsa: Bowers (1965), 79, 160. There, residence is usually matrilocal and clans matrilineal, and there is clan inheritance of most ceremonial rites and patrilineal inheritance of a man's ritual bundles.
[7] Berndt (1964), 281.
[8] Here we must remember the 'joking relationship' between certain classes of close kin, found in almost all these societies.

members of the family but also members of local groups, lineages, clans, moieties, societies and age-grades, and often the factious opposition between such bodies[1] and the growing violence and the avenging passions; and the peace-making activities of chiefs, headmen and councils. Also we must not forget the effect of awards, such as military honours,[2] and the increasing quantity of goods now available to provide gifts that subserve all the above peaceful processes or purchase peace after a breach of good order; and the power of magic and to a lesser extent religion with its supranatural sanctions, for both serve chiefly to reinforce the devotion to traditional norms of conduct,[3] but also to set avenging forces in motion to punish a breach. We must also remember that there are societies where the forces of social control are not efficient and the societies tend to destroy themselves.[4]

Turning to offences against good order, we see almost everywhere (as among the Food Gatherers) a distinction (or at least a difference) between conduct which is an offence to all and conduct which is only an offence to individuals.[5] Death caused by witchcraft is now added to the former list and is the most serious offence,[6] and the others are incest[7] (namely, marriage or sexual intercourse with a person whom one cannot properly marry), sometimes adultery by a wife (and especially elopement with or theft of a man's wife)[8] and a number of other offences, varying from people to people,[9] and including offences against good order in the buffalo hunt, military raids and tribal gatherings among the Plains Indians, and a number of sacral offences. The private (or civil) offences are mainly the other cases of homicide, wounding (of which we hardly hear), adultery of a wife or elopement with a

[1] Akwĕ-Shavante: Maybury-Lewis (1967), 165, 169.
[2] Plains Indians: Provinse (1937), 354f.
[3] Berndt (1964), 251f. For the Plains Indians, especially the Omaha, see summary in Provinse (1937), 359f.
[4] e.g. Akwĕ-Shavante: Maybury-Lewis (1967).
[5] For an analysis in which a similar distinction is basic, see Radcliffe-Brown, 'Social Sanctions' in *Encyclopaedia of the Social Sciences* (1935), 13.
[6] Australia; Eskimo: Birket-Smith (1959), 149; California: Kroeber (1925), 843; and everywhere else, e.g. Opler (1955), 237.
[7] Australia: Berndt (1964), 85.   [8] Berndt (1964), 170f.
[9] Among some Eskimo, also persistent homicide and persistent lying, see Hoebel (1954), 90.

wife or girl, and theft.[1] The most frequent disorders arise out of charges of witchcraft and disputes about women.

For a number of reasons this distinction between 'public' and 'private' offence is not easy to draw at this stage. For one thing, the public offences, such as incest, are often avenged by the same groups as would avenge a private wrong, namely, the nearest relatives, the clan or other group to which the victim or offended person belongs. There are a few or no rules or practices fixing sanctions for either type of conduct and some of the 'public' offences like the 'private' offences are often not avenged or compensated at all: a pair committing incest often suffer no punishment, except perhaps public disapproval or ridicule, and a strong man or group may be able to escape revenge for either type of wrong. There is hardly anywhere a trial or an individual or group with authority to decide or punish guilt, and in neither types of wrong does the whole community act, though there are cases where death is inflicted by a person after obtaining the approval of others[2] and we must add the rare Australian case and the Plains Indians. Some, indeed, of the public offences are hardly even of the nature of crimes: when a woman or child is killed in Australia because she or he has seen the sacred *tchuringa* (or bull-roarer), or an old or sick person is killed as being unable to travel, or an unwanted girl-child or one of a pair of twins or a man who is brutal or for other reasons unpopular, it is difficult to equate any of such cases with the punishment of a crime. Moreover some punishments of public offences resemble war as much as vengeance for crime,[3] for the more serious offences – for example, killing by witchcraft – are usually alleged against members of a foreign group. Nevertheless the distinction between public and private offence is to be seen. For example, in the more developed economies when an allegation of killing (except by witchcraft) or wounding is settled by acceptance of goods, the

---

[1] In many places unheard of, e.g. Australia: Berndt (1964), 288; Eskimo: Birket-Smith (1959), 149; Akwē-Shavante: Maybury-Lewis (1967), 179f.; Upper Tanana: McKennan (1959), 131. Among the Ponca, a thief is whipped by the buffalo police: Howard (1965), 96f. Among the Hidatsa, stealing from household or individual is a matter for the household and clan to handle: Bowers (1965), 185.
[2] Or even of the whole community: see some collected Eskimo cases: Hoebel (1954), 88f.   [3] Berndt (1964), 299f.

chief and council will offer no objection;[1] and in the few cases where chief and council or the hunt 'police' or 'soldiers' do claim authority to decide guilt and impose punishment, it is for a public offence, namely, an act which, committed at that time and place, is an offence against public order.

There are other ways of obtaining satisfaction for a serious wrong. We notice in the least developed economies a continuation from the Food Gatherers of regularized and controlled and ritualized modes of obtaining relief for the wounded feelings of persons aggrieved, including their group, without doing too much injury to the pride of the offender's group. They take place when a serious offence has been committed and the offender is thought to be known and the passion for revenge is likely to give rise to violent retaliation. In Australia there are many forms[2] but in most cases the groups of the offender and aggrieved take part. Spears may be thrown by the latter group, sometimes at first with the blades removed, or boomerangs are hurled at the accused, who is given a limited opportunity to defend himself (usually by a shield), and a local headman, assisted to some extent by relatives of both sides, presides to limit the violence and preaches restraint, and as soon as the offender is speared in the thigh or side or blood is otherwise drawn, the headman's signal ends the affair.[3] Sometimes the form is that of an armed duel between the two protagonists in the presence of their groups,[4] or a regular bout of fisticuffs among the Central Eskimo, or the parties take turns at giving and receiving blows on shoulders or temples.[5] The sanction of public ridicule is widely employed to the same end, for example by the singing of lampoons in verse. Outraged feelings may thus be assuaged or resentments may remain and a group may prefer to move and settle elsewhere.[6]

<hr />

[1] e.g. Chippewa: murderer killed or adopted, and chiefs do not interfere: Densmore (1929), 132. Ponca: retaliation for murder left to relatives: Howard (1965), 95f.

[2] Australia: Berndt (1964), 293f.

[3] See B. Spencer and F. J. Gillen, *Across Australia* (1912), 1, 199f.

[4] Berndt (1964), 295.

[5] Birket-Smith (1959), 150.

[6] Birket-Smith (1959), 150; Hoebel (1954), 92f.; Berndt (1964), 298. For satirical sanctions among the Plains Indians, sometimes organized and formal, see the following – Blackfoot: Wissler (1916), 27; Omaha: Fletcher and La Flesche (1911), 404; for the plains generally: Provinse (1937), 352f.

There are other ways of endeavouring to ascertain the identity of a miscreant than by a trial. There are only the beginnings of the use of an ordeal by oath[1] for the purpose of ascertaining guilt, but with the development of magic goes also a wide use of divination to that end, often with the assistance of the *shaman*, or medicine-man,[2] and specially where death or illness has occurred and where (as is usual) it is attributed to the use of witchcraft. The forms of the procedure are numerous – the deceased is held on the shoulders of two or more men, and a movement of the corpse is noted in a certain direction or at the mention of a name; or the exudations fall from it in a particular direction; or a small hole is observed in the ground where the spirit of the deceased has emerged in the direction of the murderer's country, or a stick is put in the hole and it is seen in what direction it slants.[3]

For most wrongs, public or private, there is no recognized sanction. In the event of a serious wrong, such as killing by witchcraft or other means, the victim's group will seek to put the offender to death if they have the chance. A husband, among the Plains Indians, is commonly entitled to mutilate his unfaithful wife (usually on the nose) or will cast her away, and may seek to kill the adulterer or ignore him according to local standards of worthy conduct. But now in the more developed economies of North America the possession of surplus wealth enables peace to be obtained by its means, and goods may be accepted if the offer is large enough;[4] or the aggrieved group, if they cannot kill the miscreant, will try to seize belongings of his or his group's, or

---

[1] Among the Plains Indians. For example, among the Comanches a man accused by an irate husband of adultery and denying liability might discharge himself by an oath by the sun: 'Sun, if what I say is not true, strike me dead. If I am not guilty, strike my accuser dead' (Wallace and Hoebel (1952), 228). See also Wissler (1916), 76, where a woman in the 'Owns Alone' ceremony, whose public claim to fidelity was challenged, might require her accuser to swear an oath.

[2] See Spencer and Gillen, *Across Australia* (1912), II, 400.

[3] Australia: Berndt (1964), 296f., Elkin (1964), 310f. Eskimo: Birket-Smith (1959), 158.

[4] Not in the Food Gatherers nor among Australians nor Eskimos, but frequently met with in the majority of the Indians of the plains. In some places the settlement by acceptance of compensation has acquired a name, e.g. the Comanche, *nanewoka*: Wallace and Hoebel (1952), 226f.

even of some other group (which will then complain and take action against the former's goods), or the offender may escape abroad for a time or be forced to go abroad.[1] Long-lasting feuds exist but are unusual:[2] a man who has killed a husband to obtain his wife is as likely as not to rear his victim's son as an affectionate parent, ignoring the possibility or likelihood that when he grows up he will kill his foster-father in revenge.[3]

To what extent, then, and in what sense is law to be found in these phenomena? Law can be recognized where, firstly, there are accepted canons of conduct; secondly, the community enforces them, that is to say for breaches of these it will impose or recognize the imposition of sanctions; and thirdly, there is some regularity in the processes of imposition of sanctions and their character (for if, for example, the only result of a public or private offence is that a community, chief, council, kinship group or individuals impose whatever punishment they think fit, this may be executive action or mob violence and not law). Seas of ink have been exhausted by jurists in discussion of the further question whether there must be courts, or whether, on the other hand, if there are customary rules of behaviour, obeyed because they are customary, there is already law. But many kinds of rules of conduct (for example, rules of etiquette) are obeyed because they are customary and we are concerned only with canons of conduct in certain fields; we cannot say that they are enforceable unless there are breaches and sanctions follow breaches; and a certain growth of the community brings about a sufficient number of breaches to create some regularity in sanctions and necessitates courts to determine facts and liability; and all this emerges and develops together – canons of conduct, breaches, sanctions, regularity of sanctions and courts – even if there is a certain time-lag between the first-named and the last.

We can give some plain answers to the question posed. There is no law among these peoples in the field of private offences, for if the first condition is satisfied the second and third are not: the

[1] Cheyenne: Hoebel (1954), 311; or be excluded from the social life of the community – Hidatsa: Bowers (1965), 173, and see 74f.
[2] Eskimo: Birket-Smith (1929), 151. For the close relation between feud and war, see Berndt (1964), 299f.
[3] Eskimo: Birket-Smith (1959), 150; and see cases cited in Hoebel (1954), 87f.

community neither imposes nor recognizes particular sanctions. Some authors lightly and loosely answer that there is a 'law of retaliation', but their 'law' is not law (but rather a statement that an irregular practice exists) nor their 'retaliation' retaliation (in the proper sense of the 'talion' – that is to say, the infliction in return of violence to the like extent). As for public offences, we have seen sundry cases where the first two conditions are satisfied, in that a chief and council, a hunt 'police' or 'soldiers' impose punishments, and perhaps the third. Hoebel makes a case for including instances (for example, among the Eskimo) where one man kills another having obtained a general consent,[1] and similar cases. These are hardly the beginnings of law, for there is no compliance with the third condition. They smack too much of murder. So many wrongs give place to a variety of violent reactions and to charges of witchcraft[2] and death for witchcraft (if it can be imposed) or even the counter-application of witchcraft, and much of this is part of a wider phenomenon of the killing of unpopular persons.

Finally we must ask, in regard to marriage, property and inheritance whether there is law here. There are beginnings, to the extent that incest, an offence of vague limits, is punishable, with considerable irregularity, as a public offence. There are no disputes in regard to inheritance or property.

We have said little of magic or religion in this chapter because it is rarely necessary to a description of these legal, pre-legal and para-legal phenomena. As at all stages in the development of law they are relevant only to procedure (for example the ascertainment of the identity of a witch) and sacral offences, but we may add in regard to procedure that there is now a beginning here and there of the institution of the asylum or refuge, not necessarily religious,

---

[1] Hoebel (1954), 88f.; F. Boas, *Central Eskimos* (B.A.E.R., 1887), 688. Hoebel defines law 'for working purposes', in the following terms: 'A social norm is legal if its neglect or infraction is regularly met, in threat or in fact, by the application of physical force by an individual or group possessing the socially recognized privilege of so acting' (*op. cit.* 28).

[2] Akwĕ-Shavante: Maybury-Lewis (1967), 186. (The plaintiff brought a charge of adultery against the defendant without evidence. The defendant fell ill and the council came to the conclusion that the plaintiff was using sorcery against him. They condemned the plaintiff to death and he was killed by the young men's age-set when out hunting.)

to which an offender may flee for safety.[1] There are in regard to certain serious offences corresponding religious doctrines – for example, the pollution of the land by the presence of a murderer or the killer's need to be purified – but so far as we have knowledge the legal or pre-legal rule preceded the religious.[2]

[1] Cheyenne (Holy Hat Lodge); Kiowa (Ten Medicine *tipis*): Hoebel (1954), 169, 175. Winnebago (Sacred fireplace of Tribal Chief): Radin (1923), 209.
[2] Cheyenne.

CHAPTER 15

Agriculturists, Hunters and Pastoralists of the Second Grade

In contrast to the Early Agriculturists (A.1) of the previous chapter, with whom a rudimentary agriculture was a minor and subsidiary means of livelihood, the agriculturists of the Second Grade (A.2), whom we shall chiefly consider in the present chapter, find in agriculture (or rather horticulture), no longer rudimentary, their main means of subsistence. They are distinguished, on the other hand, from the peoples of the next agricultural grade (A.3) by their lack of cattle and flocks and metals.

The peoples of the Second Grade of agriculture are widely spread around the globe and there are great differences between them in their degree of economic development. As we move north from the Food Gatherers of Tasmania and the Hunters of Australia towards the old civilizations of India and China, we find these peoples represented by the bulk of the populations of New Guinea, Melanesia and Polynesia and many peoples of Indonesia. From these we may take as examples, in New Guinea, the Papuans of the Trans-Fly (especially the Keraki) in the Morehead district[1] and the Kuma[2] and the Kapauku,[3] of Western New Guinea. We may instance, from Melanesia, the peoples of the Trobriand[4] and Dobu[5] off the north-east coast of New Guinea, and the island of Malekula in the New Hebrides[6] and between Melanesia and Polynesia other islands of the Southern New Hebrides,[7] and in Polynesia, Ontong Java (a coral atoll north-east

---

[1] Williams (1936).   [2] Reay (1959).   [3] Pospisil (1958).
[4] See the works of Malinowski, especially those listed: (1922), (1926), (1935). Also Uberoi (1962).
[5] Fortune (1932).   [6] Deacon (1934).   [7] Humphreys (1926).

of the Solomons)[1] the small island of Tikopia in the Polynesian fringe of the Solomons,[2] and peoples of Tonga, Hawaii and Samoa.[3] In North America, as we move southwards from the Hunters and Early Agriculturists of the Northern Plains and Eastern Woodlands towards the old civilizations of Mexico and Peru, we find agriculturists of this grade represented in the bulk of the inland peoples of the South-East United States from Virginia to the middle of Florida, and from the Mississippi to the east coast, especially the Powhatan of Virginia and the 'Five Civilized Tribes': the Cherokee (chiefly of Tennessee), the Choctaw and Chickasaw (mostly of Mississippi), the Creeks (of Georgia and Alabama) and Seminole of Florida;[4] and in South America, as we move northwards from the Food Gatherers, Hunters and Early Agriculturists of the south towards the civilization of the Andes, we find peoples of this grade in the basin of the Amazon and its tributaries, the central parts of the Tropical Forest culture area of South America.[5] The sunny climates of all these areas are in general far more favourable to man than those of the two previous chapters, for example, the South-Eastern States form one of the richest regions of North America and the warmest area of the north temperate zone.[6]

There are, however, two economies that have developed in other directions. As we move northwards, from the peoples of California along the north-western coast of the United States, Canada and Alaska we meet the rich fishing cultures of the Second Grade of Hunters (H.2) which wholly lack agriculture. Of these we may

---

[1] Hogbin (1934).   [2] Firth (1936).
[3] Hogbin (1934); Gifford (1929); W. Mariner, *An Account of the Natives of the Tonga Islands* (1817); Williamson (1924); W. De Witt Alexander, *A Brief History of the Hawaiian People* (New York, 1891); J. J. Jarves, *A History of the Hawaiian or Sandwich Islands* (4th ed. Honolulu, 1872); D. Malo, *Hawaiian Antiquities*, trans. Emerson (Honolulu, 1903); Turner (1884); Stair (1897); Mead (1920).
[4] Swanton (1946); Swanton (1952); for the limits of this area, Swanton (1946), 1.
[5] See *H.S.A.*, vol. 3; for its relation with the Circum-Caribbean Culture Area, see vol. 4, 1-40.
[6] We do not include in this grade the peoples of Central and West Africa who live mainly by agriculture and, because of the presence of the tsetse-fly, have no large cattle. They have metals and their economy is in other respects more developed. They are represented in later chapters (see *post* pp. 274, 314).

H

instance, in order going north, the Yurok of California,[1] the
Twana of the State of Washington,[2] the Coast Salish,[3] Nootka,
Kwakiutl, Bella Coola and Tsimshian of the coast of British
Columbia, the Haida of Queen Charlotte Islands and Tlingit of
the Alaskan coast.[4] Similarly the coastal populations of the
South-Eastern States show some resemblance to these in their
development.

Of the Second Grade of Pastoralists who have no agriculture
and live by their herds and flocks, we shall say something later.

All these peoples, taken as a whole, are to be equated in their
cultures and economies with the Neolithic Age of the past and
have no metals except that in the South-Eastern States a little
copper is imported from the north or mined locally and worked
cold,[5] and the Indians of the coast of British Columbia have a
few copper ornaments acquired by trade.[6]

These agriculturists and hunters have substantial and sometimes
elaborate houses of timber, rectangular or round, thatched or
covered with leaves, grass or reeds, and in many cases long-houses
that accommodate more than one family,[7] and also in some
South-East American areas one house for the public purposes of
a town:[8] and they have all less-solid houses or shelters for
temporary stay or in gardens which they will cultivate only for
a period. Apart from sundry pets they have no domestic animals
except the dog, which is used to a small degree for hunting,[9] and
in the South Seas pigs and fowls, in many places introduced in
recent centuries and not yet found everywhere,[10] and while some

[1] On the Lower Klamath river and along the coast.
[2] On the shores and drainage area of the Hood Canal and on the salt-water
inlet west of Puget Sound: Elmendorf (1960).   [3] Barnett (1955).
[4] See generally as to these tribes Jenness (1934) and Swanton (1952).
[5] Also a small amount of gold and meteoric iron; Swanton (1946), 490f.
[6] Jenness (1934), 78.
[7] Trans-Fly: Williams (1936), 12f.: the best houses are about 30 feet long.
Kuma: Reay (1959), 120 feet. The coast Indians of British Columbia built
enormous houses of beams and planks of cedar sometimes several hundred
feet long, and 50 or 60 feet wide, decorated with paintings and carved posts
or totem poles, and holding several families. In South America there are
longhouses in many places.
[8] For the houses of the South-Eastern States, see Swanton (1946), 386-421.
[9] In some areas of America, some breeds of dogs, now extinct, were kept
for eating and others for wool.
[10] In South America acquired from the Europeans.

peoples only catch and fatten the wild pigs[1] others breed and rear them. In some places pig culture is an obsession and pigs a general medium of exchange.[2] Some, but not all peoples, have pottery,[3] and most or all weave mats, baskets or textiles out of a wide variety of materials,[4] and primitive looms are found in many places.[5] There is a growing list of manufactured articles, mainly of dress and personal adornment, household utensils, tools and weapons, hammocks and stools,[6] boxes, boats and musical instruments. Among the agricultural peoples there is a superfluity of land for gardens and pig-rearing, the plots commonly lying fallow for years after a short cultivation, but there is also some rotation of crops and here and there some irrigation. Among most agricultural peoples there is a substantial diminution in the extent of food-gathering and hunting.[7] The main agricultural implement is still the digging-stick, the same stout pole some three or four feet long, and the chief hunting weapon remains the bow and arrow (in South America chiefly the blowpipe and poisoned dart) as well as the club or spear. Fishing is still by bow and arrow or spear, by poison where the rivers are not fast-flowing, and nets, traps and weirs.

Except as between the sexes there is little economic specialization in the community. There are shamans and sorcerers and experts in boat-building and other skills[8] but

[1] e.g. Trans-Fly: Williams (1936), 18, 224.
[2] e.g. Kuma: Reay (1959), 20. Malekula: Deacon (1934), 196f. where pigs are graded elaborately in 11 grades of value, at first according to size, and then development of the curvature of the tusks.
[3] South-Eastern States: Swanton (1946), 549, 555; and South America; but not on the North-West Coast, nor in parts of the South Seas, e.g. Trans-Fly, Kapauku.
[4] Trans-Fly: see list of materials, Williams (1936), 432. South-Eastern States: Swanton (1946), 602f. North-West Coast: Jenness (1934), 67, 213. The Kapauku have no weaving, little basketry, but good string-making and netting; they have no clothes and few ornaments.
[5] e.g. South America; Ontong Java: Hogbin (1934), 98; not in Tanna or Eromanga: Humphreys (1926), 64, 164.
[6] South America.
[7] Not of hunting in the South-Eastern States. Food gathering, hunting and fishing are the main sources of livelihood among the Hunters on the North-West Coast; they live mainly on salmon and other fish, sea mammals, land animals, waterfowl, molluscs and plants.
[8] e.g. Kuma: Reay (1959), 14. The Kapauku have specialist traders, shamans, sorcerers, surgeons, and dentists: Pospisil (1958), 128.

all derive their main subsistence from the same sources. Pottery and weaving are in most places the province of the woman.[1] The men do the heavy work of clearing the land, burning the bush and breaking up the clods, and the women the bulk of the cultivation and pig-rearing, but in many areas husbands and wives have separate gardens, and if so the men's plots are generally smaller than the women's and often produce different crops. In many places the whole town or kinship group cultivates all the plots in succession. In the building of houses the women usually carry the timber, the men erect the framework and the women do the thatching. Perhaps because of the increased importance of the economic role of the woman in the agricultural peoples there is a rise in her lowly status in the more developed of these economies.[2]

Trade plays a much increased part, mainly in natural products used for food and adornment, but also in partly manufactured goods. Often it is the exchange between neighbouring inland and coastal communities of vegetable produce for fish, individual transactions between a man and his trade-friend, but often it is the exchange of standard trade goods that travel over vast distances on regular routes from hand to hand. In some areas of the world, notably the Kula Ring of the Massim[3] in Melanesia, it is the ritual exchange of two highly prized, non-perishable commodities that travel in opposite directions and seem to serve none but social purposes, knitting together in alliances persons of different communities and islands, and providing means of social intercourse, emulation and prestige. Such a ritual system may co-exist with a trade of a contrasting mercantile nature.[4] There are still no markets.

There is also a considerable advance in calculation, record and communication. Systems of numbers and divisions of the year are

---

[1] e.g. Coast Salish: Barnett (1955), 118.
[2] Among the Kuma and in the Trans-Fly the position of women is low. Among the most advanced Polynesians (especially in Samoa) it is much improved. In South America the status of women varies much.
[3] The group of islands off North-East New Guinea.
[4] Malinowski (1922); Fortune (1932); Worsley (1957); Uberoi (1962).

found and mnemonic devices[1] especially notches in sticks, bundles of sticks or pebbles, knots in vines and cords, strings or leather thongs tied in knots of different colours, reminiscent of the quipus of Peru, and even the beginnings of picture-writing; articles and animals are used as currency or media of exchange; methods of communication are developed between peoples of different tongues, for example, in North America smoke signals and 'sign languages'.

Except in the least developed economies[2] the extent of war is enormous. As before, it mainly takes the form of sudden raids at dawn by parties having the general approval of their communities and leaders. War is a perennial occupation of these peoples and success in war one of the chief measures of status and prestige. In North America it is commonly measured by the acquisition of scalps, in Oceania and South America often by the possession of heads. The weapons of war are the weapons of the hunt with the addition of war clubs, shields[3] and, in America, sometimes armour.[4]

War and the use of labour now create a class of captives, that is to say slaves,[5] though most of the vanquished are slain, often after torture; those retained as slaves are mainly children, while some women are kept as wives. In many places the majority of the captives are eaten. Cannibalism now appears in many of these agricultural peoples, both in Oceania (e.g. Fiji), the South-Eastern States and South America:[6] indeed, except where it is merely

[1] e.g. Kuma: Reay (1959), 98. South New Hebrides: Humphreys (1926), 164. South-Eastern States: Swanton (1928), 400, 446, 453, 704, Swanton (1946), 610f. North-West Coast: Jenness (1934), 113f. A little of this was already to be found among the Plains Indians and in the Eastern Woodlands and the North Athapascans. The Kapauku have a highly developed decimal system and count into thousands.
[2] e.g. The Keraki; Williams (1936).
[3] In the Trans-Fly the Keraki and their neighbours have no spear or shield: Williams (1936), 436, 411; but the Kapauku have small shields.
[4] Of various materials; for the South-Eastern States, see Swanton (1946), 588.
[5] There were, however, already a few instances among the peoples of the previous chapter; for example, in the Pre-Columbian era, the Mbayá bands subjugated the Guana farmers and enslaved them: Métraux, 'Ethnography of the Chaco', H.S.A. I, 304f. A few slaves, chiefly captives, were held by the Comanches: Wallace and Hoebel (1952), 241f. All Kapauku consider themselves equal, and they have no slaves or social classes.
[6] See, for a nauseous example, Métraux, 'The Tupinamba', H.S.A. III, 119.

ceremonial (as in Australia) it seems only to be found in agricultural peoples without large cattle, in this and later grades.[1]

Magic and religion continue to perform the same social functions in these communities. Magic increasingly shows itself as pseudo-science, a supranatural means of bringing desired results, especially in important economic undertakings where success is uncertain, as in horticulture and fishing for certain species. Religious phenomena that are familiar in the old civilizations begin to appear – temples whose walls are lined with images of gods, temple priests, human sacrifice and widows of chiefs strangled to accompany their spouses in the hereafter. There are shamans and sorcerers engaged to further social purposes, but there is also witchcraft employed by all and sundry for anti-social ends. Sorcerers, like the later priests, are the main supporters of the regime, resisting change, but it is rare to find sorcerers or priests among the leaders and rulers. Sickness and death continue to be attributed to witchcraft, and apart from disputes about women, death by witchcraft is as before the chief source of intestine disorder and inter-community wars. But it is doubtful if the savage goes more in fear of the supernatural than we, and unlikely that religious sanctions determine his conduct more than ours.

Among the agricultural populations the density of population has much increased, though it is difficult to measure because in great inland areas there are always large tracts of uncultivable or uncultivated land, mountains and lakes, apart from bush needed for hunting or pig-rearing, and on the other hand the density of population on rivers and coasts is high. So, over the half-million square miles of the South-Eastern States the population was only about 170,000 or one person in 3 square miles, though from the time they took to agriculture the inland population had increased. Over the whole of New Zealand with its extent of some 100,000 square miles, the Maori population was little more than one person per square mile. The population of the Morehead district of Papua, with its large area of unusable land, is about one person to 2 square miles. The island of New Caledonia, of about 10,000 square miles, has a density of over eight per square mile. Smaller islands of about 300 square miles, such as Tanna in the New

[1] See *post* pp. 275, 314.

Hebrides, have a density of about thirty per square mile, while at the other extreme an islet like Tikopia, of about 3 square miles, numbers some 400 persons per square mile. The Kuma in the west highlands of New Guinea are about 200 to the square mile in the area actually settled.

Looking at these populations as a whole – for there is great variety in detail – we can see a progressive increase in the size of the political entities among the agricultural peoples, both as compared with the societies of the previous chapter and from the less to the more developed economies of the present chapter, and this, as we shall see, is accompanied and made possible by a progressive growth in the authority of central government. This increase is necessarily subject to the limitations of geography, for coastal and fishing communities tend to remain small and isolated in their bays, creeks, lagoons, inlets and drainage areas. So, while the tribes of New Guinea and the South Seas (except in the most advanced economies of Polynesia) are small and difficult to distinguish and rarely extend to cover the whole of any island, and the coastal communities of the South-Eastern States remained small in historic times, and only sporadically gathered into larger masses, inland the development of agriculture integrated the peoples into larger and larger tribes and confederacies – the tightly governed Powhatan confederacy of Virginia, the Catawba of South Carolina, the Choctaw, Chickasaw, Natchez and Cherokee and the Creek confederacy.[1] The fishing communities of the North Pacific coast were little smaller[2] but the strength of central government much less.

All these facts betoken the decreasing isolation of man, the wider degree of communication and the quickening tempo of development and change. The linguistic facts are of a piece: while in New Guinea and Melanesia a land journey of five miles brings often a new dialect and a Melanesian island of 250 inhabitants has

[1] These populations were estimated by Mooney (1928) as follows: Powhatan in 1600, 9,000; Catawba in 1600, 5,000; Choctaw in the eighteenth century, 17,000; Chickasaw in the eighteenth century, 8,000; Natchez in 1650, 4,500; Cherokee in 1650, 22,000; Creeks about 12,000. See also as to figures Swanton (1952).

[2] Coast Salish 15,000; Nootka 6,500; Southern Kwakiutl 4,000; Bella Coola 1,400; Tsimshian 5,500; Haida 9,800; Tlingit 10,000; Further south the Yurok in the eighteenth century were 2,500, Twana 1,000. See Mooney (1928) and Swanton (1952).

commonly its separate language divided into a couple of dialects, over the vast expanse of the South-Eastern States, with its striking uniformity of culture, some seven groups of languages were spoken by the bulk of the 170,000 inhabitants, and the vast oceanic expanse and innumerable islands of Polynesia,[1] traversed only by the frail barques of the islanders, speak languages which once formed a single tongue.

Kinship is still the cement that chiefly binds society. The biological or nuclear family is still the basic social unit but it is never politically independent and rarely economically self-sufficient.[2] It is in most places part of the clan, the chief kinship organization, a group connected by putative descent in one line either patrilineal or matrilineal, though the relationship with the other line is never disregarded and the bond between nephew and mother's brother is almost everywhere intimate.[3] Where, as usual, the clan structure exists, the clan is sometimes totemic and sometimes not; usually it is exogamous, sometimes not; and with the growth of the settled community the clan tends to divide and the sub-clan and even the sub-sub-clan to be an important organizational entity, a sub-sub-clan of a large clan often facing a sub-clan of a smaller clan in the same community. The lineage becomes of increasing authority, and on the other hand clans may be linked into a phratry or moiety which in some areas is more important than the clan. But in a surprisingly large minority of communities the clan seems to be absent, and a system of bilateral kinship takes its place.

But the emergence almost everywhere of the settled life of hamlets, villages and towns produces local groups that are fitted with some difficulty into the structure of kinship groups. Usually they are reconciled by the fact that a dominant clan is represented in the local village and the fiction (for it is usually a fiction) that the village was founded by that clan. The two moieties sometimes become two groups of villages or towns. The tribe in many of

[1] Stretching 5,000 miles from Formosa and Hawaii in the north to New Zealand in the south, and 14,000 miles from Madagascar in the west to Easter Island in the east.
[2] Practically so in the Trans-Fly: Williams (1936), 108. Among the Kapauku there is little economic co-operation outside the household of two or three related families: Pospisil (1958), 114.
[3] e.g. Trans-Fly, where the clan or section is patrilineal: Williams (1936), 114.

the less developed economies continues to be a vague, hardly definable and mainly linguistic expression, but in the bulk of these agricultural and even fishing communities tends to coincide with a village or small group of villages, and here and there to merge into a confederacy or nation. The variety in the social structure is vast even between neighbours.

One of the outstanding features of these peoples is their preoccupation with wealth, created partly by the increased availability of food and goods, the difficulty of keeping much of it, the expansion of trade and the pride of the gardener or fisherman in his skill. Next to warlike exploits, prestige depends mostly on wealth and conspicuous waste declares its possession. The right to share freely in food is limited to small kinship groups, but gifts of food and manufactured goods accompany every important social, domestic or ritual event. Great feasts and distributions are held (familiar under the name of the *potlach* or *klanak* of the North Pacific coast and almost as familiar in the South-Eastern States and Oceania)[1] when the boasting hosts (having called in the return gifts due to them or having borrowed from others) give to each guest nicely calculated quantities, reflecting every relationship in the size and nature of the gifts. A return must be rendered in due time of equal value, sometimes with added interest, and ambition or prestige commonly increase the repayment.

A second conspicuous feature, except in the most backward of these communities, is the emergence and preoccupation with rank,[2] till in some of the most developed economies we reach the familiar mediaeval distinctions of kings, nobles, commoners and slaves.

Slavery is not found everywhere as an institution, as it is on the North Pacific coast,[3] for in the South-Eastern States and parts of South America prisoners of war are traditionally burnt or eaten and women and children are adopted if they are not killed on the spot. But it is widespread in Oceania except in the more backward economies. The slave's lot varies much: it is abject in some places and hardly a human lot, but many of the women are taken in

[1] e.g. Trans-Fly: Williams (1936), 230f.
[2] Seen already in one or two peoples of the previous chapter. Mbayá society was rigorously stratified: Métraux, 'Ethnology of the Chaco', *H.S.A.* I, 304f. For the Kapauku, see note 5, p. 203.
[3] Swanton (1928), 167.

H*

marriage and the children of slaves are commonly free and equal members of the community.[1]

Above the commoners, rank among the less developed economies is bought rather than inherited. Prestige is acquired in high degree by the amassing of wealth and its distribution, though a leader is often a man who has impoverished himself by generosity. And just as we saw in North America in the previous chapter the privileges of successive age-grades being bought by the incomers through the course of a man's life, in Oceania in many places rank as well as prestige are bought together with the insignia that appertain to it.[2] But rank is also inherited and in some places shows signs of becoming a caste. Marriage, for example, between members of the chiefly class and commoners may be prohibited. The ranks of noble and commoner each have their names.[3] Everywhere along the North Pacific coast of America are the ranks of nobles, commoners and slaves, and influence accompanying wealth.

A third conspicuous new feature in these societies is the great increase in the power of the chiefs. On the one hand, in the undeveloped economies of New Guinea there is no change from the bulk of the peoples of the previous chapter. In the Trans-Fly, where the biological family is almost self-sufficient, the head of the family has a vague authority over its members and the headman of the local group a little more, but even to call a man a headman is something of an exaggeration and it is not always clear who the headman is, there are so many.[4] Among the Kuma, where the clan is the political unit, there is no centralized authority to co-ordinate the actions of its members, only a loose association of the leaders of its segments. There is no distinctive term even for a leader of a sub-sub-clan and hardly any insignia. It is merely said that he is 'first' and that 'people listen to him'. But he is more

[1] Swanton (1928), 167.
[2] New Hebrides (Malekula): Deacon (1934), 199f, 270f.
[3] e.g. South New Hebrides (Eromanga): no woman of the *fanlo* (chiefly) class may marry a man of the *taui natimono* (commoners') class; but the reverse is permitted and the man's children succeed to his rank: Humphreys (1926), 142.
[4] Williams (1936), 113, 236f. Among the Kapauku the leader (*tonowi*) is merely a *primus inter pares*, and acquires his temporary position by good physical appearance, wealth, generosity and eloquence; and a reputation for bravery and shamanism enhances it.

likely than not to be succeeded by his eldest son or patrilineal kin, and the next in succession often assists him, supporting him in public discussion and urging the people to carry out his instructions. There are also unauthorized leaders – strong,wealthy, polygamous men – but their influence is less.[1] In the islands of the Massim and Melanesia generally there are usually no hereditary political authorities nor even hereditary rank or status, but status develops here and there in the Trobriand.[2] It is only on the Polynesian fringe, in the Southern New Hebrides,[3] Fiji and New Caledonia[4] that chiefs of any power are to be found, and in Polynesia the development continues. Even in the small atoll of Ontong Java two hundred years ago a chief or king arose of each of its two villages.[5] The four clans of the island of Tikopia, numbering each some four hundred souls, are each headed by a chief to whom ultimately the land of the clan belongs and he administers it. If a man falls foul of his chief and cannot make his peace with him, there is nothing for it but to take a boat out into exile and death on the high seas.[6] In Samoa the *matai* (elected chiefs) and their *fono* (assembly) had in criminal matters powers of life and death over their dependents, and in the kingdoms of Tonga and Hawaii, where authority is more centralized, a feudal system of government has already been reached. The whole archipelago was considered to belong to the king, and part he reserved for himself and part he allocated among the great nobles who paid regular tribute and did military service for it, and they, in turn allocated land to their lesser subordinates, who gave tribute and performed military service for the permission to live upon it. In North America, in the South-Eastern States, the rulers of many nations had absolute power and the contrast with the modest status and influence of the chief in the plains of the north is striking.

[1] Reay (1959), 113f.   [2] Uberoi (1962), 5f.
[3] In the Southern New Hebrides the power of the chief was practically absolute over his village (Tanna, Futuna, Eromanga and Anaiteum: Humphreys (1926), 35f., 106f., 114, 129, 132f., 141). Contrast Malekula where, in the north-west, such chiefs as there are have no judicial or administrative function, and in the south-west any influence they have is due to wealth and lavish gifts and feasts; status is obtained by purchase of high rank in graded societies: Deacon (1934), 47f.
[4] Krieger (1943); Humphreys (1926).
[5] Hogbin (1934), 224f.   [6] Firth (1936).

Among the fishing cultures of the North Pacific coast of America the chiefly authority is far less. Moving northwards from California, though rank, based especially on wealth, is everywhere, we find among the Yurok and Twana peoples no political organization of the speech community and no governmental organization of the village nor any traditional patterns of unified action between villages.[1] Usually each village recognized one upper-class leader of a household as leader of the community. He was usually also the richest man of the village and possessed personal qualities of leadership but no control over anyone. The position tended to be hereditary but there was no rule to this effect.[2] Further north the only political unit is the village,[3] or even the extended family,[4] and government is little developed. People looked up to the head of the principal house in a clan. If the clan predominated in a village he was head of the village and if his village was more powerful than neighbouring villages he was the most important man in the district.

Marriage practices change accordingly. With the accentuation of wealth and ubiquity of gift-returns, marriage is one of the occasions celebrated by great exchanges of property between the two extended families. Though there is a certain initiation of presents from the bridegroom's side they are generally followed by gifts of equal value from the bride's, and as, among the more advanced agricultural peoples, the women's status has risen, the picture is rarely that of a unilateral payment of bridewealth. Gifts, perhaps especially on the man's side, continue for many years or throughout life.[5] Indeed, marriage itself is usually an exchange of sisters (either in the narrow or classificatory sense) and a man who has no woman to provide in return will usually have to find one.[6] Marriage by capture is rare but in a few peoples (for example,

---

[1] Elmendorf (1960), 255.   [2] Elmendorf (1960), 313.
[3] Jenness (1934), 147; as in South America where generally each settlement is autonomous.
[4] e.g. Coast-Salish: Barnett (1955), 241: no tribal officers or council.
[5] On the North Pacific coast of North America the husband's kin normally pay in a series of feasts and the wife's repay similarly in the years that follow: Jenness (1934), 155f. Of marriage in the South-Eastern States too little is known but the payments seem to be chiefly from the man's side: Swanton (1946), 446, 701-9. The Kapauku, however, have the brideprice marriage: Pospisil (1958), 52f.
[6] e.g. Trans-Fly: Williams (1936), 132, 166.

in Tikopia) it is the regular and prevailing system, so that the gifts that follow from the man's side take the form of peacemaking payments for abduction.[1] Religious ceremonies of marriage are rarely if ever found. As the power of the chief grows it is he who arranges the marriages (as in the Polynesian kingdoms). Among the bulk of our peoples marriage is by custom virilocal here and uxorilocal there, inheritance being patrilineal where marriage is virilocal and matrilineal where marriage is uxorilocal, though there are a few peoples among whom marriage is virilocal but descent matrilineal.[2] In New Guinea and Polynesia marriage is generally virilocal and descent patrilineal; in Melanesia there is much variety. In the South-Eastern States, marriage is generally uxorilocal and descent in the female line.[3] In South America, in the west marriage is chiefly patrilocal, in the east matrilocal residence prevails. But there is great variety between the closest communities: for example in the small atoll of Ontong Java, marriage is matrilocal on the main islands and patrilocal in the others.[4] Polygyny is found among most or all peoples.[5]

Ideas of property in land have developed greatly in these agricultural communities but vary vastly from place to place and it is only possible here to describe some general features. Land, unlike goods, is permanent and the chief source of livelihood, but a different piece is used in different years or seasons or it is used differently in the same or different years or seasons. It is cultivated or fallow, has trees or homes upon it. Different groups or persons have interests in the same land and may use the same land for different purposes. There is always a superfluity of land and tenures are loose, fluid and easy.[6] There are few disputes as to use or title and in most of these peoples no authority to hear and decide them.

Ideas of property in land vary chiefly according to two sets of

[1] Firth (1936), Chap. XV.   [2] e.g. in the Trobriand.
[3] e.g. Creeks: Swanton (1928), 79, 368f.   [4] Hogbin (1934), 117.
[5] The extent of polygyny varies, but the variation is not important. In the Trans-Fly, Williams (1936), 149, gives a sample group: men with one wife, 55·1 per cent; with two wives 37·2 per cent; with three wives, 5·1 per cent; with four wives, 2·6 per cent; average 1·55 per married man. This proportion is explained by the late age at which a second wife is taken, the existence of bachelors but not of unmarried women, the greater mortality of men through war. In the more developed economies, kings and nobles have many wives, but the commoner somewhat fewer.
[6] Kuma: Reay (1959), 6.

facts: the uses to which land is put in a community and the local system of organization, administration or government. Starting with the second of these criteria, we notice that in the communities where there are as yet no chiefs of power or authority there is commonly an overriding interest of tribes,[1] clans,[2] joint or extended families,[3] villages or towns,[4] and they may be the same in the public estimation as, for example, often a village contains predominantly one clan. Here the land of the community may consist of tracts considered to belong to a particular tribe, clan, sub-clan or village, and these may be divided into tracts belonging to smaller kinship groups – for example, lineages or the heads of extended families.[5] As the authority of chiefs increases, the land may come to be considered as belonging to the chief of the tribe or clan;[6] in Tonga the sacred king, and in Hawaii the king, was considered the owner of the land of the community and divided it among the lesser chiefs (apart from what he retained) in return for tribute or taxes, and these divided theirs on similar terms. Inside these main holdings of clan or other kinship group, village or king, individuals – senior members of lineages or extended families – are at the same time considered to own their portion of the land, except for uncultivated land until it is cultivated – for example, bushland for pasture of pigs or hunting – and this belongs to the general community of village, clan or sub-clan[7] or is no man's land. But rarely if ever is the owner absolute owner in the sense of modern law: rarely can he permanently assign the land[8] and others have at least a qualified

[1] e.g. Trans-Fly: Williams (1936), 51.
[2] e.g. Kuma: Reay (1959), 6.   [3] Hogbin (1934), 94, 130.
[4] e.g. Creeks: Swanton (1928), 336. Yet there are exceptions, and among the Kapauku, who are intensely individualist and commercially minded, all productive land belongs to individuals, men, wives and children over eleven. The latter may even trade this produce with their father. An owner may work, lease or sell his land, except that if he has adult sons he must ask their permission to sell or the transfer may be held invalid after his death. But such land is transferred mainly by intestate succession. The only common property is the barren mountain tops, the large streams owned by the sub-lineage and the small lakes owned by the lineage. Even bridges are not owned in common, for the parts contributed by a man continue to belong to him: Pospisil (1958), 98, 115f., 129. But every forest is free hunting ground for all: *ibid.*, 181.
[5] e.g. the *yure* of the Keraki: Williams (1936), 211f.
[6] Tikopia: Firth (1936), 376f.
[7] Kuma: Reay (1959), 8.   [8] But see Reay (1959), 8.

right to make use of it. Turning to the first criterion, we notice that land and the houses upon it may be considered to belong to different groups – for example, in some places women and in some places the members of the matrilineal group own the houses, while the members of the patrilineal group own the land.[1] The trees upon it may again be differently owned according to their species or they may all belong (as in New Guinea generally) to the person who planted them. Land is obtained by discovery, occupation, distribution by superiors or gift for consideration. For example, a man who clears bushland may thereby become owner, even to the point of a right to alienate,[2] but this is unusual and more commonly an owner can only give a temporary right of cultivation in return for a share in the produce at harvest.[3]

Little new is to be said on the subject of property in goods. Women are considered to own things made by them or belonging to their sex – bags, baskets, fish-nets, bark skirts and such,[4] and all that a man acquires by his labour or uses belongs to him.[5] Crops grown by the wife in her garden are often hers and she has a large say in the disposing of them. Household furnishings and the house itself are often the woman's.[6] There are also widespread ideas of property in 'incorporeal' things, especially songs and dances.

Rules of succession to goods have made little or no progress. As before, in most places most of the goods of the deceased are destroyed or buried at his death, sometimes to accompany him, sometimes for sentiment or to avoid the imputation that his sons killed him by witchcraft to obtain his property[7], or kin outside the immediate family may seize his possessions indiscriminately.[8] For the rest, a woman's things, if they survive, will usually go to a daughter or in a virilocal community even to her daughter-in-law living in the same village.[9]

[1] In some places the husbands and wives have separate houses near their work: e.g. Kuma: Reay (1959), 3.
[2] Keraki: Williams (1936), 211. Kuma: Reay (1959), 8.
[3] e.g. Malekula: Deacon (1934), 172f.
[4] e.g. Trans-Fly: Williams (1936), 148.
[5] e.g. Creeks: Swanton (1928), 335.
[6] Kuma: Reay (1959), 8, and see note 1, *supra*.
[7] e.g. Creeks: Swanton (1928), 337.   [8] e.g. Kuma: Reay (1959), 96.
[9] Trans-Fly: Williams (1936), 148. Among the Kapauku, her eldest son is her main heir: Pospisil (1958), 201f.

Succession to chieftainship is now commonly to the eldest or a chosen son, or the senior or a chosen member of a chiefly family or class, even where succession is otherwise matrilineal, but where it is matrilineal it will descend to a sister's son.[1]

Succession to land in these agricultural communities has grown greatly in importance. The rules or methods of succession are generally part of the rules of 'ownership'. If the head of a family is owner for the family of a plot or strip of land within an area owned by a sub-clan or other kinship or local group, his land or interest on his death will commonly descend, where land is owned in a patrilocal group, to his sons,[2] or brother and then sons,[3] according to the ideas of the community, or in a matrilocal group to a sister's son or other matrilocal relatives, but where the family increases there are apt to be new distributions of land or acquisitions from the waste or settlement on the land of others, and where the family diminishes, relatives or affines or strangers are easily admitted.[4] We find also in a surprisingly large minority of cases bilateral systems of ownership and descent.[5] In some peoples, houses may descend matrilineally and even to wives, while the land on which they stand descends patrilineally.[6] Daughters do not usually inherit, but may inherit with sons[7] or in default of sons obtain the right to cultivate till marriage or for life, after which the land reverts to the brothers or sons of the deceased.[8] In a patrilineal system we frequently see sons inheriting and working the land jointly till they partition (e.g. on their children's marriages). Adopted sons may be given land. Sometimes though property is inherited it must be paid for.[9] Widows are commonly inherited.

[1] Among the Keraki from an elder brother to a younger brother, then to the son of the elder brother: Williams (1936), 242. In the South New Hebrides, in Anaiteum, chieftainship is inherited from father to son, or in default of sons, to a son of a brother or sister, and there have been female chiefs: Humphreys (1926), 107; in Futuna, to a sister's son, or a sister's daughter's son: *ibid.*, 114.

[2] Kuma: to sons jointly till they divide: Reay (1959), 9. Among the Kapauku the eldest son is the main heir: Pospisil (1958), 201f.

[3] e.g. Trans-Fly: Williams (1936), 211.

[4] e.g. Seniang, S.W. Malekula: Deacon (1934), 172f.

[5] e.g. Samoa, South America.   [6] Ontong Java: Hogbin (1934), 118.

[7] e.g. Anaiteum, South New Hebrides, where male and female children inherit equally: Humphreys (1926), 108.   [8] Trans-Fly: Williams (1936), 211.

[9] e.g. Trans-Fly: Williams (1936), 153. Eromanga: Humphreys (1926), 185f.

There are few wills, except that in some matters, within the general system of inheritance, the deceased may have given instructions before his death which are carried out: he may, for example, have spoken of a tree as belonging to a particular child.[1]

Among the fishing and hunting peoples of the north-west coast of North America ideas of ownership of land are far less developed. The bulk of them live in substantial plank houses containing one family or a number of connected families as well as smaller habitations, and in most places they form a winter village from which the population scatters in the summer to less substantial and less permanent dwellings. The villages are usually few and small and in some peoples (for example the Yurok of California) of little importance, in others (such as the Twana) they are the chief economic units and politically they are always independent. But there is usually no governmental organization even of the village – no tribunal, officers or council – nor between villages, nor any unified action of the villages, nor is there any tribe or state; the chief social unit is the family. There is no clear village ownership of hunting land nor is it considered to be owned by kinship groups nor usually by families. In most peoples (for example, among the Twana) a man may hunt wherever he will;[2] in others there is great distrust between groups and war between villages. But sometimes there is use and 'ownership' by individuals, on behalf of their families, of spots especially productive of food,[3] and weirs erected by a winter household may be considered its property or that of the headman of the chief local upper-class family on behalf of his family. The extent of this individual or family interest in hunting sites, or means of exploiting them, varies much within the same ethnic group. In many places the plank houses belong to the individual or household who built or lived in them in the winter settlement, or (if occupied by several families) the ranking upper-class family head among them, and when the house is dismantled at seasonal moves the maker is often entitled to receive the planks. Furnishings, like the canoes, articles of excess and ostentation (such as blankets, skins and slaves), dress and personal adornment belong to those who made, acquired or use them. Incorporeal things such as personal names,

---

[1] Kapauku: Pospisil (1958), 205f.   [2] Elmendorf (1960), 260.
[3] Yurok, Twana: Elmendorf (1960), 266, 268.

songs, dances, spirit powers, ceremonial privileges and professional lore are chiefly owned by the men, but sometimes by women, who acquired them from their mothers or other older relatives or from their husbands. Most of the things a person makes or acquires can be disposed of as he wishes. Rules of succession are vague. The head of an upper-class family will commonly give articles to particular children during life, but most (especially clothing and ornaments) is burnt at death. Otherwise goods are commonly shared between the sons, or a brother succeeds in default or holds for young children. But in many places the eldest son, or the thriftiest or most capable son succeeds, especially to names, songs and ceremonial displays and devices for hunting and fishing, and may succeed for the benefit of the family to lands traditionally exploited by it. Much of the rules or ways of succession, here and elsewhere, is merely the continuity and contiguity of a group of males in a virilocal community continuing in possession in the patrilineal line of the property of a member. The clan is not of great prominence: in the northern tribes the phratry exceeds it in importance, and except in the extreme north succession is to a large extent bilateral[1] and among the Kwakiutl property even passes from a man to his son-in-law and then back to his son.

We turn to the topic of crimes and civil injuries, and first to jurisdiction: who are they that enquire into alleged wrongs and remedy them by punishment, compensation or otherwise?

Among the least developed of these agricultural communities, such as the people of the Trans-Fly,[2] as among the bulk of the early agriculturists of the preceding chapter, there are no well-established chiefs. There are hereditary or other headmen of the family and local clan with a certain prestige among the members. Such a man, normally at least, gives the word for certain movements or undertakings to begin when they have been generally discussed or agreed upon, but there are no formal meetings of elders and he issues no order. He should be an energetic gardener, a man of wealth and generosity and some public spirit and eloquence, and has the greater prestige if he is a successful head-hunter, but he is not necessarily a sorcerer or rain-maker though he takes the leading part in public rites of magic and presides over

[1] e.g. Coast Salish: Barnet (1955), 182f., 242.
[2] Williams (1936), 113, 236.

the ceremony of initiation, even if he takes no active part, and he issues invitations to feasts and accepts them on behalf of his group.

Where, then, is there a law-making or law-administering process? F. E. Williams has an able chapter on the Regulation of Conduct among them.[1] He begins by describing a code of conduct which is well understood and necessary to the continuance of the society, and to which the majority conform though they observe it differently and in different degree. One man is more industrious than another in his garden; he may marry within his moiety with or without social odium, or orient a corpse for burial in a different way. It is a flexible code and a man decides many things for himself. Most of it is inculcated in the child, partly by initiation and seclusion but mainly by the practice of life. The code comprises conduct of the nature described in the present chapter but also embraces more general social behaviour; within limits it is observed though there is no police, no one has jurisdiction and there is hardly any action by the community or any part of it to punish breaches. Some of the 'rules' are supported by formal public expression, sometimes with ritual symbolism – for example, by boundary stones or boundary lines, the publicity of a marriage and the participation of both groups. They are supported also by certain psychological factors – the tendencies towards conservatism and uniformity and the sentiments of fellowship and kinship: a man does not want to fall out with his friends and even less his kin. They are also sanctioned by the violent reaction of an offended person with or without partisans and still more by fear of public opinion and some of them also by the punishment of Gainjan, who is supposed to be able to strike a man with sickness by capturing his soul. There are also inducements or encouragements to conform – for example, the fact that the social structure is a more or less organized system and gifts may not follow. Malinowski, in the Trobriand, puts above all else the factor or 'law' of reciprocity.[2]

Some social anthropologists would say that this code of conduct is the code of law of such a people, and we may agree that they have no other. But if we call these 'rules' of conduct and the law of a modern people by the same name we are confusing different

[1] Williams (1936), 244f.   [2] Malinowski (1926).

things. Certainly some such sanctions are the chief forces of social
control in the Trans-Fly, but they are such also in a modern
state, at least in a modern village, and this situation that we see
in the Trans-Fly is not law but the perpetual foundation upon
which the edifice of law is reared.

A code of law is a set of sanctions: it defines the sanctions and
the circumstances in which they are to be imposed, and the
sanctions are on the whole of a different kind from those just
mentioned, for they are in effect concerned with breaches of good
order, with wrongs, not rights. To these ends there must be a
person or body with the authority of the society to investigate,
when necessary, the facts said or call for sanctions, and to
impose them. It is true that in the course of investigating the
facts and imposing the sanctions the authority may ultimately
have to decide whether the conduct of plaintiff or defendant was
right or wrong in some respect, whether certain land was his to
use or he was entitled to certain valuables, but this is not the
first object of the proceedings, which is to restore order. We saw
this plainly in the first manifestation of law in the previous
chapter, where the intervention of the soldiers among the Plains
Indians was to restore order, and it remains in the written codes
of law when they first appear.[1] It is also true that when the
sanctions for wrongs have been imposed with sufficient frequency
their imposition becomes a new course of conduct and therefore
rightful. It is also true that the functions of law are a specialization
and centralization of functions in the community, but of particular
functions, namely, the violent reactions of groups and individuals
to conduct that offends.

As the authority of chiefs grows, with it emerges and grows the
jurisdiction to hear and determine disputes. Already among the
Kuma[2] the leader of the sub-sub-clan adjudicates informally in
disputes between its members, and if the disputants belong to

[1] See Chap. 5 supra.
[2] Reay (1959), 5of., 117, 122, 126. Similarly in a Kapauku village, the leader
of the main local sub-lineage, who therefore may be called a village headman,
who is wealthy and the political and war leader, settles most of the local
disputes. Usually he does this in accordance with what is generally considered
to be the rights of the parties, sometimes equitably but not in accordance
with these rights, and sometimes unjustly and in his own interests: Pospisil
(1958). His influence is usually sufficient to cause his decisions to be obeyed,
and a law of crimes and torts is well developed in this remarkable people.

different sub-clans within the same subdivision of the local 'parish'[1] the orator of the locally predominant sub-clan, the spokesman of that subdivision, adjudicates and the audience is drawn from the entire subdivision. If the disputants belong to different subdivisions of the parish, the leaders of the affected subdivisions jointly preside at a meeting of the local populace. There is no central authority to maintain law and order in the parish. Decisions are taken in the light of group interests and local standards of what is right conduct (*hab'g*). It is right for a man to be a good worker, to control his wives without making public issues of any disagreement he has with them, to be always honest, to be co-operative and agreeable towards fellow-members of the clan and community. It is wrong (*kets*) to quarrel with clansmen, still more to quarrel with members of the smaller groups and wrong indeed to quarrel with brothers. But people admire a man of renown, whether or not his conduct is right. The leader rarely attempts to impose a judgment that is not in accordance with public opinion as expressed by the participants in the dispute and their interested supporters. The proceedings are prolonged and the public, members of the disputants' groups not directly affected, take part in the discussion, reiterating maxims of good conduct ('It is not good for brothers to quarrel', and the like) and are listened to with some respect if they voice the correct sentiments and clichés. Settlement of disputes by reference to these standards helps to maintain and reinforce them. Precedents are cited if they can be turned to the advantage of a group, and between members of the two disputing sub-clans recriminations recalling previous offences are exchanged. At the close shells are commonly exchanged to compensate for false accusations, harsh words and blows exchanged in the course of the proceedings. If compensation is to be given, the group as a whole is responsible for providing it and, led by the leaders, decides who will supply the goods.

From Melanesia to the fringe of Polynesia the jurisdiction of chiefs grows with their authority and the aura of reverence that surrounds them. This is reflected in the nascent criminal law.

[1] 'Parish' is used in the sense of the largest local group which can be regarded as having any permanent political unity; see Hogbin and Westwood, 'Local Grouping in Melanesia', *Oceania*, XXIII (Sydney, Australian National Research Council: 1952-3), 243, 253.

Among the Trans-Fly and Kuma, killing by witchcraft is almost the only offence of a criminal nature. In the Trobriand the chief and especially the highest ranking chief, the chief of Kiriwina, can punish breaches of a subject's duties towards him – adultery with one of his wives, theft of any of his private possessions, or such a personal insult as placing himself above the chief's head, alluding sexually to his sister or using certain filthy expressions in his presence – and for any of these he might be speared by an armed attendant of the chief.[1] In the New Hebrides, in Malekula, while in the north and north-west there are a few men who can be called chiefs and members of a class of chiefs, whose influence is derived from wealth and purchased rank, they have no judicial or administrative functions.[2] In the Southern New Hebrides the power of the chief of the village was almost absolute: he judged and punished serious delinquency by death, and if the offence was committed between members of different villages the respective chiefs met in council and punished the offender after discussions and agreement.[3] In many places there were paramount chiefs, exercising similar jurisdiction over wide areas and adjudicating and punishing in their tribal council of local chiefs.[4] In the small Polynesian atoll of Ontong Java, until a king or permanent chief arose some two hundred years ago, the priest chiefs appointed the *polepole* (police) to punish the only crime, the theft of coconuts or taro from the common land. Since then the idea of a king's peace has grown and the list of criminal offences has expanded to include adultery.[5]

In the kingdoms of Tonga and Hawaii, as has been mentioned, a feudalism resembling that familiar in Western Europe has been reached.[6] Among the ranks or classes of nobles was that of the *matapule*, the principal attendants and hereditary advisers of the chiefs. The father had a right to punish his children, the head of the extended family its members, the chief his subjects. The commoner had an appeal from the decision of a minor chief to the matapule of a higher chief, and the oppressed subject an

[1] Malinowski (1926), 91f.   [2] Deacon (1934), 47.
[3] Tanna: Humphreys (1926), 35, 55.
[4] Futuna, Eromanga: Humphreys (1926), 114, 132. The authority of the high chief is said to have been absolute.   [5] Hogbin (1934), 210.
[6] In Hawaii, the islands were united under a single king at the beginning of the European era.

ultimate right of appeal to the king. Disrespectful or disobedient conduct towards the chief,[1] including non-payment of land tax or tribute, was punished by him or his matapule. In Samoa authority was less centralized but legality more advanced. The local *matai* (or heads of kindred groups) formed the *fono* or assembly of each village or district and had in practice the main authority. The kinship group was bilateral, and there was no chiefly class; the titles of the matai were not hereditary but elective on merit, validated by large distributions of goods. In criminal matters (that is offences against the village chief or high chief) the *matai* in *fono* had powers of life and death over their dependants and tried them and the sentences were executed by the age-group and gild of the *aumanga*. The criminal offences included disrespect to a high chief, failure to conform to a village edict, insulting the village god, habitual theft, incest. Adultery, as often, was on the boundary between crime and civil wrong. The chief punishments for crime in Polynesia were death, beating, binding in public and banishment.

In general the degree of development of the law in the South-Eastern States of North America is much the same as that in Polynesia, and there is a broad similarity throughout the area. The chief wrong of a criminal nature is killing by witchcraft[2] (for which the punishment is death), and sometimes incest (which, if it obtrudes, is irregularly punished by death, mutilation, ostracism or banishment) and adultery[3] (which is sometimes criminal but usually a private wrong). Sodomy is rarely found in the law: in some peoples, as in Oceania, it is said to be unknown, in others sodomy and male concubinage are an institution.[4]

[1] e.g. adultery with the wife, and seduction of a relative, of a great chief.
[2] And also among Siouans, persistent killing by poison. In most of the peoples of the present chapter, death is usually attributed to witchcraft and, in many, sorcerers are employed to 'smell out' the witch. Among the Creeks the murderer is killed by the same kind of weapon, even the same weapon, if the relatives of the deceased demand it, though they can also accept a commutation: Swanton (1928), 344. In Samoa, death is the usual punishment for murder: Hogbin (1934), 178.
[3] Also, among the Creeks, the offence committed by a widow or widower who remarries too soon. In Samoa the usual punishment for adultery was death: Turner (1884), 178. For the Alabama, see Swanton (1928), 351.
[4] e.g. Trans-Fly, where sodomy is considered necessary to a boy's growth: Williams (1936), 158. Malekula: Deacon (1934), 169f. Sodomy was common among the Chickasaw and unpunished.

Fornication before marriage is in varying degree ignored. Theft is hardly known before white contact[1] but subsequently persistent theft becomes capital.[2] Where central government is less in evidence, as, for example, among the Cherokee, the chiefs can impose no punishment and most offences are sanctioned by irregular retaliation of individuals or groups; but where authority is well centred in a powerful king or paramount chief, as in the Virginia of Powhatan, the list of crimes shows a similar spread, and those guilty of murder and their accomplices, and robbers, thieves and adulterers caught in the act are put to death with every mediaeval circumstance of barbarity and torture, and king's guards failing of their duty are corporally punished; but it is right to add that, like any other absolute monarch, Powhatan treats in similar fashion anyone who offends him.[3]

The rest are the civil or private wrongs against individuals and their kinship groups. The chief civil wrong is homicide, for which the sanction is now in most places the performance of the duty to take a corresponding life. The strictness with which it is applied, and the extent to which it is compromised by a payment of goods, varies from people to people. In some places it is felt to be also a religious duty towards the ghost of the slain. So keenly is the duty felt among the Creeks that, after white contact, Hawkins with difficulty persuades the Creek Council to declare as law that when a man is punished by the law of the nation and dies, it is the law that killed him: 'No man or family is to be held accountable for this act of the nation.'[4] In some places, on the other hand, the feud strictly applies only when the killing is of an adult male of some account and is intentional.[5] In the Trobriand *lugwa* (vendetta) is seldom carried out and the payment and acceptance of *lula* (the peace-making price) is traditional.[6] In Samoa the *fono* intervenes only when injustice is being done, as when retaliation is threatened for accidental death or the feud threatens to disrupt the village.[7] In most places most other injuries are

---

[1] Theft is commonly such a disgrace – for it implies a consciousness of inability to earn a living – that it usually is regarded as the act of weak-minded persons: Malinowski (1926), 117f.
[2] Creeks – death for a third offence of stealing: Swanton (1928), 344.
[3] Swanton (1946), 730f.
[4] Swanton (1928), 343.   [5] e.g. Malinowski (1926), 118.
[6] Malinowski (1926), 115f.   [7] Hogbin (1934), 274.

sanctioned by the threat of action between individuals and their supporters and a peace-making gift.[1] Adultery is mainly a private wrong:[2] an adultress is usually left to her husband and his friends to punish by death or the disgrace of mutilation, mass rape or extrusion from the group, or to forgive; and the adulterer if caught is assaulted or killed if he is not too strong.[3] Theft where found is a private offence unless it is persistent.[4]

In the most developed Polynesian economies and in the South-Eastern States the advance of religion brings with it in many places the institution of the sanctuary: in Samoa, cities of refuge where a man may be free of the feud and be allowed to pay a heavy fine in the form of food, though his house and gardens might be destroyed in his absence and he might be prohibited from returning;[5] among the Creeks, sanctuary can be taken in the White Towns.[6] Among the same peoples ordeals can be seen sometimes in the form of an oath in the name of a divinity, imposed on the defendant and usually in the absence of direct evidence.[7]

In this chapter religion and magic have hardly been mentioned, and this is because he who begins to describe the usages and practices that are in the field of law or precede the field of law, does not find himself in the field of magic and religion and their usages and practices, except that there is contact on the frontier at the same points as always, namely in certain offences of a criminal nature, and especially sacral offences, and also offences where the law cannot operate, namely within the family (for the avenging and defending group is the same) and certain procedures that take advantage of the existence of magical and religious beliefs and practices, namely sanctuaries and the ordeal. Assuming

[1] e.g. Hogbin (1934), 210f., 273f.
[2] There is loan or exchange of wives at a feast in the Trans-Fly: Williams (1936), 160; and some other places.
[3] For the South-Eastern States see Swanton (1928), 346f.
[4] e.g. Creeks: Swanton (1928), 338-58; (1946), 730f.
[5] Turner (1884), 178f.
[6] Swanton (1928), 344, quoting Gregg.
[7] Samoa: Turner (1884), 184: 'In the presence of our chiefs now assembled, I lay my hand on the stone. If I stole the thing may I speedily die,' etc. For Tonga see Gifford (1929), 326. Ordeals are also to be found in Hawaii. For the use of the oath in the South-Eastern States, see J. Adair, *History of the American Indians* (1775), 51.

that religion and magic are among the means of social control, and assuming that they operate to deter men from committing murder, physical injury, sexual wrongs, theft and damage to property, the question remains what is to be done when they are committed, and this is the function of secular sanctions and ultimately law. If one looks for rules of conduct sanctioned by religious or magical as well as legal or secular sanctions, there are few of these, for magic and even religion (except in the most advanced peoples) have little ethical content. And even in such cases we merely say, and content ourselves with saying, that a certain rule of conduct is both a secular, legal or pre-legal rule and also a religious rule. We shall return to this topic later: let us however take one example.

In the small Polynesian atoll of Ontong Java, where religion is well developed and the headmen of several joint families are priests, there is a belief in the *kipua*, the immortal spirit of a person, and if there is sickness the question is, what conduct incurred the anger of the spirits, the *kipua* of ancestors. Conduct of four kinds offends the *kipua* of a person's ancestors: failure of duty towards members of the joint family and neglect of other relatives (especially poor relations) outside it; murder and adultery between members of the same joint family and displacement of a true heir (for example as headman) in a joint family; incest; and neglect of ceremonies and breaking of taboos. In such cases no action is taken by the community;[1] justice is confidently left to be vindicated in punishment by the *kipua* of the ancestors. Sexual relations and even marriages do take place within the prohibited degrees but nothing is done save by the *kipua*, who also punish with death the offspring of the incestuous. Nor do the *kipua* visit only unrighteous conduct: their mean spite is also active, and, for example, the envious spirit of a dead woman may kill so many children of a family that it rises up in its wrath and vents its feelings by digging up her body and burning it. Yet the natives go no more in fear of the supernatural than we: some fear and some do not, and public disapproval and ostracism are more powerful deterrents.[2]

[1] The only crime in the atoll is the stealing of coconuts or taro from common land.
[2] Hogbin (1934), 143, 151-64.

CHAPTER 16

Cattle Keepers – The Third Agricultural Grade, First Stage

We have now pursued our enquiry up to the beginnings of law and it is worth while pausing here to consider what we have found.

We have found that by and large there are parallel developments in all these peoples towards the emergence of law, but in detail great differences everywhere. We note, first, that there are great changes and advances on the roads to law between most peoples of the least developed and the most developed economies in each chapter, and there is great development between most peoples of one chapter and the next, but that there is overlapping. It is plain, for example, that the most backward of the peoples mentioned in the last chapter (namely, those of the Trans-Fly of New Guinea) are on the whole behind the most developed of the preceding chapter (namely the American Indians of the Northern Plains) in respect of the progress in law, while the Polynesian kingdoms, though they possess no cattle, have reached a stage in the development of government and law reminiscent of our Central Codes. It is also plain that peoples of apparently similar economic development in other respects are not always similar in their degree or kind of legal development. In New Guinea the Kapauku, little endowed with goods, are precocious in law. Among the Polynesians, the Samoans, though behind the Tongans and Hawaiians in centralization of government are more advanced in their jural conceptions and administration of justice. There is also a vast difference between the trends of the development towards law of the agricultural peoples of the last chapter and the fishing cultures of the north-west coast of North America.

We note also certain obvious resemblances in economic and legal development between some peoples of the same culture area, not shared in other culture areas, and on the other hand great differences between peoples of the same culture area notwithstanding similarities in legal development with peoples of other culture areas.

Nothing of this is surprising. Our criteria of economic development, mainly the means of subsistence, are rough and imperfect. The information is often scanty. Reconstructions of the past cannot always be accurate, and the accounts of observers are in a measure matters of opinion and the extent of the area to which they apply is not always defined. Some advances may be acquired by learning from others, some by independent invention. It is not to be supposed that there is only one solution to the problem how man is to gain control over a particular environment or maintain order in it: and it is plain that peoples without cattle or metals are capable of large progress towards civilization. Above all, it is not to be supposed that economic development wields the sole influence on law, and yet it has plainly appeared that it must wield a great and perhaps the chief influence. Looking at the picture as a whole and in its simplest terms, we can see clearly that, for example, the Food Gatherers, in any part of the world, by the nature of their economy are incapable of producing the development of law that we have recorded, or even making use of it. And it is only this correlation of visible economic and legal development that can enable us to achieve our ambition of drawing some outlines of the pre-history of law before it appears in the old Codes, even if this pre-history was never enacted wholly in one place or in the full order of events that we have sketched.

At the point we have now reached, namely at the commencement of our Third Agricultural Grade (A.3 (1)) there begins a great leap forward in material culture caused by, or accompanying the combination with agriculture of two great inventions, the domestication of cattle (that of sheep and goats being less important) and the winning and use of metals. We have already witnessed two recent, smaller but spectacular advances – the changes wrought in the life of the Food Gatherers and Hunters of North America by the acquisition of the horse from the European in the seventeenth century and after, and the development of the agricultural economies of the South Seas by the introduction or domestication of the pig. The advance to which we now refer is much greater, and old in the history of man.

But our Third Agricultural Grade embraces economies of a long stride of development ranging between peoples little more advanced than the least developed economies of the last chapter, and States and Empires standing at the close of what we have chosen to call the Primitive Age, and we must subdivide them. But there is difficulty, at least the present author has difficulty, in separating steps of material development within it; also law, found almost everywhere except in some of the most backward economies, shows rapid development and degrees of progress which are easier to distinguish, namely the stages we marked out among the peoples of the Codes. Accordingly, while the stages will be defined in both economic and legal terms, it will be especially by the legal. Examples will be taken chiefly from the African continent, because the bulk of the known peoples of the grade are found there, and because the African information is contemporary and far fuller and more precise than elsewhere, and relates to peoples living, or recently living, politically independent lives. The inference that these stages are stages of economic advance is reinforced by consideration of the area where these tribes are found: the successive stages are often between those where white contact has been most recent and those where it is of earliest date.

We began then with the first stage (A.3 (1)), the least developed economies of the Third Agricultural Grade. In economic terms they are peoples who practise agriculture (or horticulture), have cattle and perhaps sheep or goats (and in Germany horses) and are familiar with the winning, smelting and use of iron. But this triple combination is hardly complete in the most backward of these economies. Some have few head of cattle,[1] others little or no agriculture,[2] some have acquired iron in recent times and do

---

[1] e.g. Anuak, Kikuyu, Tallensi. Among the latter 95 per cent earn their living wholly on the land and the remaining 5 per cent partly so, and only a rich man has more than a couple of head of cattle: Fortes (1945), 9.
[2] e.g. Pastoral Masai, Pastoral Suk.

not smelt it. Their technology is little and crude except in a few more forward economies; they have no writing, their manufactures and arts are at first few, and none in Africa have the wheel, the cart or the plough.[1] There are no markets[2] except among some of the Bantu. With almost all of them central government is wanting and the authority of chiefs and headmen is weak. The village or settlement with a population of 50-500 persons is generally the basic economic and political unit. There is little hunting, fishing[3] or gathering.

In legal terms we define this stage as follows. There are in most but not all places persons possessing jurisdiction, but their powers are generally very small. We do not hear of legislation. Homicide (where law exists) is everywhere a civil wrong for which the legal sanctions are compensatory, consisting mainly of a fixed number of cattle or goats but sometimes (where cattle are few) the handing over of a person to the family of the slain. Among the most forward peoples an unwritten code is to be found, consisting of a tariff of a fixed number of animals payable for homicide, wounding, sexual wrongs and theft. The bridewealth marriage is everywhere, the marriage settlement is unknown and marriage gifts from the bride's side few or none. Marriage is generally virilocal and descent patrilineal. Ordeals are to be found everywhere for cases where evidence is insufficient. The criminal law is very undeveloped and criminal offences consist chiefly of witchcraft (especially witchcraft causing a death), incest and persistent theft. The sanction, where it is imposed, is usually death by lynching, stoning or drowning at the hands of the general public and destruction of the offender's home.

These peoples are represented in the old world by the tribes of Germany as we read of them in the accounts of Julius Caesar[4] and Tacitus,[5] and in the first quarter of the present century by the following peoples of East Africa – such Nilotic peoples as the

---

[1] As indeed had no peoples south of Egypt, except Ethiopia.
[2] At one time the Kamba had had a sort of unperiodic market day when women met and exchanged their products (especially pottery), but the practice disappeared: Lindblom (1920), 580. For the Bantu of North Kavirondo, see Wagner (1951), II, 161f.
[3] Except e.g. the Nuer in the dry season.
[4] *De Bello Gallico* IV, 1-3, VI, 21-24, published 51 B.C.
[5] *Germania*, published A.D. 98.

Nuer, Dinka (of closely similar culture), Anuak,[1] Shilluk[2] and Lango[3] (the last three speaking closely similar languages) and the Jaluo Nilotic Kavirondo;[4] such so-called Half Hamitic peoples as the Masai[5] and Nandi,[6] and such Nandi-speaking peoples as the Kipsigis[7] and the Suk (or Pokot),[8] and such Bantu peoples as the Kikuyu,[9] Kamba[10] and Bantu of North Kavirondo.[11] We may add an example from West Africa, namely the Tallensi,[12] in what was in the 1930s the Northern Territories of the Gold Coast, living a few miles north of the White Volta River and west of the Red Volta. In the absence of cattle there are no corresponding peoples in North or South America or Oceania, and the evidence from Asia is deficient.

The size of these populations, though not always of the political entities, shows considerable increase. The Nuer population, for example, totalled in 1930 about 214,000, the sizes of most of the individual 'tribes' varying between 7,000 and 42,000 souls; the Anuak about 40,000; the Shilluk Kingdom about 100,000; the Lango (1923) about 250,000; the pastoral Masai about 80,000; the Nandi about 48,000; the Kipsigis 80,000, the Suk or Pokot (1950) 25,000; the Kikuyu (1931) 603,697; the Kamba (1910) 235,000; the twenty or so tribes of the Bantu of North Kavirondo (1937) 312,000 and the Tallensi only 35,000. The sizes of the German populations were probably of the same order.[13] The growth of

---

[1] South Sudan, all three inhabiting the swamps and open savannah at or near the junction of the White Nile and the Sobat and Bahr-el-Ghazal.
[2] Mainly west bank of the Nile from Lake No to about 12° N.
[3] Of Uganda, immediately north of Lake Victoria.
[4] North side of the Kavirondo Gulf, north-east of Lake Victoria.
[5] Kenya and Tanzania, east of Lake Victoria, in two sections, one of which is purely pastoral, the other also agricultural. We are concerned chiefly with the former in this chapter, and the word Masai used without qualification indicates the pastoral Masai.
[6] Nandi Plateau, Kenya. North-east of Lake Victoria.
[7] Highlands of Kenya, south of Nandi Plateau.
[8] North of Nandi Plateau, on boundaries of North-west Kenya and Uganda.
[9] Kenya, between Mount Kenya in the north-east, the Great Rift Valley in the west and Nairobi in the south. The Bantu prefixes are omitted in this book from all names.   [10] Over a large area south-east of Kikuyu.
[11] Kenya, north-east of Lake Victoria.
[12] See, as to the Tallensi, Fortes (1940), (1945) and (1949).
[13] For the sizes of the German tribes, see Krzywicki (1934), 79-83, and for some other figures of East African peoples, R. R. Kuczynski, *A Demographic Survey of the British Colonial Empire*, vol. II (1949).

populations and the greater extent of intercommunication is shown by the evidence of fission and merger in Germany and East Africa and a history of almost continual movement. Few, if any, of these German and African peoples can have been for as long as three centuries in the territories in which we find them and many have altered their means of subsistence. The Nuer and Nandi with all their passion for their cattle, say they were formerly hunters, and even the pastoral Masai and the pastoral Pokot in all probability at some time abandoned the practice of some agriculture. The Kipsigis say they were originally pastoralists and their agriculture was the invention of the women. The tempo of change continues to quicken, though the influence of civilized peoples has hardly begun to operate. And though the Food Gatherers, Hunters and Agriculturists, whom we mentioned in early chapters, died out or were sadly reduced in numbers on the advent of civilized man, the peoples of the present chapter are adaptable and on contact with civilization their rate of increase has accelerated.[1] The facts of language tell the same story. The German tribes all spoke close dialects of one Gothonic group of the Indo-European family of languages, the Nilotes one Nilotic branch of the Sudanic group of languages, of whom the Nuer and Dinka speak substantially one language, as do the Shilluk and Lango notwithstanding the great distance that now separates them, and the Anuak a closely similar language. The Nandi, Kipsigis and Pokot all speak the same language with dialectal differences, and the Masai a connected tongue. The Kikuyu and Kamba are considered by themselves and others to have been formerly one tribe, and all these Bantu-speaking peoples are among the most northerly of a group of mixed Hamitic, Negro and Bushman descent, speaking one closely connected group of languages, that have spread during the last 1,500 years or so from this area to the whole of the southern third of Africa and parts of the western and eastern coasts. The Tallensi and many of their neighbours speak one and the same Sudanic dialect.

This combination of agriculture and cattle-keeping produces in Germany and East Africa communities of smallholders, in which the basic economic unit is the homestead, a household

[1] See for some figures of high fertility among the women, Driberg (1923), 146-7.

consisting generally of a hut for husband, wife and children (or in polygynous families a hut for each wife and her children) and some goats and sheep, and often on a second floor a small granary, and sometimes in a separate room on the ground floor accommodation for more animals, and a large byre where the cattle can shelter, all often surrounded by a hedge or stockade. Outside it are the fields of the homestead, the cattle being herded further off, in many cases jointly by boys and youths of a wider group. The huts and byre usually consist of wattle and daub on a framework of stouter branches, the whole thatched; and there is commonly a distance of a hundred yards to a mile or more[1] between homesteads, which may form a local cluster that may be called a hamlet or settlement, the hamlets forming in some peoples a village,[2] sometimes walled or fenced. The local concentrations of population are much greater in some parts than elsewhere. Kenya, for example, contains on the Kavirondo Gulf some of the most fertile land in the world, and further north much desert; on the other hand in Southern Sudan, at the confluence of the White Nile and the Bahr-el-Ghazal, a seasonal alternation of drought and flood brings about a migration of village communities to dry-season camps and back. The density of population varies much accordingly, in these different habitats.[3]

On the whole, the economic progress is from pastoralism to a growing extent of agriculture. So, according to Caesar, 'the Germans are not interested in agriculture and live principally upon milk, cheese and meat'.[4] In the pages of Tacitus,[5] 150 years later, the tribes are described as also growing grain. Yet still their cattle 'are indeed the most highly prized, nay the only riches of the people'. 'They are mostly, however, undersized: it is chiefly their number that they value.'[6] All these peoples esteem wealth highly

---

[1] e.g. Tac. Germ. 16; agricultural Pokot (Peristiany (1954), 18); Nandi; Kipsigis; Kikuyu; bulk of Bantu of North Kavirondo.
[2] Nuer villages consist of small groups of habitations each separated by fifty to several hundred yards: Evans-Pritchard (1951), 2. No villages among Nandi. For agricultural Pokot, see Peristiany (1954). The Tallensi live in settlements consisting of irregular blocks of homesteads without fixed territorial boundaries: Fortes (1945), 159f.
[3] Nuer, about 6 persons per square mile; Kamba 19; Nandi 66; Kipsigis 97; Bantu of North Kavirondo 140, varying between 54 and 1,137; Tallensi (in 1931) about 100.
[4] Caesar, D.B.G. VI, 22.   [5] Tac. Germ. 5 and 25.   [6] Tac. Germ. 5.

and pursue it, but the thoughts and emotions of the mainly pastoral peoples are concentrated on their cattle, which are basic to every aspect of their lives. They despise the agricultural peoples and regard themselves as tillers by necessity. Among the Germans the cultivation of the land is by slaves.[1] These peoples rarely kill cattle for food alone and they live principally on milk and milk products. The amount of cattle possessed by each of these peoples and their tribes varies accordingly.[2] The cows are usually milked by the women, girls and small boys. The status of the woman has fallen much, less among the Lango and Germans and most among the Bantu.

Among most of the peoples of this chapter the men do the heavy work of burning and clearing the land and breaking it for cultivation and the women do the bulk of the rest, with some help from the men in sowing and harvesting; but in the more agricultural peoples the men cultivate their own fields. There is some rotation of crops[3] and land left fallow, but there is much surplus land and after a few years new land is cleared.[4] In some places, as among the agricultural Masai, Kamba and some of the Pokot, the practice of irrigation is well developed. The digging-stick, still in use for virgin or rocky ground, begins to be supplanted by an iron hoe.[5] The crops grown in Germany are almost entirely grain: in Africa mainly millet and eleusine[6] and recently maize,[7] introduced by the European, and among the Bantu, beans, peas, sweet potatoes, bananas, sugar cane, manioc and other crops introduced by the European. There is substantially no growing of fruit in Germany or Africa. Hunting and fishing is men's work: the women collect wild plants and fruits and do the bulk of the

---

[1] They occupy their home on terms of supplying their master with a stated quantity of grain, cattle or clothing. (Tac. Germ. 5.)
[2] See figures, post p. 244. They vary from the Masai, estimated to possess about twelve head of cattle per person, to the Anuak and Kikuyu who possess hardly any.
[3] Among the Kamba, Kikuyu and Lango, not among the Nuer or other Nilotes.
[4] But the essential feature of Tallensi agriculture is fixed cultivation: Fortes (1940), 248.
[5] Usually in the shape of a spear-head set into a short handle, by which the ground may be prised up. The area entered the Iron Age in the early years of the century, not having known bronze.
[6] Traditionally, in some places, discovered by the women.
[7] Grain, in Germany and Africa, is mostly eaten in the form of porridge.

domestic work and the men make the hunting and warlike weapons and the other implements they use. The brewing of beer, which is of great social importance, is mainly the work of the women.

Among the more developed economies of the Bantu tribes the manufactures have increased and include stools and other domestic utensils, pottery (the work of some of the women),[1] basketry (men's work), chairs and bracelets. Only among the Bantu is trade developed. There is hardly a beginning of markets except among the Kikuyu,[2] but Kamba travel far with their wares. Apart from the magicians or diviners and the specialization between the sexes, almost the only industrial specialization is that of the smiths, among the more pastoral peoples a despised and often foreign class or hereditary gild, and sometimes the drum-makers.[3] The chief transaction is barter[4] but cattle and goats and often grain play a prominent part in the estimation of values and as medium of exchange. An agreement for the making of an article by a smith is often on the terms of supplying him with the charcoal and other needed materials, a lump sum in the form of a cow or goat, and sometimes grain for his support during the work. Mnemonic devices[5] and methods of calculation and divisions of the year into months and seasons are prominent in the Bantu tribes and here and there is a *lingua franca*.

It is not the object of this book to attempt to shed any light on a history of religion, but it is difficult to avoid seeing in the more pastoral peoples a single-mindedness which expresses itself in something approaching a monotheism.[6] There is no cannibalism, except of a ceremonial character and little of human sacrifice,[7]

---

[1] But among the Kipsigis mainly confined to some Jaluo immigrant men, though some Kipsigis women have learnt the technique: Peristiany (1939), 148.
[2] See a list of goods sold in a Kikuyu market about 1908: Routledge (1910), 106.
[3] Lango.   [4] Tac. Germ. 5.
[5] e.g. Kamba, notched sticks or a bundle of pegs recording animals paid for bridewealth.
[6] 'They do not think fit to contain the magnitude of these celestial beings within four walls, nor to simulate them by any human likeness: they consecrate groves and call by the name of gods that abstraction which is only visible to the eye of reverence.' (Tac. Germ. 9.)
[7] Some in Germany, and some among the Nilotes, e.g. Shilluk, Anuak: Seligman (1932), 92f., 98, 111.

but a belief among most or all of these African and German tribes in an all-pervading spirit, God and creator, usually associated with the sun or sky,[1] to whom they address occasional prayers for cattle, children and wives and sacrifice animals.[2] The name of the God often transcends the boundary of a people, a language or a race. There are also prophets who have received the will of the God in visions or trances, and oracles who give answers on his behalf, and sometimes 'priests' also officiate at a sacred grove or tree or intercede with him for the people. Even witch-doctors may derive their powers from him. But there is also a belief in the existence of spirits, mainly of deceased ancestors, who can be mischievous. There is also in Germany and Africa a widespread practice of taking auspices as to the success of a raid or journey or even of the correctness of the decision of a court, by examining the entrails of sacrificial animals or the behaviour of birds or by casting lots.[3] Religion and magic do not impinge upon the fields of law except at the points mentioned in earlier chapters; but where there is no law (as among the Tallensi) religious sanctions operate to support order.[4]

Partly, perhaps, because of the passion for cattle and its vulnerability to attack and capture, war is the almost perpetual relation between neighbouring groups of the more pastoral peoples, even between 'tribes' or villages of the same people if they are traditional enemies. The common type of offensive is still an approach by a raiding party at night to striking distance after taking the auspices, and an attack at dawn; the chief change is a great advance in tactical skill and military organization. The Germans, who are sufficient to harass the Roman Empire and break down its frontiers, commonly attack, according to Tacitus, in wedge-shaped formation. The Nuer, Masai and Nandi terrorize their neighbours. In a battle of any size the Lango attack proceeds generally in three columns, the two wings in advance of the

[1] In East Africa the names of the God are *Asista* (Nandi, Kipsigis, Bantu of North Kavirondo), *Eng-Aï* or *Ngai* (Masai, Kamba, Kikuyu), *Juok* (Shilluk, Anuak, Acholi, Lango), *Kwoth* (Nuer), *Nhialic* (Dinka) and also among the Kamba *Mulungu*. The name of a god spreads beyond the bounds of a language or race. Eng-Aï is Masai for 'the sky, the rain', and has no meaning in Bantu. Among the Tallensi (as in many peoples of West Africa) the cult is of the Earth Goddess.
[2] Not the Kamba.   [3] e.g. Germany, Nandi, Kipsigis, Lango, Kamba.
[4] e.g. Fortes (1940), 241, 243; (1945), 243.

centre, which contains the best and most seasoned warriors and awaits the advance of the enemy centre when his flanks have been crushed. In a Kamba raid on the Masai one column, consisting of the best troops, attacks the kraal of Masai warriors and holds them off while a second column attacks the kraals of the married and the cattle, handing them over to a non-combatant column whose retreat with the captured cattle, girls and children is covered by the first two columns.[1] The warriors are now commonly organized on a kinship,[2] village[3] or other territorial basis,[4] and whatever be the political organization or lack of central authority there are mostly permanent[5] or elected[6] war chiefs or generals, who are given great authority in war.[7] Slavery is mild and there is little of it.[8]

The age-grade system is perhaps more prominent at this stage in East Africa than in any of the peoples of the preceding or subsequent stages; but round this natural and close relationship between persons, and especially males, of the same age, and a natural deference to elders, in the manner familiar in human society there has clustered in different peoples, and often in different tribes of the same people, a different assortment of incidents and functions. For example, among the Nuer[9] it is chiefly a system which determines social relations, mainly kinship and domestic, and not political, by establishing degrees of seniority. Among other peoples the system is a military,[10] political and administrative organization. Among some of these the system is integral with the practice of circumcision, so that, in the familiar male grading of boys, warriors and elders, a boy passes into the

---

[1] The weapons of war of the Nilotes, Nandi and Kikuyu are spears, swords, clubs and shields. Among the Masai, Nandi and Kikuyu the older men and boys use the bow and arrow (mostly poisoned). The Kamba do not use spears or shields: Hobley (1910), 43f.; Lindblom (1920), 449.
[2] Hollis (1909), 9, 11; Peristiany (1939), 164.
[3] Evans-Pritchard (1940), 254 (village and tribal section).
[4] Peristiany (1939), 164f.; Evans-Pritchard (1940), 254.
[5] Peristiany (1939), 164f. Here the forces are differently organized for everyday defence and for offensives.
[6] Tac. Germ. 7.
[7] Among the Tallensi there is no central authority, no law and no regular military organization.
[8] Kamba: Hobley (1910), 48; Lindblom (1920), 160, 196. Kikuyu: Routledge (1910), 16.
[9] Evans-Pritchard (1940), 253f.   [10] e.g. Dinka.

grade of warrior on circumcision.[1] Among others of these peoples membership of an age-grade is given on maturity irrespective of circumcision, though it is practised.[2] In others these grades are further subdivided into a series of minor grades.[3] Among some peoples at a certain stage in the age-grades there is a formal handing-over of the country to the new age-grade, which thus comes into power and is entrusted with its safety.[4] Among the Kamba[5] there is erected upon the senior grade a system of ranks which are obtained by purchase, the price varying according to the rank. Among the Tallensi, where there is no age-grade system, the chiefs buy their offices.[6] Nobility is found in many places, but its influence and power varies much, as we shall see.

The clans (totemic only in certain peoples and areas)[7] are in evidence everywhere, and as the population and clans expand in size the lineage is perhaps more prominent than before. As the economic status of the woman falls, and marriage is everywhere virilocal and the clans everywhere patrilineal, the paternal relationship is at the centre of the structure of society though the maternal relationship, and especially that between a man and his sister's son, is everywhere recognized and appreciated.[8] Since the sons on marriage take up residence on or next to the paternal homestead, in most or all of these peoples there is in the hamlet one lineage or joint or extended family, and in the village or settlement a lineage which is dominant in numbers and prestige, notwithstanding the admission into residence of some cognates, affines and strangers to the clan, and is sometimes considered to own the soil.[9] It is therefore usually at the level of the village or similar unit[10] that the kinship relation combines with the territorial

---

[1] Nandi: Hollis (1909), 11. Kipsigis: Peristiany (1939), 29f. Masai: Hollis (1905), 261f. Bantu of North Kavirondo: Wagner (1949), I, 28.
[2] Kamba: Lindblom (1920), 142f. Hobley (1910), 49.
[3] Masai: Hollis (1905), 262. Some Bantu Kavirondo: Wagner (1949), I, 375.
[4] Nandi: Hollis (1909), 12.   [5] Lindblom, ibid.   [6] Fortes (1940), 255f.
[7] Usually not totemic among Nilotes, nor, probably in Germany; totemic e.g. in Nandi, Kipsigis, Kamba (Lindblom (1920), 114, Hobley (1910), 4), Kikuyu (Routledge (1910), 22f.) but doubtful in Bantu of North Kavirondo (Wagner (1949), I, 198f.).
[8] Especially among the Lango and in Germany (Tac. Germ. 20).
[9] Nuer.
[10] Nuer (village or settlement), Anuak (village), Shilluk (settlement). Irrigation Pokot (village: Peristiany (1954), 18). There are no villages among the Nandi or Kikuyu, only homesteads surrounded by hedge or stockade.

principle of division, and the village is the lowest and basic political unit of the people. Above this level, however, the kinship and territorial systems continue though they vary in strength and scale between peoples and even between tribes. The village is part of the district (with possibly a shire intervening) within which the villagers have social contacts of various kinds, within which they intermarry or combine in rites or dances, feuds or raiding parties, and such a district may be a whole tribe or a segment of it[1] according to the size of the tribe and other local conditions, and may be bound up with a dominant clan or sub-clan of the tribe or a lineage of it. The smaller the segment the greater is the sense of unity within it and the more effective is, for example, the age-grade system. The districts, like the villages and tribes, are in most places politically independent.[2] There is also, as we said, an independent kinship organization above the village (for the lineage dominant in a village is part of a clan) and the clan does not coincide with a district and may extend beyond a tribe and sometimes even a people. A tribe is the largest group which combines for raiding or defence. But there is much variation of this picture from people to people and these varying features are especially important incidents of the judicial system. Though, to take an extreme case, every Nuer regards all Nuer as being distinct from other peoples, and theoretically compensation for a wrong can be obtained between members of the same Nuer 'tribe', sometimes the relations between one village and another of the same Nuer tribe can be called international in the sense that for an inhabitant of one village to obtain compensation for homicide from inhabitants of another, inter-village war is requisite. At the other extreme the Kipsigis regard some other Nandi-speaking peoples (the Nandi, Keyo and Suk) as so closely related to them that they pay and receive bloodwealth between them. Overall, the relations between members of a lineage, clan, district or segment, tribe and people are matters of degree and in some aspects of life are sometimes closer than in others.

[1] Nuer, primary, secondary or tertiary segments according to the size of the tribe, a tertiary being a division of a secondary segment and a secondary of a primary, each possessing a separate name and territory and some common sentiments: Evans-Pritchard (1940), 142. The segments are territorial but in the main also follow the general lines of kinship cleavage.
[2] Evans-Pritchard (1940), 142.

In respect of organs of government and the authority of chiefs or headmen, we see between people and people differences as great as in the previous chapter. Among the Nuer and Tallensi there are no governmental or judicial organs of people, tribe, tribal sections, village or settlement and nowhere developed leadership except on the part of the lineage head, and therefore strictly speaking, there is no law. The so-called leopard-skin chiefs of the Nuer are merely ritual experts whose almost sole function is to settle a feud. Children are subject to parents and a wife to her husband; a man who has been initiated and has begotten children may have a good social standing and give advice on occasion upon a ritual or secular matter; in their raids Nuer follow courageous leaders; but whatever other leadership exists among Nuer and Tallensi must be found in family and kinship relations.[1]

Yet in a neighbouring Nilotic people speaking a kindred language, the Shilluk, there is the central organization of a kingdom. The hamlet of 2 to 50 homesteads (5 to 200 persons) belonging to one joint family or small lineage, has a headman who is head of the lineage, and the hamlets are grouped in some 100 settlements, each of 400 to 2,000 souls with a common chief and council on which the headmen of the hamlets sit. The chief is a member of the dominant lineage, which enjoys prestige as owners of the soil, and the settlements are political units. Above them are the two chiefs of North and South Shillukland and above these the Shilluk king, the descendant of a long line of kings. Lesser disputes are brought before the chiefs but all disputes can be brought to the king. Nevertheless his office is chiefly ritual and priestly. He is a peacemaker rather than a judge and it does not appear that he exercises his judicial powers frequently, though he exacts tribute and taxes and may intervene by force to put down

---

[1] Evans-Pritchard (1940), 172f. Subsequently under the Chief's Courts Ordinance of 1931, such courts were set up, administering 'native law and custom', see Howell, *A Manual of Nuer Law* (1954), 2. This remarkable book shows vividly how the provision of courts may lead to the development into law of inherent principles of native custom. Similarly among the Tallensi, where the British gave administrative and judicial powers to chiefs and headmen whereby custom and law were developed: see Fortes (1940), 266; (1945), 12. The former method of settling disputes between Tallensi was by negotiation between heads of lineages backed by armed self-help: Fortes (1945), 13.

recalcitrants and burn their homes and he takes the bloodwealth and other compensation and keeps most of it for himself.[1]

On the other hand the neighbouring Anuak, though reputedly of a common origin with the Shilluk, are now mainly agricultural. The village, with a population of 50 to 500 souls, is associated with a locally dominant lineage. It is self-subsistent and independent and is the largest political and economic unit. In some areas of the country there is a hereditary headman of the village, sometimes of considerable power and judicial authority, in others a hereditary noble of varying authority, the possessor of certain ritual objects. There is theoretically a kingship of the Anuak but the king is difficult to find: there are royal emblems, which are competed for by the nobles but there is no Anuak word for 'king' and no central government.[2]

The Lango, too, pastoralists engaged of necessity also as agriculturists, are believed to have a common origin with the Shilluk, but before the year 1914[3] they had no settled or constituted tribal authority and were divided into a number of factions unrelated to their clan system and often mutually hostile. The organization of the country was essentially a military hierarchy, the village leader (*jago*) combining with the leaders of other villages under the column leader (*rwot*), the functionary most resembling a chief and often the elected head of his clan, and the column leaders combining under the war leader (*twon lwak*), all owing their position chiefly to military success and prestige. In other respects the only administrative or judicial bodies were the informal gatherings of the village elders to settle intra-village and inter-village disputes in co-operation with the *jago* or *rwot*. But there was no power to enforce their decisions except public opinion and only within the village or between friendly villages in the same district was it possible to obtain satisfaction without violence.

Turning to the Nilo-Hamites, we find among the Kipsigis,[4] the largest of the Nandi-speaking peoples, that the political structure is territorial rather than kinship, and that the judicial and administrative officers loom largely in it. The hamlets are combined in a *kokwet* or village of some fifteen to sixty huts (60 to 300 persons), which is the basic political and economic unit. In every division

[1] Shilluk: Evans-Pritchard (1948).   [2] Anuak: Evans-Pritchard (1940).
[3] Driberg (1923), 204f.   [4] Peristiany (1939), and especially Chap. X.

(*temet*) of the village there is an elder of judicial and legal experience, who endeavours to reconcile disputants and, if he fails, sends them to the village judge and headman (*poyot ab kokwet*). The latter, after further attempts at reconciliation, tries small disputes with his assistant and council of elders. There is also a village economic leader (*kiptayat ab kokwet*) and as the village is also the unit for military defence it has a war leader (*kiptayat ab muenek*) but the *poyot* heads the whole. Beyond the village comes the unnamed grouping which we may call the shire, consisting of a number of villages headed by the Great Judge and governor (*Kiruogindet neo*) with his assistant and council, on which sit the village judges and other elders. They decide questions concerning the welfare of the community, all cases which come before the village *poyot* and were not completed by him, and in the first instances all cases of divorce, homicide and witchcraft. There is also a chief of warriors of the shire (*kiptayat neo neb omurenek*) and a religious head (*poyot ab tumda*), independent officers except that the military chief must in all important matters consult the Great Judge and obey him. Beyond the shire is the province or district (*emet*), the largest organized judicial and military unit, of which there are four, administered by the Great Judge and the leaders and elders of the military. This council hears questions relating to more than one shire and cases between persons of different shires, and here the judges of the two shires preside. So that, among the Kipsigis, the elected judges are in effect the administrators.

There is a system among the Nandi which contains some similar general features, except that there are no villages – only homesteads, parishes and districts. The *kiruogindet*, the spokesman or councillor chosen by the people, is the administrative head of each district, but of recent times the country has acknowledged the overlordship of the *orkoyot*, or chief magician. But though his prestige and influence is great, his functions are religious and the chief authority is that of the kinship leaders of each district. The *orkoyot* corresponds to the *ol-oiboni* of the Masai, amongst whom the kinship leaders of the district and the leaders of the age-sets wield the chief influence.[1]

[1] Since the beginning of the present century, a territorial system of division has overlaid the Masai kinship system which has decayed. See Hollis (1905), 299, for a description of an election of a chief of the warriors of a sub-district.

When we turn to the Bantu peoples we find a similar degree of variation. In two large tribes of north Kavirondo, the Vugusu and Logoli, pastoralists in varying degree,[1] there are no chiefs and such influence as exists is based upon kinship. The main judicial authority is exercised by the old men of the sub-clan, but there is no organized judicial assembly and no means of enforcing a judgment except public opinion. If a feud ensues the head of the relevant clan or sub-clan endeavours to reconcile the parties, and if they belong to two different clans the elders and warriors of both clans. If the offence is of a more serious character the elders of the different sub-clans may assemble to prevent fighting and discuss and decide the matter, and opinions of strong personalities, possessing prestige as warriors and generous givers of feasts, carry special weight. Between tribes, war is the only arbiter.

On the other hand among the Kamba and Kikuyu, who are mainly agriculturists, such government as existed was that of the leaders of the seniors' age-group, forming local councils of elders without heads or chairmen. The Kamba had no chiefs,[2] though a rich man of rank and intelligence and commanding personality might attain to leadership over a neighbourhood; nor were there chiefs among the Kikuyu though a dozen or so homesteads might unite under a leader or headman, whom they would usually disobey. In neither country was there a council of the whole people; the local councils[3] heard and decided disputes and claims between individuals and charges of crime and also matters of public order and welfare such as the maintenance of religious practice and public sacrifice.[4] There was also in most places in both countries a voluntary official police,[5] consisting of members of a younger age-group, which supported the council by enforcing the attendance of litigants and carrying out the council's decisions, if necessary by seizing the defendant's goats. And yet even here the courts are weak. A court of Kikuyu elders, to avoid

[1] Vugusu: land less fertile, population 40,000 in 1940, 9 head of cattle per family. Logoli: 45,000, land more fertile but one-seventh the area, 2 or 3 head of cattle per family. See Wagner (1949).
[2] Lindblom (1920), 151.
[3] Kamba, *nzama*; Kikuyu, *kiama*.
[4] Lindblom (1920), 150.
[5] Kamba, *kizuka*; Kikuyu, *njama*, consisting of former leading warriors, with often an elected head. See Lindblom (1920), 152f.

announcing its decision against a party, usually advises him to consult his friends, and he then retires with his supporters and returns having admitted his guilt to them and asks for leniency.[1]

Among the Germans of the times of Caesar and Tacitus there was little of the democratic spirit of the Nuer and these other modern peoples of East Africa. Above the serfs, that is to say slaves attached to their master's lands, came the general body of freemen, and above them the hereditary nobles, and the most prominent of these were the chiefs, who led by virtue of their prestige and influence, largely derived from the possession of a retinue of free, mostly noble, warriors who adhered to them and gave them allegiance, but also by their eloquence and military achievements.[2] In some places, at any rate in wartime, there was also from time to time a recognized chief of the whole people, who might properly be called a king, though he exercised an influence to persuade rather than the power to command. The chiefs made the minor political decisions and discussed the major questions before bringing them before the general assembly of the freemen of the tribe for their approval or rejection. Punishments for crime and some serious private wrongs were imposed in regular meetings of the assembly, but it also chose chiefs to administer justice in their several districts (*pagi*) and villages with their informal councils of elders. Priests maintained order in the assemblies and imposed the capital sentences.

Summing up these brief and superficial accounts of the government or want of government of these peoples, from the Nuer, who have no apparent government, and the neighbouring Shilluk with their ancient monarchy, to the Kikuyu and Kamba, with their purely local government, it is difficult to see any common features. One thing at least we are taught, that we are not looking in the only direction, or perhaps even the best direction, to find government. The other forces supporting order must be recognized: the power of the father as owner of the family property over wives and sons, after his death the influence of the eldest son over his brothers, the bonds with members of age-sets, agnatic kin, affines and maternal relatives, the personal relationships between individuals and groups with common interests, economic, social and ritual, the personal influence of a few rich

[1] Routledge (1910), 208.   [2] Tac. Germ. 11 (5).

men, successful warriors and sages, all of which cut across other groupings, the desire for public approval, the fear of violent reprisals by offended groups and individuals, and all the other factors mentioned in earlier chapters, making for social control.[1]

Applying the criteria mentioned in an earlier chapter[2] we must conclude on the facts stated in this chapter and the two that follow that there was no law among the Nuer or Tallensi in the 1920s, but there was law in the other peoples mentioned, and we shall presently see its extent and its rules.

Litigation is the delight of the Kamba and Kikuyu, and now of the Nuer under the new dispensation instituted by the Sudan Government.[3] There is a facility for law and what we may call a legal mind in these peoples. But very few, if any, of them have a notion of law in the abstract. Most are familiar with customs and courts and actions in the courts and judgments, but they have no word for law. The Nuer have the terms *cuong* (right) and *duer* (wrong) but no word for law,[4] and even the Kamba have no word for law.[5] But we are told that the Kipsigis word *pitet* signifies law and custom, including the body of customs which carry with them definite material punishments for breach.[6]

---

[1] For a brilliant analysis of social control among the Arusha (Agricultural Masai of Northern Tanzania) see Gulliver (1963).
[2] Chap. 14.
[3] Lindblom (1920), 152f.; Evans-Pritchard (1940), 162f.; Howell (1954), 225.
[4] Evans-Pritchard (1940), *passim*; Howell (1954), 225.
[5] Lindblom (1920), 153.   [6] Peristiany (1939), 183.

CHAPTER 17

Cattle Keepers – The Law

Turning to the rules of law, and rules of conduct adjacent to the field of law, we find between these peoples of our First Stage of the Third Agricultural Grade a close resemblance both in East Africa and Germany.

Marriage is accompanied and validated by bridewealth (sometimes inappropriately called the brideprice), a sum of property, chiefly in the form of animals,[1] transferred from the groom's to the bride's people and usually of enormous size. For example, among the Nuer there are on the average about $1\frac{1}{2}$ head of cattle per person, or about 8 per family,[2] and the bridewealth is ideally 40 and in fact about 20 to 30 head. It seems unlikely that the Lango own as much as an average of half a head per person, yet the bridewealth varies from 4 to 10 head and 5 is normal.[3] Among the Bantu Kavirondo, the Logoli own an average of half a head per person or 2 to 3 per family and the bridewealth varies between 1 and 4 cows (apart from goats and hoes); the Vugusu own 2 head per person or 9 per family and the bridewealth is between 5 and 15 head. Among the Kamba the bridewealth is usually 2 cows and 2 bulls and a variable number of goats (a rich man may give 100 or more) and in the South East (where cattle cannot be kept owing to the prevalence of tsetse-fly) 60 to 100 goats.[4] Among the Kikuyu (few of whom have cattle) it is usually 40 goats and 5 sheep. Among the Tallensi few men have more than 2 head of cattle and the bridewealth is about 4 head apart from some initiatory gifts, and the father customarily pays the bridewealth for a son's first

[1] But e.g. paid in lumps of iron among the ironworking clans of the Dinka: Seligman (1932), 160f.   [2] Howell (1954), App. I.
[2] In the west, where no cattle can be kept, forty-five to eighty goats together often with spears, hoes and even chickens: Driberg (1923), 159.
[4] Lindblom (1920), 72f.

wife.[1] As an average in all these peoples the bridewealth is larger than the total herd possessed by the groom's father and its payment commonly impoverishes the family for a time and would be impossible but for the contributions of relatives. As the father owns practically all the family's possessions for the benefit of the family, it is out of the question for a youth to obtain a wife unaided.

The bridewealth includes in many peoples a variety of articles of property. The Shilluk, for example, possess about $1\frac{1}{4}$ head of cattle per person and the bridewealth is commonly 17 (or some smaller number) of cows, upwards of 7 sheep, 4 hoes, 2 fish spears and 4 other spears, a basketful of tobacco and a bundle of firewood,[2] and among the Germans of Tacitus it consisted typically of a number of oxen, a caparisoned horse, a shield, lance and sword.[3] The amount of the bridewealth usually varies much in each tribe according to the wealth of the families (especially of the groom's) and from season to season according to the ravages of disease and the scarcity of cattle.[4] Before the severe outbreak of rinderpest in the early 1890s the number of cattle paid in East Africa was greater.

In many or most peoples the property is allowed to be transferred by instalments, sometimes over a period of many years, and in many cases cohabitation is allowed to begin before the total has been paid. The conclusion of a marriage is usually a progressive transaction, gifts, called by special terms, being made to the bride's relatives at different stages in the negotiations and at their close, and in several of these peoples the wedding, and sometimes also the betrothal, the consummation of marriage and the birth of a child, are marked by ceremonial rites. In some peoples the young couple continue to reside with the wife's family for a time, till the first or second child is born[5] and in some a marriage is not considered to be concluded and complete till

[1] A man with a dozen sheep, a few goats and three or four head of cattle is considered wealthy: Fortes (1949), 86.
[2] Anuak: beads, bracelets, old spears, sheep and goats.
[3] Tac. Germ. 18.
[4] Also according to the number of relatives claiming to share in it: Evans-Pritchard (1951), 82. In some peoples, however, it is almost invariable in amount – e.g. Kipsigis, eight cows and twenty-three goats paid, but a rich man will pay more quickly and perhaps add two or three goats: Peristiany (1939), 56.   [5] Nuer: Evans-Pritchard (1951), 56f., 93. Kamba.

the birth of a child.[1] Invariably, although there is some prior understanding and attraction between the boy and girl, the negotiations for the marriage begin with a formal approach by the boy, or his father or mother or elder brother on his behalf, to the girl's father and family or (if he is dead) to the brother or other guardian. A girl marries at about 17 and the man's first marriage is at about 20 years of age and, if he takes a second wife, usually at about 40. Generally there are a few bachelors but no unmarried women. Most men have only one wife but a substantial number have two, and apart from chiefs, who have many, there are few men with more than two.[2]

[1] Nuer: Evans-Pritchard (1951), 56f., 93.
[2] There are few reliable figures of the number of wives that a man has. Wagner (1949), I, 50, exhibits tax returns showing that 88 per cent of 11,039 men had only one wife each, but points out that these figures underestimate the number of wives (cf. some figures for Basutoland and Swaziland in Kuczynski (1949), II, 31). Lindblom (1920), 87, gives figures showing that of twenty-six men all but nine had only one wife but in both lists an insignificant number had more than two wives. According to Fortes (1949), 65, of 100 married Tallensi men 60 per cent had one wife, 27 per cent had two and of married men under forty-five years of age 75 per cent had only one wife. In the whole of Tongo he knew of five men who had never married, but no woman. Five chiefs would have thirty wives between them in 1920. In Germany we are told that the possession of more than one wife is limited to a small number of men of the class of nobles (Tac. Germ. 18). There are more reliable figures of the proportion of the sexes among these African peoples, but not of the time when there was fighting. No doubt the proportion of the sexes varied from place to place: see also Driberg (1923), 146. There is now generally a greater proportion of female than male adults and the disproportion must formerly have been greater. It seems likely that among these peoples (as now) and indeed among the generality of polygamous peoples (i.e. the great bulk of the peoples concerned in this book) there was a number of adult bachelors but practically no spinsters; that 70 to 85 per cent of the married men had only one wife at any given time; that about 15 per cent of the married men had two wives; and the number of men with over two wives was insignificant, though a few chiefs and wealthy men had several or many. Widows were mainly inherited and are included in the above figures. More males were born than females, but infant mortality (which was probably about 25 per cent in the first year, 30 per cent in the first two years, and 40 to 45 per cent by the time maturity was reached) was higher among males than females and the mortality among adult males much higher than among adult females. If so, polygamy was a workable and convenient system and the fact that there was no access from pregnancy and during the period of lactation (about three years) underlined its convenience. The expectation of life at birth was probably about thirty-five years on an average. The women gave birth to five or six children on the average. A serious famine or cattle-pest might reduce the population by 30 per cent.

The facts and forces that have built up this mass of property are mainly the demand for the girl and the need to obtain the consent of her father or brothers to part with her, and also the solidarity of near kin. But the bridewealth is from one aspect merely the greatest of the gift-payments that we see so frequently in primitive society, marking this supreme occasion in the life of man and woman. And, on the other hand, the father parting with his daughter will be enabled to secure by its means a wife for a son, and the father parting with his property will secure a wife for his son and she will produce girl children on whose marriage the family will recoup its fortunes. The bridewealth is therefore at once the medium of exchange of a woman for a woman and also the means of a large-scale circulation of capital, with the results that follow. This great gift-payment takes its place in the context of the social structure and takes from that its colour and incidents, and helps to form it. The peoples among whom the payment is retained by the father or brother are few:[1] almost everywhere, in Germany and Africa, the cognatic as well as agnatic relationships of the bride are recognized by payments to her maternal as well as paternal kin, usually in well-recognized proportions,[2] and similarly the paternal and maternal kin of the groom will contribute a traditional share.[3]

The necessity of finding the bridewealth gives a spur to the young man's industry and postpones his marriage to maturer years. It causes him to value more highly the wife it is so difficult to acquire and on the other hand the knowledge that her marriage brings so much wealth to her family increases her self-respect. In the past the payment of bridewealth was sternly put down at many mission stations and the result was often sloth in the men and desertion of wives. Bridewealth reinforces the dependence of the son on his father and helps to knit together the relatives on whose assistance he must rely. The marriage is stabilized by its payment, as well as by the affection of the spouses, the goodwill

---

[1] Evans-Pritchard (Anuak), 109.
[2] See e.g. Nuer: Evans-Pritchard (1951), 74. Lango: Driberg (1923), 158f. If, on death or divorce, the bridewealth or part is returned it will be distributed among the group who contributed it or their heirs: Vugusu, Wagner (1949), II, 113.
[3] But e.g. among the Logoli: Wagner (1949), II, 115; the payment and receipt of bridewealth is usually confined to the family.

of the families and their desire for public approval. It is a security to the woman against ill-treatment, for if she should leave her husband for good cause he would not be entitled to its return and might be unable to acquire another wife. On the other hand the prospect of having to repay it if she left without cause induces her relatives to influence her to remain with him. The receipt by them of shares in the bridewealth places upon them a corresponding duty and interest to protect her against ill-treatment and even, in case of calamity, to support her and her children, though vice versa if, for example, she insulted or ignored her husband, they might have to compensate him.[1] The payment of bridewealth helps to join the families of the spouses. With the birth of children the affines become in a sense cognates, and for some purposes she joins her husband's lineage while never ceasing to belong to her own family.

It is therefore usually fallacious to describe the bridewealth marriage as a sale of the woman: it is too fundamental and too much coloured by every aspect of life to be fairly described by analogy to another transaction, and especially to a modern commercial transaction the spirit of which is not even altogether that of a primitive exchange or sale.[2] It might be said with more truth that the economy of these peoples and their human propensities create the bridewealth marriage.

Little of this is law; it is rather the social and economic foundations of the law and the facts upon which the growing law operates. No law, for example, fixes the amount of the bridewealth or lays upon a relative the obligation to contribute to it or right to share in it. The families and individuals must arrange this between them. But there are prohibited marriages – usually, in brief, with close cognates – and sexual intercourse within the prohibited degrees of marriage is incest, except that there are degrees of repugnance to marriages[3] and some forbidden acts are, by reason of distance of kinship, peccadilloes, especially if there is little

---

[1] See Wagner (1949), I, 47: adultery. Nuer: Evans-Pritchard (1951), 104: assault and wounding.
[2] There is no Nuer word for 'buy' or 'sell'. On the other hand some Bantu peoples speak of 'buying' a wife (see for Kikuyu, Routledge (1910), 126) as does the Code of Aethelberht. But there the word has this extended meaning, as does 'give away' in our phrase 'giving away a daughter'.
[3] See e.g. Evans-Pritchard (1951), Chap. II, and (1954), 183f.

publicity: and the offence of incest is, as before, irregularly punished and the punishment is mainly left to religious sanctions.

The chief disputes that began to arise for law to settle in this field (apart from allegations of adultery) are claims for repayment of bridewealth.[1] One type of case is where after payment of part of the bridewealth the girl refuses to marry the man and the father fails to return the cattle (which he may have consumed or distributed). Another familiar type of case is where the bridewealth has been paid but the husband is entitled to divorce his wife and recover it.[2] The circumstances in which he is entitled to do so vary from people to people and are not precisely defined, but usually he may divorce her for repeated infidelity or laziness.[3] A third case is where she leaves him for another man. Usually the latter must pay bridewealth to her father who must return the husband's payments, but in some places he pays the husband direct. In peoples where the marriage is not complete till a child is born, the husband till that event occurs can recover the property paid and her father will commonly have postponed its distribution meanwhile. The wife can divorce her husband for impotence[4] or neglect of her such as to prejudice her chances of becoming a mother,[5] and in these cases the bridewealth is not recoverable. Where she dies without issue before leaving her father's house, among some peoples the husband is entitled to the return of the bridewealth or to a sister of hers in marriage.[6]

The payment of bridewealth entitles the husband to all children

[1] And less commonly for payment of promised bridewealth: Evans-Pritchard (1940), 167.
[2] Bridewealth is not recoverable for the wife's barrenness, e.g. Kamba: Lindblom (1920), 78.
[3] Among the Kipsigis, however, laziness is no ground for divorce: Peristiany (1939), 88. The man's grounds are adultery (proved by the parties being caught in the act or the wife eloping with the adulterer), her witchcraft and her threats to his life, and even then only if the marriage is childless. Divorce cases are here regarded as of the highest importance and tried by the Kiruogindet neo. If the wife dies childless the bridewealth is repayable: Peristiany (1939), 198.
[4] e.g. Kamba: Lindblom (1920), 82.
[5] e.g. Kipsigis: Peristiany (1939), 88.
[6] Among the Nuer, if the wife dies in her first pregnancy the husband is liable, and the bridewealth he has paid becomes bloodwealth: Evans-Pritchard (1951), 93. If the matter is in dispute, a special official mediator settles it: Evans-Pritchard (1940), 168.

born to his wife whether he is the physiological father or not. There are substantially no employees and the wealth and status of a household consists of its wives and children[1] by whom cattle and crops can be obtained. A wife of mature age will consequently encourage her husband to take a second wife and thereby also lessen the burden of her domestic duties. The status of the first or great wife is higher than the rest.

These peoples show their capacity for law by the institution of several other analogous types of marriage.[2] One is the levirate. In most of these peoples, in Africa and Germany, there is a quasi-inheritance of a widow by one of her late husband's next of kin, usually a younger brother or in default of brothers a son by another wife, and she goes to live with him. In other peoples, for example the Nuer (among whom a widow cannot remarry) the brother or son takes her to live with him, especially where he is unmarried and the widow is childless, and her children by this union are considered children of the deceased. This is the levirate, properly so called, and no bridewealth is paid. There are intermediate types of cases in other peoples.[3] But there are also, in some peoples, many cases where a man dies without wife or child, and a near kinsman, being under an obligation to do so, marries with bridewealth a wife to his name.[4] The deceased is considered both the husband and father. Stranger still is the less frequent case where a wife (usually barren) marries a woman[5] who will, through the help of some male, raise issue to her husband, and she is considered for many purposes a man, husband and father with the rights belonging to that status, including the right to inherit property and receive bridewealth on the marriage of children[6] and compensation for injuries to them.

[1] Tac. Germ. 20.
[2] All found among the Nuer, as well as concubinage: Evans-Pritchard (1951), 104.
[3] e.g. Kamba, a practical levirate; the widow inherited by the eldest brother who can transfer her for bridewealth or give her away, and, if so, any child born belongs to the new husband. If the brother keeps her, he is called 'uncle' by any child born to her and the child, if male, succeeds to the first husband's estate (Lindblom (1920), 83) though the brother receives any bridewealth paid in respect of the child, if female.
[4] Nuer, Dinka: Seligman (1932), 164.
[5] Nuer; Kipsigis: Peristiany (1939), 81, 206.
[6] Evans-Pritchard (1951), 121f.

We turn to ideas of property in goods. As among the peoples of the previous two chapters, the idea of the individual ownership – or, more properly, of the exclusive individual right of possession – of certain goods is familiar; but such a right, coupled with an unrestricted right of alienation, is among the more pastoral peoples limited to the few articles of clothing and personal adornment – for in most of them both sexes go nude – and such weapons and domestic utensils and tools as are easily made of available materials and regularly used by the individual. Such things are considered to belong to men and women alike and they are free to dispose of them by gift or barter. More valuable articles, made by one of the few local craftsmen or imported, might be given to relatives or exchanged with them, and compulsory gifts of such articles[1] or of food between relatives, and sharing of meat with relatives and fellow-hunters, is common. Property in cattle is of a different character: they are mainly held by the father of the family by virtue of membership of the family or close kinship group.[2] If he acquired them by his own efforts he can usually dispose of them freely during his life,[3] but if they came to him as bridewealth or bloodwealth or as a trustee or are inherited, they commonly came on terms of being used in the group for specific purposes, if as bridewealth, to acquire a wife for the bride's unmarried brother,[4] if as bloodwealth, for the benefit of the deceased's kin or to acquire a wife to raise up an heir to him; if inherited from a father, to provide for brothers and sisters and widow and ultimately to divide with the brothers; if inherited from a brother, to provide for the infant children and widow of the deceased till a son reaches maturity. Though a man may refer to 'my cow' or 'my things' they are usually his only in this limited sense. Among the Bantu, who are mainly agricultural peoples with a more developed economy, the wife's rights have diminished: she owns nothing except her clothing, ornaments and domestic utensils; cattle given

[1] e.g. Evans-Pritchard (1940), 183f.
[2] Wagner (1949), I, 45f.
[3] e.g. Kipsigis: Peristiany (1939), 203.
[4] Among the Kipsigis, for example, bridewealth cannot be used by the girl's father to acquire another wife for himself: 'it would be like sleeping with your daughter': Peristiany (1939), 205. Among the Lango, though a wife does not own the property she can veto her husband's disposal (e.g. by loan) of cattle acquired on her daughter's marriage: Driberg (1923), 172.

her by her husband for the support of herself and her children remain his. If for any reason the marriage is dissolved, in North Kavirondo the wife has no right even to the custody of the children.[1]

As for land, in many of the more pastoral peoples (for example the Nuer and Kipsigis and most of the Nandi)[2] there is no notion of the individual ownership (or exclusive right to possession) of land. For one thing, among all peoples of this grade there is land to spare and no one interferes or wishes to interfere with another's occupation or use of it. Gardens and fields after a year or a few years' cultivation are deserted for new ground, and complex or elaborate rules of land tenure will not evolve in such circumstances nor will they lead to litigation. In varying degree the land is considered, among the more pastoral peoples, to belong to the members of a lineage, clan or clan-division as such and the head of it controls the land by virtue of his status. Often this system is thought (with insufficient historical warrant) to originate in a settlement by an original founder and inheritance by his lineal descendants.[3] Within it fields and gardens are cultivated by occupying families, either by allotment from time to time by the head of the clan or clan-division, or by common accord of the members.[4] Arable land is more suited to occupation by households with assistance at certain seasons from the local groups[5] grazing land and water rights to use by local populations,[6] fishing and hunting territories to exploitation by local groups and individuals[7] by right of membership of them, and these tendencies are seen in the developing law. In the less pastoral peoples the clan right tends to diminish[8] and village or lineage right of occupancy to take its place, and within it the occupancy of heads of household for the benefit of their households. There is no right in a community or individual to transfer or bequeath the

---

[1] Wagner (1949).
[2] Hollis (1909), 86.
[3] For example, in many or most places relatives, affines and friends (even aliens) may be allowed to settle, e.g. Kipsigis, Lango.
[4] Lango: Driberg (1923), 171.
[5] e.g. Lango: Driberg (1923), 171.
[6] Lango: Driberg (1923), 171: communal to the village.
[7] Lango, hunting rights private but the owner must allow anyone who wishes to build or cultivate.
[8] Lango: practically none: Driberg (1923), 170.

land and after a few years the village moves elsewhere and occupies uncultivated or deserted land as before, each household by agreement, or allotment by local chiefs, occupying its own portion[1] and village parties assisting at times in its cultivation. There is much development and change among the Bantu. The Logoli of North Kavirondo are still to a substantial extent pastoralists. The possessor or owner (*omwene*) has a permanent right of use of the land he holds, and can till or leave it fallow and pays no tribute or harvest dues. But ancestral ('grandfather's') land he must cultivate and cannot let or part with, and land given to him by his father ('father's land') he divides among his sons during his lifetime and cannot let unless he has otherwise provided for them. It is only in respect of land acquired by his own efforts (for example, by being the first to cultivate it or by 'purchasing' it) that he may let or sell his personal right of user, and even in this case his heirs can redeem it by repaying the price.[2] The Kikuyu and Kamba are mainly agriculturists and the local community does not move as a whole to new territory as the old is exhausted. Here a man has individual ownership of his cultivated field or garden, whether inherited or appropriated from the waste, and anything surplus to his requirements he can give or sell to anyone who needs it. Only the uncleared land upon the outskirts of the community, which is used for general grazing or has never been marked out by an individual for his own cultivation, has no private owner.[3] But since the emergence of chiefs during the British administration the local chief's consent is required for sale or gift and the occupier can be dispossessed for serious misconduct or neglect.

[1] Tacitus describes this fully in *Germania* 26 and Caesar in *D.B.G.* VI, 22. It appears from both accounts that the chiefs assign land to the heads of the local or kinship groups and the latter distribute among the householders.
[2] Another intermediate case is that of the Tallensi, an agricultural people without government or law. There is land to spare, fixed cultivation and something like full proprietorship in the family head. There is no profit in obtaining additional farm land if a man has not enough labour in his household to work it. Land, therefore, is never rented, but is bought in some areas (where it is not sacrilege to sell) subject to the consent of potential heirs of the seller. A chief may speak of 'my land' but this only signifies land in his care, and no tribute or rent is paid: Fortes (1940), 248f.; (1945), 240.
[3] Routledge (1910), 39; Hobley (1910), 82; Lindblom (1920), 164. Wells and water sources are often common property: Lindblom (1920), 165.

The rules of inheritance, emerging more clearly among these peoples than before because of the possession of the all-important valuable, cattle, exemplify well the fact that their chief basis and origin is that the deceased's property remains where it was. That which normally happens ought to happen and therefore these various kinds of property should go to the person or class of persons most likely and able to take them. In all these peoples marriage is patrilocal and so descent is patrilineal, the property going to the member or members of the household, or in default of such to the nearest agnates, most likely and able to take them. For example, as ascendants usually predecease the father, ascendants do not inherit.

But there are differences between these incipient, tentative systems of inheritance and the crystallized rules of modern law. The modern rules are enforced by courts of law, so that they are easily recognizable as law, and they award the ownership or other interests of the deceased to a successor (or successors). The successor may be under an obligation to support other members of the family, but this is no part of the law of inheritance or, in a measure, of any law. The primitive rules of inheritance, on the other hand, are applied in case of dispute by the lineage head or elders, and rarely come before a court, so that a son's right to inherit is no more law than his obligation to support his brothers' or clansmen's attempt to find bridewealth, or to maintain the deceased's daughters or widows, or give a fair share or maintenance to the other members of the family. Consequently, also, the primitive rules are subject, and able to be subject, to wide variation to meet the needs and justice of a particular case.

Again, in modern law there are sharp distinctions between *donatio inter vivos* or *mortis causa* and testamentary and intestate succession. A person has a right to alienate his property during his life or to provide by a written will how his property shall pass at his death, and he can and does within wide limits make a complete departure from the rules of intestate succession. In the peoples of the present chapter a man can and commonly does before death divide his property or give his sons oral directions how it is to pass on his death, but it is only within the narrowest limits that he will depart from the normal incidents of succession and if he did his directions would not be carried out. Accordingly what we describe here as the rules of inheritance are in the main a description of the manner in which a man's property commonly passes, by gift, will or intestate succession. This is not to say that these peoples have not well-understood principles as to how property should pass but, as we have said, they are subject to wide variation to meet a particular case.

This situation is well illustrated among the Logoli, a large Bantu tribe of North Kavirondo, representing a middle degree of development as compared with the other peoples of this chapter. Here the father, shortly before his death, usually gives instructions to his sons as to the destination of his property after his death, and after his death and after a ceremony of purification and a prolonged debate at which claims by and against the deceased have been ascertained and assessed and charges of witchcraft causing his death have been fully discussed, a public announcement is made of the terms of division of the estate, a division which may even take some years to complete. The chief elements that serve to increase or decrease a son's share are his receipt, actual or prospective, of that mass of property, bridewealth, and his liability to provide it. For example, if the deceased left sons and daughters all unmarried, the eldest son will receive a larger share of the 'estate' – including in that term actual cattle and their prospective increase and the bridewealth to be received in respect of the daughters – than the other brothers, as representing the fact that he will have to find bridewealth before his brothers and will then be under an obligation to help them to find it. If, on the other hand, he is already married and his brothers are single, the largest share would go to the second son. But if, at the death of the father, the eldest daughter was married, but all the sons unmarried, the eldest son's share would be considerably larger than that of the others, as representing his share of the bridewealth already received, or still to be received, in respect of his sister. If then one of the daughters should later die unmarried the eldest son would be obliged to assist a younger son more liberally on his marriage. If all the sons were married at their father's death, they would receive a roughly equal share, with a slight increase to the eldest representing the probability that his sons would marry earlier than his brother's sons.[1]

Summarising the rules of inheritance observed in all these peoples, let us begin with the widows.

At first sight widows seem to pass, as though they were a species of property, by quasi-inheritance to such of their deceased husband's agnates as would be most fit and likely to possess them. Usually they go to a brother of the deceased or in default of brothers to a paternal cousin or to a son of the deceased by another wife.[2] In some peoples if there are several widows the elder or eldest go to a brother and the younger or youngest to the deceased's eldest son by another wife.[3] In some places all widows go to the eldest son by another wife[4] and only if there is no son old enough do they go to a brother of the deceased.[5] But this is by no means a complete picture, nor are these hard and fast rules. She sometimes seems to go rather for protection than by way of inheritance[6] and often, especially if she is beyond the age of child-bearing, retains a choice – she may go to live with a son or her father or one of her brothers[7] or a lover,[8] and no one will object. But it must be remembered that bridewealth was given for her by the deceased and his near agnates with a view to the rearing of children, and in many or most of these peoples it is recognised that she remains the wife of the deceased and if a child is born to her by a brother or other agnate or even by a lover[8] it is considered the child of the deceased.[9] Indeed the genitor is often called by another name than father,[10] which is reserved for the

---

[1] Wagner (1949), I, 451, 485f.; II, 117f. It follows from what has been said that in most of the societies mentioned in this chapter sons are expected to marry in order of age, Nuer certainly so even in polygamous households: Howell (1954), 191. See *ibid.* for the complicated rules of succession to claims to bridewealth. These do not apply to succession to bloodwealth: *ibid.*, 194.

[2] *Kipsigis:* a brother (preferably an unmarried brother) or in default of brothers a paternal cousin; *Nandi:* the next elder or next younger brother; *Masai:* a half brother by the same father; *Kamba:* usually the eldest brother, or if there are several widows, to different brothers and in default of brothers to the nearest agnate; *Lango:* a brother, and in default of brothers to a sister's son, or, if she is a young widow to a son of the deceased by another wife; *Tallensi:* no son inherits a widow.

[3] Kamba of Kitui; Jaluo Nilotic Kavirondo.

[4] Kamba of Thaaka. He does not necessarily keep them all.

[5] Bantu of North Kavirondo; Kamba; Kikuyu.   [6] Kipsigis.   [7] Nandi.

[8] Kipsigis.   [9] Nuer.   [10] Kipsigis: 'Kipkondit'; Kamba, 'uncle'.

deceased, and the child inherits from the deceased and not from the genitor.[1] Such a marriage is the true levirate marriage and not a case of inheritance. In some places the widow is allowed to marry outside the agnatic clan, but if so the new husband must give bridewealth to the deceased's agnates[2] or, if she lives with a lover, the child will become his if he pays an affiliation fee.

Turning to property, and especially property in cattle and goats, in polygynous households – which, as we have seen, are the minority – it usually happens that, apart from the other possessions of the deceased, he has entrusted to each wife, who has a child, a hut, animals and land for their sustenance. In most peoples this is inherited by her sons[3] (including the land, where land is heritable). But among the Kipsigis the property of the deceased is divided equally between each hut (that is to say, the family of each wife) not immediately but in course of time according to each person's needs.[4]

There remains the rest of the possessions of the deceased, including any cattle in the possession of childless wives. Here we find that the sons generally inherit, with a varying preference in favour of the eldest son of the chief, i.e. the first wife, and in default of sons the nearest agnates – that is to say, the brothers or failing them paternal cousins of the deceased.[5] The preference in favour of the eldest son is not found everywhere,[6] but where it exists it takes different forms. In some he succeeds to the whole, as the new head of the family for the benefit of the family, or distributes the property between himself and the other sons equally or according to their needs (e.g. to provide bridewealth).[7]

[1] Dinka, Masai, Kipsigis, Kamba, Kikuyu. Not Shilluk or Lango.
[2] Kamba: the brother of the deceased who 'inherits' her can give her for bridewealth to anyone he pleases.
[3] Masai: Hollis (1905), 309; Nandi: Hollis (1909), 73; Lango: Driberg (1923), 173. Among the Suk, the youngest son gets the bulk of it. Among the Kikuyu and Kamba she generally succeeds *de facto,* and her eldest son generally succeeds her with an obligation to give a share to his uterine brothers.
[4] This is apt to be very unfair, for one wife may have three sons and one daughter, and another three daughters and one son, and in the former case the sons seeking to marry have the assistance of one-third of the bridewealth of a sister, and in the latter case the son is helped by the bridewealth of three sisters.   [5] Nuer, Lango, Masai, Nandi, Akamba of Kitui.
[6] Not among Nuer or Bantu of North Kavirondo.
[7] Kipsigis, Jaluo, Nilotic Kavirondo, Lango, Kikuyu, Kamba of Machakos. Among the Kamba of Kitui he distributes under the supervision of his uncle.

Among others he receives the bulk of the property;[1] among others he gets a somewhat larger share than the rest.[2] If any of his brothers are too young he acts as trustee for them till they come of age.[3] If the eldest son is incompetent the brothers may in some tribes choose another son in his place.[4] If all the sons are young, the deceased's brother acts as trustee till they come of age, accounting strictly for the young of cattle.[5]

Generally speaking, women cannot inherit and the daughters of the deceased receive none of his property. As marriage is patrilocal the property would be lost to their father's lineage.[6] But an unmarried daughter must be supported and she will bring in bridewealth to the family. She is supported by the eldest son,[7] usually the eldest son of her own mother,[8] or in default of adult brothers her eldest uncle.[9] The bridewealth received on her marriage will usually go to him or be shared between her full brothers[10] and such other relatives as are entitled to share, and even the cattle received on her marriage by her father during his lifetime is often inherited by her full brothers (subject to their own original claim to share in it).[11] Though daughters do not inherit from their fathers they often succeed to their mother's ornaments and household utensils.[12]

Though ascendants do not as a general rule inherit, a father may inherit from a son who has not reached man's estate.[13] Slaves

---

[1] Dinka: eldest son of first wife gets the majority of it on division by the father and is bound to take charge of the family: Seligman (1932), 175. Nandi: Hollis (1909), 73. Suk: Beech (1911), 35.
[2] Kamba of Thaaka: he receives one animal of each species more than do his brothers.
[3] Masai, Lango, Bantu of North Kavirondo.   [4] Masai, Lango.
[5] Masai, Lango, Bantu of North Kavirondo. Among the Kikuyu the brother must be younger than the deceased.
[6] Or clan-subdivision: Peristiany (1939), 212.
[7] Kamba of Machakos.   [8] Nandi; Kamba of Kitui.
[9] Some Kamba, Jaluo, Nilotic Kavirondo.
[10] Nandi, Kamba of Kitui and of Machakos, Kikuyu, Bantu of North Kavirondo.
[11] Nuer: Howell (1954), 191f.; Nandi, Kipsigis, Lango, Kikuyu.
[12] e.g. Nandi; where they even share the plantations worked by their mother till they marry. Lango: ornaments etc. go to daughter or in default of daughters her husband sells them; her granaries, food, household utensils go to her co-wives or, if there are none, her husband sells them: Driberg (1932), 176.
[13] Nandi: Hollis (1909), 73.

sometimes inherit as though they had been sons.[1] Maternal relatives do not inherit except in default of near agnates in a few peoples.[2] Where headship or chieftainship exists and is heritable it descends generally in the same way as property.[3]

Oral 'wills' are common[4] and among some peoples (e.g. the Nuer)[5] a father is expected to divide his possessions before his death. Feeling its approach he will commonly, in all these peoples, call his sons together and announce his wishes regarding the disposal of his property including land (where land is heritable) partly to avoid disputes and partly to avoid injustice, limiting himself to details of the customary rules of succession and provisions supplementary to it. He might give his weapons or other cherished objects to particular sons.[6] He might declare what property of his was in the possession of others or what he owed, and give instructions for payment of his debts, though his heirs would in any event be considered liable to pay them. He might declare what share was to be given by the eldest to the younger sons, saying, for example, that each of them was to have ten goats, and telling them 'when they want meat or fat or dowries for wives to ask the eldest brother; but anyone not behaving himself is to take ten goats and go'.[7] He might make different gifts to each of his wives, and if children were young say which brother or brothers were to take the property as trustees.

These, then, are the general rules of succession, and already, it will be seen, they contain the bases of the modern law of inheritance, including, for example, in the person of the eldest son or brother, the executor, administrator and trustee, and in these oral instructions the modern written will and testament. We know little of the rules of succession among the Germans, but their subsequent history suggests that they were much the same.

[1] Lango.
[2] Lango: a sister's son may inherit in default of a son or brother of the deceased. But it may be made a condition that he shall come and live in or near the deceased's village. Not permitted among the Masai: Hollis (1905), 309.
[3] e.g. Lango: Driberg (1923), 175.
[4] e.g. Nuer; Dinka; Kipsigis, where the oral will is called the *kararget*; Lango; Kamba; Kikuyu.   [5] Howell (1954), 190.
[6] Among the Kipsigis he can ask his sons to give cattle to a member of the clan-subdivision. Among the Lango the gifts are not valid till confirmed at a meeting of members of the family and clan at a festival: Driberg (1923), 173.
[7] Routledge (1910), 144. For the Kipsigis see Peristiany (1939), 212.

CHAPTER 18

Cattle Keepers – Crimes and Civil Injuries

The distinction between crime and civil wrong is to be seen everywhere among these peoples.[1]

The criminal offences are everywhere very few.[2] Death by witchcraft continues to be the main such offence, and is usually punishable by death at the hands of the general local community, when they are strong enough to inflict it, and the destruction of the offender's home.[3] Incest is irregularly punished by ostracism or worse if it becomes public and can no longer be ignored,[4] and there are two comparatively new offences of unnatural sexual intercourse[5] and, above all, persistent theft, especially of animals. The latter crime is regularly punished by death – lynching at the hands of the local community.[6]

When we turn to the civil injuries we find, subject to degrees of development, an almost complete unanimity in the incipient law of these peoples – a uniformity that we have not witnessed before – and especially in homicide; we begin to see that the law

[1] Tac. Germ. 12. Lango: Driberg (1923), 209.
[2] See Evans-Pritchard (1940), 68, who doubts if there are any crimes among the Nuer.
[3] Suk: Beech (1911), 30: organized lynching. Nuer: Evans-Pritchard (1940), 167. Lango: Driberg (1923), 241. Bantu of North Kavirondo: Wagner (1949), I, 275f. Kamba: Lindblom (1920), 279. But in some of these societies there is a tendency to sentence to payment of bloodwealth (on the basis of homicide) after trial and condemnation: Wagner (1949), I, 275f., Peristiany (1939), 193. This treatment of witchcraft is found in a number of peoples of very different economies.
[4] Nandi: Hollis (1909), 76 (flogging by the women of the village who strip for the purpose, and destruction of the offender's house). Among Nuer it is mainly a religious offence and requires sacrifice: Evans-Pritchard (1940), 173.
[5] Tac. Germ. 12; Bantu of North Kavirondo: Wagner (1949), I, 108. It is practically unknown among the Nuer: Howell (1954), 218f.
[6] Kamba of Kitui and Mumoni. Kipsigis: Peristiany (1939), 190f. Nandi: Hollis (1909), 75.

of civil injuries, and especially homicide, is at the heart and centre of the legal system. These are the wrongs that law arises to sanction, for this is the chief source of the disorder which the law arises to assuage. This is the explanation of the almost total preoccupation of the Codes of our next stage with the civil injuries, and already we find among the most developed economies of the present grade, namely the Kamba and Kikuyu, oral Codes in form and content familiar to us from the most primitive codes of the past.

Upon a killing taking place the slayer takes to flight from the vengeance of the next of kin of the slain. But first he hides his cattle, commonly by mixing them with the herd of a friendly group outside his clan,[1] for the victim's relatives will seize any cattle of his or of any member of his clan or clan-division, on which they can lay hands.[2] Then he himself takes refuge – among the Nuer at the hut of a leopard-skin chief (whose person is sufficiently revered or respected to prevent the shedding of blood in his presence) – but the next of kin are watching for him and if he leaves the hut will spear him. The Masai hides wherever he can; the Nandi takes sanctuary under a tree or by a river, for no Nandi will kill a man who takes refuge in this way.[3] The slayer also in many places requires ceremonial cleansing from the blood of the slain.[4]

A feud begins or threatens, and before any attempt to compose it can be made the slayer or a member of his clan might be killed. Among the Kipsigis at this point the father or son of the slayer brings a cow by way of ceremonial apology to the next of kin to obviate revenge. But whether or not cattle have been taken or a man has been killed in reprisal, the function of the elders or clan leaders or Nuer leopard-skin chief[5] is to make peace. They urge and entreat the avengers not to resort, or maintain the resort, to violence. On the one hand, the pride of the clan and its

[1] Nandi: Hollis (1909), 73.
[2] Kipsigis: Peristiany (1939), 193. Masai: Hollis (1905), 311.
[3] Masai: Hollis (1905), 311. The pursuer changes garments with him and the latter is his prisoner or slave till ransomed by the subsequent payment.
[4] Nuer: Evans-Pritchard (1940), 152f.
[5] For the procedure see Evans-Pritchard (1940), 152f., and for the elders' part, p. 178.

sense of duty to avenge the dead urge it to retaliate;[1] but the resort
to vengeance is not approved by public opinion[2] and on the
other hand, instigated by fear of avenging violence – the true
sanction of this law or practice[3] – and swayed by the entreaties
of elders or chief, an enormous sum of bloodwealth is offered.
Sooner or later,[4] with a show of reluctance, real on the part of
the younger clan-members at least,[5] they capitulate and agree to
accept it,[6] having lost no dignity in the process; but hatred may
continue and violence recur. Among a few of these peoples the
bloodwealth is fixed by the elders to meet the circumstances of
each case,[7] but among the rest it becomes fixed by practice in the
settlement of disputes, as with us the market-price of an article
is shaped by supply and demand, and each people or tribe has a
definite figure of composition for homicide,[8] with some variation
between different districts of each people and between periods
when cattle are more and less plentiful, and according to other
circumstances to be mentioned.

But, as has been said, political relations determine within what
territorial limits bloodwealth can be claimed with a good prospect
of recovery. At one extreme, for example among the Anuak, who
are mainly agriculturists with few cattle, the villages, associated
with a locally dominant lineage, are self-subsistent and independent
and compensation for homicide is only paid to fellow-villagers
and not for inter-village fights.[9] Within each Nuer tribe bloodwealth is paid, but between tribes war is the only arbiter,[10] and
even between two villages of the same tribe relations may be such
that inter-village war is requisite to obtain satisfaction for homicide.
At the other extreme the Kipsigis pay and receive bloodwealth

[1] See Brutzer's description of a Kamba feud in his *Begegnungen mit Wakamba*
(Berlin, 1902), 3.
[2] Among the Suk there is no killing, says Beech (1911), 29f.
[3] Evans-Pritchard (1940), 150.
[4] Among the Masai for two years the dead man's 'head is still fresh' and they
will not accept the cattle for that time: Hollis (1905), 312. For the bloodwealth
among the Arusha (Agricultural Masai) see Gulliver (1963), 127f.
[5] Lindblom (1920), 155f.
[6] Tacitus describes the situation precisely (*Germania*, 21).
[7] e.g. Suk and Bantu of North Kavirondo.
[8] Tac. Germ. 21: 'Luitur homicidium certo armentorum ac pecorum numero.'
[9] Anuak: Evans-Pritchard (1940), 26. Only between fellow-villagers is it
kwar (an act for which compensation can be made).
[10] Nuer: Evans-Pritchard (1951), 151.

between themselves and some other Nandi-speaking peoples, the Keyo, Nandi and Pokot.[1] And on the other hand, for homicide of a close relative (for example, a paternal cousin) either a lesser amount or no bloodwealth is paid, for there is no separate avenging and defending group and no good purpose is served by further reducing the strength of the kinship group or paying out cattle from persons who will receive it; and often nothing is done save to carry out rituals of purification or provide the deceased with a wife.[2]

These rules and practices are shaped by two main factors, apart from the natural grief and anger on one side and fear of vengeance on the other – namely, the existence of cattle, the invaluable possessions that are the capital of the community and provide its revenue and support and are so easily seized; and secondly the absence of common, central authority; in its absence no other workable sanction could be envisaged but only the all-destroying feud. The extreme case of authority is represented by the Shilluk monarchy where, by a new and important development of which we shall see much more in the next stage, a large part of the payments for homicide and other serious injuries are collected by the king, who keeps for himself most of the cattle he seizes[3].

[1] See *supra*, p. 237.
[2] *Nuer:* nothing is paid for a brother or wife: Howell (1954), 62, 235; perhaps half the usual amount for a paternal cousin: Evans-Pritchard (1940), 156. *Lango:* Driberg (1923), 210f.: have a bilateral kinship structure, and if a man kills his mother no compensation is paid as the killer is nephew to the family of the deceased and belongs to it as much as to his father's. Other killings within the clan are not compoundable, as the loss is to the clan and the killer is usually put to death, but two bulls must in any case be sacrificed to remove the blood-guilt and propitiate the spirit of the deceased. If a husband kills his wife he pays bloodwealth to her relatives. *Nandi:* Hollis (1909), 73f.: a Nandi killing a man of the same clan is unclean for the rest of his life unless he can kill two other Nandi of a different clan and can pay the bloodwealth for them himself. He may never enter a cattle kraal except his own. A Kamba father who is so unfortunate as to kill his son pays sums to the mother and nearest relatives. If he kills his wife he pays bloodwealth to her father, who then repays him the bridewealth, but this only applies when she has borne him children: Lindblom (1920), 155. *Kipsigis:* Peristiany (1939), 199: a killing within the clan is not paid for. Bridewealth is repaid if a childless wife kills her husband but not if she has borne a child, 'for a boy will raise seed to his father and cattle will be given for a girl'. *Tallensi:* homicide even in self-defence is sinful and requires ritual purification: Fortes (1945), 235.
[3] Evans-Pritchard (1948), 13. Out of the ten or so head payable he is likely to keep all, except one or two, which he will let the next of kin have.

K

The Germans were similarly advanced, for Tacitus tells us that 'a part of the impost (*multa*) is paid to the King or State and part to the man who is being vindicated or his relatives'.[1]

The amount of bloodwealth is, as it needs to be, enormous. It is at least as large as the amount of the bridewealth in the same people and usually much larger and would commonly be impossible for one man to pay without assistance. For example, among the Nuer, who possess an average of one and a half head of cattle per person, the bridewealth is about twenty to thirty head and the bloodwealth about forty. The Lango own about half a head of cattle per person and the bridewealth is about five head and the bloodwealth seven.[2] Accordingly the killer seeks the assistance of his relatives who, in the ordinary way, will contribute in recognized proportions provided he pays what he reasonably can,[3] and in the same way the bloodwealth received will be shared by the relatives in well-known proportions, so that, for example, among the Kipsigis every member of the clan-division of the victim ultimately gets some share of the cattle or its calves.[4] In this way the structure and solidarity of the kinship group, and to a lesser extent the cognates, express themselves in the rules that evolve. The killer's clan has a powerful interest in buying peace, for otherwise the persons and property of its members would be liable to violent attack. But if the same man committed the offence a second time they might decline to assist, saying 'Your blood be upon your own head', that is to say, 'Meet your blood-liability

[1] Tac. Germ. 12.

[2] Of the following figures, the first is the bloodwealth for a male adult, the figure in brackets is the bridewealth: *Nandi:* 5 cows, 4 bulls, 15 goats (1 cow, 1 bull). *Shilluk:* over 10 head (over 10 head) – cattle owned by the nation about 1 head per person. *Kipsigis:* 10 head, 50 goats (8 cows, 23 goats). *Pastoral Suk:* 50 cows (10 cows, 20 sheep). *Pastoral Masai:* 100 head (50 head) – cattle reputedly owned about 12 head per person. *Akamba of Kitui:* 14 cows, 1 bull (3 cows, 2 bulls). *Akamba of Thaaka:* 60 goats (28 goats). *Akamba of Mumoni:* 5 cows, equivalent of 50 to 60 goats (28 goats). All these figures seem to have been higher before the epidemics of rinderpest in the early 1890s.

[3] Kipsigis: Peristiany (1939), 195. A Kamba must give at least a cow or his relatives will not help him: Lindblom (1920), 155.

[4] Kipsigis: Peristiany (1939), 197; Tac. Germ. 21. There is often a connection between the relationship where bloodwealth is paid or received and where marriage is forbidden. For example among the Kamba, where parts of the same clan are so distantly related that they do not help one another to pay bloodwealth, marriage is permitted between members: Lindblom (1920), 122.

with your life'[1], and if the killer cannot pay, the next of kin of the victim will kill him or possibly a relative, or will seize, or be given in satisfaction, an unmarried sister or daughter[2] (or even a son of the killer himself). Especially is this so among the more agricultural people, who have fewer cattle: for example among the Anuak (who have few oxen and only small flocks of sheep and goats) the giving of a sister or daughter is the usual payment.[3] We shall see more of this type of sanction in later chapters.

Because there is little of nobility or rank among most of these peoples, corresponding distinctions in the amount of bloodwealth are hardly found.[4] Among some peoples less is paid for the killing of a woman:[5] more often the amount is the same.[6] The death of children is usually compensated at a lower rate,[7] but sometimes the payments are according to sex.

The difference between intentional and accidental killing is appreciated and among the Kamba the latter has a separate name (*mbanga*) and the sanction is half. There are no peoples, however, where accidental killing is free of bloodwealth and more commonly the payment is the same.[8] They also appreciate the difference between killing by stealth or ambush and killing openly in fair fight, but commonly in all these cases the bloodwealth is the same and the only difference made is in the forbearance shown to

[1] e.g. Kipsigis: Peristiany (1939), 199.
[2] e.g. Shilluk; Lango: Driberg (1923), 211; Pastoral Suk: Beech (1911), 29; Kamba; or he will dispose of a daughter for bridewealth to raise the money: Lindblom (1920), 155.
[3] Anuak: Evans-Pritchard (1940), 26.
[4] For the Nuer, see Evans-Pritchard (1940), 217f., 155.
[5] Half among Kamba and Kikuyu. For the killing of a married woman the question who has the right to compensation depends on the status of the marriage. For example, among the Kipsigis if the marriage has been consummated by the birth of children, her family receive nothing, the husband receives two cows and eight goats and the rest is distributed among his family in the usual way. If she had no children, the whole of the bloodwealth goes to her family who must return the bridewealth to the husband (as she died childless). Similarly if a murder is committed by a married woman who has borne children, her husband's clan-division is liable. In the rare case where she was single no compensation is usually demanded till she marries and bears a child, when the husband and his clan-division become liable: Peristiany (1939), 198. If a childless woman kills her husband the bridewealth is returned but not if she has borne children: *ibid.*, 199.
[6] e.g. Lango, where the position of women is unusually high.
[7] Masai, half for a boy.
[8] Suk: Beech (1911), 29f. Kipsigis: Peristiany (1939), 202.

the slayer.[1] In many places payment is made over a number of years: in some a wealthy offender is made to pay a little more than a poorer man because more can be got from him.[2]

The Nuer consider that bloodwealth is paid to acquire for the kinship group of the slain a woman who will rear a child to take his place, and therefore bloodwealth should be of the same amount as bridewealth. Other peoples lay less stress on this aspect of bloodwealth, which, as we have seen, is more commonly larger and is distributed to (as it is paid by) specific members of the agnatic and cognatic group. Nevertheless several peoples use part of the property as bridewealth to marry a woman to a member of the family or, as the Nuer say, to marry a wife to the deceased, who shall bear a child to take his place;[3] and where a sister or daughter of the slayer is taken in place of cattle she is commonly married to a member of the family, or he may adopt her and take the bridewealth received for her, or if a son of the slayer is taken he may on growing up return to his family provided he leaves a female child in his place.[4]

Compositions for injuries less than death become similarly conventional (though less constant)[5] within similar territorial limits and outside the family, and they vary in proportion to the severity of the injury. There appear to be no cases where the amount payable varies according to rank, age or sex of the injured. But among some peoples[6] no compensation is paid even for loss of eye or limb, but the offender must feed his victim while he suffers the effects of the injury and from time to time slaughter animals for that purpose. Among some peoples there is no compensation for flesh wounds but only for breakages.[7] In all of these peoples if a man is considered to have died from the injury, albeit many years afterwards,[8] it is a case of homicide and visited as such, and among the Kamba a post-mortem examination is held to ascertain if the injury caused the death.

---

[1] Kipsigis: Peristiany (1939), 193, 202.   [2] Kamba: Lindblom (1920), 156.
[3] Half the Nuer bloodwealth is used for the purpose: Evans-Pritchard (1951), 98.   [4] e.g. Anuak: Evans-Pritchard (1940), 26; Nandi: Hollis (1909), 75.
[5] Nuer: Howell (1954), 60; and more likely to vary with offender's means. Kamba: Lindblom (1920), 156.
[6] Some Nandi-speaking peoples (Nandi, Kipsigis, Pastoral Suk).
[7] e.g. Nuer: Evans-Pritchard (1940), 162.
[8] e.g. Kipsigis: Peristiany (1939), 193.

The sanctions for seduction, adultery and rape are usually small, something near the amount payable for loss of a toe. Seduction of a young unmarried woman is not frequently paid for:[1] if she becomes pregnant in consequence, he is expected to marry her, giving the usual bridewealth, and any cattle paid for the seduction count towards it. But if she dies in consequence or dies in pregnancy the payment is for homicide.[2] But the act of fornication may be no wrong or may be a religious offence. Among the Masai, for example, sexual intercourse with a woman or girl of the same age is no offence, but if of his father's age he is cursed and pays two oxen and prays the elders to remove the curse, and if of his daughter's age it is a serious crime punished by destruction of his kraal and cattle.[3] In the small villages of the Nuer and some other peoples, sexual intercourse with a girl of the same village is likely to be more or less incestuous and if she belongs to a different village no compensation is likely to be obtainable. Among several Nandi-speaking peoples there is no recognized compensation for seduction.[4] For adultery, the sum payable is again not large,[5] and not frequently paid, but in several peoples a man caught in *flagranti delicto* may be put to death by the irate husband,[6] though such a reaction is not generally approved. Adultery of a wife is often also a religious offence for it causes pollution in the two parties and the husband.[7] Again, among Nandi-speaking peoples there is no recognized material sanction for adultery. We hear little of rape,[8] and the absence of consent by the woman seems to make little difference to the sanction. You must be strong if you are to get compensation for seduction, adultery or rape.

[1] But Nuer: Evans-Pritchard (1940), 167: a heifer and a steer; Lango: varies between six goats and one bull plus fifteen goats in different localities: Driberg (1932), 160.
[2] Nuer; Kamba: Lindblom (1920), 157.
[3] Masai: Hollis (1905), 312.
[4] e.g. Nandi: Hollis (1909), 76.
[5] But it varies much. In Nuerland it is six cows, but if the adulterer can show that there is fruit of his adultery he can claim back all but one cow. Lango: one cow, one heifer and one bull: Driberg (1923), 161. Kamba: one goat: Hobley (1910), 79, Lindblom (1920), 158.
[6] e.g. Nuer.
[7] Nuer: Evans-Pritchard (1954), 185f.; Tallensi: Fortes (1949), 117.
[8] Kamba: one big goat: Hobley (1910), 78.

For theft the sanction varies much between different classes of property. Theft of property other than animals, if it is of no great value, is not significant except that it is commonly regarded as contemptible. But theft of valuables, including animals, is usually paid for by the return of the article and its single[1] or double[2] value, and a man caught stealing cattle may in some places be lawfully killed on the spot.[3] For repeated theft of any property there is generally an increasing sanction[4] and for persistent theft the punishment is usually death. If a thief has no money to pay for his theft his relatives will pay[5] or he sells cheaply a daughter or sister,[6] and women and children who steal and have nothing to pay with are usually beaten.[7] In a few places thieves are banished.[8]

These, together with claims for damage to property[9] (especially by trespassing animals) and occasionally defamation[10] are the main civil injuries with which the law concerns itself, and these added to claims in respect of bridewealth exemplify the main disputes which arise in litigation.[11] The following is an example of a code of civil sanctions (of course, unwritten) taken from the Kamba of Kitui.[12]

[1] Kamba: Lindblom (1920), 158f.: usually double value, but death for incorrigible thief, or theft of cattle, produce of field, or honey. Similarly Kikuyu.
[2] Lango: for theft of a canoe its return together with one goat for each man it can carry.
[3] e.g. Lango, Kipsigis.
[4] Nandi: Hollis (1909), 75: first offence, payment of four times the value of the thing stolen plus a beating; second offence, torture, confiscation of half his property, destruction of his grain and a branded mark on his forehead; third offence, strangled and his cattle slaughtered.
[5] Nandi, Kipsigis.
[6] Kamba: Lindblom (1920), 158f.
[7] Nandi: Hollis (1909), 75.
[8] Kamba: Lindblom (1920), 60.
[9] For which there are in some places conventional payments, e.g. Nuer: Evans-Pritchard (1940), 162; Kamba: Hobley (1910), 80; Lango: Driberg (1923), 211f.
[10] e.g. in recent years Nuer (imputations of witchcraft and sometimes adultery): Howell (1954), 71; and also Lango: Driberg (1923), 213.
[11] For examples of common disputes, see e.g. Evans-Pritchard (1940), 151, 167.
[12] See also, for the Kamba, Lindblom (1920), 156; Hobley (1910), 79. Nuer: Evans-Pritchard (1940), 167, Howell (1954), 70; Lango: Driberg (1923), 210f.; and for corresponding codes in different districts of Kikuyu: Routledge (1910), 215f.

Homicide (except by accident)
    Of a man   14 cows, 1 bull[1]
    Of a woman   7 cows, 1 bull
    Of a child (formerly; now[2] according to sex)   6 cows, 1 bull

Homicide (accidental – mbanga)
    Of a man   7 cows, 1 bull
    Of a woman   4 cows, 1 bull
    Of a child   according to sex

Injuries (accidental or not)
    Loss of a finger   1 cow, 1 bull
    Loss of a toe   1 bull, 1 goat
    Loss of a leg or arm   7 cows, 1 bull
    Loss of both legs or arms   14 cows, 1 bull
    Loss of an ear   5 goats
    Loss of an ear (accidental)   2 goats
    Tearing an ear   1 goat
    Loss of an eye   1 cow, 1 bull
    Loss of both eyes   14 cows, 1 bull
    Loss of a tooth   1 goat
    Loss of a tooth (accidental)   pot of *tembo*
    Loss of nose   1 cow, 1 bull
    Loss of a testicle   4 cows, 2 bulls
    Loss of both testicles   14 cows, 1 bull
    Loss of penis   14 cows, 1 bull

Homicide or injury by a person of the same village or family
                              Half composition

Adultery   1 bull, 1 goat
    If a child is born and dies before composition
       for adultery is paid   2 bulls, 2 goats
    If woman dies   Bloodwealth

[1] One bull goes to the tribunal (*nzama*) as a court fee in the cases where it is mentioned above. Hobley (1910), 78, and Lindblom (1920), 154, put the figure at thirteen cows and one bull, and for the Kamba of Ulu at eleven cows and one bull. See those authors for differing versions of this code and for the way in which the bloodwealth is distributed.
[2] Early twentieth century.

Rape   1 large bull equal to 1 cow

Bridewealth   3 cows, 2 bulls

Theft
    General   Restitution plus 1 bull
    Honey-barrel stealing or habitual stealing   *Kingole* (lynching)

Of procedure there is very little, though all tribunals have their well-recognized ways of getting through their business. Cases are heard with little formality, but in the most developed economies (especially the Kikuyu) there are distinctions between the types of wrongs tried by different tribunals. All claims are heard by unsworn oral evidence, but where, and only where, evidence fails while suspicion remains, ordeals are resorted to for the decision of the dispute and they are found everywhere except in the most backward economies. The ordeal is undergone by the defendant, and if he is successful in it he is acquitted. It is not applied to a mere witness. Because in some types of cases (especially charges of witchcraft and adultery) evidence is commonly wanting, certain types of ordeal tend to be used for particular charges;[1] but all ordeals tend to fall into two classes: in one the defendant undergoes a dangerous test, the other is an oath by which he imprecates against himself if he should be guilty. The former class is exemplified by the use of hot iron and of hot water among the Germans and the Kikuyu.[2] Typical examples of the latter class are: 'May this (animal, spear, human skull, *kithito*, etc.) kill me if I do not tell the truth', or 'May I die like this *sengi*' (beating a goat to death at the same time);[3] or 'I swear by my sister's garment'[4] or 'by the dead',[5] or 'by my dead father'. There seem to be few, if any, ordeals by the name of the God of the people. The sorcerer commonly administers it so as to render its use the more impressive.[6]

---

[1] Theft: Kamba: Hobley (1910), 78, 81. Witchcraft: Agricultural Suk: Beech (1911), 28.   [2] Routledge (1910), 212.
[3] Kikuyu. Cf. Kipsigis: Peristiany (1939), 188.
[4] Masai (cf. Lex Frisionum, Tit. 12) or, in the case of a woman, 'by my father's garment': Hollis (1905), 312.
[5] Lango: Driberg (1923), 213.
[6] e.g. Kamba: Lindblom (1920), 173. Kikuyu: Routledge (1910), 213.

CHAPTER 19

The Recent Peoples of the Early Codes –
Third Agricultural Grade, Second Stage

We turn from the First Stage of our Third Agricultural Grade to peoples of the same degree of economic and legal development as those of the Early Codes of the past. They show some close similarities to the peoples of early Anglo-Saxon England and Merovingian France in both respects.

In economic terms we define this stage as we defined that of the Early Codes of the past.[1] These peoples live by agriculture and cattle-keeping with subsidiary hunting. Their cattle (where cattle can be kept) are still their chief pride and the centre of their thoughts and aspirations, giving them milk and occasional meat and materials for clothing, shields, receptacles and other articles of daily use and attire and constituting an important criterion of social and economic success and status. But except in the less developed economies[2] their principal sustenance is from agriculture.[3] They are fairly settled in their territories but there is frequent migration and now conquest. Kings of nations (or chiefs of tribes) are to be found in most places, called kings or chiefs of their peoples and not yet of their land,[4] just as the tribe is often

[1] See *ante* Chap. 5; but the present and the following chapters refer to the peoples of the Early Codes of the past as well as the present, and in particular to their economic, social and political conditions.
[2] e.g. North-West England, Wales and Scotland.
[3] Among the Rega, from hunting.
[4] Clovis is 'Rex Francorum' and so is each of his successors, whatever part of France he rules. Hlothhere and Eadric are 'Kings of (the) Kentishmen', Alfred is at first 'King of (the) West Saxons' and later calls himself 'Angul-Saxonum Rex'. In our next period Canute boasts himself 'King of all England and King of the Danes' (I Canute). Even William I called himself on occasion 'King of the English' (the Ten Articles of William I). The King or Paramount Chief of Basutoland is the 'morena e moholo oa basotho' (The Great

named after its chief or one of his ancestors. But the power or influence of local lords or sub-chiefs is substantial and rank and nobility are almost everywhere. There are signs of a movement towards feudalism. Except in the more developed economies, such as that of the latter half of our Anglo-Saxon period, the basic local, kinship, social and economic group is in most places the homestead and not the village.[1] There is no sale of land and there are substantially no markets. Rarely do laws fix prices, for they change but slowly. Cattle are the chief medium of exchange, and though there is often some use of a currency acquired from civilization,[2] it is tied to cattle, and cattle are the chief means of payment of bridewealth, court fines and compensation, and there is a traditional ratio of values between the domestic animals and goods commonly exchanged. As there is still little specialization except between the sexes and all can make almost everything they require, there is little regular trade and little exchange, and foreign merchants are treated with suspicion and require permission to trade, which they obtain in return for gifts or dues from the king or chief or his deputy. But there are a few specializations, including those of the smiths and sorcerers (and in Europe the priests) and a few other artisans.[3] These too, however, live largely on the produce of their cattle and land. Almost the only commercial transactions are sale and exchange: there is no hiring or commercial deposit, but there is a little employment of men or boys to herd cattle (where cattle can be kept) in return for payment of an occasional heifer. In addition, as in some of the peoples of the previous chapter, there is a practice (Nguni, *ukusisa*) among

---

Chief of the Sotho) though he only rules over the southern Sotho: Schapera (1937), 173. There are no chiefs of tribes among the Mandja, only chiefs of villages and clans; among the Rega, chiefs of villages and districts and sometimes of a tribe.

[1] The Mandja and Rega have no cattle and no homesteads, only villages of an average size of about 175 persons.

[2] In England sometimes copies of Roman or Arab coins, with little addition (reminiscent of the newly minted Maria Theresa dollars, dated 1780, now or recently current in Aden and the Yemen). In the absence of cattle, arrows are used by the Mandja as measures of value, and the Rega use salt, iron, native cloths and, since the coming of the Arabs, pearls, cowries, copper and circles cut out of local snail shells.

[3] At the end of this period the number of specializations has increased, chiefly at the courts of kings: Whitelock (1952), 104f.

wealthy men to place cattle in the keeping of others in return for permission to take the milk. The institution of slavery is everywhere in Europe and but for its abolition in the modern world would be everywhere in Africa.

We define these peoples in the same legal terms as those of the Early Codes of the past. Courts are almost everywhere, held by the tribal chief[1] or king and his political subordinates, usually the heads of local communities, and the leading members of the local families have the right and duty to attend as members of the court, though all who wish can be present and take part in the trial. We now hear of legislation in most or many places[2] though the volume is not large,[3] and as the legislators are the kings or tribal chiefs with their councils, who also largely compose his court in litigation, the processes of legislation and the administration of justice are not always clearly separated. Criminal offences and civil wrongs can be readily distinguished. The sanctions for civil wrongs (including homicide and wounding) are pecuniary. There are no prisons and hardly any mutilations except of slaves; but the king or tribal chief has a right and interest to protect his people and a serious wrong (a 'blood case') to a subject is an affront to him and, in pursuance of a tendency which we witnessed under the Shilluk monarchy, to a degree varying in different peoples, he demands and receives a fine or compensation for the more serious injuries to his subjects as well as other wrongs against himself. Homicide, when tried, is only tried in his court. Accordingly homicide and wounding take a first step towards becoming criminal offences. Apart from this the criminal law is in its infancy and the crimes remain such as they were. Though theft is a civil injury, often persistent theft, and sometimes all theft of cattle, is criminal and punishable by death. There is an appeal on all matters from lower to higher courts and, in addition, cases started before a headman or other inferior tribunal will be sent

[1] The Mandja have no tribal chiefs and the Rega have only occasionally had a paramount chief.
[2] Not among the Mandja and Rega.
[3] The contents of some legislation are well known: for example Chaka, the Zulu chief, abolished circumcision; and Kreli, chief of the Gcalekas (a section of the Xhosa) altered the law by providing that if a wife died childless at her husband's kraal the bridewealth should no longer be returnable: but if a childless widow left and returned to her father's kraal the husband's heirs could demand its repayment.

on for hearing to a higher court if the matter is too serious or too difficult. As before, ordeals, where evidence is wanting, are employed almost everywhere.[1]

The bridewealth marriage is everywhere,[2] and there are no marriage settlements as yet. Marriage is virilocal and descent mainly patrilineal but the matrilineal relationship is also important. As the forms and incidents of marriage remain as in a previous chapter[3] we shall say little of it here. We note, however, a new conception in South Africa that the origin and main purpose of bridewealth is to afford support for the wife and children if they return one day to her paternal group in need, and to place on the recipients of the bridewealth the duty of support.[4]

As examples of these peoples let us take the whole of the Nguni peoples of South Africa as at the middle of the last century. They consist of a few hundred Bantu tribes, having certain physical affinities with the Bushman, Hamites and Negroes, living in a long belt of South-East Africa from Swaziland in the north through Natal and down to Port Elizabeth in the south, and from the escarpment of the Drakensberg to the sea. The Southern or Cape Nguni consist mainly of the Xhosa, Thumbu and Mpondo, and the Fingo and other recent immigrants; the Northern Nguni are the Nguni of Natal, who number more than two hundred independent tribes, including the Zulu, and whose economy is on the whole somewhat more developed than that of the south. We also include, partly by way of contrast, two further examples taken from the peoples of Central Africa who are unable to keep cattle mainly because the equatorial rain-forest is inimical to the spread of grassy plains, and because of the ravages of tsetse-fly. One is the Mandja, in the Haut Chari of the French Congo, between the Rivers Fafa and Kumi;[5] the other the Rega on the eastern side of the Belgian Congo between the Lualaba and Lake Kivu.[6] The results of the absence of cattle

---

[1] Not among the Mandja, and among the Rega only for witchcraft.
[2] See e.g. Aeth. 77, 83. Ine 31.
[3] Chap. 17. In England the attitude of Christianity towards polygamy (a system not permitted in the Roman Empire) was a substantial cause of its repudiation by kings and nobles in the seventh century.
[4] Cape Commission, *passim*.
[5] Gaud (1911).
[6] Delhaise (1909).

are fundamental throughout the economy. They keep goats and poultry and practise horticulture or agriculture, but the main occupation of the Rega man is the hunt. With the absence of cattle, cannibalism is probably more practised (in the last quarter of the nineteenth century) than in any other area of the world, and the same may be said of the Ngala and Ngbetu (referred to in later chapters). The Mandja and Rega kill and eat all prisoners of war.

As compared with the peoples of the previous three chapters, the evidence shows a progressive increase in the speed and extent of communications, migration, population growth, merger and fission, as well as in growth of the power of central government and capacity for administration and organized war, and now conquest by war, and other changes.[1] This development has been illustrated by the history of the barbarian peoples that overran the countries of the Western Roman Empire in the fifth and succeeding centuries. It can equally be illustrated in the history of the late eighteenth and early nineteenth centuries in South Africa.

Until the eighteenth century, wars between the tribes of South Africa arose usually out of disputes over boundaries or water-rights, the lifting of cattle, ill-treatment of a visiting subject, refusal to deliver up a refugee, and the like. They were common enough, and took the shape, now so familiar to us, of raids upon an enemy settlement which was reached by night and rushed at dawn. As many men as possible were killed, the cattle, young women and children were taken and the huts burnt, and the raiders beat a hasty retreat. The chief kept as much of the booty as he desired and distributed the rest among his warriors and council. Raid and counter-raid continued until the weaker chief sued for peace, and, if it were granted, paid a regular tribute of cattle or other property in token of submission and allegiance, being commonly permitted to retain a large measure of autonomy. Or then (or later if he discontinued the payment of tribute and was attacked and once more defeated) his whole territory might

---

[1] For authorities on the Nguni, with special reference to their law, see I. Schapera, *Select Bibliography of South African Native Life and Problems* (Oxford, 1941); First Supplement by Holden and Jacoby (Cape Town, 1950); Second Supplement by Giffen and Back (1958); also Bernice Kuper, 'Bibliography of Native Law in South Africa', 1941-61, *African Studies*, 23 (1964), pp. 155-65.

be absorbed and he himself retained as district chief, unless the victor substituted a relative of his own.

But by the third quarter of the eighteenth century the process had grown in scale and changed in character. An era of wars of conquest began, and tribes overcame and absorbed their neighbours and kingdoms emerged. The familiar story of Chaka and the Zulu kingdom shows what the peoples of this chapter are capable of. The Zulu in 1750-75 were a tribe or clan of some 2,000 tribesmen. In the ensuing struggle for supremacy Chaka, their king, by ruthless determination and military and administrative foresight, made himself in the ten years from about 1815 to 1825 master of a kingdom some 80,000 square miles in extent, covering the whole of the present Natal. The slaughter was on a scale unprecedented; chaos reigned throughout native South Africa and many of the smaller tribes were utterly destroyed. Many thousands of refugees, sometimes entire tribes, fled in every direction and fugitive tribes drove other tribes from their homes. Even Zulu generals with the forces under their command themselves sometimes fled and established kingdoms elsewhere. Out of this chaos were founded the Rhodesian Ndebele, the Shangana, the Basuto and other nations. The Zulu nation was built up from the remnants of over a hundred tribes. The men of the same age-groups were organized into regiments and quartered in great barracks about the country and trained for war while they herded the king's cattle and worked his fields. No man could marry till the king gave the word to the whole regiment to marry into a specified age-regiment of girls. War was perennial and the assassination of the cruel despot in 1828 afforded relief to his people. Long before the British deposed Cetewayo in 1880, the whole of the Zulu nation had become so homogeneous that, although it had broken into over two hundred tribes, there was one uniform Zulu culture throughout Natal.[1]

If the size of these populations, for reasons to be given, shows little increase from those of the previous chapters, the power of central government has grown much. The tribe or kingdom

[1] During the same century, further north and west, the more developed communities of the Central and Late Codes (with whom at present we are not concerned), the South Sotho under Moshesh, the Rhodesian Ndebele under Mzilikazi, and the Ngwato under Khama, similarly reduced their neighbours under their rule.

(Nguni *isizwe*) is now not only a people with its own name, occupying its own territory, but it also manages its own affairs and acts as a united body in war, and primarily this unity is expressed through allegiance to the same chief, after whom in Africa it is often named;[1] and though even the smallest includes many alien families or groups, the main stock is generally composed of persons all claiming descent from the same line of ancestors as the chief.[2] The tribes are everywhere small, and in South Africa some number no more than a few hundred souls and most are only a few thousand strong.[3] The nations into which tribes were incorporated in these areas by conquest or otherwise are much larger. At the beginning of our period the average size of the seven English Kingdoms was of the order of 100,000 persons,[4] but the Mercian, the Merovingian and the Zulu Kingdom at their height each numbered over 300,000 souls. The density of population continues to be governed by ecological conditions: South Africa has always been thinly occupied, mainly because of shortage of water and erosion of the soil, in Zululand at a rate of only about $3\frac{1}{2}$ persons per square mile,[5] whereas fertile England was probably populated by some 10 to 12 persons to the square mile.

The division of functions between the sexes in agriculture, cattle-keeping and the home remains much as in previous chapters, save that in South Africa women do not milk or handle the cattle, and this is the task of boys under the supervision of the men. Europe is rich in cattle, sheep and horses; the Africans have fewer cattle and also goats. In both areas land is plentiful everywhere and a largely shifting cultivation is practised. The arable fields are close to the homesteads or village, the pasture land further off, and in Wessex and possibly areas in Mercia and Yorkshire there is evidence of the large, open arable fields of Mediaeval England in which the ceorl (or peasant) has his strips.[6] The Cape Nguni's chief tool is some variety of digging-stick, wooden spade or iron-bladed

---

[1] e.g. 'X's people'.   [2] Schapera (1937), 173.
[3] The total population of the Mandja tribes is only about 25,000.
[4] In the south of England, Sussex, Essex and probably Middlesex, were independent kingdoms which early became shires of larger kingdoms: Whitelock (1952), 78.
[5] The density of population of the Mandja is only about 6 per square mile.
[6] Ine, *c*. 42; Stenton (1943), 277.

hoe,[1] but the Europeans have also a heavy ox-drawn plough acquired from civilization, and the slave ploughman is a familiar figure among them. The variety of crops has increased (the Germans of Tacitus grew corn alone) though many of them have been learned from civilization.[2] All keep fowls and the Europeans pigs. Pottery and brewing are chiefly women's work and metal work is the men's. All specialization is only partial, in the sense that some have special skills but even the magicians and priests and the smiths, as well as the wood workers, leather-workers, basket-workers and potters, and in Europe the stone-carvers, merely acquire additional income by these skills and live chiefly on their land and cattle and make their own huts. Skills tend to be confined to families but there is some paid apprenticeship for magicians and smiths.

The goods in use have increased much. The household goods include pots made for various purposes – there is no wheel in Africa – bowls, platters, headrests, and spoons, and horns of animals used for a variety of objects, and there is woodwork and ironwork, spinning, rope-making, dyeing, a little weaving and tanning. Articles of personal adornment are few – the males in Africa go nude – but there is some barbaric jewellery in Kent, perhaps made by Roman-British craftsmen. Metals – iron, some copper (and in Europe, bronze), lead and a little gold, found or traded – are in use for ornament or the lashing-on of spears and clubs.[3] Hoes and spears are of iron and so are most tools. Iron is mined but, in Africa at least, they cannot melt iron ore, and only produce sufficient heat, by bellows and charcoal or clay, to reduce the ore to a bloom and then shape with a stone hammer.

Age-grades do not form the basis of an organization in all these

---

[1] The Mandja and Rega use the iron hoe (about 6 to 7 inches long on a wooden handle) which has recently (1900) displaced the digging-stick.

[2] The Nguni grow Kafir corn (*sorghum vulgare*) which is indigenous, maize (from America via Europe), eleusine and several species of melons, pumpkins, peas, beans, ground-nuts and sweet potatoes, and brew beer from sorghum and also maize. The Anglo-Saxons grow rye, barley, oats and wheat (the quantities in that order).

[3] Anglo-Saxon weapons for hunting and warfare: spear, bow and arrow, shields of wood covered with hide: Hodgkin (1935), 24f.; also presumably clubs and axes. The Nguni weapons (for hunting and warfare): spear, axe and club (no bow and arrow) and shields of untanned hide: Schapera (1937), 141. In both peoples the spears are of wood, with iron heads.

peoples. Among the Southern Nguni, as in Western Europe so far as we know, there is no organization based on age, extending through a tribe, though the hierarchy of age is important. But in the Northern Nguni this gradation is the basis of Zulu military organization: between the ages of eighteen and twenty each age-grade is enrolled by the king into a distinct regiment and also performs civil duties for him as his councillors, district administrative officers and messengers.

The clan[1] continues to be a social group of high importance in South Africa and among the Celtic peoples, commonly taking its name from a putative ancestor in the male line. It is not always totemic, nor is it wholly territorial: in South Africa, for example, the same clan may be found in different tribes, especially among the Northern Nguni after the disruption wrought by Chaka. The character and extent of the part it plays in the social structure varies much from people to people, but on the whole its significance begins to diminish with the growth of the territorial principle of government and the strength of central authority. For example, among the Celtic peoples, more pastoral than the English, central government is weak and the clan strong, while among the Anglo-Saxons, who probably came to England rather in parties than as whole kinship groups, the kinship group of which we hear is the *magas* or *maegth*, which, like the Frankish *parentela*, seems to comprise near patrilineal and near matrilineal relatives,[2] and government is by kings. In South Africa (and apparently in Europe) the lineage, the members of which have usually one common grandfather, is more important. The paramount chief or king is the leading representative of the dominant, the royal clan or other kinship group and most of the influential chiefs below him belong to it also. In social relations the clan or near kindred remains a group of great significance. As among the peoples of the previous three chapters, they subscribe to the bridewealth and bloodwealth and receive their due shares of each; they support the oath of their kinsman when

---

[1] Whereas the Germans of Tacitus fought largely as kinship groups, as do the Xhosa, among the bulk of the other Southern Nguni and in England and France the military are organized territorially, and among the Northern Nguni by age-grades.

[2] England: Alf. 30. France: L. Rib. 12[2]; L. Sal. 58, de Chrenecruda. Norway: the Frostathing Law.

it is taken in litigation and they are often held responsible by government and injured persons for his good behaviour.

Especially in the less developed economies – those of the Southern Nguni and England and France when first settled by the barbarians – the basic local and territorial, social, administrative, military and even judicial and to a large extent economic unit is the homestead or kraal,[1] a group of huts housing a man, his wife or wives and unmarried children together with some married sons and their families, other near patrilineal relatives and such other persons as may attach themselves to its head[2], a total of anything between four and forty adult males, and also the cattle kraal, though animals may live with the household. The whole group of huts of wattle and daub or mud and straw is surrounded by a fence or stockade,[3] and in a polygamous household the hut or 'house' of each wife and her children and the property allocated to her or acquired by her are separate and distinct units and may be separately fenced. The Nguni do not form villages (which are characteristic of the more developed South African economies) and villages were probably few at the coming of the Anglo-Saxons and Franks[4] as they were in Tacitus' Germania. Consequently, in the settlement of England whatever Roman-British towns had not already been deserted in the economic decay of the third to the fifth centuries dissolved into desolation and ruin, and plantations sometimes grew up in their midst or beside them. The same fate overtook to a large extent even the remaining cities of Gaul. It was mainly the *villae* or *fundi*, the self-sufficient Celto-Roman estates, which survived. Later in our period villages of two to six households along the same stream or hillside were common in Western Europe,[5] and there were also, from the middle of our period, larger villages of up to forty and more households; but by the time of Alfred, at the close of this period, the population was mainly divided into villages, though there were still innumerable isolated farmsteads in the less profitable lands, many of which remain to this day with their Old English names.[6]

In South Africa a number of such kraals, along the same stream

---

[1] Xhosa and other Southern Nguni, *umzi*; Northern Nguni, *umuzi*.
[2] Nguni, *unumzana*.   [3] Hodgkin (1935), 218.
[4] Stenton (1943), 276, 284f.
[5] Clapham (1949), 44.   [6] Stenton (1943), 283.

or hillside, usually closely connected by kin, form again a distinct social, territorial, political, administrative, judicial and military unit which may be called a sub-district[1] under the control of a headman, and sub-districts may be grouped into larger districts[2] under the headship of a sub-chief. Such districts are called by Bede and others in England in the eighth century *regiones* or *provinciae* and in Wessex *shires*, but there is little known of their composition except that many probably originated in the smaller settlements of kindreds, for the Latin term is often translated by the English *maegth* (kindred) and among the Southern Nguni the districts tend to be occupied by members of the same clan. Above is the King or Paramount Chief. In different areas the number of units intermediate between kraal and chief will vary and the sub-district may be missing and in England in Aethelberht's time the *ceorl* (peasant) appears to be subject to no lord save the king.[3] Let us now look more closely at the administrative, political and legal relations between the various units of the population and their various heads.[4]

The members of the kraal or household in all lands owe to the head respect and obedience and he can inflict corporal chastisement on his wife. He is responsible for their good behaviour to the head of the district and the chief or king and is liable for their wrongs to the persons injured.[5] He represents them in litigation, supported by them, and indeed a wrong to one of them is a wrong to him. He decides disputes between them with the assistance of senior males. These relations are to some extent continued into the sub-district or district, which is the smallest effective political unit.

The headman or sub-chief, English aeldorman (*praefectus*) or reeve of the district, region or shire[6] is appointed or confirmed

---

[1] Southern Nguni, *ibandla* or *umhlaba*; Northern Nguni, *isigodi*; in France, the hundred, under its *centenarius*, *thunginus* or *vicar*.

[2] Northern Nguni *isifunda*; Frankish *pagus* under its *comes*, *graf* or *grafio*.

[3] See Aeth. *passim*, and Stenton (1943), 274.

[4] See especially, for the Nguni, Schapera (1937), Chap. VIII.

[5] So that a husband is liable for his wife's torts.

[6] In Mercia, according to the land books, the shire is governed by 'dukes' or 'princes' and sometimes a man is called 'dux' as well as 'comes'. In France the pagus is governed by a *comes* or *grafio* and the sub-district or hundred is under its *centenarius*, *thunginus* or *vicar*, each with his *rachineburgii* (council of notables). In England the shire begins to divide into hundreds at the close of this period.

by the chief or king, of whom he is often a relative, and is responsible to him for its order and good government. He must give his people assistance in their problems and difficulties and sponsor them before the chief. If he is not popular, they will desert him and go to another district and district chief.[1] On the land allocated to his people by the chief, or traditionally occupied by them, he regulates the division between the heads of families, re-allocating from time to time, as needed by families, land available when a family diminishes in numbers; but there is land to spare and he regulates the settlement of strangers in his area. He is, of course, not liable to individuals for the wrongs or debts of one of his people, but he decides disputes (law cases) between its members with the assistance of an informal council of elders, being the heads of local clans, families or other kinship groups.[2] These disputes are of two kinds: those sent up by the headmen of kraals or sub-districts as being too difficult or serious to decide and those started in his court, and there is an appeal from him to the court of the chief or king, to which he will also refer cases too difficult or serious for him to decide or traditionally heard in that court. He will see that his people pay the customary tribute to the chief or king and collect it, and that they perform the customary services to him at one of the king's estates and will carry out the latter's orders. He visits the king from time to time to act as a member of his council and report on the problems of his people. Before the adoption of Christianity he will on their behalf conduct or preside at religious ceremonies. He is entitled to certain services from his people on his land or in the building of his house.

The chief of the tribe or king is the object of veneration and adulation and is extremely wealthy. He receives a large share of the cattle looted in war and his herds are the largest in the land. Before the advent of Christianity he has many wives and he has many slaves and young men come from all parts of his kingdom to serve at his court and labour for him. He is also entitled to certain tribute in kind and services, the nature and extent of which varies from people to people and from one area to another, but in most places include certain free labour on his estates and in the

---

[1] In England this movement is restricted (see Ine, 39).
[2] England: Stenton (1934), 296. Folk moots are mentioned in the laws of Alfred and *popularia concilia* in Mercia at the beginning of the ninth century.

building of his homestead. In England it consists chiefly in the repairing of bridges and defences, the cartage of goods, and above all service in the fyrd,[1] and in the earlier period the rendering of the king's *feorm*, namely provisions sufficient for his maintenance and that of his retinue for twenty-four hours, due once a year from a group of villagers and rendered at a royal village or estate near by and applied to the king's use by his reeve.[2] It also includes the quartering and free entertainment of his servants and messengers, from greatest to least, as they pass over the country on his business. The rendering of service is commonly in proportion to the holding of land, and in England, except Kent, the unit of land known as the *hid* (hide) or *hiwisc* – that is to say, the holding sufficient to support a ceorl's household – is the basis of social and political organization.[3] The grants of land by king or chief to his nobles and companions on conquest or other occasions, with the right to receive the dues that ought to be payable by the inhabitants to the king, or subject to specified tribute and services to the king, go some way to create the English manorial system of later centuries.[4] He also receives the fines and compensation payable to him for crimes and wrongs (of which more anon) and fees in litigation. But he is under a corresponding obligation to use this wealth for the benefit of his people and everywhere royal generosity continues to be the most admired of his virtues.

The chief or king is such by heredity, in the sense that the eldest son (or, among the Nguni, the eldest son of the woman married as the 'great wife') will succeed if he is competent, but otherwise, like Alfred the Great, a brother is likely to be chosen in his place. Among the Franks, sons succeed to equal shares of the kingdom. A woman does not usually succeed, but everywhere,

[1] When in the charters, from the eighth century onwards, a donee of land is exempted from services, this exemption does not normally extend to the repair of bridges and fortresses and service in the fyrd: Stenton (1943), 286f.
[2] *Gerefa* – sheriff.
[3] Stenton (1943), 267. In Kent it is the larger unit of the *sulung* or plough-land, the area which could be kept in cultivation by a plough-team of eight oxen (*ibid.*, 278). In France the Merovingians inherited a system of taxation which fell into desuetude, but tribute was paid in various forms and on various occasions of which too little is known.
[4] Stenton (1943), 298. Another factor may often be the consolidation or spread of a king's authority, whereby an independent king may decline to the status of the former's sub-chief, or in an English charter from rex to *sub-regulus* and finally to *dux* or aeldorman (*ibid.*, 301-2).

if the customary heir is too young, may be appointed regent to rule for him till he reaches years of discretion (in France the age of twelve). Often, in Europe and Africa, the king's mother (like the redoubtable Brunhild, wife of Sigebert) is a powerful and able regent, especially if, as is frequent in Africa, she was married with bridewealth contributed by the people generally. More usually, however, the regent appointed is the eldest surviving brother of the deceased.

The king of the nation, or tribal chief, is the ruler in peace and leader in war, the supreme judge and (until Christian times) the chief priest and magician. Let us look at these functions in a little more detail, remembering that there is development between the South and North Nguni and between the beginning and end of our period in Western Europe.

First, he is the ruler, or head executive and administrative authority, with rights and obligations as such. He is generally assisted by a number of advisers – a few relatives (such as uncles, cousins and brothers) and a few of his district chiefs or headmen (who may be the same persons) and a few other friends. At his accession there were advisers of his father whom he might retain till he finds his own counsellors. He need not take their advice but he would be foolish not to consult them and he would rarely oppose their united opinion. They are to some extent held responsible by the general community if he goes astray. They should keep him informed of public opinion and events within the tribe or nation and matters that call for attention. Included in his entourage are some officials, who may be commoners, and the Merovingian monarch of the sixth century and the Zulu king will have a few such, dividing departments of the household between them. One is his minister or chief adviser – among the Northern Nguni the *induna*, among the Xhosa *umphakathi omkhulu*, and in Merovingian France the *mayor of the palace*. His office is not usually hereditary but tends to become so, especially when the king is weak, often the case in Zululand and in Austrasia among the descendants of Arnulf and Pepin I. He is head of the administration and of the courts and the district chiefs tend to fall under his authority. Among some of the Xhosa, for example, the kraal of the chief councillor, which is near that of the chief, is a refuge or asylum for anyone fleeing a sentence of death for any offence, and normally, if he can reach it, he suffers no more than the payment of a fine, and indeed anyone considering himself unjustly punished, even by a chief, will there obtain an investigation of his case, and even a chief may be required to release the cattle that he has seized.[1] But in England the typical aeldorman of the eighth and ninth centuries seems to be a member of the king's household who has been put in charge of a *regio* or shire and is removable at pleasure. Among the many persons who resort to the king's court, or take up permanent residence in the capital village, there are (apart from his councillors, advisers and messengers) local chiefs and headmen and their indunas, who come for instruction, or to explain away a matter that has come to the king's ears, those who have come in the hope of making a career in the royal service, and the king's bodyguard, which eats at his table.

In the Germania of Tacitus we noted that 'upon minor matters the chiefs[2] deliberate, and upon greater matters the whole tribe, except that even those matters that rest upon the decision of the whole people are first discussed by the chiefs'.[3] It remains the general situation that the king or tribal chief rules, but there is a tribal council,[4] consisting of the district sub-chiefs and headmen and his other advisers, including some commoners of ability, and other relatives, or some of these, and also there are important occasions when the whole tribe is specially assembled to hear and debate a proposed change in fundamental policy. Again the king need not act upon their advice if they differ, but he would not act contrary to their united counsel. When, however, the Franks first invaded Gaul, because of the great distances to be travelled, these national councils ceased to be held for a time, and it was only when a great military expedition assembled that they were able to express their opinions. They met, indeed, voluntarily from time to time in meetings of ecclesiastics and meetings of laymen to discuss affairs of common interest, and the king no doubt took note of their views. At the end of our period, when order returns for a time under the Carolingians, the national council meets again and becomes a significant part of the new constitution.

[1] Cape Commission, Evidence 83-85 (Gaikas).
[2] i.e. the tribal chief and his council of district chiefs or sub-chiefs.
[3] Tac. Germ. 11. [4] Nguni *ibandla* or *inkundla*; English *witan* or *witanagemot*.

In brief, the power of an individual ruler depends largely on his own ability and ruthlessness, but it has grown vastly. Many Merovingian rulers were, like Chaka and some others in South Africa, despots, and the system of government has been well described as a despotism tempered by assassination. Nevertheless it is well known in Europe and Africa that the king or tribal chief, even if he has the right to make changes in the law against or without advice, would be foolish to attempt to do so. Cetewayo, ex-king of the Zulus, giving evidence before the Cape Native Laws Commission, said that he had not, as king, the power to make a change in any law in Zululand unless the chiefs were consulted and agreed.[1] Indeed he relies on them, when they return to their territories, to publish it so that it may be obeyed.[2]

As ruler of nation or tribe, the king or chief controls the distribution and use of its land. It is considered to belong to him,[3] but it is his in a sense intermediate between a legal ownership and administrative management. He could not sell it even if there were anyone to buy it.[4] Especially when the community moves to a new territory, but indeed in all cases, he controls the division of the land among the chiefs, and as representing him they control the division between the heads of the households,[5] but grazing is common to all. In theory the king could deprive an occupier of his land, at least for neglect of it, but in fact, in the words of Cetewayo, he merely 'tells him he ought not to do such a thing because his father did not'.[6]

All able-bodied adult males are liable to military service (English, in the *fyrd*) – that is to say, to be called out for military service (but not for training) and normally only within the district of their homes (in England within their shire).[7] Service by the occupants of homestead or kraal in their clans or other kinship groups, as among the Germans of Tacitus and Xhosa, is giving place in the second half of our period to other organizations – among the Zulu by age-grades and in Europe according to land-

---

[1] Cape Commission, 530.
[2] Sir Theophilus Shepstone giving evidence to the Cape Commission well describes the constitutional position of the Nguni chief, especially in Zululand, at p. 4 of his evidence.
[3] This rule survived in England till 1925.
[4] Cape Commission, 443.   [5] Cape Commission, 49.
[6] Cape Commission, 523.   [7] Stenton (1943), 287.

holding, the village being liable to the supply of men according to the number of hides at which it is rated, and the district chief or lord being responsible to provide them. The ceorl is hardly armed during most of our period: the noble arrives better equipped on his modest horse but dismounts to fight.

Lastly the king, or tribal chief, before the introduction of Christianity, is the chief priest and magician of his people. What this means and what effect Christianity had upon the power of the king and the development of legal procedure in Europe, we shall consider in a later chapter.[1]

[1] See *post* Chap. 21.

CHAPTER 20

The Recent Peoples of the Early Codes – The Law

In the previous chapter some of the rules of law characteristic of the recent peoples of the Early Codes have already been noticed, in particular their constitutional rules, defining the relations between the authoritative bodies in the state or tribe. We continue with the other branches of the law, including the law of the peoples of the Early Codes of the past, partly for comparison, and partly because in our chapter on the Early Codes of the past[1] we were considering those Codes at their face value and we possess some further knowledge of the law of those peoples.

The institution of marriage, until the adoption of Christianity and contact with civilization, remains substantially what it was at our previous stage[2] and we need add little. It is the bridewealth marriage, consummated by payment of bridewealth and cohabitation (or, more precisely, the handing over of the girl). The institution is known to the Nguni as *ukulobola*, and *lobola* – or, more properly, *ikazi* – is the bridewealth itself, payable in cattle where cattle can be reared.[3] The amount is a matter for agreement, and is normally something between ten and seventeen head of cattle, all paid before cohabitation, but in temporary scarcity it may be much less and often part is left as a debt. Marriage is generally patrilocal, and the character and incidents of the marriage remain much as before except that we notice in South Africa the insistence, by native and European observer alike,[4] on the notion that

---

[1] See *ante* Chap. 5.   [2] Chap. 17.
[3] North of Zululand, where cattle do not flourish, it is usually payable in corn or iron hoes: Cape Commission, Evidence, 35. The Mandja bridewealth usually consists of about 360 arrows, five copper bracelets and two knives of jet.
[4] e.g. Cape Commission, *passim*.

the origin and main purpose of bridewealth is to provide maintenance for the wife and her children if she should return to her
father's home in want, or even need support during the subsistence
of the marriage; for every kinsman of hers who received any part
of it is obliged to maintain them in those circumstances, an
obligation which, in some places at least, the courts will enforce.[1]
But, as before, there is more than one rationale of the institution.[2]
Polygyny is everywhere and the proportions of men who have
one, two or more wives remain much as before – the bulk (about
75 per cent) of married men have only one wife, and the proportion
who have more than two is insignificant and confined to the
chiefs and the wealthy.[3] The levirate marriage (*ukugena*) remains
in some places, and in some places the inheritance of wives
(usually by the next younger brother of the deceased). Of the
marriage settlement, that is the provision of property or money
by the girl's father for her support and that of her children, there
is as yet no sign, except that the recipients of bridewealth are under
the obligation referred to above, and it is common or usual for the
bride to bring with her an animal or other gifts on entering her
groom's home, and sometimes they may even approach the value
of the bridewealth. Of the bridewealth marriage in the Early
Codes of the past we have less information, but it probably
survived in England till the Norman Conquest at least, and there
is no reason to think that it differed in important respects from
that described above.

Apart from claims for death and personal injuries, women and
bridewealth are the chief sources of litigation. Unpaid *ikazi* is
recoverable in the courts, but more common and difficult are the

[1] e.g. Cape Commission, Evidence, 94.
[2] The following statements were made by native witnesses to the Cape
Commission – 'I paid *lobola* to make a knot of alliance' (100). 'He brought
her up and I took her away' (81). 'A father expects something for his
daughter as she has to perform the duties of a wife and give birth to children.
As these things are inflictions on the girl the father must get something in
compensation' (*Ibid*.). 'There would be no relationship without the cattle,
for there would be no friendship between the two kraals' (93).
[3] The population of the Mandja was stationary. Thirteen men had between
them twenty-nine wives, who had sixty children, of which 40 per cent died
before maturity. Three Mandja chiefs who completed their career had ten
wives and by them nineteen sons (of whom twelve survived) and nine
daughters (of whom four survived.) Out of these eighty-eight children,
therefore, only fifty-two (59 per cent) survived to maturity: Gaud (1911) 262f.

husband's claims for its repayment in a variety of circumstances. There is the case where, after payment, the lady has not been delivered; or where after betrothal – constituted by an agreement for bridewealth and some formality or festivity – and payment of part on behalf of the boy, she is seduced by another or runs away with him. Here there is a question whether the latter pays the boy compensation or he or the parents repay the boy the bridewealth. *Ikazi* may also be repayable where the wife dies childless, or where she leaves her husband without good cause. Divorce, in some places only recognized if given by the chief's court, can be obtained by the husband for sorcery, repeated adultery, desertion, refusal or inability to give conjugal rights, or other serious misbehaviour, and in such cases he is entitled to repayment. But any children that have been born to the wife are always his, and he may have to make an allowance on that account. And on the other hand he will not secure repayment if his wife is entitled to a divorce, which she can obtain for cruelty, desertion or refusal or inability to render conjugal rights. The law on these matters varies in detail from people to people.

We turn to ideas of property. The rules of law relating to land were touched on in the previous chapter. The land is generally considered to belong to the king or chief, who has the right to dispossess the occupant without cause, but for reasons of state and public opinion he is rarely likely to do so and the holding descends in the families[1] according to the local rules of inheritance. An occupier dispossessed by his local chief or headman has a right of appeal to the king, but there is no right of appeal against dispossession by the king. There is no notion of the individual right of property in land save in the king, and no one sells or purports to sell his holding. But the king or chief makes grants of territory to his *comes* or *gesith* (companion) in France and England and his sub-chiefs in Africa, especially when newly conquered territory is distributed, and also in Europe to bishops and abbots who are building up the great ecclesiastical estates of later centuries. The combination of this rule that the land belongs to

---

[1] There is no inheritance of land among the Mandja and Rega. The land is vested in the clan or chief and reverts to them on being abandoned. A man requiring land for himself and family will usually apply to the chief of the village or territory in which he desires to live and land will be assigned to him.

the king and the knowledge of writing and of the Roman conveyancing forms of the sixth century gives birth, from early in the
eighth century to a practice of the grant of charters by the kings
to their companions and nobles, and to churches and abbots,
giving them territorial lordships (especially over newly conquered
lands) and empowering them to exact there the dues and services
formerly rendered or that would be payable by the local peasantry
to the king; *bocland* (bookland) becomes the name for an estate
secured to its holder by a royal charter in such Roman form. The
charter may even include a clause empowering the recipient to
transfer the lordship or bequeath it and often that the heir shall
be a religious community. The form of the charter becomes so
significant and regular that in the ninth century when a king
wishes to devote his land to religious uses free of tribute and
dues to himself, he enters into such a charter granting the land
to himself free of the specified burdens.[1]

But the notion of the individual property in goods is, of course,
everywhere and chattels are exchanged and sold. The few things
used or acquired by a woman, single or married, are considered
to belong to her, but cattle allotted to each of his wives by a
polygamous husband are considered to belong to her house.[2]

The African rules of inheritance show no change from the
peoples at the close of the previous stage and we need add little
to what has been said.[3] Where there is more than one wife the
eldest son of each inherits the property allocated by the deceased
to that house, including the right to bridewealth in respect of
each sister, with the obligation to support his mother and unmarried sisters and to help unmarried brothers to find bridewealth,
and the eldest son of the Great Wife inherits the rest with a
general obligation of support. Females do not inherit.[4] But among
many or most Nguni peoples a sister and a brother are paired off
from the rest and he is bound to support her with necessaries and
is entitled to receive the *ikazi* in respect of her. In default of sons

[1] Stenton (1943), 298f.
[2] But among the Rega, household utensils brought from home by the women
or later acquired by them are considered to belong to the husband's mother
or his first wife. [3] See *ante* p. 257f.
[4] But among the Mandja the few goods go to the eldest child, male or female
(unless she is married). Among the Rega the eldest brother usually takes
them.

the nearest patrilineal relative (usually a young brother of the deceased) takes subject to the same obligations, and in default of relatives, the chief. In the few cases where a commoner has more than one wife, the first wife is the Great Wife, but not among the chiefs. Here the Great Wife is married as the Great Wife, often with *ikazi* contributed by the people, or is appointed such by the chief after consultation with his advisers.[1] Among most Nguni however, the home and most of the personal belongings of the deceased are destroyed at his death. Much of this must have been law among the Germans and English at the commencement of our period, but the evidence does not survive. The law of later centuries sheds little light even on the question to what extent primogeniture was law in earlier days, but it does suggest that there were differences between the territories of earlier kingdoms and tribes, and in England especially between Kent and the rest, and that in most places sons inherited their father's possessions equally, and perhaps daughters in default of sons and that, as in Africa, the household continued undivided for some time after the father's death.[2]

In the absence of writing there is no formal will and testament in Africa, but a father's last words and instructions in respect of his household are scrupulously obeyed. They do not normally depart far from the traditional rules of succession and rather provide supplementary details thereto. In Europe the possession of writing, confined to clerics, and the practice of leaving property to a religious foundation for the redemption of the soul of the donor, creates a written will, later enforced by ecclesiastical courts.

We turn to the civil wrongs and crimes, noting first that, as at all stages since law first appears, there is a palpable distinction between the two, though the Nguni have no term for either.[3] With the growth in the power of the chief it is best described as a distinction between wrongs committed against individuals and

---

[1] Among Gaikas and some other Nguni a second Right-Hand Wife is also recognized and a third wife, the Left-Hand Wife, who is a 'rafter' to one of the other houses; the son of the Great Wife or Right-Hand Wife would inherit the property allocated to that house and so with other wives. (See e.g. Cape Commission, Evidence, 116.)

[2] Stenton (1943), 314.

[3] Cape Commission, Report 21; Evidence, 5, 25.

wrongs committed against the chief, though there is an element
in the latter group of wrongs against the chief as representing the
state or tribe. Serious crimes are only tried in the chief's court and
a man is bound to report to his superior the commission of any
crime of which he may become aware,[1] and an attempt to compromise a crime is punishable by fine, nor does the compromise
bind the chief, who may still exact the due sanction in respect of
the offence.[2]

In the most serious civil wrongs, especially homicide, we notice
in these tribes of South Africa a palpable advance against the
generality of our peoples of the previous stage,[3] an advance already
foreshadowed in the Shilluk monarchy and some of the German
tribes and already reached in the peoples of the Early Codes of the
past. The foundation and justification for the rule of pecuniary
sanctions for homicide is the impracticability of any other rule –
that is to say, the absence of any developed central authority in
the society which could punish or prevent it, the absence of
prisons in these undeveloped economies, the strength and
solidarity of the kinship group (the chief power in the tribe) which
would resent physical interference from any authority external to
it and yet may not have the strength to obtain revenge or to resist
it, and the common interest in the maintenance or restoration of
peace. Any other sanction would be the unrestricted violence of
the feud, and indeed the feud remains in the background as a
force that supports the rule. Nor is there as yet a sufficient public
spirit and social conscience to regard homicide as religiously,
ethically or socially evil; or is it better to say that the inability to
enforce any other sanction makes it impossible to see homicide
in that light? Now the power of the clan or other kinship group
is diminishing in favour of kingship, and kingship brings about
the change that homicide is an offence against the king, for it
lessens the number of his subjects and therefore his strength, and
against his kingdom. We saw[4] that the effect on the sanctions for
homicide was somewhat different between the English and Continental Codes, and it is different again among the Nguni, but
these are differences in detail and the stage of development is the
same. Among the Germans of Tacitus we read that 'a part of the

[1] Cape Commission, Evidence, 8.   [2] Cape Commission, Evidence, 86.
[3] *Ante* p. 26of.   [4] *Ante* p. 68.

impost (*multa*) is paid to the king or state and part to him who
is being vindicated or his relatives'. We are told no details and
need not doubt that the position differed in different peoples. Only
under the strong Shilluk monarchy – the most advanced of
our peoples of the previous stage – did we find a rule that the
king (though acting spasmodically and not with regularity)
through his messengers collected the pecuniary sanction for
homicide and the other serious injuries and kept most of it for
himself, but would let the next of kin or injured victim have a
portion.[1] Turning to the past peoples of the Early Codes, we
found in the Code of Aethelberht a doctrine under which the
generality of individuals are under the *mund* or protection of some
superior (parent, husband or king) and compensation (*mundbyrd*)
is payable to him for breach of his right to protect. In regard to
the king, apart from wrongs which are in a special sense breach
of his *mund* (for example, molesting one of his lieges called before
him, robbing the king, slaying a man on the king's premises or
lying with a maiden belonging to him) there is *mundbyrd* when any
freeman is slain or robbed anywhere, or any freewoman is raped.
A fine is payable to the king but (with the possible exception of
robbery) there is also payable to the victim or his family the sum
of compensation (called by a different name) defined by the Code.
The Continental Codes generally express the matter somewhat
differently and provide for the more serious cases a payment of
fridus (peace money) to the king in addition to the *faidus* (feud
money, or compensation) to the person wronged.[2] The Nguni go
further and in their law the payment for any blood case (that is,
homicide or serious personal injury) goes wholly to the king,
though he may in his discretion give something to the person
injured, and no compensation is payable to the victim or his
relatives. Accordingly the hitherto civil wrongs of homicide and
serious personal injury among the Nguni become criminal
offences, while in Europe they are still civil and also criminal.[3]
Unintentional killing among the Nguni is, equally with 'killing

[1] Among the Mandja and Rega the sanctions for the civil wrongs are
generally pecuniary, and the amount of the sanction is assessed in each case.
There is no table of fixed compositions.
[2] *Ante* p. 68.
[3] Religion has little power among the Mandja and Rega, and there are no
sanctuaries in which a man may take asylum.

in anger', punishable by a fine payable to the king and only triable in the king's court, though the fine will be smaller. In most cases there is no trial but the king's sheriff (*umsila*) calls and collects the fine. There is a right to kill a murderer caught in the act.

Nothing need be added here on the subject of the traditional fines or compensation for personal injuries. Adultery, always on the frontier of crime, is both a civil and criminal offence. Compensation is payable to the husband (increased in some places from three to five head if the woman becomes pregnant) but the king may still, if he learns of the offence, inflict a fine. An adulterer may be killed in *flagranti delicto*. Seduction is met by compensation to the father or other nearest kinsman, usually in the amount of one head of cattle, but it is rare that the man does not marry her.[1] Rape is both civil and criminal, in that it is tried in the chief's court and the fine imposed is payable to the chief, but the parties are permitted to compromise. Theft is in general civil, and can be compounded by payment of a multiple of the value, but theft of cattle is a criminal offence. A thief caught stealing in the night may be killed with impunity. It is interesting to find a similar spoor law to that in the Early Codes of the past: if the trail of a recently stolen animal leads to a certain kraal and stops there, the inhabitants must explain the matter away or pay. The only other civil wrong of which mention need be made is the occasional slander, tried in the chief's court, which imposes compensation in cattle according to circumstances.

The criminal offences, apart from those already mentioned, are witchcraft and the making of a false charge of witchcraft by a witch-doctor, treason[2] (that is to say, such offences against the chief as planning his death or making war against the tribe), burning a man's home, incest[3] and other unnatural offences, and in some places abortion. They are all tried in the chief's court and the sentence varies between a fine, banishment (rarely) and death and confiscation of the defendant's possessions, according to circumstances.

[1] A witness stated to the Cape Commission (Evidence, 132) that he had never known such a case.
[2] And acts of contempt of the chief or his court. For the Mandja, see Gaud (1911), 421.
[3] Among the Nguni all marriage between relatives by blood or clan members is prohibited.

L

The only transactions among the Nguni that can be given the name of contracts are exchange, sale, loans between friends, *ukusisa*,[1] the temporary care of children by a foster parent, services of magicians and a few artisans, and betrothal and marriage. It does not appear that the law recognizes any executory contract among any peoples of the Early Codes – that is to say, any agreement which is as yet wholly unperformed on either side. The debts due under such transactions are recoverable in the courts.

The procedure of trials among the Nguni is informal and by unsworn evidence. There is no torture of defendants or witnesses,[2] and the accused, women and children can all be heard.

To sum up the contents of this and the previous chapter we see that there is no great difference between the law of the Nguni and of our peoples of Europe, and no greater difference than between one European people and another, however much they may differ in the other elements of their culture.

But whereas everywhere among the Nguni ordeals are employed at a trial only where evidence is wanting,[3] in Western Europe the ordeal underwent an abnormal development that is probably found nowhere else. We shall attempt to outline this history, and the reasons for it, in the following chapter.

[1] See *ante* p. 272.   [2] Except slaves.
[3] But a witness may on occasion voluntarily seek to strengthen his evidence by such a form of words as 'This is true in the name of the chief'. (Cape Commission, Evidence, 159.) See *post*, similarly among the Lamba (Chap. 24). Among the Mandja the ordeal is not employed.

CHAPTER 21

Trial by Ordeal in the Early Codes

In the previous two chapters on the Recent Peoples of the Early Codes nothing was said of their religious beliefs or observances or magical practices and this is because we found no occasion to refer to them in an account of their substantive law. The situation is such as we observed among peoples of less developed economies than these, namely that there is no confusion or mingling of law with religion or magic. Magic and religion in their relation to law continue to operate as conservative agents which go to retain or reinforce the loyalty of a society to its traditional norms of behaviour, but not to reform or amend them. The ethical content of magical and religious ideas is in any case small, though when a community has adopted or evolved a new social or ethical outlook on any matter and a corresponding rule of law, it may also become a religious rule – that is to say, a rule whose sanction is divine displeasure, but it was not religion or magic that created or amended the ethical or legal rule. The only borderline we have found, here and earlier, between law and religion is at two points: one, where certain criminal offences (known as sacral offences) are also religious offences; and the other where magical or religious beliefs and practices are employed by the law to deter perjury. The means used is the ordeal.

We have seen that about the year A.D. 700 the Early Codes undergo a great change in England and France, namely in the introduction into the written laws in some places of religious matter,[1] and plainly economic development will not explain it for it occurs at the same time in both countries though economically England is still a century behind France. We will also find, at a somewhat earlier date, great changes in the development of the

---

[1] See *ante* p. 48f.

ordeal, and we should compare and contrast the religion and magic of Western Europe with that, for example, of the Nguni in order to understand the causes.

The South African Bantu is a cheerful and extrovert person. Religion[1] means less to him than to many other peoples and he is far more interested in the mundane things of this world than in metaphysics and the after-life. Magic and witchcraft are nevertheless conceptions of importance. All the Nguni distinguish between the witch (Zulu and Xhosa *zumthakathi*) who is more commonly a woman than a man, and seeks to cause the death of an enemy by magic, especially poison, and the wizard (Zulu *inyanga*) who practises the profession of magician and is at the disposal of any member of the public for a fee. The methods of witch and wizard are often the same: the difference lies in the purpose.

Various forms of ordeal and divination were occasionally resorted to by the Nguni to ascertain the guilt or innocence of a defendant. But, as in our previous stage, they were only used in the absence of evidence, and therefore chiefly in charges of witch- craft and adultery (where direct evidence is usually wanting) but also in theft (which now becomes so serious a wrong) and other cases where evidence is wanting. The poison ordeal was used for the capital offence of witchcraft (for if the defendant dies, justice is done); the other main forms of ordeal were two: the ordeal by hot water and the ordeal by hot iron.[2] They were not applied to witnesses and the oath was unknown.

In the religion of the Nguni, ancestors figure more vividly than the god. They believe in a soul that wanders in sleep and survives as a spirit after death, and the most important spirits for them are the souls of those who were of chief importance to them in life, namely their parents and ancestors. These continue, as they believe, to interest themselves actively in the affairs of their descendants and their people, to resent breach of custom and to expect attention, by gifts and sacrifice. They can send blessings if pleased, and disease, drought and disaster if slighted. The more important and powerful they were in life, the more important and powerful they remain, and most important of all are the

[1] For the religion of the Nguni see W. C. Willoughby, *The Soul of the Bantu* (1928, New York); Schapera (1937), Chaps. X and XI.
[2] Picking stones out of hot water, and licking a red-hot knife.

ancestors of the chief, the ancestors of the senior lineage of the tribe. They are pleased by sacrifices made by the senior living member, and therefore it is for the chief, and him alone, to perform the sacrifices to his ancestors. They declare their desires in various ways, and sometimes through prophets, persons prone to see visions, who become recognized as such by having once seen a vision or undergone a great spiritual experience.

The sacrifices are for the most part stereotyped, slight, ceremonious and unemotional affairs. There is nothing of a burden of sin, repentance or self-abasement and hardly of ethical conduct dictated by religion, except that it is right to adhere to the old ways, and that the ancestors will be angered and may do mischief if custom is forsaken.

There is also a vague but universal belief among the Nguni in a Supreme Being connected with the sky. He is the creator of all and can deal out punishment, especially by sending disastrous weather. But he is never worshipped nor is prayer or sacrifice offered to him. The ancestors can approach him as mediators on behalf of their descendants, like some important headman approaching a chief, or, as we might say, like a patron saint mediating with God[1] and in particular, they can appeal to him for rain. It is the function of the chief to obtain rain for his people by interceding with his ancestors by means of one of the rain-making rites. He is also the custodian of various sacred objects and medicines, and magicians work at his command. He conducts other important religious ceremonies for the whole tribe. In this sense he is the chief priest, but there is no priestly caste or order.

These beliefs, and the belief in various mischievous local spirits of divers sorts that beset the traveller's step, are the main religious tenets of the Nguni. There are no places, hallowed by religion, to which a man may flee to save his life. The sanctuary among the Nguni is the kraal of the chief counsellor, who also acts as a sort of appeal court against arbitrary actions of the chief.

The tribes and confederacies of Germany, when we first see or can infer their legal practices, employed ordeals only for the same

[1] W. C. Willoughby, *Race Problems in the New Africa* (Oxford, 1923) p. 78f.

purposes and to the same extent as the generality of primitive peoples of the same material stage elsewhere and in other times. They tried disputes upon the informal oral and unsworn evidence of the parties and their witnesses, and later, when they learned the use of writing, the inspection of such documents as were available; but in the absence of a sufficiency of evidence they resorted to other means to assist the search for truth, namely the application of an ordeal to the party whose story was in question. The expression 'a sufficiency of evidence' must not be understood in any technical sense – the recent English rule dating from the eighteenth century and now almost wholly repealed, which excluded hearsay evidence with certain exceptions, had, of course, no place – but the ordeal was generally used only where the evidence of the defendant was alone available and it was applied to him. As among the Nguni the most common ordeal was that of the cauldron of hot water (Old English *ceace*) and that of the hot iron was also employed: the party who was burnt was guilty, the successful party was in the right.[1] The ordeal by an oath in the name of a god is rare among peoples of this stage of development, and it must be considered unlikely that these tribes had possessed it.

With the diffusion of Roman culture and the adoption of Christianity came the oath,[2] taken commonly in church at the altar, often on sacred relics, consecrated arms or the gospel, with an accompanying ritual growing in elaboration and designed to terrify and deter the dishonest, but the oath was only used to the same extent and in the same circumstances as the ordeals previously employed. It was an oath of purgation – that is to say, it determined the issue: the defendant who took the oath successfully was acquitted: he who failed to take it was guilty. The use of the

---

[1] Other ordeals were, later at least, by drinking cold water or being immersed or thrown into it; and there were also methods of divination.

[2] The oath of purgation had survived throughout the history of Roman law, though the extent of its use is not clear. The plaintiff might in certain cases offer an oath (of different forms) to the defendant, and if the latter took it the action was lost; if he refused it he was condemned. He might, however, offer it back, in which case the same alternative lay before the plaintiff: W. W. Buckland, *A Textbook of Roman Law* (Cambridge, 1932), 633. Generally the oath appears to have related to matters within the sole or special knowledge of the party to whom it was offered. Among Christians the use of the oath was probably reinforced by such biblical texts as Ex. 22[9-11].

oath spread rapidly, and on the Continent tended to replace the older ordeals, but less so in England.[1] To follow the course of the story we must look at the texts of the Codes in the order of their date, and have hardly any other source of information, for the Codes are anterior to other legal literature and usually to all other literature. Above all we must not read into them, as many a scribe wrote into them, the developments of later centuries.

The extant fragments of Euric's Visigothic code (*c*. A.D. 483) – a Late Code of a people long influenced by Roman culture and converted to Christianity, and applying to disputes between Goth and Goth and Goth and Roman, contains no reference to oath or ordeal except those typical of Late Codes,[2] namely in claims against a bailee for loss of animals, goods or money, lent, deposited or hired. He is to 'provide'[3] an oath that the loss was not by his fault or negligence. There is, however, one development – in one case he is to provide the oath 'together with his witnesses'.[4] These clauses imply that here, as elsewhere, the evidence of parties and witnesses was normally unsworn, otherwise the provisions would have been unnecessary, and the oath is in each case an oath of purgation.

The Ostrogothic code, the Edictum Theoderici, of A.D. 500 also belongs to the economic stage of our Late Codes. The Ostrogoths had adopted Christianity and absorbed much of Roman culture, and many of the provisions of the Code have counterparts in late Roman law. There is no reference throughout to oath or ordeal except two applications of the oath: one, § 106, providing that where a case is decided by oath on the consent of the litigant or the order of a judge, the decision is final and no claim for perjury may be brought;[5] the second (§ 119) that where property is lost in an inn, those who were there are to take an oath of their family's innocence, and the plaintiff takes an oath as

---

[1] For some texts in the laws showing the ritual used in England in the ordeals, see Ine, 37, and (nn.) thereto in Attenborough (1922), II Aethelstan, 23; Liebermann, vol. I, pp. 374 *et seq.*; and, on the Continent, for the use of the oath see e.g. Ed. Roth. 359.
[2] Chaps. 278-85 De Commendatis vel Commodatis.
[3] 'Praebeat'.
[4] 'Una cum testibus' (they would usually be kinsmen).
[5] See also Lex Romana Burgundionum XXIII.

to the amount he has lost. These, then, are again apparently cases where no evidence will generally be available on the other side, and the taking of the oath decides the issue.

The Lex Burgundionum, another code of native law of a people influenced by Roman culture, a Late Code of similar date produced for the barbarian subjects of that realm, contains five instances[1] of the application of the oath, directed in each case because of the absence of any evidence except the defendant's. In four of the cases the question is as to his knowledge of a fact and he escapes liability by taking an oath[2] that he did not know it; and in the fifth instance a criminal charge is brought against him, based on suspicion, and he is acquitted on taking an oath of innocence together with eleven of his nearest kinsmen.

But there is also the celebrated Chapter XLV, which is historically so important that it should be quoted in full in translation:

> Many of our people are so far corrupted by the stubbornness of the litigant and the impulse of greed that they commonly do not hesitate to offer oaths on matters of doubt and continually to perjure themselves on matters unknown. To remove this criminal practice we decree by the present law, that as often as a case arises among our people, in which the defendant denies, with the offer of oaths, that he owes what is claimed from him or has done what is alleged against him, an end should be put to their litigation in manner following: if the side of him to whom an oath has been offered is unwilling to accept oaths and says, confident in the truth, that his adversary can be convicted by force of arms, and the other side does not yield, permission to fight shall not be refused. One of those witnesses who had come to give oaths shall fight, God judging, for it is right that if anyone says without hesitation that he knows the truth of the matter, and offers oaths, he shall not hesitate to fight. And if a witness of the side that offered oaths is defeated in the contest, all witnesses who promised to swear shall be made to pay 300 shillings each by way of punishment and without any indulgence of time. Whereas if he who rejected the oath is killed, whatever was

---

[1] L. Burg. VI, 3, 6; VIII, 1; XX; XXXIX, 3; LII, 4.
[2] L. Burg.; in LII, 4, with eleven witnesses.

owing shall be yielded up ninefold in full from his estate, so that they may delight in truth rather than perjury.

It bears a date equivalent to A.D. 502. We notice that at the date of this law the practice of a number of witnesses supporting the defendant's oath of purgation (of which we have seen two instances in the code) must have become common in Burgundy, and we notice the royal legislator's lack of faith in its invariable efficiency. This is the first trace and beginning of the ordeal by battle. The barbarian legislators were much concerned to put an end to feud and disorder and to punish an aggrieved person taking the law into his own hands, and several clauses of the *leges barbarorum* are expressly devised to this end. Hence the expression 'pugnandi licentia non negetur'. The present law, by which an angry king imposes the sanction of an enormous sum which few could find, surprises us by its early date, if indeed it is so early. It purports to be a law enacted by Gundobad after the main code (which dates from before 490) and it does not appear in the Lex Romana Burgundionum, which was also later than the main code. It was the subject of the passionate attacks in the ninth century of Archbishop Agobad of Lyons, who without success urged Louis II to abrogate it.

When we turn to the Lex Salica, one of the most primitive of our Early Codes, we see that this situation has not yet been reached. The earlier part of the code (II-XXXVIII) may be of about A.D. 500 and edited in Clovis' time. Like the rest of the code it is to be found in eleven texts of the eighth and subsequent centuries. It contains no provisions relating to procedure and none relating to the oath, with two interesting exceptions which are only to be found in one of the texts.[1] In each case the oath is only applied *si certa probatio not fuerit* ('if there is no definite proof'), and the defendant is to discharge himself with a fixed number of swearers (twenty or twenty-five, presumably kinsmen) *medicus electus* – that is to say, the opposing side is to have the right of nominating half of them. If the defendant cannot provide the oath-takers, in one case (a suit between two Romans) he is to undergo the cauldron test, in the others he pays the sum specified

---

[1] In the earlier part of the Code:— XIV, 2, 3, and XVI, 3: only found in Cod. 2 of Hessels and Kern (1880).

L*

304 PRIMITIVE LAW, PAST AND PRESENT

by the clause. At the beginning of the later half of the code are two other provisions in similar terms, one only found in one of the texts, the other found in two.[1] There are, however, five more clauses to be mentioned, which are found in the later parts of the code in all texts.[2] Three of them are probably cases of oaths of purgation, and probably only apply where there is no definite proof; the last two relate to witnesses giving sworn evidence as to certain facts. There is, therefore, evidence that the use of the oath is spreading and traces of the oath-helpers becoming in some cases merely sworn witnesses. There is no mention of the ordeal by battle and no evidence of it among the Franks for nearly three centuries after Clovis.

The enormous Visigothic Code of Reccesswinth ('the Law Book') was promulgated about A.D. 654 to all subjects of the kingdom. It is one of our Late Codes – an excellent compendium of Visigothic law as influenced by contact with Rome. It contains no references to the ordeal of battle or the cauldron. In most mentions of the oath, it is an oath of purgation taken where there is no sufficient evidence of any other kind, and this outlook is clear in several chapters. We read, for example, in II, 1.21:[3]

> Let the Judge, so that he may grasp the case well, first question the witnesses and then ask for the documents, so that the truth may be more surely discovered, lest it may easily come to an oath. . . . But let oaths be given in those cases where the judge's investigation elicits no writing or proof or sure signs of the truth.

And II, 2.5 provides that

> the Judge should ask for proof from both parties, plaintiff and defendant alike, and competently decide which ought

---

[1] L. Sal. XXXIX, 2 (only in Cods. 1 and 2) and XLII, 5 (only in Cod. 1).
[2] L. Sal. XLVIII, 2 (imposes a fine for perjury on the party and each of his oath-takers); XLIX (fine on a person who refuses to give sworn evidence where a party must produce witnesses); LIII (a person summoned to the cauldron finds it convenient to redeem his hand and furnish swearers instead); LVI (defendant refuses to obey a summons; twelve witnesses are to prove on oath that they were present when each step in the process took place); LVIII (a homicide has not enough to pay; twelve to swear that he has no more means). The cauldron test is also mentioned in LVI.
[3] In substance, copied by L. Bai. 9, 17.

the rather to be accepted. But if by proving the matter the truth cannot be ascertained, then let the defendant clear himself by oaths that he has not and never had the things claimed from him, or had no knowledge of the matter asked or in truth knew nothing about it or has not done the thing spoken of or to the party spoken of; and when the defendant has so sworn the plaintiff should be made to pay five shillings to him.[1]

The clauses referred to provide in a few cases for the oath to be taken by the plaintiff (usually as to the amount of his loss),[2] but more commonly by the defendant, and usually as to the absence of the guilty knowledge or intention charged against him,[3] but there are also the clauses relating to bailments (taken from the Code of Euric with little variation).[4] However, there are also in a few cases oaths to be taken by witnesses as to facts in issue.[5]

The Lombard Code, the Edictus Rothari (which belongs to the beginning of our stage of the Central Codes) was promulgated in A.D. 643 but amended in slight degree by his successors and may be taken as law of about A.D. 700. It is, as we said, the best of all codes of native law, hardly influenced by Rome. Here are vast changes. There are a number of clauses providing for the oath, and in all cases it is an oath of purgation, only taken where normally there would be no real evidence except of one party. They consist of types of cases now familiar to us.[6] In some of these a number of

---

[1] V.C.R. II, 4, 2 seems to signify merely that after the oaths have been taken the judge is to hear no one else – a provision found elsewhere in the leges barbarorum.
[2] V.C.R. VIII, 1, 5 and 2, 1.
[3] e.g. V.C.R. II, 1, 17 and 18; IV, 4, 2; VI, 5, 5; VI, 2, 8 and 5, 12; IX, 1, 4 and 8; IX, 1, 13; X, 1, 6.
[4] V.C.R. Tit. V; and see VIII, 4, 8.
[5] V.C.R. II, 4, 3, and 5, 15 (evidence of handwriting): VI, 5, 12; X, 3, 5 (position of boundaries).
[6] These are the following: (a) oaths denying charges of sexual misconduct (179, 202, 213); (b) oaths denying a guilty knowledge or intention (Ed. Roth. 198, 229, 230, 231, 248, 265); (c) oaths denying liability where the defendant is charged with a capital crime before the king (presumably on suspicion – Ed. Roth. 9. If the accuser cannot prove the charge it is capital for him); (d) other cases where no independent evidence would be available (Ed. Roth. 195, 227-8, 262, 362, and 365. In the last two cases the alleged debtor is dead and the oath of denial is taken by his heir).

compurgators, who will swear with the defendant, is specified[1] and the other side is entitled to nominate half.[2] It is provided that in future a defendant who admits the claim is not to be allowed to deny it on oath.[3] But in most of the clauses providing for the oath, the party has the option to choose the ordeal by fighting[4], and in one that is the only ordeal provided.[5] In most of these cases the party can choose a 'champion'[6] to represent him, and it appears that there is already a class of professional champions. There is even a clause forbidding champions to go into the fight carrying secreted upon their persons herbs intended for bewitching the adversary.[7] Accordingly the number of cases in which oath or battle may be chosen is limited, but there are and have been enough to create a class of champions.[8] Not that the practice escapes criticism. Luitprand (*c.* 118 of A.D. 731), amending the law, laments: 'We are uncertain of the judgement of God[9] and we have heard of many unjustly losing their property through a fight, but because of the custom of our nation, the Lombards, we cannot repeal the law itself'. It seems that among this spirited people the ordeal by fighting had spread at this date somewhat further than elsewhere.

We end the continental story with seven codes and some fragments, which come to us from the period following the dark age of about A.D. 650 to 750 and are mainly of the second half of the eighth century and early ninth. They are all of the stage between

[1] It varies between three and twelve according to the amount at issue (Ed. Roth. 165, 179, 359).
[2] See details in Ed. Roth. 359.
[3] Ed. Roth, 364.
[4] *Per pugnam ad Dei iudicium* (Ed. Roth. 195, 202, 213, 228 and 365). It is not the position here, as in the Burgundian Code and some others, that the one party is given the right to swear, but the other can decline to accept it and challenge to battle. The party has usually the option to swear or fight. There is no option to fight in contests between relatives (Ed. Roth. 164, 165, 166) or where the denial is of knowledge or intention.
[5] Ed. Roth. 198 (slander of a woman, where the defendant says he can justify it).
[6] *Camfio* (M.H.G. Kampf—fight).
[7] Ed. Roth. 368.
[8] Later legislation limits the weapons to cudgels and shields; Charlemagne, Capitulary, 65; Lothar, 32; Lud. Pii, 15 (all in *M.G.H.*, Legum, Tom 4.)
[9] An expression which signifies the result of a trial by ordeal and especially by battle.

the Early and Central Codes, and some are hardly of better quality than the Salic Law, and they purport to set out the laws of different peoples of the Frankish Empire (which has now also swallowed up all the peoples that have been mentioned in this chapter except the Visigoths, now relegated to Spain). The provisions relating to oath and ordeal show continued deterioration to the following point. The use of the ordeal by oath is no longer confined to cases where there is no evidence except of the one party, or where *certa probatio non fuerit*, and such an expression is now rare. The oath avails as a defence in a growing bulk of all kinds of claims, and especially crimes and the more serious civil offences, till its ambit is very large, but it is not possible in these codes to see the precise limits of its application. Most of these provisions fix the number of swearers that the defendant must produce, and it varies according to the gravity of the charge or size of the claim from three to eighty. It is to be assumed that these compurgators are usually members of the party's kinship group that stands with him at the trial, but apart from the earliest of these documents there is no provision giving the other side the right to nominate half. The ordeal by hot water or iron is rarely mentioned and seems to have become of little moment. The ordeal by battle is of frequent but limited application and 'champions' are mentioned in several codes.

In detail, in the earliest of these documents, the fragments known as the Pactus Alamannorum (of perhaps the close of the seventh century) after setting out the offence, the general form is *solvat solidos (40) aut cum 12 medicus electus iuret*[1] ('let him pay 40 shillings or swear with 12, half nominated'), but it is found only in a minority of cases.[2] The number of compurgators varies between three and eighty. One fragment[3] provides for a choice between the oath and the ordeal by battle.

In the Lex Alamannorum, of the first half of the eighth century, the situation is much the same. There are only a few provisions

---

[1] The words 'medicus electus' are often missing.
[2] The form varies: Pac. Alam. fragment, 2, *c.* 39 'aut cum 24 medicus electus aut cum 40 qualis invenire poterit iuret'; in 42 'aut cum 24 totus electus aut cum 80 qualis invenire poterit iuret'.
[3] Pac. Alam., 2nd fragment, *c.* 34, which relates to a charge of evil conduct against a woman. The phrase is *cum spata tracta* ('with drawn sword').

giving a right to swear, if the offence is denied, with a fixed number of witnesses (half, sometimes all, to be nominated by the other side),[1] and two cases where the defendant is entitled to choose battle *cum spata* (or *spada*) *tracta*, with drawn sword.[2] In later additions to the law (the second book) the right to swear and the right to battle are more frequently given.[3]

In the Lex Baiuvariorum, of the second half of the eighth century, the provisions for the ordeal by battle increase in number and there is much reference to champions.[4] The later material here contains some lengthy and unconvincing procedural matter.[5]

In the Lex Ribuariorum, the code of the Ripuarian Franks and one of our Early Codes, dating from about A.D. 800 though it draws on materials of earlier centuries, it appears that in most cases there is now a right in the defendant, who denies the offence, to swear with a fixed number of compurgators. There are also, in the later parts of the code,[6] a few provisions for ordeal by battle, but no reference as yet to *campeones*.

Lastly come the other codes drawn up about A.D. 800 or a little later, at the direction of Charlemagne, to record the legal usages of his peoples – the Lex Saxonum, Lex Frisionum, Lex Angliorum et Werinorum (i.e. Thuringorum) and Lex Francorum Chamavorum. All these codes set out a large number of offences for which the defendant, if he chooses to deny the claim, is entitled to swear with a fixed number of compurgators, and these are especially the more serious cases, that is to say criminal offences and homicide.[7] In no instance is the right to swear limited to a case where there is no sure proof. There is an alternative right to go to battle in some of these laws, but the codes are scanty and the provisions piecemeal and the texts not accepted by all scholars as genuine, and it is not possible to see the extent of the right; but

---

[1] L. Alam., Chaps. 24, 30.
[2] L. Alam., Chap. 44(1): if a freeman charges another with a capital crime *et exinde probata res non est nisi quod ipse dixit, liceat illum alium cui crimen imposuit cum tracta spada exoniare se contra illum alium.* See also Chaps. 24, 56.
[3] L. Alam., Chaps. 87, 92, 95.
[4] L. Bai. II, 1; II, 11; XVII.
[5] e.g. L. Bai., tit. XVII.
[6] L. Rib., c. 32, 4; 57; 59 (4); 68.
[7] In the L. Fris. and L. Angl. et Wer. the defendant can swear in all cases of homicide, at least, and some cases of theft. In L. Fris., tit. III, where a slave is charged with a minor theft, the master swears 'by his garment'.

it must have been wide because of the references to champions.[1] The ordeal by hot water is only mentioned in cases of theft, in the Lex Frisionum and Lex Francorum Chamavorum,[2] and the ordeal by hot iron in the Lex Angliorum et Werinorum.[3]

What then were the reasons for this unique spread of the use of the ordeal, and the introduction of the ordeal by battle, in mediaeval Western Europe? In spite of the fragmentary character of the legislation and the differences in the dates of the codes and their contents, the general history of those centuries can be easily seen from them. Three processes were unfolding themselves in the following order, though they overlapped considerably in time, and the development is somewhat earlier in time in the Late Codes than the Early Codes.

First, the oath was adopted, at the different dates when these peoples were converted to Christianity, but at first it was only applied for the same purposes and to the same extent as the ordeal by hot water that had preceded it, namely to the defendant alone and where his evidence was alone available on the question which was in issue. Some extension occurred where it was used 'ubi probatio certa non fuerit', but this was less an extension than the employment of a dangerous form of words. For if a weak court, forced by a powerful litigant or a doubtful conflict of stories, should seek a refuge in these words, and declare that there was 'no sure proof', the ordeal by oath was capable of unlimited extension. It tended, in fact, to supplant other ordeals and to spread to all serious cases, where the offence was denied; and in a few cases it was applied to witness of fact.

But, secondly, conditions were in time imposed upon the right to swear: perjury was rife, and in many cases a fixed number of co-swearers was required. Usually they would be members of the

---

[1] L. Fris. XIV, 4; L. Angl. et Wer. 55. L. Fr. Cham. has no reference to battle or champions, but this fragmentary draft only purports to set out respects in which their law differs from that of other Franks (see § 1). L. Angl. et Wer. has no reference to champions but contains a general provision (§ 56) for decision by battle in claims for theft or wounds where the composition is over 2s. L. Sax. (§ 63) only mentions a right to trial by battle where a plaintiff claims the title to land in the defendant's possession.

[2] L. Fris. III; Fr. Cham. 48 (for seven robberies, a capital offence).

[3] L. Angl. et Wer. 55 (woman charged with poisoning her husband or betraying him to his death: battle or, if she has no champion, hot iron).

defendant's kinship group, that gathered to support him at the trial, and the number was fixed by law in an increasing number of types of cases, and the number of oath-helpers grew till it reached anything between three and eighty, according to the seriousness of the charge. Then the law gave the other side (usually the plaintiff) the right to nominate half of them – persons known to him to be less likely to perjure themselves. At first, when the number was small, they were expected to know the facts and whether the defendant was guilty – which was the matter upon which they supported his oath – but, as the number grew, few could have any direct knowledge of the facts, and certainly relatives were interested persons. Some of them could be made liable to pay, or their goods could be seized under a judgment against the defendant, and in a serious case it was commonly impossible for him to find the money without their assistance, and in practice they would usually have to help him.

Thirdly, there was growing resentment against the use and abuse of the oaths, and there was a reaction. One of the objects of the oath was to satisfy the plaintiff of the truth of the defendant's version of the facts, but the plaintiff was refusing to accept[1] these oaths and the acquittals that followed on them. The legislators began to allow him, if he wished, to challenge the defendant, to fight it out by battle. In the Lex Burgundionum, Chap. 45, he is given a general licence to fight if he is not satisfied with the oath, but the use of the oath was then much narrower than it later became. Finally a large number of cases are specified in the codes, especially of the more serious cases, in which either side is given the option to fight.

But so exceptional a history required exceptional circumstances to create it, and they were chiefly two. The first was the existence of a powerful, international religion. In many similarly primitive peoples, living, as they do, in conditions of comparative isolation, if there is a secular ruler he is also the head of the religious system. He is the chief performer of its rites and the chief and hereditary intercessor between his people and the anger of the gods or spirits, and religious sanctions support his authority. But in Europe, the power of an organized international church, which

---

[1] L. Burg. 45; and cf. Ex. 22[4]: 'the owner shall accept (the oath) and he (the defendant) shall not pay'.

was the heir of all surviving elements of civilization and claimed authority above and beyond the secular power, militated against the strength of kingship.[1] The Franks were as credulous as they were ignorant, and as devoted as they were superstitious. They flocked to church at the ringing of the bells, and they dreaded the torments of hell. It was a weak kingship that faced the church and faced the local chieftains, and in France the areas of the kingdoms were wide for economies so backward.

The second circumstance was a disposition to violence and an admiration for prowess in the fight, not found in all peoples. The result of the fight was *iudicium Dei* (the judgment of God) and the popularity of the spectacle among the masses helped it to spread across the Continent far and wide.

Yet it was only at the Norman Conquest[2] that the ordeal by battle was foisted upon a reluctant, small and insular England. The Anglo-Saxon laws of the English kingdoms had begun in much the same way as the continental codes. The Laws of Aethelberht of Kent (about A.D. 600) contain no word of procedure. Those of Hlothhere and Eadric of Kent (about A.D. 690) have a few clauses on this topic, including four[3] which provide for an oath of purgation to be taken by the defendant (sometimes supported by a number of oath-helpers called 'witnesses'),[4] and it is evident that oaths are taken in a number of cases, usually (but not always) where there will be no evidence except the defendant's. There follow two contemporary codes, the Laws of Wihtred of Kent, and Ine of Wessex, of about A.D. 700, where the ecclesiastical authorship and interest is pronounced. They contain a substantial number of clauses providing for the procedure of the oath,[5] and in these and the subsequent Anglo-Saxon Laws (which say little of the oath and as much about the other ordeals) we see a use of oath and ordeal which does not

---

[1] The introduction of Christianity similarly weakened the power of kingship in many African peoples.

[2] See William I, *Regulations regarding exculpation*; text and trans. Robertson (1925), 232.

[3] H. & E., Clauses 2 and 4 (harbouring a fugitive homicide who has disappeared); 5 (stealing a man and selling him abroad, evidence available on both sides); 10 (unintelligible).

[4] H. & E., Clauses 2, 4 and 5.

[5] Wihtred 16-24.

change after A.D. 700 and has not even developed as far as that found on the Continent in 600 A.D. They apply only in a limited number of types of cases, now familiar to us,[1] and usually apply to the defendant alone and where his evidence is alone available. There is little sign of the application of the oath to mere witnesses of fact. The references to compurgators are few, and there seems to be no right in the opposing party to nominate them. And there is no ordeal by battle.

The evidence from the rest of Christian Europe and Asia Minor corroborates this account. There is no ordeal by battle in Scotland or Wales till it is introduced from Norman England in the twelfth century or in Russia till it enters from Germany in the thirteenth, and it is missing from the mediaeval codes of Asia Minor. Indeed, in the Ancient Laws of Ireland even the use of the oath is scant and there is hardly a mention of it.[2]

---

[1] Capital criminal offence of treason (Alf. 4; II Aethelstan 4); oaths denying guilty knowledge or intention (Ine, 16, 21; Alf. 36; Edward the Elder, 1[5]); sexual misconduct (Alf. 11[4]); failure of the defendant to produce his vendor when the plaintiff claims that goods in the defendant's possession are his (Ine, 25, 53; Edward the Elder, 1); harbouring a fugitive (Ine, 30; II Aethelstan 2[2]; H. & E., 2, 4, *supra*); witchcraft (II Aethelstan 6).

[2] *Scotland:* Leges inter Brettos et Scotos, nothing of procedure; Assisē of David I and Laws of the Four Burghs, general resemblance to English law of the first half of the twelfth century as to oaths and co-swearers, and see Assisē David I, § 2, option to defendant charged with theft to choose twelve co-swearers or battle; and see §§ 8, 20, and L.B. 12, 13, 22; *Wales:* much of oaths and co-swearers, but no reference to battle till the later additions (Ancient Laws of Wales (1841), p. 548, § 9, where battle and a champion are once mentioned); *Norwegian Laws:* In Gulathing and Frostathing, ordeals by hot iron for men and hot water for women and oaths in serious cases with a number of co-swearers increasing according to the gravity of the offence, chosen by both sides (Gulathing, 132f., Frostathing, IV, 8), but no ordeal by battle; *Russia:* ordeals by hot water, iron or oath for theft and homicide (Jaroslav's Pravda, Expanded Version, 21, 22, 37, 85-7) usually in the absence of other evidence; but ordeal by battle unknown till, after German expansion in the Baltic and lively commercial intercourse with Northern Russian cities, it is first mentioned in a treaty of 1229 between the city of Smolensk and some German cities, and is prominent in the fifteenth century Charters of Pskov and Novgorod: Vernadsky, pp. 12, 18. *Armenian Laws:* normal use of oaths as in Central Codes and no battle; *Georgian Codes:* no battle, and little of oaths, but in Law of Beka, 27, oath with oath-helpers denying adultery.

CHAPTER 22

The Recent Peoples of the Central Codes–Third Agricultural Grade, Third Stage

Now we turn from the second to the third stage of our Third Agricultural Grade – the peoples of similar degrees of economic and legal development to those of the Central Codes of the past. In its economic and legal aspects, therefore, we define this stage in the same terms as that of those Codes. It is essentially a stage of transition between our Early and Late Codes, and if the previous two stages[1] are those of barbarism this marks the beginnings of civilization.

There are, mainly in Central Africa, a great number of peoples from which to take our examples, for civilization travelled mainly from the west of Africa to the peoples of our last six chapters. If we start from the area of East Africa from which we took instances of the Cattle-Keepers – the homes of the Nandi, Kavirondo and Lango – and move westwards round the north side of Lake Victoria, we reach a fertile and well-watered corridor bounded on the east by Lake Victoria and on the west by the chain of Lakes Albert, Edward and Kivu and the mountain mass of Ruwenzori. Here are to be found the nations of Buganda,[2] Kitara (or Bunyoro) and Ankole, all of which belong to the later half of the Central Codes. This corridor has been a highway whereby Negro-Hamite pastoralists have migrated southwards from the

---

[1] *Ante*, Chaps. 16-21.
[2] *Buganda* is the name of the African country or kingdom; *Baganda* the inhabitants; *luganda* the language. Uganda is the European protectorate, subsequently established, which consisted chiefly of the above three kingdoms and Toro (which had been formed out of Bunyoro), and is now the name of the African state. Ganda is a conventional abbreviation.

region of the Upper Nile to the plateaux of Rwanda and Tanzania. Still further to the south, peoples of the first half of this stage are to be found in Zambia. We may take as examples the Lamba, who dwell partly in what is now North-West Zambia and partly inside the projecting corner of the Republic of the Congo; and the Bemba, who live in the centre of the plateau of Northern Zambia between the four great lakes of Nyasa, Tanganyika, Mweru and Bangweolu. If we start again from our East African tribes and instead of travelling westwards move south-east towards the civilization of the coast of the Indian Ocean, we reach, in an area stretching from Kilimanyaro to the hinterland of Mombasa, the Teita, Taveta, Digo, Giriama and other Nyika peoples,[1] all of which are of the beginning of the same stage of development. Again, if we start from the Nguni peoples of South-East Africa, whom we took as instances of the peoples of the Early Codes, and move to the north and inland from the less advanced Nguni of the Cape through the Northern Nguni of Natal, we reach the South Sotho of Lesotho, the Northern Sotho, the Venda and the Shangana-Tonga of the Northern Transvaal, who are all of the stage of the Central Codes. Further north and west, in Central Africa, we may take two further examples from the Republic of the Congo, namely the Ngala on the banks of the Middle Congo around Nouvelle Anvers, and the Ngbetu, between the valleys of the Vele and Bomokandi (both peoples being notorious cannibals).[2] Some of the more backward peoples of West Africa also belong to the same stage and of these we may take one example, the Tiv[3] of Northern Nigeria, living along both sides of the Benue River, about 150 miles from its junction with the Niger.

In economic terms then, we define this stage of development as follows. These peoples live mainly by agriculture with sub-

---

[1] The Nyika tribes in 1914 occupied a tract of country, a few miles inland and parallel to the coast, extending some 140 miles north from the Kenya-Tanganyika boundary. The largest tribe is the Giriama, as to whom see Champion (1967). These tribes show clear evidence of a deterioration in economic status, though their law retains characteristics of the Central Codes.

[2] See *ante*, p. 275.

[3] See as to the Tiv, Bohannan (1953), (1957) and (1968) and Akiga's Story (1939).

sidiary hunting,[1] and with cattle-keeping where cattle can be reared, and keep sheep or goats and poultry. Though there is much migration and conquest most are firmly settled in their territories and the occupiers in their holdings and their kings (or paramount chiefs) who are almost everywhere, are sometimes called kings of their land and sometimes of their people.[2] The population is often of different ethnic characters, so that such societies can be called states. The increase in population is substantial and the area of the state has increased and, subject to ecological limitations, the density also. There is still enough land for everyone and to spare but the superfluity diminishes. Towards the end of this period there is a beginning of the sale of land and of a landless class. Feudalism, if we use the term in its widest sense, is found in varying degree in most of these peoples and towards the end of the period is at its height. The unilinear clan diminishes in power and importance. The basic local, social, economic and administrative unit is now generally not the homestead or kraal but the village,[3] and towns are common, and with towns and increasing wealth, markets commence[4] and are often controlled by the state, township or village,[5] and often there are

---

[1] Many, however, of these peoples of Africa, where game is so plentiful, are enthusiastic hunters, and the Ngala and Ngbetu may be described as hunters first and foremost.

[2] See *ante*, p. 271.

[3] In Buganda, the main crop is the banana and the houses and plantations may spread as much as two or three miles along a hillside. These settlements might rather be called parishes than villages, but there were markets recently introduced by King Mutesa when the Europeans entered. The Bemba, on the other hand, have no cattle, and their assets are slavery and service. There are no markets and little trade and no organized system of barter or sale: Richards (1939), 22, 213. The Tiv live in homesteads or compounds, and blocks of compounds, fairly evenly scattered about the country. The settlement pattern may be described as a series of small blocks of agnatic kin, held together and separated by the lineage system. There are traditional markets: Bohannan (1968), 36f.

[4] In England, Southampton and Worcester were *ports* (i.e. market towns) as early as the mid-ninth century, and by Edward the Elder's time (early tenth century) a *port* was usually also a *burh* (i.e. fortified). See also the previous note. The Ngala and Ngbetu have markets but there is little or nothing in the way of markets in the other African peoples we have taken as examples, except the Tiv, where markets are well developed.

[5] In England by the 'port reeve' or other royal or local official; in Buganda and Tivland by a special chief: Roscoe (1911a), 452, Bohannan (1957), 152f.; 1968), 146f.

316 PRIMITIVE LAW, PAST AND PRESENT

market tolls[1] and borough or market courts.[2] All these peoples are familiar with the use of a number of metals and some are skilled smelters[3] and many are skilled workers in iron.[4] Currencies of some kind are almost everywhere[5] and sales increase as against barter, with consequent changes in prices, and prices are sometimes fixed by law.[6] There is, on the whole, a greater variety of crops[7] and more trade, more manufactured goods[8] and wider communications.[9] The specialization of occupations is still, however, mainly between the sexes,[10] and the line of division remains much as before, but there is an increased specialization of artisans and sometimes attempts are made by law at the close of our period to fix their pay;[11] and there is a beginning of gilds.[12] Yet artisans number only some 3 per cent of the population, and apart from

[1] Ten per cent on the value of the goods brought in, Buganda; Roscoe (1911a), 452. The King of the Ngbetu levied a toll on sales. There were market tolls on goods brought in at Worcester before the end of the ninth century. See also IV Aethelred 2.

[2] In England there were borough courts at least from the middle of the tenth century (Edgar III, 5, 1) and by the end of our period all the larger boroughs had courts. The Tiv now have market courts: Bohannan (1957, 1968).

[3] e.g. The Bakitara.

[4] The Ngbetu are fine builders in wood, among the best iron workers in the Congo and skilled workers in ivory and copper.

[5] For large transactions cattle, where cattle are to be found. But already among some of the peoples of the Early Codes certain commodities which are imperishable, in common use and demand and of a common size or easily measured, began to figure in the exchanges more frequently than other goods, because they could always be kept and traded away without loss for something else as occasion offered. Consequently they began to figure as measures of the value of goods (in Central Africa, arrows, salt, iron, squares of barkcloth, copper). Later, after the Arabs came, cowrie shells and other ornaments. The Ganda used ivory discs, then beads, then cowrie shells for small debts and cows for large: Roscoe (1911a), 456. The Ngala and Ngbetu used spears, shields, arrows, knives, hoes, squares of standard coarse cloth, small copper cylinders, rods or ingots (cf. early Rome). For the Hittites see *ante*, p. 72. The Tiv now use money.

[6] e.g. Hittite Code and some English laws.

[7] For the Lamba, see Doke (1931), 95f.

[8] Ngala and Ngbetu: good huts, pottery, woodwork, ironwork, spinning, rope-making, dyeing, a little weaving and tanning, painting, sculpture and the making of musical instruments.

[9] e.g. A Bangala jargon (not to be confused with the Ngala tongue) has spread over the Congo, dropping much of its grammar in the process, including the Bantu alliterative concord.

[10] See n. 7 *supra*.   [11] H.C. 158f.

[12] In England there is a gild in Canterbury in the ninth century.

the priests, sorcerers and diviners over 90 per cent of the population earn their living wholly or mainly on the land. Religion increases in power and here and there is a class of ecclesiastics of sorts, of growing influence,[1] and among peoples of the past who have acquired writing at this stage, as it is within the province of the scribes, who are an ecclesiastical order, their influence grows the more.[2] There is widespread human sacrifice,[3] and the slaughter of wives, subjects and slaves to minister to their kings and chiefs in the hereafter.[4] The practices of divination increase and the taking of auspices has spread far and wide.[5] Nobility,[6] slavery and serfs[7] are almost everywhere, and the status of the free peasant falls towards serfdom, especially in Europe and India.[8] At the close of this stage there is a beginning of a great advance in the arts: there is in particular good sculpture and military architecture, and painting.[9]

In legal terms we define this stage as follows.[10] The more serious

[1] For the Bemba, see Richards (1940), 99.
[2] See *ante*, chap. 4.
[3] Not necessarily for religious purposes or reasons.
[4] See, for the Bemba, note (1) *supra*; for the Ganda, Roscoe (1911a), 284, 331; for the Ngala and Ngbetu, see *Les Bangala* and *Les Mangbetu*.
[5] For our South Bantu peoples, see Hoernlé (1937), 234f. Among the Ngbetu no one would commence a journey or military operation without first taking the auspices, and there is an official to foretell the future on important matters of public interest. For the Ganda, see Roscoe (1911a), 338f.
[6] But there is a continuing tendency for the chiefs, i.e. feudal lords, to take the place of aristocracy and in Buganda there is only the royal family and commoners: Roscoe (1911a), 86. There are no serfs nor any great differences of wealth among the Tiv.
[7] Slaves consist mainly of the following classes: (1) war captives, mainly women and children, for the male captives have mostly been killed, or (Ngala and Ngbetu) eaten; (2) slaves acquired as such; (3) debt-slaves (see below); (4) persons self-enslaved, for inability to maintain themselves; (5) persons enslaved by order of a court on conviction, (6) serfs. Slavery is mild. Among the Ganda, slaves are merely non-members of the clan; Mair (1934), 32. A Ngala slave might have several wives or male slaves of his own.
[8] See *ante*, Chap. 9.
[9] Western Europe: in the Carolingian Empire, especially the Eastern provinces, church building and sculpture (largely Byzantine), book production and decoration and handwriting, finding its way into England in the following century (tenth to early eleventh). The Ngbetu are fine builders in wood, among the best ironworkers in the Congo, and skilled workers in ivory, and also in copper, of which most of their ornaments are made. The Ngala and Ngbetu have some paintings as well as sculpture and the making of musical instruments (late nineteenth century).
[10] But the Tiv have no law.

civil wrongs, especially homicide, continue the process of their conversion into criminal offences, and the pecuniary sanctions for homicide begin their change into the capital sanction for intentional homicide. At this intermediate stage they take a variety of forms, the most characteristic being the handing over of a number of persons. Indeed, this sanction is the characteristic mark of the age. The sanctions for wounding remain pecuniary. Adultery (which in former ages usually partook to some extent of the nature of a crime) becomes generally capital. With the rise in the quantity of property, theft becomes a heinous offence, and the thief caught in the act is guilty of a capital offence, otherwise the sanction is generally a multiple of the value of the thing stolen. There is an increase in the list of crimes which are commonly punishable by death and the confiscation of all property, subject to mitigating circumstances. Capital charges are only triable in the king's (or paramount chief's) court unless he has granted the jurisdiction to others. Two further sanctions now become important for the first time – outlawry (or banishment) and mutilation, for there are still no prisons except for a few dungeons for political offenders, whose food must be found by them or their relatives.[1] There are, however, everywhere, stocks for those awaiting trial,[2] and occasionally for the punishment of offenders, and here again the offender must feed himself. As theft is common and important, a practice of requiring a possessor of goods, alleged to have been stolen from the plaintiff, to produce his seller, becomes familiar and institutional and gathers its rules around it. Consequently, as the transactions of every day are oral, they take place, at least if they are substantial, before a number of witnesses (about five or six on the average) and the law enjoins, and purports to require, the practice. In addition to cash sale and ready barter the borrowing and even hire of goods becomes common and there is much litigation about it, and sometimes attempts are made by the law, towards the close of the period, to fix charges for hire. It is characteristic of the age that the ordeal begins to be commonly used where goods lent or hired are

[1] Alfred 1, 2. But among the Ngala and Ngbetu there is imprisonment in chains.

[2] In England, already in Alfred 35 (2); and see e.g. Roscoe (1911a), 22, 264; Mair (1934), 188; Doke (1931), 53. There is also in some places torture to secure the confessions of adults: Roscoe (1911), 261f.

alleged to have been lost, damaged or destroyed without the borrower's fault in the absence of witnesses. He must swear to it, and if he swears successfully is acquitted. The ordeal by poison becomes common for capital crimes and is therefore in all lands used chiefly in charges of witchcraft. Sanctuaries are almost everywhere and sometimes begin to take the form of 'cities of refuge'. There is a beginning of the loan of money for a lump-sum interest, and credit and debt on a growing scale and suretyship.[1] and everywhere, except in Western Europe,[2] the pledging of the persons of debtors or their dependants (usually children or unmarried sisters but sometimes mothers) as security for repayment.[3] Similarly the creditor becomes entitled to seize the persons of the debtor and his family in execution, and heirs are liable for the debts of their deceased father. These rules are consonant with the law (referred to above) of the handing over of persons as the sanction for homicide. It is characteristic of this period (partly because of the progressive incorporation in the state of old kingdoms and different ethnic groups) that there are difference in the law in different areas,[4] and particularly in the law of inheritance; in some places a man is considered in some respects to carry his personal law with him and can demand that it should be applied. There is little change in marriage. There is still hardly a beginning of the marriage settlement.[5]

This is the type of the states of the Central Codes. Again, it need not be said that there are differences between one economy and another and between those at the commencement of this stage and at the end. All these characters are not to be found in any one people so far as our information goes. And notwithstanding the account, contained in this and the following two chapters, of the economy and law of common types of nations of the stage of our

[1] e.g. Baganda: Mair (1934), 188 – on the release of a defendant on bail.
[2] The fifth-century Code of Euric, c. 299, prohibits parents from selling, giving or pledging children.
[3] Also still, in several places, a practice to seize the persons or property of innocent third parties to put pressure on a debtor to pay (*inkole*), see Doke (1931), 65. But such practices, and the general taking of the law into one's own hands, are strictly illegal in most places, as among the Lamba and Ngbetu.
[4] For example, in England there were differences between the law of Mercia, Wessex and the Danelaw (Stenton, 498f.; Liebermann, I, 638).
[5] See *ante*, p. 75.

Central Codes, we must remember that there are peoples like the Tiv, whom we have assigned on the grounds of their economy to the beginning of this stage, and who have no government, no court with any power to enforce its decision or advice, and no law, and where order is supported by entirely different sanctions – by loyalty between certain clans and lineages, and other social forces with which we are now familiar, by the belief that certain serious breaches of order will bring danger from mystical or supernatural sources, and by wars of reprisals between the clans of the offender and the victim. Such peoples are often of special interest to the legal historian. The view has been expressed in this book that law and courts of law emerge together, and this view is powerfully supported where, upon such a people being given courts by the British administration, with power to enforce their decisions (whether they exercise it or not)[1] the people's vaguely expressed ideas of right conduct are rapidly transformed into a coherent and expanding system of law.[2]

The average size of these societies has continued to enlarge. The Ganda probably numbered between two and three millions in the third quarter of the last century, but as a result of civil war, famine and the scourge of the tsetse-fly had in the census of 1931 dropped to 870,000. The population of Bunyoro diminished by 1919 to 102,509, of Ankole to 149,469, and of the neighbouring kingdom of Toro to 126,000. The total populations of the four kingdoms probably exceeded six millions in the middle of the nineteenth century, reduced to 3,500,000 in 1931. The Bemba population in 1940 numbered about 140,000.[3] The Ngala early in the century were about 110,000 and the Ngbetu a little over a million.[4] Tiv in the 1930s numbered half a million. The population of England at the close of the period was about 1,500,000

---

[1] A Tiv court has not been successful unless it has brought about a settlement in which both parties can concur: Bohannan (1957), 63.
[2] See Paul Bohannan's remarkable book *Justice and Judgement among the Tiv* (1957); and among the peoples of the Early Codes, compare with Prof. E. E. Evans-Pritchard's pioneering work on the Nuer (1940), Howell's valuable book (1954); and see, as to the Tallensi, Fortes (1940), 264.
[3] See, for some collected figures in regard to Uganda, Kuczynski (1949), vol. II, Chap. IX; for figures relating to the Nyika and Teita, vol. II, p. 150; in regard to the Sotho *ibid.*, p. 31, and for the peoples of Zambia, Chap. XI.
[4] The Nyika tribes are now (1914) small, and the largest, the Giriama, about 70,000.

and the subjects of the Hittite State (or Empire) at least several hundred thousand. The density has also risen but varies vastly with local ecology. The density of population in South Africa remains low – of the Bemba in 1940 an average of 3·75 persons per square mile. In England it was about 20 per square mile. Of the Kingdoms of Uganda, the density in Ankole in 1919 was about 25 per square mile, and that of Buganda, and the average of the four provinces of Uganda, in 1931 about 44 persons per square mile. In the fertile and well-watered country of the Ngbetu the density early in this century was about 250 per square mile. Most of these populations no longer consist wholly or mainly of homesteads but the bulk live in villages, usually climbing the slope of the same hill or occupying the bank of the same stream, and the village is the basic local, social, administrative, military and judicial unit. It is often largely a kinship group, apparently formed by the expansion of a lineage, and indeed many villages are formed by a founder with a sufficient following of relatives;[1] and as there is land to spare in all or almost all of these peoples, he can usually do so provided he remains in the territory of the same chief or obtains permission to go outside. The Bemba village contains an average of 30 to 50 huts;[2] the villages of Lesotho from 10 to 50 independent households with a population usually of 20 persons or less and rarely more than 250.[3] In England, even in the eleventh century, only a very substantial village had 30 households, though a few here and there were much bigger. Villages and hamlets of from 2 to 6 households were very common.[4] Water supply has much to do in determining the size of villages. In the north and west of England, where there are good springs of water everywhere, the hamlets were very small: in Eastern England villages tended to form on a suitable water course. The same contrast is manifest in different areas of South Africa, but the Ganda homes and their plantain gardens are along the hillsides, not the streams. The largest Ngbetu villages contain about 1,500 persons. There are also towns of growing size. In 1086 London had perhaps a population of 13,000; York, 8,000, Lincoln

[1] Not the Ganda village, which consisted of those who had elected to attach themselves to some particular chief but the peoples taking the lead in a particular village tended to be related to one another: Mair (1934), 34.
[2] Richards (1940), 89.   [3] Hoernlé (1937), 70, 88.   [4] Clapham (1949), 44.

and Norwich 6,000, Thetford 5,000 and Gloucester, Ipswich and Oxford over 3,000; and there were several others of importance such as Winchester. The Ngala towns contain 5,000 to 12,000 souls.

The economies of these peoples differ widely. In the kingdoms of Uganda the general picture is of a native Negro agricultural people (the Bairu) ruled by a conquering, immigrant Hamitic or Negro-Hamitic pastoral people (the Bahima). In general there is the same picture as in Western Europe, of a non-tilling nobility and tilling serfs and slaves, and only the details differ; for in many areas of Western Europe, too, invading pastoralists had established themselves as a ruling class over native agriculturalists. Among the Ganda the immigrant nomads were comparatively few and the populations merged so that only the royal family boasted its pastoral descent. But in the more pastoral kingdoms of Bunyoro and Toro (Toro having been separated from Bunyoro in recent times) and even more in Ankole the cleavage remained strict. Intermarriage generally was unthinkable; the Bairu had, indeed, no cattle to pay bridewealth nor were they allowed to acquire any or even to herd their lord's cattle. The nobility of the kingdom continued to live almost entirely on milk and eschewed vegetable food. Some favoured individuals, however, of the Bairu were rewarded by the king with freedom and land for conspicuous service and could intermarry with a willing family of the nobility. The despised artisans were all of the Bairu.

The Bemba and Lamba peoples of Zambia present a different picture. Most of their land is infested with tsetse-fly, so that the Lamba have no cattle except in parts of the south-east and the Bemba none, and neither have pastoral traditions.[1] Accordingly the Lamba and Bemba are agricultural peoples with subsidiary hunting. Consequently goods are few and trade little and there are no markets and no currency. On the other hand the Ngala and Ngbetu, who also have goats but no cattle,[2] are hunters with subsidiary agriculture. The Ngbetu were formerly a group of tribes conquered by the Ngbetu, who now form an aristocratic ruling class. The Tiv again, are a fairly, homogeneous Negroid

---

[1] The Lamba have a few goats: the Bemba a few sheep and goats; both have fowls.
[2] The Ngala also keep sheep.

population of subsistance farmers with a primitive agriculture, but they have cattle and markets. No one has authority over the whole people and the Tiv organized themselves on the basis of a segmentary lineage system, and before the British came in 1907 there was no head of a Tiv lineage or of any group larger than the compound, a group of huts of close kinsmen, containing between 7 and 170 persons.[1] Like all African peoples south of Egypt, with the exception of Ethiopia, the technology of these populations is very low in comparison with that of Western Europe, and none have the plough, the wheel or the art of writing, and none of the peoples described in this chapter have the horse or other riding animal. This difference in the level of technology should not surprise us: we have already seen how backward were the Romans in this respect in comparison with Western Europe.[2]

The system of agriculture and land tenure differs from country to country. Among the bulk of the African peoples the soil is poor, though often well watered, and any family wishing to settle in an area will obtain land from the local chief, and the men with their iron axes cut down the trees or brushwood and burn it and the women with their iron hoes turn up and cultivate the ash-fertilized soil with some help from the men at the commencement; and when the land is exhausted a new site is similarly opened. The Lamba and Bemba are perhaps the most backward of these agriculturists. The population is everywhere under four persons per square mile and the land poor though wet and hardly anywhere can cattle be kept. A Lamba village headman, when after a few years the soil in the vicinity has become exhausted or insanitary, will move the whole site with his villagers to a place in his territory or, with permission of the paramount chief, beyond it.[3] Similarly a Bemba village will move every four or five years, and in addition it is liable to disruption at the death of an important member or the loss of popularity by the headman. Moreover every man is liable to live in a different village at different times – that of his birth or his mother's people, or his wife's at his marriage, or the village to which he removes a few years later, or one in which he succeeds his maternal uncle as headman, or elsewhere – with whatever permission is required, though the bonds of kinship

[1] Bohannan (1957), 8.   [2] See *ante*, p. 24.   [3] Doke (1931), 85.

chiefly tie him, the bonds with his maternal kin or his *ulupwa*.[1] Among the Ngala and Ngbetu, where the land is well watered and the chief occupation is the hunt, and the population is dense, and in our more southerly peoples where it is thin and the soil poor and dry, land is obtained by the head of a family from the local chief. All these populations are, on the whole homogeneous. In Buganda, Bunyoro and Ankole the land is generally as fertile as anywhere in the world, the density of population considerable and there is little or no movement of villages. In Ankole and Bunyoro the despised Bairu, who cultivate the soil, are free to move to another chief. It seems a general truth that wherever a population at this stage consists of pastoralists as well as cultivators the former despise the latter as they despise the smiths and other artisans. Similarly in England and Europe generally the cultivation is largely by slaves or serfs. The population has become ethnically homogeneous but the status of the free peasant, who in Aethelberht's time knew no lord but the king, continues to fall as he gradually loses economic and personal independence. Domesday Book gives the impression that the greater part of Southern England is divided into manors exclusively inhabited by serfs and slaves, though there were more freemen in England than would there appear, and there were fewer slaves in Normandy and in the Danelaw.[2]

The nation-wide organization by age-sets is hardly found except among the Sotho. The clan remains and amongst most of these peoples, those partly pastoral and those who are mainly hunters, the clans are patrilineal[3] and marriage patrilocal. On the other hand among the Bemba and Lamba, who have no cattle and are mainly agriculturists,[4] they are matrilineal and marriage is matrilocal in the sense that for some period, at least, after the marriage the young people take up their residence with the girl's parents. Also the bridewealth, instead of cattle, consists of service by the bridegroom and the giving of a few miscellaneous articles.[5] In the same peoples succession to chieftainship and inheritance of property is matrilineal. But this general statement requires

[1] Richards (1940), 90; (1939), Chap. VII.
[2] Stenton (1943), 463f., 507.
[3] Apparently mostly totemic and exogamous.
[4] As well as the Digo, among the Giriama peoples.
[5] Lamba: until recent times, hoes: Doke (1931), 79.

qualification: the cognatic principle of organization shows some advance, for not only in Europe but also in these African peoples both groupings are important. For example, among the Bemba there is also a bilateral kinship group (the ulupwa), which consists of the near relatives on both sides of the family and also relatives-in-law; these are the people with whom he may choose to live and who gather together at important events in his life.[1]

Though, on the whole, religion shows development and an increase in power among these peoples, there are differences from one nation to another at least as great as in any other aspect of culture. Some of them, notably the Ganda (the most advanced of these economies) are deeply religious, others (for example, the Ngala and Ngbetu) are secular in their attitude to life. In all of them there is a belief in spirits, to whom they attribute the power to protect, help and injure, and to whom they pay most reverence, especially spirits of deceased relatives and departed chiefs, to whom their descendants, and particularly the reigning chiefs, perform ceremonies or service. In Central Africa, including Uganda, and West Africa there is also the cult of fetishes[2] (and sometimes amulets) objects of all shapes and sorts, including favourite fetishes of chiefs, well known by name, and obscure objects possessed by common folk, and all credited with powers to protect and injure. In addition most believe in one supreme sky god, who is often the Creator, but in most of these peoples there is no worship of him and hardly a prayer to him. No temple or shrine is dedicated to him and no priests serve him. He is too far off and too great and uninterested. But the Ganda and some others display many of the conspicuous religious phenomena of the beginnings of civilization in the ancient world. The Ganda have many gods, some national and some private and obscure, and most have their estates along the hillsides and their temples or shrines on the hilltops at which rites are performed and festivals celebrated and human and animal sacrifices rendered. Their priests, largely hereditary, are in charge of temples and rituals and some fetishes and even the reigning king is godlike, and there are prophets, mediums and oracles, the mouthpieces of their god, and even vestal virgins who attend the shrines. With these religious

[1] Richards (1940), 88.
[2] Including the royal drums of Ankole.

beliefs and observances, however, are intertwined the ideas and practices of magic, hard to disentangle.

A mere glance at the rules of law to be found in these nations will indicate to us again that there is still little in common between the injunctions and prohibitions of their religion and magic and the rules of their law.[1] The ethical content of their religion is much smaller even than in modern man. At its plainest we are told of the Lamba[2] that their high god Lesa, creator of all, whom no one worships and to whom few address a prayer, is angered when men sin deeply, when they commit murder, adultery or theft. These acts he punishes by sending leprosy or smallpox. Among the Tiv, murder and adultery are religious offences calling for ritual reparation. The explanation of such beliefs and practices is that murder and adultery, and sometimes theft, are becoming criminal offences, and, as we have seen before, the contacts between law and religion are two: one where certain wrongs are so abhorrent to the community that they become both crimes and breaches of religious norms of conduct, and the second where religious sanctions or the belief in magic are used in legal procedure to ascertain truth by the application of an ordeal or some mode of divination. Otherwise religion serves chiefly to reinforce the devotion of the people to its traditional code of conduct, and it must be rarely, if ever, that it leads to new law or amendments of the law. But we can also see that as the more serious of these old civil wrongs become crimes, and the list of crimes generally expands, these two contracts are widening, and this expansion of the criminal law is caused mainly by the progressive enlightenment of a social conscience – even though it be the enlightenment of self-interest – and the growing strength of central authority that can enforce it.

We said that there are, here and there, among these nations ecclesiastics of sorts with growing influence. There are priests, persons having, as members of a calling or occupants of an office, custody of sacred places or objects and supervision of rites performed in regard to them.[3] They are to be seen among the Ganda, Kitara and Bemba, and they have influence and authority. For

---

[1] The Tiv have no law.   [2] Doke (1931), 228.
[3] In West Africa there is a widespread belief in the Earth Goddess, and there are priests or custodians of the Earth and sacrifices at her shrines.

example among the latter, the *bakabilo*, hereditary priests whose main duties are ritual, are also the king's advisers, with considerable powers to check his exercise of his authority, and some of them sit with him on his court; and among the Ganda the *Kimbugwe*, who is the priest and guardian in charge of the sacred royal umbilical cord, has his own court, which ranks next in status to that of the king and the *Katikiro* (his prime minister and chief justice), and, as far as we know, applies the general law of the realm. We also see here and there the ordeal in litigation being applied by priests as well as the sorcerers or medicine-men. In countries which have acquired the art of writing at this stage, for example, the Hittite Empire and Brahman India, we can see the influence that proceeds from its exclusive possession, but it is only in the Christian nations that we can witness the power of great ecclesiastical landlords, the building up of an elaborate and separate system of ecclesiastical law and ecclesiastical courts and the presence of ecclesiastics on the secular tribunals and councils. For this phenomenon we can now see the reasons more clearly, and among others they are the monotheistic religion and one united priesthood, an international religion that dwarfs local rulers, and an ecclesiastical system of administration of justice that originated long before under a higher civilization. We shall say more of this later.

M

CHAPTER 23

The Recent Peoples of the
Central Codes – Feudalism

At the close of our period[1] in most of these peoples the king (or paramount chief) is at the head of a feudal society and it is appropriate at this point to endeavour to describe the system and how it has come about. It is created by economic development and needs.

These large political systems cannot be built up and these populations cannot be held together, without a sufficiently strong and central government, and in most of the societies which we are considering, central government is well developed, and strong by the standards of our previous stages, and takes the form of rule by a king. Like other important institutions of society, kingship is supported by mystique and the national religion, by the king's divine right to rule, by the people's belief in his supernatural powers over the prosperity of the land and welfare of his subjects, by his inheritance of the guardian spirits of the line of the dead chiefs, by his possession of sacred relics, by his power of approach to national deities, by his responsibility for the rites on which the people's food is thought to depend.[2] The king in most of these peoples represents a curious combination of the absolute monarch, possessing, in theory, an arbitrary and absolute power over the lives and property of his people – for he can take them in a moment of anger without reason and can in Africa, at least, enslave and sell his subjects – and the man with a desire and need for popularity and a reputation for fair and just dealing. Government also

---

[1] Namely at the close of the eleventh century in England, and in Africa in the Kingdoms of Uganda, which stand at the very end of our period and perhaps even at the beginning of the next.
[2] Bemba: Richards (1939), 25.

cannot be carried on except by the means and interposition of district, subdistrict and village chiefs or lords. This is an economic and also an historical development, for many of these districts (as we have seen) were former independent kingdoms absorbed and conquered with or without their rulers. We may add that these chiefs or lords must have power and form a hierarchy of powers, otherwise the government cannot be effective. A system, for example, under which the intermediate chiefs are mere agents of the king is not usually possible, for the power of the king is not sufficiently strong to hold together a state of this size in so primitive an economy. Government also cannot be carried on without supplies, especially as largesse is expected of the ruler, as it has been from the first and always will be. The king's supplies cannot be provided by money, for there is not yet sufficient of it, and accordingly must be provided in kind by tribute or taxation, and must take the form of goods (mainly food) and services. In an agricultural or largely agricultural community (and almost all our peoples are such) tribute can only be got from the occupier of land, for on it he lives and finds his food, and this is commonly so even if he belongs to the small minority of the craftsmen. The king is king of the land, and in almost all these peoples the land is considered to belong to him – and sometimes in our peoples of Uganda the cattle also[1] and even the crops and food[2] – and in theory he could dispossess anyone and take any of this property without a reason.[3] One of his main functions is the administration of the land and its fair division among the heads of households. For this purpose – and to the extent that it has not already been done – he must divide it into districts and allot it among district chiefs (many of whom are for reasons of safety and good government his relatives) who in turn allot to sub-chiefs of villages (usually appointed or confirmed by him), or, more often, of groups of villages, who allot among village headmen, and they among heads of households; but there remains outside this division a large share of the land which he retains as his demesne (that is to say, which he occupies and works directly) and the

[1] Ankole: Roscoe (1911b), 2.
[2] Bemba pay tribute on all crops and also game and wild honey taken: Richards (1939), 251.
[3] He is also possessed of certain monopolies – e.g. Bemba: ivory and salt.

large shares which the district and sub-chiefs similarly retain, and much of all this is unoccupied and unused. Everyone, for his protection and for reasons of good government, must have a territorial chief.

It depends largely on the personality, ability and popularity of the king, as well as upon the degree of coalescence of the peoples making up the state, whether his chiefs enjoy a measure of independence; the householder pays his tribute of food, according to local circumstances and practice either to the king's officer direct at a royal village or estate, or to his immediate chief, who pays it over, taking what he is entitled to take; the householder also pays his tribute of service partly to the king direct and partly to his chief.

The family head who requires land in a particular district must go to the chief of that district and will usually obtain it, for the strength of a chief depends on the number of his tenants. In return he must perform the duties arranged or customary, for example pay an arranged proportion of the harvest, or, if he desires the sole right to fish in a reach of a river, pay his duty in fish. As in the peoples of the Early Codes and even towards the end of our present stage, the householder has the freedom to leave an unpopular chief and ask land from another, to whom he then comes under similar obligations; but when the density of population increases so far that the superfluity of land disappears, that situation must end.

This relationship between man and chief and king extends not only to rights in land and obligations to pay tribute, but also to a third aspect – the maintenance of order and decision of legal disputes. In each court sits the local chief or his judicial officer, with a group of councillors who are commonly heads of leading families. A case too serious for the court is sent up to a higher court, and there are certain serious and especially capital offences reserved for the king's court unless he has expressly granted to a subordinate chief the right to hear and punish them; there is also a system of appeal from the lowest to the highest court and sometimes a separate system of courts for the largest towns, and sometimes separate courts held by great figures in the state. The general basis of all these jurisdictions is that only a chief who has power over the parties can enforce his decision.

There is a fourth aspect of government. The king's functions include that of defending the nation's land, and this necessarily involves the military service of the able-bodied men (who are not necessarily or solely the heads of households) and so every such man is under a duty of military service which is part of his general tribute of service. The armed men must feed themselves till they reach the frontier and in some lands take their wives to cook for them.

Human beings erect their economic relationships into divers philosophies. For example, in the kingdom of Ankole (one of the conquests of the Bahima) the state was, in the mind of the freeman, built upon a relation of *okutoizha* (clientship, homage or dependency).[1] A Muhima cattle-owner would go before the *mugabe* (king) and swear to follow him in war, and undertake to give him periodically a number of cattle to keep the relationship alive. He was free (provided he did not combine with others to do so) to put an end to this relationship by ceasing to pay homage, but till that occurred he was under a duty of military service, a duty to attend the king's kraal bringing periodic gifts of homage, and a duty to give cattle when the king was in temporary or special need.[2] When the client died, his heir reported to the mugabe and renewed the bond of clientship by giving a 'cow of burial.'[3] In return for military service and homage the client was entitled to protection by the king's forces from cattle-raiders, and retaliation by the king against those who raided his cattle, and in case of a breach of the peace to have the transgressor tried before the mugabe; the king might give his kinsmen the right to punish murder by blood-revenge and was under a duty to maintain peace between his clients. The Bahima were cattlekeepers, not agriculturists, and could pasture their cattle anywhere; on the other hand, in the neighbouring agricultural kingdom of Buganda, each person held his land from his superior on terms of service. These developed forms and relations are characteristic of the more advanced economies of the present stage. They are to be found, for example, at the present stage, in large measure in the Hittite Empire[4] and in Russia[5], Armenia and

[1] Oberg (1940), 128f.   [2] Known in Europe as a feudal 'aid'.
[3] In Europe, a 'relief'.   [4] See *ante*, p. 81.
[5] In the expanded version of Jaroslav's Pravda.

Georgia[1] as well as in Western and Central Europe,[2] India, China, Japan, the Arab world and the empire of the Turks.[3]

But in the view of many historians of Mediaeval Europe, the term 'feudalism' is properly applicable only to that institution which grew in France from A.D. 700 onwards and extended as far as the Rhine, and, adopted by those able administrators the Normans, was brought by them to England at the Conquest, and flourished in Western Europe during the tenth, eleventh and twelfth centuries. In their view the term is not even properly applied to Anglo-Saxon England, Southern France, Italy or Central Europe beyond the Rhine. They use the term in its narrower, technical or legal sense, to signify a body of institutions characterized, firstly, by the personal relationship of vassalage between two free men, namely the obligation of obedience and service (chiefly military) by the one (the vassal) and the obligation of protection and maintenance by the other (the lord); and secondly, and usually as a result, the grant by lord to vassal of a piece of land known as a fief or benefice.[4] But there were wide and important differences in the nature and incidents of feudalism in many different areas of Western Europe and at different periods during the five hundred years beginning in A.D. 700, just as there are wide differences in the types of government of our African peoples; and the analysis given at the head of this chapter is but a type to which no African nation exactly conforms. Too little is known of the details of their systems of government and too little also of the governments of Europe, for the volume of legislation is trivial at this stage and says little of government and even charters omit much that is assumed to be known. Through lack of information we are prone to exaggerate the resemblances between different areas and periods in Europe and to exaggerate the differences between Europe and other lands. It would be more useful to our present purpose, as well as essentially true, to describe these various phenomena by one name and call these societies feudal.

Omitting, then, these differences between the developed feudal

---

[1] See *ante*, p. 81.
[2] See Bloch (1940); Sir F. M. Stenton, *English Feudalism 1066-1166* (2nd edn, 1961); Ganshof (1952).
[3] See a few authorities cited in Ganshof (1952), xvif.
[4] Ganshof (1952), XVIf.

societies, can we see any common steps by which they are brought or come into being? One is, of course, the general process of development of such a political structure. For example, among the Lamba, one of the least developed economically of these peoples, the position of the paramount chief is still weak, so that while the usual gifts are made to him, they are still considered to be voluntary, and not by way of tribute but respect; the four group chiefs, as well as the paramount, have jurisdiction to pass sentence of death, and the village chiefs pass up a capital charge to them or to the paramount chief at their will. Though there are sometimes appeals from group chief to paramount, he rarely reverses their decision, out of consideration for their dignity. With the Ngala the position of the paramount chief is no stronger. The Ngbetu, on the other hand, were a group of tribes conquered by Ngbetu (now an aristocratic ruling class) and here the paramount or king has, we are told, unlimited power. The nations of Uganda are feudal.

A second type of step is taken towards feudalism when a king (as often in Anglo-Saxon England) grants lands to a chief as immediate lord of a village or district, with the right to receive the tribute that the king would have received, and jurisdiction to try the cases reserved to his court.[1] A third and more important type of step is taken when chiefs and peasants in danger of losing their land in evil days, put themselves and their households in the hands of lords who can at least give them food, and they receive back their lands for the length of their lives without payment of rent and on terms arranged. This, the European *commendatio*, is seen as early as the Frankish settlement, when Gallo-Roman landowners are putting themselves in the hands of barbarian chieftains for their protection. In later times the process accelerates and is employed by lords, who, unforced by want, desire to increase their lands. Lastly, in many nations, one of the purposes of this system of administration is military, and the services to be rendered are, above all, military services. It is common that the rise of a specialized and costly type of weapon has limited its use to a wealthy class. For example, the Ganda warriors, according to Roscoe, had spears and shields: the peasants joined them as bearers or followers with only clubs or heavy sticks. Among the

[1] Stenton (1943), 492f.

Ngbetu the freemen were armed with lance or throwing-spear and shield, the lower classes with bow and arrow.[1] Before A.D. 700 there was introduced into the Eastern Roman Empire over its Asiatic border, and there developed, the use of heavily armed and protected soldiers mounted on an improved and heavy breed of horse with a high-peaked saddle. Till then, as in England, till 1066, the horse in Western Europe was a mere pony, suitable for transport to the battlefield but not for riding in battle. About A.D. 700 began the introduction of the heavy cavalry man into France, and by the middle of the ninth century the process was complete. The required training was intensive; the cost of horse and equipment was great;[2] only the class enjoying the produce of wide lands and much cattle could indulge in such a pursuit. The only method available, at this economic stage, of strengthening the levy of the able-bodied by the introduction of those able to turn out at need properly trained, with horse, equipment and weapons, attendants, foot-soldiers and food, was to give land to suitable young men on terms of 'knight's (that is to say, boy's) service', and still better, to grant a fief to a vassal on terms of providing a stated number of knights and their complement. Upon the existing administration was engrafted the new system as William engrafted it in England after the Conquest, men holding on terms of knight's service side by side with men holding on other terms of tribute. The new system gathered its rules about it. Like other benefices knight's tenure soon became hereditary. While other tenants for the most part (except in Kent) transmitted rights to land divisible among their sons, land held by knight's service came to descend by primogeniture, for to divide the land would frustrate the purpose of the holding. New brooms sweep clean and in England, after the Conquest, the status of the free sokeman (or free peasant) was depressed and dwindled to a small class confined to a few districts, as William granted lands to his Norman vassals. Finally, almost all land in the country came to be held either on knight's service or serjeanty (that is to say, to provide foot-soldiers, horses, arms or other military needs) or by religious foundations in frankalmoign (that is to say, as the term

[1] *Les Mangbetu* (1909), 527f.
[2] See L. Rib. 36[11], according to which the total cost in the eighth century was 45s. equal to the cost of half that number of oxen.

was applied in England, on a free tenure owing only the service of prayer). The Hittites became one of the three world powers of their day by the possession of a new weapon, the heavy horsed chariot, and we can be sure that the need to grant lands on terms of providing charioteers, chariots, horses and their equipment and complement, served to solidify and spread the feudalism of the nation.

We must not forget that these new weapons have their effect on the law in divers ways. For example, the war-horse came to France between A.D. 700 and 850, and with it a developed form of feudalism and knight's tenure and ordeal by battle; the war-horse only came to England in 1066 and with it the Normans brought a new and extreme and highly organized form of feudalism and knight's tenure, and ordeal by battle.

M*

CHAPTER 24

The Recent Peoples of the
Central Codes – The Law

We will add little to what has been said of marriage among these
people, for the marriage by bridewealth remains (or in some
societies, which have no cattle, marriage by service and gifts).[1]
But there are signs that here and there the amount of the bridewealth is diminishing,[2] and here and there is a beginning of the
marriage settlement, the gift from the girl's father to her or the
young couple.[3] There have always been small gifts from her side
on marriage, but they have usually till now been insignificant in
amount compared with the bridewealth.[4]

We have no space to enter into the details of the law of inheritance, which varies much even in the same people. There is still

[1] Bemba and Lamba: Richards (1940), 95; Richards (1939), 207f., 225f.;
Doke (1931), 79 (service for a period of years and a few articles). Ngala:
2 or 3 slaves, 2 or 3 necklaces and 2 or 3 empty bottles. Ngbetu: slaves,
goats, iron, spears, knives, dogs. As to peoples possessing cattle: *South
Bantu:* cattle usually paid over an indefinite time and not final in amount.
Ankole: pastoralists, 2-20 cows according to the man's means; agriculturists,
a cow calf and a young bull or 14 goats: Roscoe (1911b), 124f. *Kitara:*
pastoralists, 10-20 cows; agriculturists, usually 1 cow or 5 or more goats:
Roscoe (1923), 267f. The Giriama have lost most of their cattle and the
brideprice has been altered from 6 cows and a bull to 65 goats and sheep
and 15 calabashes of beer (as an average).
[2] Ganda, in recent past, ten goats or at most two cows, ten pots of beer and a
set of barkcloths. It would take a year to collect by begging from relatives:
Roscoe (1911a), 88f. Now (A.D. 1934) among the educated Ganda the suitor
may give whatever he desires of his own free will (as in England, eleventh
century, II Can. 74) but the cost of the wedding to the groom is large:
Mair (1934), 81f. The Tiv system of marriage by exchange was prohibited
by the British, and bridewealth took its place and purchased the bride who
would formerly have been exchanged.
[3] See *ante*, p. 75. Hardly yet in Africa.
[4] But often large among the Cape Nguni.

usually little to inherit. In the less developed economies of this stage, where land is poor and to spare, and the village moves every few years as the site is exhausted or insanitary,[1] the near relatives of the deceased can reap his crop and continue to use his garden site as long as they please. Crops are sold or bartered but not the land.[2] In the more developed economies of the feudal societies the land usually belongs to the king and could in law be recovered by him without cause and reverts to him on being abandoned. By the end of our period, in Europe and Africa, there is a tendency for feudal holdings to become hereditary and descend by primogeniture, but the change is not completed in this period. Nor has the occupier generally acquired the right to assign such a holding.[3] There remain the other holdings of land, including allodial (i.e. individual) land in France and holdings of land in England before the Conquest. These interests are heritable and usually descend in Europe equally among sons, and, in default of sons, among daughters. But in Africa, with many exceptions, primogeniture holds sway; the eldest son (or sometimes brother) succeeds with the obligation to help his brothers to marry and to support his mother and sisters, acting as guardian of minors. Property usually descends patrilineally, but in the Bemba, Lamba and Digo[4] matrilineally and in some other places bilaterally. There is here and there a clan leader and council to settle such disputes between the members.[5] Chieftainship commonly has its own rules of succession.[6]

Personal property usually descends in the same way as heritable interests in land. It is almost exclusively vested in the male head of the household, who acquires powers of life and death over his children and almost equal powers over his wife. The sons have

[1] Lamba and Bemba.   [2] Bemba: Richards (1939), 274.
[3] Ganshof (1952), 130f; Hittite Code, *ante*, p. 81.
[4] Digo: to children of deceased's sisters (in practice, strongest nephew); in default, to children of deceased's mother, and in default to sons and grandsons of maternal aunts.
[5] Ganda: The senior member of a *siga* (or sub-clan) settles disputes on matters of inheritance, clan status, debts or subscriptions towards a fine of a member, and there is a clan council which operates as a final court of appeal: Mair (1934), 35.
[6] Lamba: a younger brother usually succeeds or in default a sister's son, or nearest matrilineal clansman in the village. Inheritance of property is generally to a brother. Ganda: a son but not the eldest son, succeeds the father, to be agreed upon between the Katikiro and the great chiefs.

no property till they marry and leave the home.[1] The proprietary capacity of wives has not yet fallen as low as in many of the nations of the Late Codes, and they are generally considered to own, in a legal or quasi-legal sense, the property given to them by their husband during life, what they make or exclusively use, what surplus of their crops remains after supporting their family, and what they acquire by bartering or selling it.[2] But the rules of property are not technical – there is too little of it – and much is destroyed at the death of the deceased or given as presents to chiefs or taken by relatives at the funeral. In particular, slavery is a vague and mild status. In some places slaves may own slaves and other property. The Ganda slave is, in effect, a person who does not belong to a clan and therefore cannot inherit from a clan member. Wills – a man's instructions as to the division and disposal of his property – are oral in Africa, and almost always in Europe, and of no great importance. If they departed materially from customary ways of devolution they would not be obeyed. But the Ganda paterfamilias regularly nominates his heir.[3] As for the inheriting of widows, the levirate is becoming less common with the diminishing importance of the clan. A Ganda wife, if of marriageable age, usually goes back to her father's family. But in many peoples widows are taken by inheritance or in marriage by a brother of the deceased, or by a son of another wife.[4]

[1] *Les Bangala* (1904), 227-35; *Les Mangbetu* (1909), 333, 339.
[2] Ganda. But among the Ngala and Ngbetu these go to her eldest son on her husband's death; and similarly among the Lamba, except for her hoes, pots, mats and baskets and her own plot: Doke (1931), 204.
[3] Mair (1934), 211f. In default, children, brothers and senior clansmen appoint him. Before Mutesa's time the heir appointed was usually a brother's son, but now a son or grandson of the deceased.
[4] e.g. Lamba. Hittite Code, 193; widow goes to brother, then father, of the deceased. The following are the outlines of the rules of inheritance of property amongst some others of these peoples: *Boni:* Children inherit equally, and failing them brothers. *Teita:* In some places widows inherit a share, except of livestock. Otherwise sons inherit equally. There is individual ownership of land cultivated for a season and it may be let or sold. *Taveta:* Sons inherit, the eldest getting the largest share. Wives do not inherit, but in the absence of sons, a plot is given to daughters. Individual ownership of forest land and letting of land. *Nyika:* Eldest brother is sole heir, or in default eldest son. If the eldest brother is younger than the sons, he inherits the wives and the sons inherit their father's property equally. *Giriama:* Eldest son inherits for the benefit of his brothers equally and in default of sons, a brother. Women do not inherit.

We turn now to crime and civil injuries, and first to the civil injuries, and note a large measure of uniformity in the law of the peoples of this stage.

In these peoples, as in the Central Codes of the past, the more serious personal injuries continue the process of their conversion into criminal offences. There are a number of new circumstances which serve to explain the changes that take place. First, there is a development of what we might call the social conscience. It is an outlook created by membership of a state – a feeling that these are not merely acts against the victim or his kinship group but against the members of the state, in that all the individuals that compose it are endangered and suffer, and the state is embodied in the person of the king. It is not merely, as in the Early Codes, that the king suffers loss or outrage by the loss of or injury to one of his subjects, and that in him the general body of the community are affected. Secondly, there is such a degree of development of the central power in the state that it can impose sanctions, and those other than pecuniary. Thirdly, and in consequence, the sanctions undergo a process of change from pecuniary to corporal sanctions including mutilations.[1] There were already such sanctions imposed on slaves,[2] partly because they had no kinship group who might be outraged and resist, and partly because they had no means to pay, and these remain.[3] Now the power of the kinship groups is slowly giving way to the power of the state. Now also it becomes abhorrent, especially in these more specialized economies with their increased discrepancies of wealth, that anyone, because of his means, might be able to inflict serious injury and escape with the payment of a money compensation for the loss or injury caused to a poor man, or with a fine; and there are no prisons. There is further, especially in regard to homicide, a growing sense of the feebleness, pusillanimity and disgrace of accepting blood money, and that it is a wrong to the state to do so. There is also a sense of the importance of endeavouring to restrain the commission of such a wrong in the future, and this involves the need to impose a deterrent punishment and therefore the need

[1] Lamba: Doke (1931), 64, 79 (mutilations and enslavement).
[2] See *ante*, pp. 67-8.
[3] Alf. 25: fine for rape of a slave by a freeman; castration 'as compensation' for rape of a slave by a slave. III Edmund 4: death or mutilation of a slave for theft.

to fix sanctions more in the light of the quality of the wrong and less in the light of the loss to the victim. All this the central authority is, within limits, able to do, and if, in any case, the offender escapes, at least it can banish him or declare him an outlaw, that is to say, one who has no protection from the law in this violent age, and can be killed with impunity; and it can confiscate his assets. But we must not exaggerate the enlightenment of the age.

First, then, in regard to homicide; and here the data observed in the recent peoples of the stage of the Central Codes enable us better to understand the Central Codes of the past. In the Early Codes the pecuniary sanction payable by way of compensation to the next of kin generally remained, but there was often also a fine payable to the king, and among the Nguni (though not yet in England or continental Europe) this was now the only sanction. The typical sanction of the Central Codes is the handing over of one or more of the following persons – the offender himself, his children, his sisters (particularly his unmarried sisters) and occasionally his mother: not usually his wife,[1] because to lose her labour would spell ruin and she is not of his clan. This sanction, as we have seen, accords well with the liability for a man's debts, for which there can be execution on the same persons; and indeed debts can be paid *inter vivos* by the same means;[2] and, as is shown by the frequency with which young females are handed over, there is often the further purpose to raise up a child to take the place of the victim. It is also doubtful whether in these economies there is generally any other equally practicable way of paying for these wrongs or other large debts: as the communities become more agricultural the number of cattle per head of the population is probably less and sometimes none: money is little in quantity, and where land is plentiful its value is little: in the feudal states land and sometimes cattle and crops belong to the king: hence the chief and most available assets are persons and their labour.

[1] But among the Ngala and Ngbetu a wife may be awarded to the creditor if the defendant does not obey a judgment.
[2] A Lamba pleading in court for his life may offer the chief his mother and sisters, and if the chief accepts the offer then unless the defendant's father can redeem his mother or the sisters' husbands redeem them, they will be taken and apportioned. Or a sister may offer herself to the court: Doke (1931), 64.

Though its details vary, such a law is almost universal in these peoples in Africa, and is the law of the Hittite Code. But for reasons not altogether clear, in Western Europe a man cannot sell a free man or woman and only the debtor himself may be taken in execution for a debt or be handed over by way of sanction for homicide. The cause is likely to be economic[1] not religious – it is difficult to imagine Christian doctrine which prohibits this law and supports slavery and serfdom, and religion does not create new law or amend it. But the sale of children was prohibited early in the Visigothic Code,[2] though it had been familiar in ancient Rome. The punitive and deterrent object is effected by a distinction, variously expressed, between more and less reprehensible forms of homicide, punished by greater and smaller sanctions, though there is some sanction in nearly all cases of homicide. However, though in fact these peoples are inarticulately cognizant of the differences between intentional, negligent and accidental killing, these are not the common legal categories. Negligence has never yet appeared in the law and does not now, and intention is difficult to ascertain. Distinctions in law, if they are to be enforceable, must be pragmatic and materialist and not psychological nor subjective, nor is the intentional the only reprehensible kind of homicide. The most common distinctions are between 'killing in anger' and killing 'when only his hand errs';[3] secret killing (including killing by poison and failing after killing to make prompt disclosure) and open killing; killing by ambush;[4] killing by one kind of weapon and killing by another.[5] In no case does the sanction vary with the status of the slain. There is appended a list of the sanctions in these peoples, so far as they are explicit and known to us.[6] A killer caught in the act may everywhere be put to death with impunity.

---

[1] Western Europe is, in general, much richer in cattle and other goods.
[2] Euric, 299; see Zeumer (1894).
[3] See H.C.; also in Africa.
[4] Both these sanctions are common in Europe.   [5] East Africa.
[6] *Boni:* the killer handed over to family of the slain to be dealt with; if killed by accident, another person must be handed over to fill the dead man's place. *Teita:* another man must be handed over, or a payment in children or cattle, or the killer handed over or put to death. But the amount of the payment varies acording to the manner in which the victim was slain – e.g. if by knife, more than ten times the penalty when killed by club; if by poison, killer takes the same poison. Accidental homicide, payment of one child and

The persons so handed over often occupy a status intermediate between slave and free,[1] but are sometimes treated as slaves.[2] Male children are often allowed to return home on reaching maturity, but girls remain[3] and may be allowed to return to their

---

cattle. *Taveta:* death, but may be compounded by payment of compensation. *Nyika:* intentional killing, two to ten persons of killer's family to be given to family of victim. In default, murderer must be handed over and put to death. *Digo:* distinction between murder in the heat of passion and in cold blood. In the latter case, four times the number of persons handed over. *Giriama:* one male and three females handed over to victim's family. Killing of own brother or father, one person handed over. Killing of wife or child, no penalty. Subsequently owing to impoverishment the sanction of one male and three females reduced to two females and now (*c.* 1914) sixty-five goats (the equivalent of the bridewealth) to the family of the deceased and fifteen goats fine to the elders. For a wilful murder these amounts are doubled: Champion (1967), 19. *Shangana-Tonga:* formerly death, now handing over of a girl or payment of bridewealth to obtain a woman to bear a child in place of the victim. *Venda:* death or banishment, and the chief confiscates all his possessions and takes the whole of his family. For accidental homicide, a fine. *Northern Sotho:* killer put to death, and his relations must also give bridewealth to acquire a woman to replace the victim (if she was a woman) or to bear a child (if the victim was male). *Lamba:* court usually takes a number of persons (sisters and mother of the accused). Some of the women are handed over to the heir of the victim (or, in the case of a child, to his maternal uncle) as slaves, others kept by the chief. But killer sometimes put to death or fined according to the seriousness of the offence. If a sister is married, her husband can ransom her if he wishes, and she becomes his slave: Doke (1931), 63, 82. *Bemba:* persons handed over, members of the *inganda* (lineage group). *Ngala and Ngbetu:* if no extenuating circumstances, killer handed over to relatives of the slain, who may kill, eat or sell him. In extenuating circumstances he may be ransomed. *Ganda:* intentional homicide, blood feud and handed over to be killed; if no malice, payment of a number of women, cows, goats and barkcloths: Roscoe (1911a), 20, 266; Mair (1934), 184f. *Kitara:* similar. *Ankole:* similar. *Southern Nigeria:* no cattle kept, and widespread practice of handing persons over (e.g. Talbot (1926), vol. iii, 625f.). *Northern Nigeria:* some of the more backward peoples, e.g. in the N.E., *Margi of Adamawa Province,* feud and giving of garments and handing over of a girl to deceased's brother to bear a child in his place: C. K. Meek, *Tribal Studies in Northern Nigeria* (1931), vol. i, 213f., also the *Katab,* vol. II, 78. *England:* 'Murder' (i.e. secret killing) is unemendable. Killer 'shall be given up to the kinsmen of the slain'. II Can. 56, 64. Other homicides, wergeld to relatives and a payment for *mundbryce* to the king. For other sanctions in the Central Codes of the past see *ante,* p. 74f. Some of the above information is very fragmentary.
[1] Nyika: they occupy a somewhat menial position, but are not slaves.
[2] Southern Nigeria: sometimes free, sometimes treated as slaves: Talbot (1926), III, 626.
[3] Nyika.

families on giving birth to a child (who will take the place of the slain).[1]

The institution of the sanctuary, because of the increase in the number of capital offences and the changes that are taking place in the sanctions for homicide, grows in importance,[2] and the growth of villages and towns creates here and there a new feature, the village of refuge – a village where an important shrine or temple is to be found. For example, among the Lamba[3] a man who has committed murder, theft, adultery or other serious offence may flee to such a village (of which there are seven in Ilamba) and is there seized and tried before the local chief, the pursuer remaining outside. The defendant may be merely fined or, if the offence is sufficiently serious, sentenced to death, for there is a beginning of the notion that the land is polluted by certain heinous offences and the shrine-village must be freed from the miasma.[4] Such a religious, as distinct from the secular, political sanctuary, is only found where the power of religion shows increase. It is not to be seen, for example, among the Ngala and Ngbetu.

Sanctions for wounding are still pecuniary everywhere and we still find short tariff-lists of payments varying according to the part of the body injured and the nature of the injury.[5] In most places the sanction consists of a payment to the injured and a payment to his lord or king,[6] but elsewhere the plaintiff may get nothing.[7]

[1] e.g. Shangana-Tonga: Junod, *Life of a South African Tribe* (1927), I, 441f.; Margi: Meek (1925), I, 217.
[2] See *supra* as to the Anglo-Saxon Laws.
[3] Doke (1931), 57.
[4] This notion accords with the practice of banishment. See, for example, Edward and Guthrum, ii. 'Wizards, sorcerers, perjurers and those who secretly compass death shall be driven from the land and the nation shall be purified.' II Can. 26. provides that there shall be no sanctuary for theft or treason.
[5] e.g. H.C. 7-16; Wateita (*E.A.L.*, vol. I, 102) and in England the Leis Willelme 10, 11.
[6] Or the elders, Wateita (half to person injured, half to elders).
[7] Ankole: the Mugabe might very rarely order a cow to be paid to a man seriously hurt: Roscoe (1911) (b), 19. Similarly among the Tonga. With the Sotho the payment ordered was payable to the victim. Among the Giriama the penalty for causing permanent injury was the same as death, but there was no payment to the elders; for a mere temporary injury, a small number of he-goats: according to Champion (1967), 19. This, if correct, is a rare distinction.

As in the Central Codes of the past,[1] so in those of the recent peoples, adultery becomes criminal and capital. Everywhere a husband who finds his wife and paramour in *flagranti delicto* is entitled to kill them both out of hand,[2] or mutilate them.[3] But the king has an interest in the infliction of capital sentences, and capital offences can only be tried in his court. A Lamba husband who has killed the pair should or must report to him.[4] But in practice lighter sentences are often passed and the adulterer is blinded or otherwise mutilated or ordered to hand over two persons[5] or a fine is imposed[6] or the court may pardon.[7]

Rape also becomes a capital offence during this period.[8] Seduction or fornication is still, and up to modern times, a common prelude to marriage and the sanction remains pecuniary.[9]

Theft generally remains a civil wrong for which the sanction is multiple restitution (the multiple increasing with the value of the thing) or restitution and an additional payment; but a person caught in the act of stealing anything of any value may be killed on the spot with impunity[10] and similarly (though the logic of it is not apparent) a thief caught in the act is liable in some courts to the death penalty,[11] or the court may impose a mutilation.[12]

[1] See *ante*, p. 77.

[2] e.g. Lamba: Doke (1931), 67; Ganda: Mair (1934), 186, Roscoe (1911a), 26.

[3] Champion (1967), 20, Doke (1931), 67f. A Lamba husband may also seize a sister and enslave her or marry or sell her.

[4] Doke (1931), 67f.   [5] e.g. Ganda: Roscoe (1911a), 261f. Ngala, Ngbetu.

[6] But a Lamba husband scorns to keep the money and passes it to her family: Doke (1931), 68. Taveta and Giriama – a fine is usual.

[7] In the inept ecclesiastical courts of Western Europe (where the capital sentence cannot be imposed) if the matter comes before them the sanction usually consists of a whipping or other bodily penance, commonly remitted for money.

[8] Lamba: death of the man and enslavement of his sister: Doke (1931), 69. H.C., death (II, 83). England: death or castration (in Alf. 25, it was only a fine). The offence is usually only triable by the chief or king.

[9] Kitara: Roscoe (1923), 66 – two cows usual and marriage. Lamba: ostracism, and no payment unless the girl was immature: Doke (1931), 69. Giriama: a number of goats.

[10] e.g. Ganda: Roscoe (1911a), 264; Mair (1934), 186. Bemba: Richards (1939), 186.   [11] e.g. Ganda: Roscoe (1911a), 264;

[12] Lamba: a hand or ears may be cut off: Doke (1931), 64. Ngala: owner may slay him or eat him or cut off his hands. Ngbetu: violent self-help not permitted, but the king often sentences the thief to amputation of the ears. Mutilation also remains as a common sanction for theft by a slave (e.g. H.C. 95 – cutting off nose and ears as well as restitution and payment of a sum of money).

The law continues to pay great attention to this offence, especially theft of animals, and almost half the Hittite Code sets out the sanctions for theft of different species of animals, agricultural equipment and the like. The sanction for theft of a great bull (that is a bull two years old), is a payment of fifteen bulls; for a great horse fifteen horses and for a great ram fifteen rams.[1]

There are other civil wrongs in a slowly lengthening list, especially trespass and slander.

We see, then, that of the wrongs that were once civil, at the close of this period adultery has become criminal as well as civil, rape criminal, but homicide is not criminal in all its forms – indeed in some of its forms it is not criminal in modern times – and in some circumstances and peoples it is both criminal and civil; nor are the circumstances in which it is criminal the same in different peoples; nor is theft in all its forms criminal, nor is wounding generally criminal. This, however, is not the whole of the increase in the criminal law. Witchcraft, incest,[2] bestiality and treason remain the chief crimes and are punishable generally by a sentence of death and confiscation of all the offender's possessions, though a court may impose lesser sanctions (rarely for witchcraft) – mutilations, or the handing over of a number of persons, or banishment. It is not easy in Africa to see what are the additions to this list of crimes, for information is meagre and relates to the past, and the power of the kings in the more advanced economies is absolute and its exercise often arbitrary. But we may say, as of Europe, that the additions are of two main kinds: first, certain acts are criminal wherever committed, and some criminal only if committed in special circumstances. For example, in many places a breach of the peace on the king's highway or disorderly conduct in the palace or in his presence or an offence against a member of his household – especially, of course, adultery with one of his wives – is criminal, as an offence to his person. The offences which are criminal wherever committed include, towards the end of our period in England, treason, murder (that is to say, secret killing), robbery, *forsteal* (ambush), *hamsocne* (armed attack on a man in his house) and *fyrdwite* (neglect of military service). The sanction for some of these offences is merely a fine, but other crimes are

[1] For the other Central Codes of the past, see *ante*, p. 77.
[2] Lamba: usually the guilty burnt, sometimes banished: Doke (1931), 70.

'bootless' (that is, not emendable by money) such as treason and murder and false coining, and most of these are punishable by death and confiscation of the offender's property.

Any lawyer is familiar with the difficulty in practice of determining whether an offence is a crime or a civil injury. A crime has been defined as a wrong for which the sanction is enforced at the discretion of the state and can be remitted (if at all) only by the state.[1] In this period, in Europe and Africa, a distinction is easily visible between wrongs only triable in the court of the king or paramount chief,[2] and those triable in other courts. Courts are jealous of these jurisdictions, for the forfeitures, fines and court fees receivable are a valuable source of revenue. Yet English and African kings, with surprising frequency, grant to various lords most of these jurisdictions,[3] nor is the king's jurisdiction the same in different parts of his realm. Nor are all matters reserved to the court of king or paramount chief necessarily criminal. We may sum up by saying that at the close of this period and in the Late Codes crime and civil injury are closer together than they have ever been before, and yet the distinction remains real.

There is no space to enter into details of the procedure of the courts. Nowhere in Africa are technicalities of procedure to be seen, but ordeals and methods of divination (such as by observation of the behaviour of animals) are in use almost everywhere where evidence on one side is wanting, and therefore almost exclusively in cases of witchcraft and (to a lesser extent) adultery. There is widespread through Central Africa the use of the ordeal by poison for charges of witchcraft, and torture is employed in a variety of cases to obtain confessions.

---

[1] J. Austin, *Lectures on Jurisprudence*, Lecture XXVII; C. S. Kenny, *Outlines of Criminal Law* (Cambridge, 11th ed. p.14.).
[2] Called in England 'pleas of the crown'; in Normandy 'pleas of the sword'; in Africa 'crimes of the chief' and similar names.
[3] By 1066 many of the pleas of the Crown which Cnut had reserved for himself – usually breach of the king's special peace, ambush and treacherous manslaughter, the reception of outlaws, violent entry into a house and neglect of a summons to the militia: Stenton (1943), 485f.

CHAPTER 25

The Recent Peoples of the Late Codes

We leave the Central Codes and turn to our final stage, the fascinating age of the Late Codes, and in particular the recent peoples of a similar degree of economic and legal development to those of the Late Codes of the past. We define this stage, therefore, in the same terms as that of the Late Codes of the past.

There is a large number of such peoples in the present century. most of them in West Africa. Continuing our journey westward from East and South-East Africa, past the peoples of the Central Codes in Central Africa, we find in Nigeria and the Gold Coast (since called Ghana) many peoples of the earlier half of the Late Codes. This is not surprising, partly because the Guinea coast has been in contact with Western Europe since the fifteenth century, partly because some of the terrain is favourable, but chiefly because, as we have seen, civilization in this part of the world has for many centuries travelled from North Africa via the West, for the Sahara Desert has offered a great obstacle to direct communication from the north.

Southern Nigeria[1] is populated by the Negro race (for the southern coast of West Africa is its home) a coast of deltas, sandbanks and mangrove swamps, and behind these a zone of tropical forest some fifty to a hundred miles wide, where because of the prevalence of tsetse it has been difficult or impossible to rear cattle or horses. Beyond, the forest gradually opens into parkland, pierced by rivers great and small, especially the mighty Niger and its tributary the Benue; and still further north, in Northern Nigeria, is a great undulating plateau, reaching a height of some 7,000 feet in parts of the Bauchi Highlands. Northern Nigeria is

[1] The terms Northern and Southern Nigeria are used in this book to denote the territories which they comprised in the 1920s. For the history of the Nigerian Colony and Protectorate, see Burns (1947).

a dry and healthier land, but much is covered with loose, heavy sand and the desert encroaches. Eastern Nigeria, from the Bauchi plateau and Adamava province to the coast, is the home of more backward peoples, of economies no more developed than those of our Central Codes, poor and often naked communities, mainly agriculturists with few or no cattle, and, till recent times, much given to cannibalism in the southern forest, and sometimes with no rulers, no courts and no law. Among the best known of these peoples are the Ibo and the Yakö. In the west of Southern Nigeria, namely Yorubaland, for many centuries large kingdoms have existed, centred on various large towns[1] and succeeding one another, but vigorous immigrant peoples, invading and infiltrating from the north, have taken the better lands and driven the Negro inhabitants into southern forest and swamp.

Long ago Hausa-speaking peoples, partly pastoralist, occupied Northern Nigeria, and some seven centuries ago they received much of Islamic culture and Islamic law. Powerful states were founded, with well-organized fiscal systems and trained judiciaries, and in a long series of wars struggled for supremacy with one another. Then over the centuries Fulani, a Hamitic pastoral people, infiltrated from the north over most of Northern Nigeria, and at the commencement of the nineteenth century conducted a *jihad*, or holy war, against the backsliding Muhammadan rulers of the Hausa states. In the result came the empire of Sokoto, to whose Sultan eleven emirates (or kingdoms)[2] acknowledged allegiance. The only exception was the old Hausa kingdom of Bornu in the north-east, whose sultan maintained his independence. At the close of a long history of British penetration the Colony and Protectorate of Nigeria was formally inaugurated in 1914.[3] The bulk of Northern and Western Nigeria is occupied by

---

[1] Oyo, Benin, Ife, Lagos, Ondo, Ijebu, Egba and others. From the fifteenth century to the nineteenth the two kingdoms or empires of Oyo and Benin alternately dominated Yorubaland.

[2] Including Nupe.

[3] Until 1959 Islamic law of the Maliki school was fully in force, with some adaptation to local custom, in the emirates of Northern Nigeria, and so, though not an exclusively Muslim country, this was one of the few parts of the world where the Shari'a, as applied, was not confined to the law of personal status and family relations, and even in criminal matters Islamic law had concurrent jurisdiction with the criminal code introduced by the British (except over persons not subject to the jurisdiction of native courts). In 1959,

peoples of our Late Codes, and we may take as an example typical of many peoples of West Africa the kingdom of Nupe, with its capital town Bida and its dependencies (including the Kyedye) in the centre of Nigeria, at the transition from the southern forest belt to the arid savannahs of the north, and we may also take the Yoruba kingdoms.[1]

The southern part of what became Ghana has for long been occupied chiefly by the Akan peoples, Negro tribes speaking dialects of one language, who at different times in their history formed a number of states. Here, too, there is movement and pressure from the north, but to a far lesser degree, and though small bands of Muslim traders settled here and there from the fourteenth century onwards, and rulers were converted to Islam,[2] the number of Muslims is small and Muhammadan law was never received. The most numerous of the Akan peoples are the Ashanti who occupy the higher ground inland. In the eighteenth century

---

however, codes of criminal law and procedure, based on the Sudanese (i.e. Indian) Code, displaced Islamic law in the field of crime, and for most purposes Maliki law became confined to matters of personal status and family relations: see Anderson (1959a). The adaptation to native customary law applied, and applies, chiefly to matters of land tenure, talionic penalties, the rate of blood money for homicide, marriage gifts and payments and the wife' ability to enforce a claim for return of dower and dissolution of marriage: see Anderson (1955), 70; Lewis (1966), 45f. There was also opposition from the West to certain other sanctions, notably mutilation for theft, stoning for adultery, and the talion for deliberate homicide and wounding, as in the Shari'a: see Anderson (1959b), 23.

[1] We do not take as examples the Ibo, Yakö or other peoples of the eastern half of the forest belt because in the 1920s, though their economies were advancing rapidly, they were still at the stage of our Central Codes. Forde and Scott (1946), 78f., sum up the differences between the Western and Eastern halves of Southern Nigeria as follows: (1) In the Western Province the crafts are more advanced and more widely practised. (2) There is more specialization, and craft work is often full time. (3) The scale of social organization is different: while in the east generally the political units are small and amorphous, in the west large loosely connected chiefdoms (i.e. kingdoms) have existed for centuries, with the population concentrated in the capitals. The towns have long been very large with the urban population a high proportion of the whole. (4) The internal trade in the west in native products is much higher per head of the population, both between town and country and between the regions. (5) In the west there is one permanent crop, cocoa, the main cash crop. The trees do not yield for several years, and then they yield for one to thirty years. Hence large sums are invested for labour.

[2] Lewis (1966), 17.

they had formed a powerful feudal state, consisting of semi-autonomous chiefdoms grouped round a central kingship, which expanded by wars of conquest against other Akan peoples and was long able to fight wars of resistance against the British. We take the Ashanti confederacy and, nearer to the coast, the small kingdom of Akim Abuakwa[1] as examples here of our peoples of the Late Codes.

In East Africa there is a small number of peoples of the Late Codes. In the south are the Tswana of Bechuanaland (since known as Botswana), a group of Sotho peoples each forming a separate political unit, of which the largest and best known is the Gwato. Further north is the empire of Ethiopia, formed over two thousand years ago by colonization from the Sabaean civilization of Southern Arabia, and long remaining isolated on its lofty plateau,[2] little affected in its culture by the peoples who have poured past along the lands below.[3] The Gallas of Southern Ethiopia lag a little way behind.

We describe all these African peoples in the condition in which they stood in the 1920s except where some other period is specified.[4]

In Central and South America, too, in terrains similar to that of Ethiopia, we find notable civilizations of the Late Codes. Here, before the Spanish conquests of the early sixteenth century, empires extended, at the time of their greatest development, over a large part of a region covering North America south of the middle of modern Mexico and reaching through South America along the lofty plateaux of the Andes, and across the area between them and the Pacific coast, as far south as the River Maule in Chile – in total, that is to say, from about latitude 18° north to 35° south. In this area were two main homes and centres of civilization both situated upon the cordillera of the Andes, which in North America spreads out as a great tableland covering inland Mexico, Guatemala and Yucatan. One of these centres was in the

---

[1] See Danquah (1928).
[2] Much of it well watered and over 7,500 feet high, in latitude stretching from 4° to 15° north.
[3] For the law and government of Ethiopia, see Perham (1969) and bibliography; C. Conti Rossini, *Principi di diritto consuetudinario dell'Eritrea* (Rome, 1916); Walker (1933).
[4] The Ashanti are described as at 1894.

valley of Mexico, which includes five lakes within its area and is situated at a height of some 7,500 feet. Here at the time of the conquest the dominant people were the Aztecs of Tenochtitlan (now Mexico City), immigrant hunters from the north into a civilization centuries older. In South America the home and centre of the highest civilization was in the Central Andes, around the valley of Cuzco and Lake Titicaca and the river-basins of that region, all at an average height of some 11,500 feet and a latitude of some 15° south. In the four centuries preceding the arrival of the Spaniard, the people of the Incas had built by conquest over numerous small Indian states an empire extending from the Andes to the Pacific coast and reaching from southern Colombia to the River Maule. Peru and Mexico were able to support themselves by the divers products of the hot, temperate and cold regions of the plains, the slopes and the highlands, and lived in the main by an intensive agriculture.

Of all these peoples of the present and past the least developed economies are those of West Africa and the English of the early twelfth century. The Tswana, Peruvians and Mexicans continue the advance with the Hebrews, the Romans of the Twelve Tables and Eshnunna; and the most forward are the Assyrians of the Middle Period, the Babylonians of Hammurabi, Ethiopia, traditional China, India of the Code of Manu and the English of the middle thirteenth century.

We said of the Late Codes of the past[1] that this is the age of the blossoming of civilization, that it gives birth to all or most of the great faiths of man, that the arts now burst into a brilliant maturity, and the great legal systems are born. This is not to say that all such peoples give birth to a great faith or mature arts or a great legal system. In comparing the cultures of Africa and other lands we must remember among other things: that these African states (omitting the Semitic, Christian empire of Ethiopia) are only of the first half of the Late Codes; that land and climate are on the whole unfavourable; that the technology of Africa is backward in all respects, especially as compared with Western Europe; that the Bantu is a cheerful, extrovert person and not essentially religious to whom the modern world has given Christianity

---

[1] *Ante*, p. 83.

and Islam and thereby deprived him of the chance of giving to
man an original faith; also that we must not attempt to compare
the merits of the art or religion of one people and those of
another. With these qualifications all these peoples, within the
field of this book, are wholly comparable.

The vast majority of these peoples (including a substantial
portion of the dwellers in the towns) live by agriculture and
cattle-keeping with subsidiary hunting and fishing.[1] There have
been and still are among them a number of mainly pastoral communities, such as Fulani in various parts of Northern Nigeria,
some of the Galla in Southern Ethiopia and Semites in the Near
East. On the other hand the peoples of the forest lands of the
Guinea coast, including almost the whole of Southern Nigeria
and Ashanti, cannot rear cattle because of the prevalence of
tsetse.[2] Also there were no cattle in America. However, these are
extreme examples, and sheep or goats are found almost everywhere in Africa, and poultry everywhere.

Both in Northern and Southern Nigeria[3] in 1921 approximately
76 per cent of the occupied adult males were farmers[4] and this
proportion is roughly characteristic of all the less developed of
these economies. The products of agriculture are now many and

[1] For the economies of Nigeria, see especially (in addition to the other works
referred to below) Forde (1934), and Forde and Scott (1946).
[2] In Nupe, cattle used to be moved from season to season because of tsetse
but have recently been given up as not worth the trouble: Nadel (1942), 201.
The Fulani herdsmen retained their cattle.
[3] In the references to Northern and Southern Nigeria in this and following
chapters it must be remembered that a large number of the peoples, especially
in Eastern Nigeria, are of the Central Codes, though subsequently they
advanced rapidly.
[4] Northern Nigeria: Meek (1925), II, 214; Southern Nigeria: Talbot (1926),
IV, 162. For more recent figures see Forde and Scott (1946) and, for Yorubaland: Lloyd (1962). Hunting is the occupation of an insignificant number:
Meek, *ibid*. In Northern Nigeria the total area of cultivated land is about 7·7
per cent. The average acreage per cultivator is 3·5 here and in Bechuanaland:
Schapera (1938), 201. Even in Northern Nigeria the livestock is scanty (2¼
million cattle, 1¾ million sheep, 4¼ million goats; total human population
9,998,314; percentage of pastoralists, 1). For Nupe, see Nagel (1942), 204.
In Ethiopia, against an unknown population of 5 to 10 million inhabitants
there are 7 million head of cattle, 18 million sheep and goats and 1,600,000
horses: see *Guida dell'Africa Orientale Italiana* (Milan, 1938), 96. In India (1911)
the percentage of persons actively engaged in farming is still 65, and in
China about the same time probably 70 per cent.

varied,[1] but less in England where root crops are not grown. In Africa and America the heavier work of clearing the land is done by the men; hoeing and planting is in some places the province of the women, in others of the men.[2] The digging-stick is still the main implement of agriculture in America,[3] the hoe in Africa,[4] except Ethiopia[5] and Botswana where the plough has recently been introduced, and ploughing is man's work everywhere. Yet a heavy ox-drawn plough was in use in Babylonia and Egypt in the third millennium B.C. and in India in 1000 B.C., and a light hand-plough was in use in China in 500 B.C.[6] The farm wagon (equally old in the ancient world) has been recently introduced into Ethiopia and Bechuanaland (Botswana); until then the wheel was unknown in Africa south of the latitude of Egypt and it was unknown in America. Irrigation canals, terrace cultivation, the use of manures[7] and rotation of crops[8] are generally familiar, but in England the absence of root-cultivation restricts the scope of rotation to an alternate cropping and fallow.[9]

The specialization of occupations shows great advance and the list of distinct callings in West Africa and Ethiopia (as well as the past peoples of the Late Codes) is very large.[10] There is a considerable rise in the number of craftsmen and artisans, now some 5 per cent of the working population. The crafts (including the priesthood) are generally hereditary,[11] but early in our period

---

[1] For a list in Nupe: Nadel (1942), 208f. Northern Nigeria: Meek (1925), I, 119-33; Southern Nigeria: Talbot (1926), III, 119f. There are few fruit trees as yet in England, Nupe (Nadel, *ibid.*) and elsewhere except Southern Nigeria and Ghana.
[2] e.g. in Nupe and much of Northern Nigeria.
[3] Vaillant (1944), Plate 38. The Peruvians also wielded a heavy hoe which may be termed a foot-plough.   [4] Nupe: Nadel (1942), 207.
[5] Where it is an ox-drawn plough pointed with iron.
[6] Sheh Ching (trans. Couvreur, Ho Kien Fou, 1896), 439.
[7] Especially in Peru, with its rich supplies of guano. Nupe: Nadel (1942), 207.
[8] Elaborate in Nupe: Nadel (1942), 208f., but no rotation of crops in Southern Nigeria (1-2 years cultivation and 5-10 years fallow) where land was plentiful.
[9] Beginning to change during the period from a two-course to a three-course rotation. (Two-thirds cropped and one-third fallow.)
[10] For a list of occupations in Northern Nigeria, see Meek (1925), II, 224f.; Southern Nigeria: Talbot (1926), IV, 162f.; Nupe: Nadel (1942), *passim.* In Mexico we are told the households were mainly self-sufficient: Vaillant (1944), 131, but see the list of crafts on pp. 122f.
[11] Nupe: Nadel (1942), 47. Peru: Prescott (Peru), 33. Ethiopia: Perham (1969), 110.

apprenticeship (where a child lives with the master for a number
of years) makes its appearance in twelfth-century England[1] and
elsewhere.[2] Traders are more difficult to number: they are said
to account for 3·6 per cent of the occupied population in Northern
and 8·6 per cent in Southern Nigeria, but everywhere in West
Africa the women are active in petty trading in the markets.[3]
Pottery, now often of great beauty in America and China, is still
their province in most places,[4] and they have a virtual monopoly
of spinning[5] and are very active in weaving.[6] They have also in
effect a monopoly of brewing.

There is a great extension in the number and size of markets,[7]
and almost everywhere the kings and the towns receive tolls on
the value of goods sold, or rent for stalls, or taxes on the value of
goods imported or exported. In the larger markets, sections are
set apart for the sale of specific commodities[8] including surplus
crops of all kinds. There are almost everywhere market courts
to deal with disputes that arise or crimes that are committed
there.[9] Foreign trade through river ports is now considerable in

[1] Clapham (1949), 133; P. & M. I. 672.
[2] Nupe: Nadel (1942), 257, 266. Apprenticeship is common in India and
China throughout our period.
[3] Talbot (1926), III, 904; Nadel (1942), 332, and see pp. 319f. for Nupe
markets generally. Peru: Moore (1958), 86.
[4] Northern Nigeria: Meek (1925), II, 224 (13,214 women and 3,443 men
engaged in pottery). Nupe: Nadel (1942), 295f. South Nigeria: Talbot (1926),
III, 933f.
[5] Peru: Rowe, 241.
[6] Nupe: Nadel (1942), 279 (the work of men). Northern Nigeria generally:
Meek (1925), II, 224 (36 per cent of the weavers were women).
[7] With the developed market comes the 'week' in West Africa, Mexico and
elsewhere. Markets must be held at well-known periods. In North and South
Nigeria it may be a four-day week or a five- or seven- or eight-day week: it bears
usually some relation to the easily recognized period of a month and usually
some reference to the market. In most places in Southern Nigeria the days of
the week are named by reference to the market – 'the day before market',
'market day', 'the day after market' and so forth. The week commonly has a
day of rest and festivity: usually this is one of the other days of the week, but
sometimes it is market-day and some English charters provide for markets
on Sundays. The stage is set for the spiritual conceptions surrounding the
Hebrew Rest-day. The Aztec markets were usually held on the last day of the
five-day week.
[8] In Nupe, as in London, every important commodity has its proper place:
Nadel (1942), 42. Mexico: Joyce (1914), 129. It is doubtful what markets
there were in Peru, and trade was little and local: Moore (1958), 86f.
[9] e.g. Nupe, Mexico, Ethiopia, England, India and China.

Babylon and Nupe, as also is investment in such and similar enterprises and expeditions,[1] and Hebrew and Ashanti kings carry on their own foreign commercial undertakings.[2] England continues her coinage, the silver penny, and a coinage appears early in China, India, and Ethiopia in our period, but among the Babylonians, Assyrians and Hebrews silver passes by weight, and copper in Egypt and Rome. Elsewhere a variety of suitable imperishables of known size serve the purpose,[3] especially cowrie-shells in West Africa. There is a beginning of banking; in Babylon, Assyria and Judah it is the deposit of silver,[4] in Ethiopia of money,[5] but everywhere currency is only in regular use in the towns.[6] There are doctors everywhere, in many places barber-doctors and barber-surgeons.[7]

In a town of any size each trade and profession tends to be carried on in a particular street or quarter.[8] The development of trade and crafts brings with it gilds of merchants and then gilds of craftsmen and they become more and more common during this stage.[9] Some of the early gilds, as in Bida[10] and in the early Buddhist literature of India,[11] partake to some extent of the nature of other feudal institutions, for the head of a gild is entitled to respect and dues from the members. In India from the fourth century B.C., in China at a similar period and in many places elsewhere they make regulations for the conduct of their members and hold courts for the trial of wrongs they have committed[12] and even enrol defence levies from among them.[13] It is by

---

[1] Nupe: Nadel (1942), 311. Also C.H. 100-6.
[2] Hebrews: De Vaux (1961), 78. Ashanti: Rattray (1929), 109.
[3] In Mexico and Peru there is no metal currency except gold dust; there is no skill in smelting: Vaillant (1944), 131f. In West Africa generally as in early Rome, copper rods are in use, and formerly cowrie-shells, beads and other valuables. For Southern Nigeria: Talbot (1926), III, 187f.
[4] See *ante* p. 86 and C.H. 122-6.   [5] Perham (1969), 215.
[6] See *ante* p. 86.   [7] e.g. Nupe: Nadel (1942), 298-301.
[8] e.g. Nupe: Nadel (1942), 41; and Babylonia.
[9] Mexico: Joyce (1914), 126f., Vaillant (1944), 122.
[10] Nadel (1942), *passim*.   [11] C.H.I, 206-7.
[12] Similarly in Mexico the gild of travelling merchants held its own court for criminal and civil matters: Prescott (Mexico), 71.
[13] Western Europe and India (Maurya Empire, fourth century B.C., Arth. 341, 346; Manu viii, 41). For the gilds of China, see H. B. Morse, *The Gilds of China* (2nd edn, 1932); and *Journal of the North China Branch*, Royal Asiatic Society, vols xii and xxi.

the combined effect of the gild mentality, a growing specialization in industry, a closer religious attachment and organization and a static economy that the caste system is now created in India. In England we hear much of gilds from the beginning of this era, not only in London but even in the smaller towns. They are treated with some of the suspicion that trade unions arouse in later days, and again and again we are told of craftsmen who are fined by the town for forming an association without charter or permission. Whether they pay the fine is not so clear.

The arts burst into sudden blossom, especially the building of royal or sacred edifices, not only in Egypt, Babylonia, Assyria and India but also in Mexico and Peru. Yorubaland has at times during the last thousand years produced works of art of the highest excellence.[1] Bida (Nupe) raised great buildings at its foundation in 1860, and the peoples of West Africa have exercised a large influence over the music of the modern world. The Mexicans, Maya, Babylonians and Chinese make great advances in astronomy.

Such advances enable the land to maintain an increasing population. The English kingdom doubles its numbers during the period to some $3\frac{1}{2}$ to 4 million inhabitants. The population of the Nupe is given in the 1931 census as 326,017. In dry and thirsty Bechuanaland according to the census of 1936, the numbers of the largest kingdom, the Ngwato, including its subsidiary peoples, are a little over 100,000, but the smallest is little more than 1,500.[2] The population of the Ethiopian Empire about the same time may be conjectured to be some 6 million.[3] The subjects of the Inca numbered 7 million or more at the conquest; and the population of the Chinese Empire in A.D. 156 is said to have reached 50 million.

The density of population continues to increase accordingly. Over the whole extent of West Africa and the highlands of Ethiopia the density exceeds that of any other large area of Africa south of the latitude of Egypt.[4] The density of the Central Andes exceeded that of any part of the rest of South America.[5] In

---

[1] For example, the famous terra-cotta and bronze heads from Ife of the twelfth to fourteenth centuries A.D. reproduced in *Man* (1949), XLIX, 1 and 61.
[2] 1936 census: and see Schapera (1938), 1-5.
[3] Perham (1969), 264-6.   [4] Fitzgerald, *Africa* (7th edn), 108.
[5] Steward, *H.S.A.* V, 663, 676.

Northern Nigeria the density is about forty persons per square mile. In Southern Nigeria it is much higher[1] and it was much higher in parts of ancient Egypt, Mesopotamia, China and India. Again, at the other extreme, the density of the Bechuanaland reserves is less than 2·2 persons per square mile.

The towns have much increased in number and size. Northern Nigeria, with 10 million inhabitants in 1921, contains five towns with populations between 20,000 and 50,000 each, forty-four towns with populations over 5,000 each and 1,087 with over 1,000 each. Southern Nigeria with a population of 8,371,459 has one town (Ibadan) with 238,094 inhabitants including its farming suburbs and twenty-three towns of over 20,000 each.[2] The town of Bida, capital of Nupe, has a population of 29,848 (having been perhaps twice as large in 1900) and more than one-quarter earn their living on the land. The presence of pastoralism, as we have seen, breaks up the population into small units, and whereas in Northern Nigeria the inhabitants of the towns are only 0·2 per cent of the total and of the urban areas 5·2 per cent,[3] in Southern Nigeria, where there are practically no cattle and no breeding of horses, 69 per cent of the population live in the towns, although 75 per cent of the population live by farming.[4] Tenochtitlan (Mexico City) holds 300,000 persons,[5] and Cuzco (the Inca capital) including its suburbs was estimated by the Spaniards at 200,000. Jerusalem and London contain about 20,000 persons. In Peru the average village probably holds about 300 persons[6] and in modern India and China the average village contains about the same number. In many lands the larger villages are divided into wards.[7]

---

[1] Nupe: Nadel (1942), 11. The density of Southern Nigeria in 1921 was 91 per square mile: over all Nigeria in 1921, 54 per square mile. Gold Coast Colony (1931 Census), 66 per square mile. On the plateau of Ethiopia the density was over 20, as it was in the Central Andes.
[2] The West of Southern Nigeria in 1931 had at least nine towns with populations over 50,000.
[3] Meek (1925), 173f.
[4] But in the Bechuanaland Reserves the villages or towns are few and large, and during the agricultural season, from November to June, the bulk of the population scatters in small family settlements alongside its fields, and moreover the cattle, instead of being kept at hand, as in most South Bantu peoples, are maintained in the veld, often 20-40 miles away: Shapera (1938), 11.
[5] Vaillant (1944), 127, 137.
[6] Rowe, 228.   [7] e.g. Mexico, Nigeria.

The huts of the inhabitants are usually made of wattle and daub and thatched, but there are some better houses of stone.[1]

The populations held together in these growing states continue to be less homogeneous in ethnic character. Many or most of them are appropriately termed 'empires' for they include in their boundaries semi-independent states of different racial or ethnic groups. There have been several such in Nigeria in recent centuries containing Hamitic and Negro stocks.[2] Abyssinia – a name that by one derivation means 'mixed population' – combines Semitic, Hamite and Negro populations. Bilalama, Lipit Ishtar and Hammurabi legislate for Semites and Sumerians. Even the Hebrews rule over semi-independent Philistine cities and Hittite and other ethnic groups. The Emperor of Ethiopia is the Negus Negusti, the King of Kings, and such also is the ruler in Babylonia and Assyria.

This development has been brought about partly by continued change in the character and purposes of warfare. Its scale is larger and it is carried on with better organization and greater art. Warfare in Nupe has its rules of etiquette and convention.[3] The objects of war are envisaged from the commencement and are commonly the gain of territory for economic ends. It was mainly to increase his receipts of tribute, to extend his private possessions and to gain land on which to settle his soldiers and followers that Menelik II, Emperor of Ethiopia, conducted the conquest of the Galla in the south of the country during the two decades beginning in 1875. But wars are also undertaken for the sake of religion. The followers of Muhammad wage it to spread the true faith of Allah; the West European to free the Holy Land from the infidel; the Inca to extend the worship of the Sun, the god of his house; the Aztec to maintain the supply of human captives for sacrifice. In religion we note the progress of customs and institutions of which we saw the rise at the close of the Central Codes. We can watch the steady increase of human sacrifice in Mexico[4] and Peru and among the Maya,[5] and the growth in all these countries, as well as

---

[1] e.g. Mexico: Vaillant (1944), 136.
[2] Nupe: Nadel (1942), 69f. For Nigeria generally see Burns (1947); and A. W. Bovill, *Caravans of the Old Sahara* (1933). Northern Nigeria: Meek (1925), I, 98f.   [3] Nadel (1942), 110.
[4] Prescott (Mexico), 38f.   [5] Joyce (1914), 261f.

Sumer, Egypt, China and India, of the slaying of wives and slaves to accompany their royal or noble master in the hereafter.[1] The embalming and preservation of the bodies of the dead is widespread in America and West Africa as well as Egypt.

All the peoples whom we have taken as our examples are feudal societies.[2] The power of emperor, king or paramount chief continues to grow; the land of the state is considered to belong to him and he controls and administers it through feudal lords, heads of districts, villages and wards and in theory it is held at his will and pleasure. According to the strength of central authority, the personality of the king, or the difficulty of communications, the ruler below him may be a semi-independent prince or, as in Peru, hardly more than an administrator ruling at the will of his absolute master, or something between these extremes. In either case he is a great landlord while he holds his office.[3] The duties of the holding are often imposed on the land, whoever holds it. Often land is held on terms of military service;[4] sometimes it is inalienable,[5] and sometimes it is tenable by women on condition that they find an able-bodied man to perform the service.[6] There is often land held by other public officials on terms of service to the throne or stool, for example the Babylonian and Ethiopian tribute-gatherers.[7] Sometimes the king grants to the knight[8] or official land held by a number of free peasant cultivators, so that he may be supported and enabled to perform his public duties by means of the fixed proportion of produce and the labour services

---

[1] In China till the seventeenth century A.D. Sutteeism is now at an end in China and India, but in many country districts of China it is still scandalous (though legal) for a widow to remarry.
[2] See *ante* Chap. 23. For feudalism in Peru, see Moore (1958), 14f. There may well be other peoples whom we should allot to the Late Codes, but which are not feudal societies, but I do not know of any. Feudalism has gone in modern Nupe.
[3] Prescott (Peru), 22-3; Prescott (Mexico), 12f.
[4] e.g. C.H. 26-39, Nupe, Ethiopia, Egypt (till the New Kingdom, at least).
[5] C.H. 36f.
[6] e.g. Ethiopia: Perham (1969), 161. Nupe: Nadel (1942), 117, 181. Nupe women can hold fiefs, and Islamic law encourages it, but few do. In Babylon the priestess (*naditum*) can hold a fief, and is excused personal service; her feudal duties may be performed by a son or other male: Driver & Miles (1952), I, 365 and (n).
[7] Ethiopian *gultenya*; C.H. 36-9.
[8] Ethiopian *farasenya*.

N

which the latter are bound to give him, as well as by the demesne in his possession.[1] Individual churches, monasteries and temples hold land by gift of the king free of duties or in frankalmoign and thereby also become lords of the peasant cultivator. The latter (now a member of an increasingly depressed class in England and elsewhere) bears the brunt of the maintenance of the state and its public services and growing body of officials, and commonly pays to the king a fixed proportion of the produce (in Ethiopia[2] and in the emirates of Northern Nigeria a tithe)[3] as well as labour dues.[4] And there are feudal aids or levies for special purposes, and reliefs.[5] Except in the king's demesne they are paid as a rule to intermediate chiefs or royal officers. So that below royalty there tend to be two classes of freeman in the state, the lords and commoners, a division perpetuated in the English Parliament. In several states it is a distinction between, on the one hand, the long-established families of the ruling ethnic group, men of means, landowners, and cattle-keepers, and, on the other hand, subject or conquered peoples or immigrant stocks, clients, cultivators, tradesmen and artisans.[6] Below are the unfree, serfs or slaves, the latter (except for enslaved criminals or men who sold themselves to obtain food) being foreigners acquired by capture or purchase. In the 1920s there are slaves on a large scale only in Ethiopia. Slavery is often light,[7] and in many countries, as in Egypt and England, slaves are few. These classes are not always hereditary (especially in Mexico) and now successful traders

---

[1] e.g. Ethiopia. In Babylon, Rome and Mexico, soldiers received grants of conquered land on terms of military service: Vaillant (1944), 130.
[2] For the revenue of Ethiopia: Perham (1969), Chap. XI; Ashanti: Rattray (1929), Chap. XIV.
[3] Nupe: Nadel (1942), 59 – the Arabic-Hausa *dzanká*. In China the land tax is the main source of revenue till our day.
[4] In Peru the tribute is mainly in the form of labour: Prescott (Peru), 36; Moore (1958), Chap. II.
[5] Schapera (1938), 64f.
[6] In Botswana, among the Kgatla, the *bakgosing* and *badintlha*: Schapera (1938), 31; in Judah and Israel the 'princes' or *śarim*, and the rest; in Peru the *incas* and *curacas* and the rest; in Rome patricians and plebeians; in Babylon and Eshnunna the *awilum* and *muškenum*; in Mexico the plebeians are the *macehual*, freemen holding as members of a *calpulli* or tenants at a rent: Joyce (1914), 117; Prescott (Mexico), 14; Nupe: Nadel (1942), 127.
[7] In Mexico, slaves might own slaves, and their children are born free: Vaillant (1944), 124; but most slaves are for sacrifice.

become landowners and begin to gain entry into the ranks of nobility.

In all these peoples the king administers and allots the land through his lords or officers. Any man who (for example, on marriage) finds himself in need of land applies to the head of the family, but if there is no spare room he must go to his chief[1] for an allotment, and so must a foreigner who wishes to settle there, or a man who has changed his chief for another, or in less advanced communities, such as the Tswana,[2] where a whole village seeks to move to a new site. The local chief, subject if necessary to royal authority, will grant it.[3]

But feudalism is not concerned merely with rights to land but also personal relationships – the European vassalage or homage. We saw a system of *okutoizha* (clientship, homage, dependency or allegiance) between king and patrician subject already in force in Ankole. We see the same system in Nupe, Peru, Mexico, Ashanti and other lands in the earlier stages of the Late Codes. A commoner of Nupe, desiring land or more land, could give himself into the service or 'patronage' of a land-owning overlord and thus secure land as well as political protection by an initial gift in kind, occasional presents, expressions of homage and a tithe from his crop.[4] The oath of allegiance by feudal lord to sovereign is institutional everywhere.[5]

There is infinite variation of this general picture. It is not to be assumed that all subjects hold land on a feudal tenure. As the superfluity of land diminishes, for example in parts of West Africa and Western Europe, there is a growing number who do not hold land, and there are employees. There are also dependencies whose allegiance to the king or emperor is somewhat tenuous. In Europe it is doubtful if there was ever a situation where all the land of a kingdom was held on feudal tenures. In

---

[1] In Mexico and Peru he applies through his local kinship group; in Mexico, the *calpulli*: Joyce (1914), 116f.; in Peru, the *ayllu*, a local group of a more or less endogamous nature: Rowe, 253f.; Pozo, 483.
[2] Schapera (1938), 197.
[3] e.g. in Nupe, Mexico, Peru, Israel and Judah, modern Eritrea and Bechuanaland. Eritrea: Nadel, 'Land Tenure on the Eritrean Plateau', *Africa*, XVI (1946), 21-2, 99-109.
[4] Nadel (1942), 59, 195f., 122f. and *passim*.
[5] See the Ashanti ceremony described: Rattray (1929), 102f.

Africa we cannot expect to see a feudal system in full force among a people that has lost its independence to a European power. Land tenure, military defence, government, the collection of revenue and administration of justice are all facets of the same economic system. If the chief is subjected to a foreign governor and a foreign system of law, and is deprived of the collection of revenue, including tribute and court fines, his authority is necessarily diminished and the system fades. Yet among the great empires and the small states of recent times, and in the independent nations of the past of whom we have knowledge, we can see it at work in varying degree. It is these circumstances in West Africa that gave origin and scope to the system of indirect rule, for feudalism is itself a system of indirect rule.

But feudalism is part of an economic system in which payments are in kind and not in money, and the advance in trade, in markets and in wealth is sounding its death-knell. There is an increasing quantity and use of money, and it is already in general use in the towns. In England we saw that from the middle of the twelfth century,[1] tenants holding on knight's service were increasingly availing themselves of the opportunity to pay scutage in place of military service, as the villeins were giving tallage instead of labour, and thus the king obtained the means to provide himself with a mercenary, professional and mobile army. There are already in early Egypt,[2] Nupe[3] and Ethiopia[4] small but growing professional forces of the nature of bodyguards, but for the time being in Ethiopia the king's forces consist for the most part of men holding on knight's service and the general able-bodied male population that can be called out to war but not to training. The knight proceeds to his rendezvous followed commonly by one or two baggage-animals laden with food, two or three tenants who owe him labour services and slaves carrying equipment. So far as possible they live on the native peasants so as to conserve their supplies, but woe upon the scattered and defeated forces if they attempt to repeat this on their way home from the battle

---

[1] Beginning with the campaign of Henry II against Toulouse.
[2] Under the New Kingdom, i.e. from about 1600 B.C., mercenaries become predominant in the army.
[3] Nadel (1942), 108f.
[4] e.g. Perham (1969), Chap. IX.

through the peasant's fields. Little by little, rents and taxes will take the place of tribute, small professional armies will supersede the enormous feudal levies that leave their holdings and devastate the native fields, the growing power of the central authority will exercise one system of administration and apply one system of law throughout the land, and feudalism will end.

CHAPTER 26

The Recent Peoples of the Late Codes – Kinship, Marriage, Property and Inheritance

Hitherto we have seen various kinship groups (to which we have not had space to devote much attention) appearing after the grade of the Food Gatherers and growing in strength and influence and, apart from their other functions and effect, shaping in large measure the law of marriage, property and inheritance and serving as an organ of government and administration. We now see changes in them, tending in the same general direction among the various peoples of the Late Codes. In particular the clan system, though in the less developed economies (for example, of the Ashanti) it remains a significant and unifying force in the political organization, diminishes in power, especially in the towns.

These kinship groups include the nuclear or biological family, the household or extended family, the lineage and the clan. The lineage and clan have usually been unilateral, that is to say that descent has been traced through females or through males, according to local ideas and practices, though it was usual to find that in a patrilineal society the maternal relationship was not ignored, nor the paternal in a matrilineal system. There was a tendency for the matrilineal principle to be somewhat more common in purely agricultural economies and the patrilineal more prevalent in pastoral and in hunting peoples. We also saw that this application of the patrilineal or matrilineal principle was closely associated not only with patrilineal and matrilineal inheritance but also virilocal and uxorilocal residence – that is, the practice of the young couple on marriage to take up residence with his relatives or hers (difficult as it is to classify communities in this respect), and also the prohibition of marriage between persons bearing that relationship (or, more recently, within certain limits of propinquity in that relationship).

So, in our peoples of the forested regions of West Africa, where cattle can hardly be kept (as, for example, in Ashanti and other Akan peoples) the matrilineal principle is dominant, whereas in states which have been created through the conquest of agricultural peoples by pastoralists (as in Northern and Western Nigeria) or by hunters (as in North America) we see clearly the paternal principle gaining upon the maternal. And now in these enlarged populous kingdoms and empires descent becomes to a large extent bilateral (as apparently in Mexico) or ambilateral (where the two principles are found in the same people and both function for different purposes). The state is never a kinship group, and towns loom large, and in them there is less space than in a village to take up residence with a particular family group. With better communications and greater mobility of the populace the clans (the large kinship groups) become scattered, and marriage takes place between more distant partners and the clan is in process of breaking up. But it is an unconscionable time dying, and as the bulk or all of our Late Code peoples of the past have pastoralist origins, it is not surprising that here too, except where (as in Western Europe) the descent group is bilateral, the clan is patrilineal.[1]

In most of these peoples the basic social and kinship unit is the household, consisting of a man and his wife or wives and their unmarried children, often married sons, and sometimes an unmarried or widowed sister of his and even a married daughter, and their children and the slaves or pawns, and an employee or apprentice – all totalling between two and thirty persons,[2] and housed in a compound or group of huts, often walled. This is the Roman *familia*, the Chinese *hu*, Hebrew *beth 'ab* and the English *mainpast* of the thirteenth century. The larger social and kinship

---

[1] e.g. Hebrews (the *mišpaḥah*), Romans (the *gens*) and probably everywhere in Mesopotamia, though it is not clear that the clan survived here, and in the north the A.C. contains evidence of some uxorilocal marriage.

[2] For an analysis of some Tswana households, see Schapera, *The Social Structure of the Tswana Ward*, Bantu Studies IX (1935), 208-18. There the household averaged about six persons.

unit of importance is the lineage, a body of persons descended from the same known patrilineal ancestor, commonly three or four generations before the living adults. More remote ancestors are in fact rarely remembered. But the basic economic and political unit is the town or village and its wards or sections, a group of villages often bearing a permanent relation to a town, which is administered under the town chief or reeve and his council, the heads of local households.[1] In many peoples the capital village or town is the centre of the state.[2] There are also other territorial units, the counties or districts, whose government remains feudal while the towns are gaining a measure of self-government and semi-independence.[3] And there remains here and there in the villages a link between the territorial and kinship bases of administration, in that the bulk of a lineage may be settled in a particular ward of a town or village.

The bridewealth marriage survives but is waning as in the Late Codes of the past.[4] It is normal everywhere in Africa, Mexico and Peru,[5] but the bridewealth is diminishing in value and it is often left to the young man's people to decide what to pay, and it is not always paid. In some areas of Ethiopia[6] and elsewhere[7] it is even considered shameful to accept it. Sometimes (as under Islamic law)[8] it is paid to the wife, not her people. And gifts from the other side increase in amount and a dowry or marriage portion begins to be paid, which is often of the same amount

---

[1] e.g. Nupe: see Nadel (1942), 40, 56, for the functions of the village chief. Tswana, Ashanti.
[2] As among the Tswana and in Nupe and the city-states of Babylonia.
[3] As in England.
[4] See *ante* p. 88.
[5] e.g. Northern Nigeria: Meek (1921), I, 201-3. Southern Nigeria: Talbot (1926), III, 633. Nupe: Nadel (1942). Ashanti: Rattray (1923), 22f. Tswana: Schapera (1938), 138-47. Mexico, Peru, Hebrews (Ex. 22$^{16-17}$), Romans, Babylonia, China, India and Western Europe.
[6] Walker (1933), 25-6.
[7] Nupe: Nadel (1942), 351; Meek (1925), I, 202. India (see *ante* p. 88).
[8] e.g. Northern Nigeria generally. Under Islamic law it becomes a settlement on her and is her property, and where the amount is unspecified the law fixes a minimum. After her husband's death she has a lien on his estate in her hands to secure payment of it to her. In Ethiopia it becomes common property of husband and wife. In Babylonia (see C.H. 164) the dowry is usually larger than the bridewealth, and it is inherited by the children on her death.

as the bridewealth, and often it is the bridewealth, paid by
the father to the young couple,[1] and sometimes with an
addition.[2]

There is a vast variety in the rules defining the classes of kin
with whom marriage is prohibited, and there is no space here to
do more than indicate two tendencies. One, in accordance with
changes mentioned above, is a tendency to prohibit marriage with
near cognatic relatives, rather than members of a unilateral clan.[3]
The second is a slight tendency towards monogamy[4] and the
third (a complementary tendency) is the existence of concubinage,
secondary or looser marriages.[5] These are types of associations
whose nature and purposes or effects vary widely. In West Africa
generally no bridewealth is paid but only gifts and maintenance;
the woman continues to live in her father's house, and the
children (because no bridewealth has been paid) are considered
to belong to her or her family. There are no obligations on either
side after the relationship ceases. The Late Codes of the quasi-
monogamous peoples of the past are concerned to regularize
these unions. In Babylonia and among the Hebrews and elsewhere
in the ancient Near East the purpose of concubinage was to
enable a man whose wife was childless to take another woman (a
freewoman or a pawn) for the purpose of begetting children
without thereby impairing the status of the true wife and without
binding himself toward the second woman by all the duties of a
husband if she should also be childless.[6] But the law was also
concerned to provide for the children's rights of inheritance and
to fix the ownership of the property of the parties to these loose
unions. In the peoples of our previous chapters we have rarely

---

[1] See e.g. Meek (1921), I, 96f.; Nadel (1942), 351. This is common in
twentieth-century China in many country districts. In Botswana the results
are strange; among the Ngwato, Khama forbade the payment of bogadi
(bridewealth). Among the Kgatla, however, a man is not considered properly
married unless it is paid, and accordingly no church will marry him: Schapera
(1938), 146-7.
[2] Walker (1933), 25-6.
[3] But not in China.
[4] As among the Chichimec.
[5] Tswana; Islamic law; Nupe and Northern Nigeria generally: Meek (1921),
I, 195f. Southern Nigeria: Talbot (1926), III, 427. Ashanti: Fortes (1950),
281; Rattray (1929), Chap. IV. Mexico: Vaillant (1944), 118.
[6] Hebrews: Ex. 21[2f]. Babylon: C.H. 144f.

N*

seen religious ceremonies of marriage, but now they are sometimes found in the most advanced of our economies.[1]

The wide-ranging economic advance referred to in the previous chapter has created large and divers developments in the law of property. Goods are increasing in number and value; money is in wide use in the towns; trade, credit and debt expand and for the first time there are great developments in the methods of utilization of land, imposing many interconnected problems. Even when the problems seem similar, the solutions are often different. To attempt to understand what is occurring let us look at one or two common and familiar situations with minds free from doctrines and preconceptions derived from mature law. It will serve at the same time to remind us of the road by which we have travelled. Let us first go back to an earlier agricultural grade and without detailing the nature of the economy consider in general terms what, if we were starting afresh, we would propose to provide by law, if such a thing as law exists or can exist there.

A, the father of a family, lives with his wife and children, and they possess certain goods and certain interests in land. We instinctively look for a single owner, individual or corporate, and would like to say who it is. But this attitude is due to our background and training, and would not necessarily fit the facts. A has certain responsibilities towards his family and they towards him and one another. They ought to have rights too. He will demand and be given more say, perhaps, than anyone else on the question what is to be done with the land and the goods, but it does not follow that he should have all the say. They all use and work on the land though their functions are different, and apart from some heavy initial work of clearing it he is likely to do less than anyone else and be often busy hunting or fishing or fighting or sitting on a council or just talking with the other men. Is he to have a right to part with a child's toy or pet or a wife's utensils or the apparel of members of the family without their consent or the goods they have acquired by their labour or trading? More

---

[1] Not Hebrews, but Rome (*confarreatio*) and Christian Europe and Ethiopia. But in England a large part of the population did not marry in church in the thirteenth century, and apart from deacons Ethiopians rarely marry in church, partly because there is no divorce in such a case and no second marriage even after the death of a spouse.

important – is he to have power to part with the land and deprive wife and children of their main source of livelihood? And who is there to transfer it to? He has perhaps two wives and has allotted to each a plot which she and her children can work, and cattle for them to milk, for their support. To whom does this belong, and should he be entitled to part with it without anyone's consent? And what of his other relatives, the brother or nephew who will succeed to his interests, at least in default of children, and to whose relatives he himself succeeded? And what of the neighbours and members of his clan or other large kinship groups? Do they want a stranger foisted upon land in which they are interested? Ought we then to say that A holds the land or goods on trust for a group – his children or family or household or lineage or clan or village? It is difficult to isolate and define the group, or say what the terms of the trust should be. And surely their interests are not the same. At least no one but he or his family should have the right to occupy the land. And if, instead of being farmers, the community were food gatherers, or hunters or pastoralists, the picture would be entirely different: the idea of anyone owning a piece of land would be even stranger.

It dawns on us that we are only beginning to look at the facts, and that they are far too complicated and at the same time far too simple for the application of our legal preconceptions. It is possible that a learned draftsman might effect something with an elaborate scheme of trusts or *fideicommissa* and legal estates, but he would need endless instructions as to what sets of facts he ought to contemplate and provide for, and what provision he ought to make in each case, and the answers he got from the question what ought to happen in such and such an event might often be 'It all depends', with a reference to the interests of other persons of whom he had never heard. In the end he might only be able to list a large number of events and say what ought to happen in each case, and that does not take us any further. He would receive his final blow on being told, perhaps, that there were no courts and no means of enforcing the law he proposed to lay down, except public opinion, which of course, some strong men successfully ignored. At least we can see that goods, being few and of little value, are easier to deal with than land, and that some (but not, by any means, all) are more capable of a simple doctrine that they 'belong' to one particular person; and we can tell the draftsman that peoples acquire legal conceptions from the facts and events of their lives and environment, and not from revelation, and we can see that there is infinite scope for different solutions and conceptions, but little scope for a doctrine of legal ownership.

Let us move on. It is a characteristic of the commencement of the Late Codes that the superfluity of land ends, though not at one moment, and states can be found where there is still surplus land in some areas and not in others.[1] The disappearance of surplus land is one of the most important facts in the development of the law of land. Let us look at one or two familiar situations at the very start of the Late Codes while a surplus exists.

A, with his wife or wives – he usually, of course, has one – and children occupies land and huts in a village, which they use for cultivation, cattle-keeping and residence, with pasture further off. The land is considered to belong to the king, who would call it 'my land', and it is distributed by him or his officers or a council among the towns, descent groups or great local lords. The village is a satellite of a town and the village land is considered to belong to the town chief or local head of a descent group, who would call it 'My land'. A obtained his on marriage by request to his father, or by grant from the town chief or kinship head, and would call it 'My land', and the other villagers would refer to the village land as the kin's, or town chief's or kinship head's according to the context, but would usually call the land occupied by A and his household A's land or the land of A's family.

It is obvious that no one is referring to legal ownership, in the modern sense, in any of these cases. After all, even in England, this word 'ownership' is not found till 1583, though the word 'own' is found with the meaning of 'to take' as early as 888, and with the meaning of 'to hold as one's thing' from 1000. The word 'belong' (which we have often preferred in this book) is found with the meaning of 'to accompany' and 'to relate to' from 1340 (after the close of our period) and with the meaning of 'to be the property of' (in a quite untechnical sense, as indeed it often is today), not before 1393. In these African peoples we can find

---

[1] e.g. Nupe: Nadel (1942), 181; and see Lloyd (1962), 74.

plenty of verbs meaning 'to take', 'to hold', 'to accompany', 'to be master of',[1] but usually nothing more nearly corresponding with 'own'. We might describe A, perhaps, as having 'possession', but (as during a large part of the life of English law) it is a possession where there is no ownership.

Perhaps A received a grant of the land from his chief (the village chief or head of some descent group) to the extent that he needed land for the support of the family, and if his family increases he will get more; or, if another family needs more land he may have to part with some of what he already has. But his interest is now heritable and there is a surplus. Then he will have to give some land to a son on his marriage, if he can spare it. As likely as not he will only cultivate part of it and leave most of it fallow. He might even leave the land and live in the area of another chief, and if so in time it might well be allocated to another family.[2] Again, the rights of his wife or wives to support themselves and their children by working a portion of the land must not be forgotten, and the rights of his relatives and prospective heirs. It might be best to say that the land belongs to the family or other kinship group to which A belongs. It might be best, as in parts of West Africa, to say that A's interest is that of a usufructuary[3] and the term is apt, except that it involves the supposition that someone else is the legal owner. This might be the village, or a kinship group, but they might equally be described as usufructuaries, as indeed kinship groups often are in West Africa. As for any right to alienate the land without permission or consent, this hardly exists as yet in any individual or body, though there is an amount of lending of land for a short period to a local inhabitant or immigrant, with the permission of the chief or kinship head, in return for a present. Again, in these circumstances, we can see endless scope for attributing the rights in the land to different individuals, corporate bodies or rulers, but little scope for modern notions of ownership.

But let us look again at A's family and land in a people of the middle and second half of our Late Codes, where the surplus of

[1] Hebrew *ba'al*; Latin, *dominus*, and also *herus* and *heres* (both from a root meaning 'to hold'). [2] Nupe: Nadel (1942), 186.
[3] The Roman jurist Paul defined usufruct as 'the right to use and take the fruits of another man's property, the substance remaining unimpaired'.

land has gone. All the land is still commonly considered to belong, in a sense, to the king or chief, but the feudal principle is waning and everywhere the holder's interest is heritable. The land in A's possession was mostly inherited by him, together with his brothers, from his father, and after his death they probably farmed and occupied it together as a joint holding, till on the marriage of a son of theirs or some other appropriate occasion they divided it. Primogeniture has mostly gone,[1] though, for example, under Hebrew and Assyrian law the eldest son gets a double share and in Southern Babylonia more than an equal share.[2] If A's father had left no son the land would probably have been divided equally between the daughters – as in the Hebrew case of the daughters of Zelophehad[3] – for as the importance of the clan has diminished, where descent is bilateral the land is less likely to be lost to a kinship group on a daughter's marriage; and in some peoples the land now goes equally to sons and daughters. Another part of the land occupied by A is held on a lease from B at a rent, often for a long or indefinite period, and often (as in Babylonia and recently in parts of Nigeria) on the metayer system, namely that B provides seed and stock and A pays him a proportion, usually a half, of the produce as rent. This is one of the few ways in which A can increase his holding. Some of his land may have been won by him out of the waste, or by cutting down forest and clearing it, but there is less of that now.[4] This last piece would be considered A's in a different sense, free for him to alienate in any way he wished – for example, by selling it: it never belonged to him as his father's heir.

But there are other changes. We saw a great expansion of trade and credit and debt, and A will need from time to time to borrow money for a variety of purposes and if he cannot pay he or his unmarried sister or child will be liable to be taken as a debt-slave or pawn.[5] This has become an unsatisfactory security. For one

[1] In Northern Nigeria largely on the adoption of Islamic law.
[2] Driver & Miles (1935), 296.
[3] Numbers 27[1-8]; but with the qualification that they shall marry within their father's tribe, 36[1-9]. See also I Chron. 23[22]. This was, it seems, traditionally a change in the law.
[4] Improvements made by him might also be thought to be his, see e.g. Lloyd (1962), 81.
[5] In Ethiopia in 1930 creditors could still be seen walking along the streets with their debtors shackled to them.

thing, the law is beginning to fix a period after which the pawn is free,[1] and in any case a man's or child's labour may not be worth his keep, at any rate for long, and in some places in West Africa it is being said that the institution of pawning is as much in the interest of the young pawnee as the creditor: it gives him an opportunity of learning husbandry or a trade.[2] Land is the chief wealth of the people and the best security, and the lender is prepared to advance money without interest on the security of a pledge of land, instead of a pledge of persons or goods. It is inconvenient to the borrower: he parts with the possession of land till repayment, but he needs the money. This transaction, however, depends on a clear right of the occupier to pledge the land.

The problem is worked out differently in different peoples. In recent decades we can see the problem and the progress made in various Yoruba kingdoms and elsewhere, and by degrees the individual holder obtains individual ownership of his land. There are at first qualifications and conditions. Hebrew and Eshnunna law give A's patrilineal relatives in succession the right of pre-emption if he desires to sell, and the right to redeem the land if he pledges it. In some peoples,[3] at first, various consents of interested persons are required. Finally, at the close of our primitive age we find a ready market in land. It is as a result of the same economic development and the end of a superfluity of land that it is common for brothers, on the death of their father, to live together and manage the estate as a whole – for example, among the Hebrews,[4] Romans, Assyrians,[5] Sumerians and Babylonians,[6] Chinese and Hindus.[7]

Within the family other developments contribute to the same

---

[1] For the Mexican restrictions see Prescott (Mexico), 18f., Joyce (1914), 133; for Ashanti, Rattray (1929), 46f. This is because the debtor is not considered to work off the debt, and his labour represents only the interest on it: Nadel (1942), 312 and *passim*; Rattray (1929), 54; Talbot (1926), III, 633.

[2] e.g. Nupe: Nadel (1942), 313.

[3] In England in the thirteenth century. In Eshnunna, L.E. 39 suggests that a man only sells his house when in financial straits.

[4] e.g. Deut. 25[5].

[5] See Driver & Miles (1935), 407.

[6] L.E. 38; C.H. 165, 166, 178.

[7] Manu ix, 104f. Then later, when they decide on partition, they take their share in all these countries.

end at the close of our period. In the first half of the Late Codes there is little further deterioration in the status of the married woman. She retains, for example, the goods she acquires,[1] and indeed in West Africa and some other areas she is commonly the chief trader in the market and sometimes in a better financial position than her husband.[2] But a daughter has still often no right to inherit, nor has a widow such a right, though even a slave inherits in many places in the absence of other heirs,[3] and the members of the household[4] can be given as pawns or debt-slaves for their father's liabilities and even seized by the creditor after his death.[5] And at the close of our period, as we have seen[6] in India,[7] China,[8] England and Rome, and in a restricted degree in Eshnunna and among the Hebrews,[9] Assyrians[10] and Babylonians,[11] in every case of a regular marriage – that is to say, a marriage evidenced by deed, payment of bridewealth, religious ceremony or permanent cohabitation in the husband's house, as the case may be – the husband and father is lord and master of the household and of every person in it. Sons have no property during his life. His wife is under his power, and in Mesopotamia,

[1] e.g. Tswana: Schapera (1938), 151-4, 220; though the husband controls his wife's and son's property, 28, 221. Nigeria: Meek (1925), I, 281; Forde & Scott (1946), 123. Mexico: Vaillant (1944), 118: the wife can enter into contracts and sue in court.
[2] Nupe: Nadel (1942), 332.
[3] e.g. Ashanti: Rattray (1929), 43; inheritance to a female slave, the descendant of the deceased or his ancestor and a female slave. For the Hebrews, see Gen. 15². Among the Romans, too, it seems likely that slaves inherited in default of clansmen.
[4] In many places, not the wife, e.g. Hebrews (but here only the husband could divorce). Contrast C.H. 117.
[5] It is only after the end of our period that the liability of sons to discharge their father's debts is limited to the assets they inherit from him.
[6] See ante p. 88.
[7] 'Three persons,' says Manu, 'a wife, a son and a slave are declared by law to have in general no wealth exclusively their own; the wealth which they may earn is regularly acquired for the man to whom they belong' (viii, 416). See Narada, V, 39 (translated by Jolly, S.B.E., vol. 33, Part I).
[8] Ch'ü (1961), 103f., 20f.
[9] Some wives are bought and he can sell his son or daughter.
[10] A.C. 3, 4, 6, 35.
[11] Under C.H. 151 a woman is liable for her husband's debts, even his ante-nuptial debts, unless protected by a covenant between her and him. But she has a certain contractual capacity and can acquire property of her own and take legal proceedings.

if she goes abroad, goes veiled.[1] Subject to the contents of a
marriage deed in Babylon, everything she brings into the house
is his property, and this was the rule in England from about 1250
to 1870. One of the objects of the law is to make clear what can
be seized in execution upon a debt.[2] Wrongs committed against a
father are punishable with the greatest severity.[3] In China a man
is well entitled to kill his wife who strikes or abuses his parent,
and in all peoples at the close of our period a woman caught
committing adultery may be mutilated by her husband or put to
death as he pleases.[4]

It is the father who takes proceedings for wrongs to members
of the family; they are wrongs to him whether in his own person
or as representing them. In English law this situation survives
till our own day, for a father has a right to sue for any wrong to
any member of his household. It is the complement of this aspect
that, among the most advanced economies of the Late Codes, the
father is liable for the wrongs of the members of the household.
But we must make a distinction between the liability for the wife
and the liability for the sons. By the end of our period, namely
in the Code of Hammurabi,[5] and in England of the thirteenth
century[6] and not before, the husband is liable for all the wrongs
and debts of his wife. But in some places sons leave home almost
as soon as they are old enough to incur such liabilities in trade
or for wrongs, and in regard to sons, there is not, in the less
developed of these economies, any general rule of a father's liability
for his son's debts or wrongs. The rule varies from place to place,
though he usually pays.[7] But at the end of our period, when
corporal sanctions are general for serious wrongs, the rule in

---

[1] A.C. Even in classical Latin to 'marry a man' is 'nubere viro' – 'to put on a
veil for a man'. The Chinese wife is generally married in a veil.
[2] A.C. 35: 'If a widow enters a man's house (i.e. comes to cohabit with him
there) everything she brings becomes her husband's, and if the man enters
the house of the woman everything he brings with him becomes the woman's.'
[3] See *ante* p. 87.
[4] L.E. 28; A.C. 3, 4, 15, 16; C.H. 129.
[5] C.H. 151, 152.
[6] P. & M. II, 132. The rule is not reached among the Hebrews nor in the
XII Tables.
[7] Tswana: Schapera (1938), 50 (father responsible except in regard to an
offence punishable corporally). Gold Coast: Gold Coast Native Courts
Commission, 31f.

Babylonia and thirteenth-century England is that the father must hand over to the injured plaintiff any subordinate member of his household (or mainpast), who has committed a serious offence (or felony), or, if he does not comply, must pay a fine.[1]

We see, therefore, that the emergence of individual ownership of land (though it is found earlier in a few places)[2] tends to be conditioned not only by the termination of the superfluity in land, but also the incorporation of the household, as it were, in the person of the father, its despotic master and the owner of its property, and we also see that at the close of the primitive age the law is assuming a new character. Its rules are becoming based on commercial and national expediency, and do not necessarily comply with moral justice. It is becoming technical – that is to say, divorced in some measure from the situation and the relations that prevail between the members of the household. For the same reasons it begins to live a life of its own based on principles surviving the circumstances that gave it birth.

We have no more space to discuss intestate succession.[3] Succession by will makes great strides in this age. In South and West Africa[4] and among the Hebrews[5] the will is oral and informal: a man at the approach of death may call his family together and announce his wishes regarding his property, departing as a rule only in details from the customary mode of succession or merely supplementing it.[6] Deuteronomy 21[15-17], fulfilling the conservative role of religion, forbids the father to give the double portion of the eldest to another son. But in the more advanced economies of Rome, Assyria, Babylon, Ethiopia,[7] India and England, wills are common. In Babylon written wills are general,

---

[1] P. & M. II, 530. Rome: Gaius IV, 75f. This liability originated in the XII Tables for theft.

[2] We saw it, for example, in New Guinea (A.2) and among the Kikuyu and Kamba (A.3 (1)); and see Vanderlinden (1969).

[3] For inheritance in Peru: Moore (1958), 91f. and 14f.

[4] Ashanti: Rattray (1929), 238. Tswana: Schapera (1938), 230. Joruba: Lloyd (1962), 290.

[5] e.g. Gen. 24[36], Sam. 17[23], 2 Kings 20[1], Deut. 21[15-17].

[6] Among the Tswana, if a man's will departs to any considerable extent from the ordinary rules of inheritance, an aggrieved person will appeal to the chief to adjust the matter: Schapera (1938), 230. For modern Yorubaland: Lloyd (1962), 290f.

[7] Walker (1933), 17, 52, 198.

and we see signs in Rome and Babylon and Ethiopia that it begins to be considered a man's duty to make a will of his property. But there are necessarily restrictions on the right of a man or woman to leave property by will, especially land held upon certain tenures, and it is rare for a man to depart, save in detail, from the rules of intestate succession.

CHAPTER 27

The Recent Peoples of the
Late Codes – Transactions and Contract

Sir Henry Maine's theory of the early history of contract[1] is part
and parcel of his religious theory of the origins of law. Because in
its beginnings law emerged everywhere from an indifferentiated
mass of religion morality, and law, and the early lawyer sprang
from the priest,[2] it retained as its fundamental characteristic a love
of technicalities and formalism, perplexed ceremonies, grotesque
gestures and symbolic acts. The early lawyer can only see law
through the envelope of its technical forms. So with the history
of contract:

> That which the law arms with its sanctions is not a promise,
> but a promise accompanied with a solemn ceremonial. Not
> only are the formalities of equal importance with the promise
> itself, but they are, if anything, of greater importance, for that
> delicate analysis which mature jurisprudence applies to the
> conditions of mind under which a particular verbal assent is
> given, appears in ancient law to be transferred to the words
> and gestures of the accompanying performance. No pledge is
> enforced if a single form be omitted or misplaced, but, on the
> other hand, if the forms can be shown to have been accurately
> proceeded with, it is of no avail to plead that the promise was
> made under duress or deception.[3]

I know of no time or place at which such a situation existed.
In many ages, but chiefly in the most developed of these economies,
men have taken or exacted oaths to do or refrain from acts,

---

[1] *A.L.*, Chaps. VIII and IX.   [2] E. L. & C. 26.   [3] *A.L.* 313.

especially such acts as are outside the sphere of law, and have uttered curses upon those who should pass a threshold, deface a boundary stone or sepulchral monument, or seek to upset a transaction,[1] and kings have enacted imprecations upon any successor who should annul or alter a code,[2] but these phenomena are irrelevant to the history of contract.

Let us briefly go back and survey, as we did in the realm of property, the road that we have travelled in this area. First, however, we must put aside the modern lawyer's conception of contract in the abstract. This is a technical and theoretical conception arrived at by a process of abstraction from an increasing number of facts and suitable for application to the innumerable forms of transactions.[3] The law of contract starts with simple and practical beginnings. Law does not develop by giving unwanted remedies. In the law of the Late Codes, in England, Rome, Babylonia and Assyria, in India and China, in Hebrew and Islamic law, we must still talk not of contract but of transactions, that is to say, transfers. The history of primitive contract is the history of primitive commerce, and the progress is small till the close of the primitive era.

In the Food Gatherers we found no evidence of trade because there were no goods surplus to requirements.

Among the Hunters and Early Agriculturists[4] we found some animals and goods (mainly natural produce) surplus to the immediate needs of subsistence, and some trade in this almost everywhere. It takes place by barter, that is to say contemporaneous exchange of one thing for another – though in a few places there are imperishable articles in use as a medium of exchange.[5] Trade takes many forms, sometimes it is between individuals, sometimes between permanent 'partners' belonging to different tribes or other social groups. In some areas types of goods and return

[1] In the Assyrian tablets, and especially the Neo-Assyrian.
[2] Epilogues of L.I. and C.H.
[3] And on the other hand it may be pointed out that even modern English law does not enforce an agreement unless there is a deed under seal, or in some cases writing, or consideration, and sometimes both the last two requirements.
[4] A.1.
[5] As for example the dentalium shell and clamshell disc bead in California and the Basin-Plateau Area.

goods go from hand to hand over thousands of miles on permanent routes. Some of this is enveloped in ritual and much exemplifies gift-exchange, that is to say, gifts for which a return of similar value is expected. This we can hardly call trade.

In the peoples of our second Agricultural Grade trade has largely increased both in barter and sale, and now includes a quantity of partly manufactured goods. Again there are individual transactions between a man and his trade friend, and also exchange between neighbouring communities, for example, of the vegetable product of horticulturalists in return for the fish of a neighbouring coastal village. Apart from this there is the exchange of standard trade goods travelling over vast distances on regular routes. There is also in some areas (especially the Kula Ring in Melanesia) the ritual exchange of two highly prized, imperishable commodities, travelling in opposite directions, that seems to serve no commercial but only social purposes and is not called 'trade' but by another name. Rarely do we find, as among the Kapauku, a developed system of credit, savings, loans at interest, hire, and leases of land.[1]

In the first stage of the Third Agricultural Grade[2] there is trade by contemporaneous barter, and cattle, goats and often grain play a prominent part in the estimation of values and as medium of exchange. There are also smiths engaged to make an article, often on terms of being supplied with the metal and charcoal needed and grain for subsistence during the work and a lump-sum payment at the close in the form of a cow or goat. There are rarely any markets, for these peoples live mainly in isolated homesteads.

In the peoples of the Early Codes[3] there is still hardly a market till the close of this period. There is some trade in produce and manufactured articles and there are traditional value-relations for the purposes of exchange, especially between cattle, sheep and goats.[4] When a metal currency is adopted it bears a fixed relation to them, so that a shilling in England is at first the price of a cow and a *sceatta* or penny the price of a sheep. There are some foreign merchants, but the chief transactions remain contemporaneous

[1] Pospisil (1958), 15, 129f.   [2] A.3 (1).   [3] A.3 (2).
[4] Even among the Tswana, after the recent introduction of European currency and the fluctuations in market prices, a heifer is generally sold among the Gwato and Kgatla for £5, a sheep for £1, a goat for 10s., corn at £1 per bag, and goatskins and sheepskins at 1s. each: Schapera (1938), 242.

barter, cash sale, loans between friends and arrangements between friends for agistment of cattle. There is still little or no hiring or commercial deposit and little engagement of specialists.

At the close of the Early Codes and among the peoples of the Central Codes there is substantial economic development. There is a great increase in trade, especially in manufactured goods. There are in most peoples markets, market towns, tolls and dues on goods for sale, and a port reeve, or market chief, in control. There are currencies of some kind (mainly metal) everywhere, but money is in little use in the countryside. For large transactions cattle are usually the means of payment, except in barter. There is hire of goods, especially farm animals and carts in the ancient world. Artisans number some 3 per cent of the working population and there is some hire of agricultural workers (paid in kind) and artisans in the towns (paid in money)[1] and at the close of the age some fixing of prices of goods and hire charges, for the value of money is beginning to fall.[2] Loan of money for a lump-sum payment begins. There is suretyship and pledging by debtors of their dependants. There is a familiar situation where A sees an animal or article in B's possession and claims that it is his and has been stolen from him, and B denies this and alleges he bought it from a third party. He is required to produce his vendor. Sales of goods of any value take place in a market town before a group of witnesses, and the law endeavours to insist on this practice but it is nowhere essential to validity.

The great and quickening development in the Late Codes has been outlined, and there is no space for details. The number of craftsmen and artisans is some 5 per cent of the working population and the traders some 6 per cent. The variety of skilled occupations is large. Agricultural workers are paid in kind, artisans in the towns often in money. Gilds of artisans and traders and markets and market courts show great development and

[1] In Nupe wage labour is still a new thing and only to be found in the towns, and the amount of it is insignificant. Many are temporary workers who subsequently go back to the family farm: Nadel (1942), 251. Assistance on the farms is given mainly (1) free, by relatives living in the same compound, (2) for payment, by collective labour of fellow-villagers and friends (p. 241), (3) by slaves and pawns, (4) by clients.

[2] From A.D. 1100 to 1300 the average silver content of a new English penny only fell from 22½ to 22 grains, but in the fourteenth century to about 15 and in the fifteenth to about 11.

foreign trade is considerable and kings engage in it.[1] There is commercial hire and deposit (including banking), investment in commercial expeditions and enterprises,[2] partnership, agency, suretyship and leases of land. There is pledging of dependants, and mortgages of land and crops, at first by pledge (where the occupier parts with possession on loan) and later by hypothec (where he loses possession only on failure to repay). There is some registration of title to land. And there is, of course, the law of marriage.

Yet in spite of this development, sale is still by far the most common transaction, and all that has happened to contemporaneous barter (which survives) is the substitution of money for the commodity on one side and the conversion of the transaction to cash sale. Nothing remains to be done or claimed (except that the law may give the buyer a claim to recover the price if a certain disease or defect in the thing sold appears within a certain period, or, of course, if it turns out not to have been the vendor's to sell). This is considered a distinct type of transaction. Even at the end of this age, in the Old Babylonian period, no transaction was considered a sale unless it was for cash,[3] otherwise it was not recorded in a sale tablet alone. So, the Roman *vendere* originally signified a cash sale, and *emere* ('to take') a cash purchase. Even modern English records the same situation, for 'sell' originally meant 'deliver', and 'sale' still primarily denotes an instantaneous and completed transaction. Indeed in even a modern market, a retail sale which is not for cash must be an unusual event.

All important transactions are conducted before a substantial number of witnesses. We have seen this in the Central Codes, and throughout our period it is universal in England, Africa, Rome, Jerusalem, India[4] and everywhere else. We have seen the reason for this – to meet a possible claim by a third person (or the seller) that the property is his and has been stolen from him. If we had any doubts that this was still the reason, the Codes of Eshnunna[5] and Hammurabi, the Assyrian Laws and

---

[1] Among the Hebrews, King Solomon. Nupe: Nadel (1942), 311.
[2] C.H. 100f. Nupe: Nadel (1942), 311.
[3] In the following references to Babylonian and Assyrian contract-tablets, I have drawn especially on San Nicolò (1931). See, for a recent Bibliography in this field, Klima (1965).
[4] Manu viii, 201, 202.   [5] L.E. 41.

the tablets tell us so in the plainest terms. As in modern times, even writing (where writing is in use) is not thought to obviate the necessity for witnesses (especially as neither party can usually write or read) but the number of witnesses is larger than with us because fraud is perhaps more rife and life more uncertain and the courts demand that evidence. In Babylonia there may be anything between one witness and twenty or more, and five or six is an average number, but neither tablet nor form nor witnesses are essential to validity. In West Africa today we have the further advantage of being able to observe that the witnesses, in some places at least, receive a customary gift-payment for their pains, which may be a fixed proportion of the price.[1]

This, then, is the universal type of the most familiar and important commercial transaction – a ready-money sale (in the more advanced economies, the metal currency weighed out at the time) before some five or six witnesses. The witnesses (and the writing, if any) are for the benefit of the buyer, not the seller (as indeed they must be on a cash sale). So, in the Mesopotamian tablet in this Old Babylonian period, the transaction is alway expressed from the buyer's point of view: 'So-and-so has taken for so much silver such-and-such a thing', not 'So-and-so has given', and the seal is always the seal which will be of use to the buyer, namely the seller's seal. The early Romans called the transaction *mancipium*, a 'taking', not a 'giving'.

Everywhere, too, among the most developed economies, the important sales tend to be of the same subject-matter – in Rome, Mesopotamia, Egypt and elsewhere, land, cattle and slaves or serfs, and among a people who engage largely in a water-borne trade, like the Babylonians and Egyptians, ships also; and in Babylonia and Egypt, where the temples retain their records for centuries, sacred offices and the income from them. We have already sought to set out steps by which land had become saleable in the middle of the Late Codes and a ready market in land appeared at the close. We are not told much in the Codes or deeds of the consents

---

[1] See e.g. Rattray (1929), 232, 234,; Rattray (1923), 368.

required from near kin or their rights of pre-emption and redemption.[1]

These sales are all sales of specific items of property – such-and-such a field (naming it) a particular slave, bull or cow, and so on. Thus it is that in Rome by the year 270 B.C. a rule is evolved by the conservative Roman mind that land in Italy, cattle and slaves are only properly transferred in the presence of five Roman citizens and a man holding a copper balance, and the buyer ('taker') declares: 'I say this (slave etc.) is mine by Roman law, and he be taken by me with this copper and copper balance' – and he strikes the balance with the copper and gives it to the transferor. The Romans were then still generally illiterate, but this transaction in later days remained an oral transaction long after writing was in general use. The Sumerians, Babylonians and Assyrians, and to a lesser extent the Hebrews and Egyptians, used writing to evidence their important transactions, the Egyptians and Hebrews mainly papyrus, and the Mesopotamians clay tablets. In twelfth- and thirteenth-century England, and among all these peoples who used writing, the general form of the document was the same. The parties were illiterate and the document was written by a scribe, witnessed and sealed by a party.[2] This is still the form of

---

[1] The following is a late Neo-Assyrian specimen (C. H. W. John's *Assyrian Deeds and Documents*, No. 172. Cambridge. 1898). It records a cash sale of a slave, Nasir Ninip, by M.M. to R.A., and commences with the seal of the seller:

'Seal of M.M.
the saknu of the horses of the New Palace,
legitimate owner of the person transferred.
Nasir-Ninip a weaver of embroidered cloth,
slave of M.M.
has made a bargain R.A.,
the charioteer of the King, and from
M.M. for a mina and a half (of silver)
royal standard has taken. The price was complete
(and) given. There shall be no retreat or
lawsuit. (Whoever in) future
shall set up a plea, etc. (penalty clause)
(There follows a warranty against epilepsy for a certain period)
In the presence of (9 witnesses).
In the month of Ululu, 20th day, in the Eponymy of Y,
the saknu of Durile.'
[2] In England it was not till the thirteenth century that the ordinary freeman had his own seal.

the modern English deed.[1] The Roman *mancipium* was an oral deed. Both finally became conveyances, the form of which gave them their validity. In England slavery now takes the form of serfdom and there is no separate selling of slaves, and the deed is mainly used for sales of land.

There is little barter of specific valuables, either in Rome or Babylon or elsewhere: these are normally disposed of in the towns and by way of sale, in the way we have seen. There is no sale of a large quantity of non-specific goods – that is to say, of produce; such transactions usually take place in the country and by barter. When a large estate disposed of its produce, say, its present produce of oil, to another estate which would deliver a quantity of its produce of corn after next harvest, this credit-barter was recorded in a loan-tablet. It was not a sale. In Rome, indeed, the transaction retained the name of *mutuum* ('exchange', 'barter') in classical times.

So much for the cash sale, but less commonly there are also sales (of specific goods) on credit, where the purchaser is to pay in the future. These were so much less common that the Babylonians did not regard them as mere sales: they drew up two tablets, one a sale-tablet recording a cash sale, and the second a tablet recording that the seller has lent the buyer such-and-such a sum ('the amount of the price'), which the buyer will repay on such-and-such a date; or recording a deposit by the seller with the buyer of the amount of the price, or an account declaring the buyer to be in debt to the seller in that amount, and recording that he will repay on a certain date. Similarly, if the transaction were one under which the buyer paid in advance and the seller agreed to deliver in the future, a sale-tablet was drawn up recording a cash sale, and a second tablet recorded the seller's debt in respect of the goods. In Rome by 200 B.C. they had arrived at the practice-book rule (which survives in the fragments of the Twelve Tables) that any of these extra terms, if orally stated at the time of the *mancipium*, would be binding.[2]

[1] Except that normally in England there are two counterparts each sealed by both parties, or each by a different party. In Babylonia, if there are two copies, they are identical, and on a sale each bears the seller's seal.
[2] For a more detailed examination of the features of the *mancipium* and the reasons for concluding that they date from about 270 B.C., that the above provision, validating terms orally added, dates from about 200 B.C., and that

There were no mere agreements to sell, in which payment and delivery were both to take place in the future – what the English law calls an executory agreement of sale – the peoples of this stage do not do business in that way. But there is quite a little here and there of the giving of 'earnest'. X may want to consider whether he will buy a certain article from Y. Y lets him consider the matter till, say, the following day, on condition that he pays him a small sum which he will forfeit if he decides not to buy. We see this practice in West Africa and England, but it is not sufficiently important to find its way into the Old Babylonian tablets or the Roman forms of transactions of our period.

In Bechuanaland and West Africa loan of money at interest[1] was not known. Among the Hebrews it was just creeping in – a loan of money remunerated by money – that is to say, by interest. Hence, in the Old Testament, religion exercising its normal function of resisting innovation (in this case, salutary if impracticable) prohibited usury, and the rule survived in England with wide exceptions till 1865. Muhammadan law struggles to maintain a consistent and practical attitude. But in all the more developed economies of the Late Codes, thirteenth-century England, Rome, Babylon, Assyria, Ethiopia, China and India, the loan of money at interest is common. In England, kings, monasteries and landowners are widely borrowing at interest, and loans upon a rent-charge of 10 per cent per annum are normal. In Babylon the rate was as high or higher – 20 per cent and more could be got. Loans by a moneylender or landlord on the security of a crop or a field (a form of security corresponding to the letting of land on the *metayage* system) were very common, and Hammurabi was concerned to check its abuses.[2] In Rome (as elsewhere) the money lent was weighed out as in the *mancipium*, at the time of the transaction.

Then there are the bailments of goods which will be returned in the future, free loans of goods to friends for use, deposit (in the East especially of silver) and hire of ploughs, wagons and oxen, with or without drivers. The process seen in the Central Codes[3]

---

the general history of the development of transfers and contract was much the same in Babylonia and in Rome, see the first and second editions of this book, Chap. XXXIV.
[1] As distinct from a share in the profits.   [2] C.H. 49-50.   [3] H.C., I, 75.

continues: the ordeal by oath is brought into use to meet the case where the borrower or hirer says the ox has died or was eaten or the property destroyed without his privity. These clauses are more numerous and more detailed in the Codes, the more advanced is the economy.

We have seen enough to realize that there has been a large-scale development in this branch of law, and there are now a good many types of transactions, but there is not yet nearly enough of this in Babylon, Rome, England or elsewhere, to call for a general theory of contract: that, for example, a contract is made by an offer and an acceptance in the same terms, or that it must be carried out, or a breach compensated by the amount of the loss incurred. It is not that these peoples do not think that a promise should be performed, but that at this stage commerce does not proceed on that basis: no one relies on a mere agreement on both sides to do something in the future, and consequently no one can be damaged by a failure to carry it out. Law does not pretend to compensate where there is no loss, and there are few, if any, cases where the loss to the plaintiff is tried and estimated. In a modern court the usual remedy for breach of a contract to buy or sell goods is the difference between the contract price and the market price, and if there is no difference there is no loss and no remedy. In the times of which we speak market prices do not fluctuate to that extent so that even if parties relied on a mere executory agreement it would usually be difficult to say what loss has been incurred by a breach. In England and elsewhere, there are claims in debt to recover money owing to the plaintiff (for work done, or the return of the price paid for goods or of bridewealth) and claims in detinue to recover his goods (hired and not returned, for example) but in England it is probably the sharp drop in the value of the coinage and the sharp fluctuations in market prices in the sixteenth century that create the necessity to rely on executory contracts, and develop the action of assumpsit.

But there are already in the Late Codes elements of contract in the subsidiary terms of these conveyances on sale – for example, the express warranties on the sale of slaves or animals against epilepsy or other disease occurring within such-and-such a time – and we saw an interesting case at the end of the Hebrew Code of the acceptance of a certain risk being implied on the hire of goods.

Professor Schapera, indeed, tells us[1] that the Tswana tribal courts in 1935 to 1940 had arrived at a general doctrine of contract, a few claims upon executory contracts, a few awards of damages and mandatory orders. Such a situation is not reported from West Africa.

[1] Schapera (1969).

CHAPTER 28

The Recent Peoples of the Late Codes—
Religion, Letters and Procedure

When we turn to the borders of the law, where the spheres of law and religion touch, there is still a correlation with economic development. The increase in the power of religion in the peoples of the Late Codes is unmistakable,[1] and in many independent empires the number of members of the various religious orders is much the same. In the latter part of our period they total about one quarter of the adult population and own about a third of the land. These are the best estimates that can be made of Mexico,[2] Peru[3] and Ethiopia[4] as of England and other lands that have been mentioned.[5] And where the priestly influence and authority over the faithful gives rise to ecclesiastical jurisdictions, there is a close competition and rivalry with the secular courts. So, too, in Ethiopia, where by a law of 1942[6] at one blow the whole ecclesiastical jurisdiction was removed except for the disciplinary authority of the church over its own officers and the infliction of purely spiritual penalties. But the division, when it takes place in our period, between the secular jurisdiction and the ecclesiastic, normally assigns the same group of subjects to the latter (mainly,

---

[1] See *ante*, p. 83. And yet the domains and conceptions of law, religion and morality remain distinct. Vaillant (1944) says (p. 125) that in Mexico religion did not enter into the field of ethics, nor, I suggest, into the domain of law. Even less is this the case in Africa.
[2] In Mexico we are told that 5,000 priests were attached to the principal temple in the capital, and there were several hundred smaller temples in each of the principal cities: Prescott (Mexico), 32f.
[3] In Peru it is said that the priesthood received the produce of one-third of the land.
[4] Perham (1969), 109.
[5] See *ante*, p. 88.
[6] Law of Nov. 30, 1942, art. 10.

389

marriage, divorce and inheritance).[1] Again, to the extent that
writing is in use, it is taught only in the schools of church and
temple and is the possession of the scribes, who are not priests
but a calling on the fringe of the religious orders. So even in Ethiopia, though the priest can read Ge'ez, the dead Semite language
in which the psalter and liturgy are written, he cannot as a rule
understand it; and in China the Buddhist priest does not understand the Pali of the Buddhist canon. The scribes are held in
great awe by the populace as the learned men of the age,[2] and the
knowledge of the mystery of writing opens a wide door to
influence and power.[3] In Mexico, as in Rome, the ecclesiastical
monopoly of letters involves a control of the calendar and correspondingly over the sittings of the courts, though at the end of
this age the possession of writing begins to extend to the layman.

The history of the ordeal in these peoples illustrates the difference between countries where the power of priesthood and
religion is great and those where it is small. Among the Tswana
the ordeal has disappeared; we saw little of it among the Nguni of
South Africa, but in the Tswana it has gone, and in China it was
of no importance at any time.[4] But in most of these peoples the
ordeal by oath continues in use for the same purposes as before,
that is to say it is applied only to the defendant, in disputes in
relation to bailments and other disputes where evidence on one
side only is available (such as charges of witchcraft, incest and
adultery)[5] and it is conclusive. In a few cases it is extended to the
plaintiff, where he has to prove the amount or value of his loss.
The use of the ordeal by oath for these limited purposes increases

---

[1] In several former British possessions these questions were either reserved
to the decision of the religious courts of each community (as in Palestine
in the period of the Mandate) or were decided in accordance with the law
administered in those religious courts (as in Aden). As to Northern Nigeria,
see *ante*, p. 348f.
[2] See an amusing account of the *dabtara* (scribe) in Walker (1933), 115f.
For the functions of the *malam* in Northern Nigeria, see Meek (1925), II,
5f. and *passim*.
[3] See the amusing account of the profession of the Egyptian scribe in the
instructions of one Tuauf to his son (British Museum, Nos. 10182, 10222,
cited by E. A. Wallis Budge in *The Dwellers on the Nile* (1926), 40).
[4] Ch'ü (1961), 209.
[5] The priests at many shrines in West Africa apply the local forms of ordeal
to test charges of witchcraft, adultery or theft and manipulate the local
oracles.

in the Late Codes to the end of our period, but otherwise evidence is generally unsworn. In Ethiopia, as in England and the Akan peoples, the oath is extended to witnesses, and therefore, since the taking of an oath is a dangerous thing, and the parties cannot fairly be expected to tell the truth contrary to their interest, they are not allowed to give evidence – a rule which lasted in England in civil cases till 1851 and in criminal cases till 1898. But the witnesses' oath is not necessarily conclusive. Finally, in England of the thirteenth century and in modern Ethiopia, the trial before chief and elders becomes a trial before judge and jurors – neighbours sworn to decide the truth.

Another curious and most interesting use of the oath is in the procedure called by the Romans the *legis*[1] *actio per sacramentum* or 'procedure by oath', with its *sponsio*, or forensic wager. The first is never found except in peoples of the Late Codes: the forensic wager appears for the first time at this point, and as part of the procedure by oath, but outlives it and survives for some time longer.

To understand them we must remind ourselves of the legal background. These peoples of the Late Codes, as we have seen, evince a deep interest in law and a love of litigation, a keen sense of right and wrong, and especially of their own right and the wrong of others. They are full of confidence in their opinions and extremely boastful. It is a necessary part of the constitution of these feudal societies, especially in the first half of this age, that territorial lords of various degree have in most matters jurisdiction over their tenants, though some disputes (called Crimes of the King,[2] or Pleas of the Crown[3]) are so serious, and some questions so difficult that, after a preliminary enquiry sufficient to ascertain its nature, the case must be sent up to the court of a superior lord or the king. In the result there remains a welter of jurisdictions, some being, indeed, conterminous with the boundaries of vassal kingdoms, and (at any rate in detail) there are different rules of law and different procedures in force in different areas of the state.[4] Further, we must remember that the body of

[1] i.e. mentioned in the XII Tables, as we are told.
[2] e.g. Nupe: Nadel (1942), 166, 172.
[3] England. For a similar system in Mexico, see Prescott (Mexico), 16f. In Ashanti these offences are called *oman akyiwadie* (lit. 'things hateful to the nation'): Rattray (1929), 294.
[4] See many examples in Rattray (1929).

392 PRIMITIVE LAW, PAST AND PRESENT

rules of law has grown vastly in extent, and the administration
and practice of the law have already begun to be something of an
art, and consequently here and there detailed and technical rules
of procedure and of law have evolved.

In civil disputes, with which alone we are at present concerned, the supply of litigation outstrips, as it were, the demand.
There are always disputants asking for their disputes to be heard.
In Ethiopia, indeed, it is a generally recognized duty on the part
of any disinterested person to accept the role of a reconciler when
asked to so do by utter strangers as he travels along the road. If
he is unsuccessful in solving their differences, at their request he
will take them to the lowest-ranking judge in the vicinity,
reporting the dispute.

This pressure of litigants is such as to increase the importance
of the institution of suretyship, which is already much in evidence
in a variety of circumstances. Litigants must often find a surety
to pay the judgment fee or the amount of the judgment before
their cases will be heard. Even this is, of course, insufficient to
gain a hearing for a trumpery dispute in the court of a great chief,
king or emperor. But a man often desires that his trivial quarrel
should be heard in the great chief's court, either because of a
sense of its vast importance, or his desire for the pomp and
publicity of that court, or his mistrust of the efficiency or impartiality of the local court. He achieves this result by swearing
the great chief's oath, or, in other words, by conditionally cursing
him.

For example, in Ashanti a man may have a quarrel with his
neighbour as to whether a particular tree is within his boundary
or whether the other has trespassed upon his land, or has struck
him, and may desire that the dispute shall be tried in the court of
a particular *Omanhene* (or Tribal Chief). He says, for example, 'I
say this tree is on my land'. The other says, 'I say it is on mine'.
The first swears, 'May fetish So-and-so kill *Omanhene* X if it is not
on my land'.[1] The other swears, 'May fetish So-and-so kill *Omanhene* X if it is not on my land'. This puts quite a different com-

---

[1] Or, e.g. 'I swear the forbidden name', or 'I swear *Omanhene* X *Wukuda*'.
Wukuda (Wednesday) is the day when a certain calamitous defeat was sustained
by the Akwapim and others. For instances of the working of this procedure
by oath, see Gold Coast Commission, 30f.; Rattray (1929), 379f.; Danquah
(1928), 69f.

plexion on the case. *Omanhene* X has a very definite interest in the matter, and, moreover, a criminal offence, a crime of the chief, has been committed by one or the other. It is now the duty of anyone who hears the words spoken immediately to arrest both parties, and he is entitled to be paid a specific fee for doing so. The two parties are reported to the chief whose oath has been sworn; in some places they are put in the stocks meanwhile, for both are *prima facie* guilty of cursing the *Omanhene*, or they may be released on giving sureties for their attendance and the payment of court fees. The question at issue – namely, which party was in the right (for example, whose tree it was or whether there was a trespass or assault) – is then tried in the court of the *Omanhene*, and whoever is found to be in the wrong is guilty of a criminal offence and punished accordingly, either by fine payable to the state,[1] or even (in former times) capitally. The successful party pays to the court *aseda* (content money) by way of thanksgiving.

This procedure is applicable to every kind of civil dispute, and is found throughout the Akan peoples of the Gold Coast and Ashanti, in Rome in the period of the Twelve Tables and for some time after, and in modern Ethiopia. There are variations in the procedure from place to place, but the essential incidents are the same everywhere: the curse or oath, the surety, and the fine. Yet the procedure arises in each place quite independently out of similar circumstances. Though general in the Gold Coast colony and Ashanti, it is not (so far as I know) to be found in Nigeria. There was no cultural contact between ancient Rome, the modern Gold Coast, and the Ethiopian highlands. Nor does its existence depend on the tenets of the national religion. Few religions could differ more than those of ancient Rome, the Gold Coast, and Christian Ethiopia. The procedure by oath spreads, and threatens to oust the simple procedure by summons in all these areas, and this is because its extension is the measure and means of the extension of the power and jurisdiction of the king or paramount chief over the whole kingdom or empire, as feudalism dissolves. But as his jurisdiction spreads and widens, the oath loses its meaning. In Ethiopia where the incidents of the procedure

[1] Often partly used to pay the expenses of a sacrifice to propitiate the fetish.

O*

are the same, the form is '*Menelik Yimut*' (Let Menelik[1] die!). It is used in joining every sort of issue in litigation in all courts, and even in concluding legal transactions. When an agreement has been made (for example, an agreement of marriage), or an allegation has been made in court and denied, the one will commonly say to the other, '*Man Yimut*' (Who is to die?) and the reply is made '*Menelik Yimut*'[2] (Let Menelik die). In other words, the old oath has become a mere method of indicating the binding character of what has preceded. So in Rome, when we hear of it, the oath is disappearing from the procedure, though its name remains.

In all litigation in ancient Rome, as in ancient India, and modern Ethiopia, the wager, too, plays a prominent part, whatever the nature of the issue to be tried. It is a result of that characteristic boastfulness to which we have referred. Any stake may be made, but in Ethiopia it is usually either a 'mule', 'a horse', or 'honey'. If, for example, a man stakes a 'mule' on the result and loses, he pays a judgment fee of twenty Maria Theresa dollars, and if he wins he receives ten dollars from the other side. No doubt a high stake impresses the court with the sincerity of the wagerer.

[1] Emperor of Abyssinia from 1889 to 1913.
[2] Question and answer corresponding, as in the Roman stipulation, so as to impress on the parties, and on the mind of bystanders who may have to bear witness to it in the future, that an oral agreement has been arrived at.

CHAPTER 29

The Recent Peoples of the Late Codes – Crimes and Civil Injuries

We have seen, at various stages, that the law of civil wrongs lies at the heart of the developing legal system, and, for example, that the first legislation of the Early Codes consists almost entirely of sanctions for the most serious of these wrongs, namely homicide and personal injuries, so that law appears to issue and spread from these wrongs. We have also seen that there is less variation in these sanctions between peoples of the same stage of economic development than in any other branch of the law. The civil injuries of the Late Codes of the past have been somewhat fully discussed[1] and those of the recent peoples might well be dismissed by saying that the law is substantially the same as that of the past. But some examples and references should be given.

The general sanction for homicide is everywhere death.[2] If tried, a charge of homicide is triable only in the king's court, but the law must rely much on the next of kin for its enforcement, and this is the true age of what is commonly called the 'blood-feud' – that is to say, death at the hands of the nearest kin of the slain – a rule which so many have mistaken for the earliest stage of law, or,

---

[1] See *ante* Chaps. 8 to 12.

[2] Southern Nigeria: Talbot (1926), III, 625f. and map on p. 627, showing that among all the Late Code peoples death is always inflicted, and see Table 19. Northern Nigeria: Meek (1925), I, 271f., and for the Islamic law of homicide in force in Northern Nigeria till 1959, articles by J. Schacht on Ḳatl and Ḳiṣāṣ in *Encyclopaedia of Islam* (Leiden and London, 1913, new edn, 1954), and Anderson (1951). For the Ashanti, see Rattray (1929), 294f.; for Mexico, Joyce (1914), 131, Prescott (Mexico), 17, Vaillant (1944), 126. For Peru, see Rowe, 271, Moore (1958), 168, and for the Maya, Joyce (1914), 183. For the Tswana, see Schapera (1938), 260f.

on the other hand, have attributed to a particular race.[1] The slayer
flees, if he can, either abroad or to some secular[2] or sacred
sanctuary whose authority will cover him for a time. So, on the
borders of Ethiopia the depredations of outlaws are as great as on
the English borders in the thirteenth century. But homicide is also
now in part a criminal offence, a wrong against the whole nation,
and in part a religious offence, causing pollution of the land or
other danger from supernatural sources, and accordingly neither
the secular nor the religious refuge will avail him long.

We have said that the general sanction for homicide is death,
and this is the rule correctly stated in Exodus 21[12], for most men
intend what they do. But a homicide may not be intentional: it
may be negligent, but negligence is not a separate category among
these peoples.[3] It may be accidental, and if so, in most but not all
cases, death will not be imposed and blood money will be accepted
or a fine paid to the king. It may be a killing in self-defence, and
here, as a rule, no punishment will be insisted on.[4] We are not
told enough of the borderline between capital and other homicide,
partly because it is vague and difficult to define, and partly because
in most places in West and South Africa (except Northern Nigeria)
the courts of 'customary law' have for some time had no jurisdiction in homicide.[5] There is more than one test of murder. In the
developed Islamic law 'deliberate homicide' is capital, and blood
money is accepted in other cases at a heavier or lighter rate
according to types of circumstances; but there are many differences

---

[1] It is often said that death for murder is the traditional law of the Semite, but
this is erroneous. The acceptance of blood money is widespread among
them, and the avenging of inter-tribal murder by the feud (traditionally the
rule before Islam) merely instances the results of the absence of a tribunal
having power over both parties.
[2] So in Botswana, where religion has little power, he flees to the homestead
of a senior adviser of the king; among the Ngwato, the homestead of the
chief's mother.
[3] But see, as to homicide by neglect in Islamic law, Anderson (1951), 823.
[4] Except in Ashanti: Rattray (1929), 297.
[5] Tswana: Schapera (1938), 26of.: death for 'culpable homicide and murder'.
No compensation to the family of the slain. Among Ngwato and Kgatla
accidental homicide is not punished: negligence is punished by a fine to the
chief. But among the Kwena, even for accidental homicide, confiscation of
all property to the widow and orphans. *Ethiopia:* Perham (1969), 48: homicide
private to the parties. Blood money may be accepted, and this rule is adopted
into the 1930 Code.

between the schools. Blood money at the lighter rate may be payable where there was no wrongful intention, and death may be imposed in certain types of unintentional homicide, but for justifiable homicide or killing in self-defence there is no sanction.

Homicide remains in all systems partly a civil, partly a criminal offence: in Islamic (as in Athenian) law mainly civil. In some systems (as in some Islamic schools and in Athenian law) forgiveness by the victim or next of kin is a bar to any proceedings. In many systems the next of kin have the right to accept blood money, but the community (as in Ethiopia) will hold the family in low esteem. In some systems (as in England) the king retains the right to proceed against the murderer whatever settlement may have been made. In many or most systems the next of kin commits no wrong if he kills the murderer without waiting for a trial: in Islamic law he merely commits a contempt of court. In some peoples (e.g. in Northern Nigeria) the question whether the homicide was intentional or not is suitable matter for an ordeal, the evidence being that of the defendant alone. In Islamic and other systems the question is often answered by considering the type of weapon used. The judgment of the court after trial is usually that the killer be handed over to the next of kin to do his duty. In Ethiopia the present emperor in 1925 devised an ingenious method of suiting the requirements of the law and obviating its apparent barbarity by a device by which the co-ordinated sights of four rifles are directed upon the condemned murderer, who is strapped to a plank, and the next of kin fires all rifles at once by a simple mechanism.[1] In some systems the murderer is killed by the weapon he used;[2] in many the method of execution is aimed to avoid a flow of blood.[3]

In regard to wounding, as in the Hebrew Code and the other Codes of the first half of the Late Codes of the past, the commonest sanctions are either payment of a fine, or payment of the plaintiff's doctor's fees and his maintenance during the period of his disability, or, less often, a sum by way of compensation. But in a

---

[1] Mérab, *Impressions d'Ethiopie* (Paris, 1929), III, 218.
[2] Botswana; and see the incident related in Talbot (1926), III, 626.
[3] e.g. by stoning (Mexico and Peru), hanging (West Africa and Peru), throwing down from a high rock (Ethiopia, Peru, Botswana). But among the Yoruba the murderer is stunned and decapitated.

substantial number of cases there are no proceedings for these injuries: the plaintiff is left to his remedy of retaliation, and in some places the court may order the infliction of talionic penalties, that is to say the same loss in the manner in which it was inflicted, for example the loss of an eye.[1]

There are, as ever, differences from place to place in the standards of sexual morality. Adultery with a married woman is in most places criminal and often also a religious offence. In Southern Nigeria the usual sanction is a fine or compensation or both.[2] In the Muslim states of Northern Nigeria the sanction is, in theory, stoning to death, but in practice a public flogging often takes its place. In other places in Northern Nigeria the sanction may be compensation, a fine, imprisonment, public whipping or enslavement.[3] Among the Tswana, too, sexual morality is lax and the husband beats his wife and claims damages; among the Mexicans,[4] Peruvians[5] and Maya[6] the guilty pair are both liable to the death penalty. In Ethiopia, under the new Penal Code of 1930, the

---

[1] *Southern Nigeria:* Talbot (1926), III, 628f. and Table 19, which refer to Southern Nigeria generally (143 subtribes and districts). To summarize his data: in 62 cases the offender must get his victim cured and pay the doctor's fee, often also maintaining him meanwhile or doing his work on the farm. (These 62 cases include 13 cases of the payment of doctor's fees plus a fine, and 9 cases of the payment of doctor's fees plus a small compensatory payment.) In 59 cases the sanction is a fine (in 13 of which the defendant must also pay doctor's fees). In 21 cases the defendant pays compensation (including doctor's fees in half the cases). In 11 cases there is retaliation. In 22 cases there is no trial for wounding. In Yorubaland the sanction is a fine. *Northern Nigeria:* usually fines and compensation, which, in the Muslim courts, is in proportion to the amount of blood lost: Meek (1925), I, 274. In some Muslim states (e.g. Hadeija) talionic penalties are inflicted by the court's order. *Ashanti:* usually a compensatory payment: Rattray (1923), 310f. *Mexico:* doctor's fees and compensation: Vaillant (1944), 126. *Tswana:* mere assaults, no proceedings. Otherwise usually fine or thrashing, or both. Recently, a tendency for the chief to give part or all of the fine to the victim as compensation. Sometimes in earlier days *talio* was ordered. If the injury is by accident, no compensation except, perhaps, a share of the medical expenses.
[2] See Talbot (1926), III, Table 19. To sum up his data from 162 subtribes or districts, in 57 cases the sanction is a fine, in 18 cases a fine plus compensation, in 13 cases a fine plus sacrifice to the offended earth goddess Ala or the ancestors, in 25 cases we are told that the sanction is damages, and in 4 cases the *talio*.
[3] Meek (1925), I, 275f.
[4] Joyce (1914), 131f.; Prescott (Mexico), 17; Vaillant (1944), 126.
[5] Prescott (Peru), 261; Rowe, 271; Moore (1958), 170.
[6] Joyce (1914), 284.

sanction for adultery is reduced to three years' imprisonment. The *talio* for adultery is occasionally found, that is to say the wronged husband may similarly treat the adulterer's wife.[1]

Rape is usually criminal, but there is inadequate information. In Yorubaland the sanction is flogging;[2] among the Tswana it appears the offence was formerly capital.[3] Imprisonment makes its appearance in several lands as a sanction for crime, but the prisons are dungeons where the prisoner's relatives are the chief source of food.[4]

Theft also follows the same course of development as in the Late Codes of the past and becomes criminal. Among the Tswana the ordinary rule is still payment of the double value, but the thief with stolen cattle in his possession was liable to be killed or mutilated in the hands.[5] In Yorubaland, the usual sanction for the first offence is flogging; for the second, mutilation (usually by cutting off ears), for the third, death, and death is also the sanction for burglary and for theft in the market or on the highway. In the rest of Southern Nigeria, in addition to the above punishments, there are a few cases of restitution or a fine, and some of public humiliation.[6] Among the Peruvians, Mexicans and Maya, according to the gravity of the offence the thief makes multiple restitution or is enslaved or killed.[7] In Ethiopia, as in thirteenth-century England, the thief of property of substantial value is normally killed, whether caught in the act or not. If the value is less, the sentence might only be the cutting off of hand or nose, or fine or multiple restitution.

These continue to be the main wrongs in an expanding list. These civil wrongs, at the close of our period, have become

[1] See above as to Southern Nigeria. It is also occasionally found in Ghana.
[2] In the rest of Southern Nigeria (which includes many peoples of the Central Codes) usually a fine or compensation (and in default of payment the prisoner is sold or pawns himself) and in some cases the sanction is enslavement: Talbot (1926), III, Table 19.
[3] Schapera (1938), 260.
[4] e.g. Southern Nigeria; the Muslim states of Northern Nigeria: Meek (1925), I, 276; Ethiopia. In Mexico defendants were only imprisoned pending trial or sacrifice: Vaillant (1944), 126.
[5] Schapera (1938), 271.
[6] Talbot (1926), III, Table 19.
[7] Peru: Rowe, 271; Prescott (Peru), 26. Mexico, where highway robbery and stealing in the market are capital: Joyce (1914), 131; Prescott (Mexico), 17; Vaillant (1944), 126.

criminal as well as civil, and the boundary between crime and civil injury has consequently become more shadowy than before or since. But there remain lesser wrongs, which are purely civil, and some purely criminal offences, tried in the king's court: treason, incest and other illicit sexual intercourse, sodomy and bestiality, often slander, witchcraft,[1] cowardice in the face of the enemy, suicide and a number of sacral offences,[2] and the sanctions are mutilation or death and the confiscation of all property.[3]

[1] Tried as a rule by an ordeal.
[2] Ashanti: Rattray (1929), especially Chaps. XXVIf.
[3] e.g. Schapera (1938), 48; Peru: Moore (1958), 166.

Index

A.1, defined, 6, 172f
A.2, defined, 7, 200f
A.3, defined, 7, 226f
A.3 (1), defined, 227f
A.3 (2), defined, 271f; *see also* Early Codes
A.3 (3), defined, 313f; *see also* Central Codes
A.3 (4), defined, 347, 351f; *see also* Late Codes
Accad, *see* Babylonia
adoption, 91, 164, 214
adultery, 27, 61, 66, 74, 77, 91, 101-3, 112, 125, 167, 191, 220-3, 249, 267, 271, 298, 318, 326, 343, 346, 390, 398-9
Aethelberht, Laws of, 31, 42, 43, 47, 49, 53, 56-9, 61, 64, 311
Aethelred, Laws of, 53, 79-80
Aethelstan, Laws of, 53, 78-9, 98
Aew, 59
age grades and age sets, 183-4, 188, 191, 196, 221, 235-7, 278-9, 286, 324
Aghbouga, Code of, *see* Georgian Laws
agriculture, 85, 174-5, 201-2, 221-3, 253, 277, 315, 323, 337, 352-3
Akan Peoples, 349-50, 393
Akim Abuakwa, 350, 392
Akwĕ-Shavante, 173-97
Akwĕ-Sherente, 173
Alacaluf, 157-71
Alalakh, 16, 83, 90
Alamannorum Lex, 24, 29-30, 48-53, 60, 307-8

Alamannorum Pactus, 307
Alfred the Great, Laws of, 52-6, 64, 312, 318
ambush, 92, 141, 149, 265, 341f, 345
America, South-Eastern States, 199-224
America, South tropical forest culture, 199
Ana-Ittišu, 15
Andaman Islands, 157-71
Angliorum et Werinorum Lex = Lex Thuringorum, 30, 70, 75, 77, 81, 308-9
Anglo-Saxon Charters, 41; Laws, 31, 47, 53-4, 77-80, 311-12
Ankole, 313, 320-4, 329-31, 336, 342-3
Anuak, 227-70
Apache, 173, 184, 188
appeals, 220, 273, 282, 330
apprentices, 85, 129, 354
Armenian Laws, 36, 71, 73, 78-81, 312, 331
armies, 333-5
arson, 79, 122, 295
artisans, 85-6, 107, 316, 353, 380-1; *see also* craftsmen
arts, the, 118, 317, 356
Ashanti, 350, 355, 361, 366-7, 373-6, 391-400
Assiniboin, 173
Assyria, 13, 16, 19, 47, 82-4, 86, 92, 98, 100-3, 351, 355-9, 365, 372-375, 379, 382-6
Athapascans, Northern, 173-4
Athens, 21, 77, 82, 92, 397

auspices, taking, 317
Australians, 172-97

Babylonia, 13-14, 19, 47, 82-90, 102-4, 351, 355-7, 360, 372, 382-7
Baganda, see Ganda
bailments, 75, 86, 145-6, 150, 386-7, 390-1
Baiuvariorum Lex, 30, 48, 50-3, 60, 308
bands, 159-71
banishment, see outlawry
banking, 128, 355, 382
Banyankole, see Ankole
Banyoro, see Kitara
barter, 56, 69, 86, 106, 233, 272, 296, 316, 318, 379-88
Basin-Plateau Area, 172-97, 379
battle, ordeal by, 302-12
Bechuanaland, Botswana, see Tswana
Bella Coola, 200
Bemba, 314-29, 336-46
benefit of clergy, 96-7, 111, 113
bestiality, 62, 76, 79, 81, 346, 400
Bible, see Hebrews
Blackfeet, 173, 193
blasphemy, 103
bloodwealth, 237, 239, 261-6, 279, 293, 396; territorial limits of payment, 262-3 see also homicide
Boni, 338, 341
Botocudo, 158-71
boundary, violation of, 80
Brettos et Scotos, Leges inter, 32, 55, 58, 61, 312
bridewealth, 57, 66, 68, 74, 87, 102, 106, 112, 147, 182, 228, 244-9, 255, 258, 264, 273-4, 279, 288, 291, 324, 366-7
burglary, 106
Burgundian Laws, 26, 43-4, 55, 82-3, 86, 91, 92, 95, 100-1, 302-3, 310
burials, 122
Bushman, 158-71

calculation, 202-3, 205, 233
California, 173-8, 180, 182, 186-7, 379
canon law, 34, 49

Canute II, 76-8, 79, 271
capital sanctions, 87, 92, 96-7, 101-103, 111-12, 121, 192, 221-3, 260, 268, 318, 340f, 346, 400
caste, 107, 111
Catawba, 205
cattle, amount of, 227, 231-2, 244-5, 264-5, 277, 341, 352
Central Codes, 28, 34-5, 55-6, 70-81, 106-7, 225, 308-9, 313-46; defined, 72-5, 314-19
Chaco, 173
Charlemagne, 30-1, 43, 55, 70
charters, land, 291
Cherokee, 199, 205
Cheyenne, 173, 195, 197
Chickasaw, 205
chiefs, 102f, 184-7, 190-3, 208-11, 216-17, 228, 236-8, 259, 273, 277, 282, 330
chieftainship, succession to, 214, 217, 259, 283, 337
China, 10, 20, 83-7, 90, 92, 96-7, 100-3, 332, 351-9, 366-7, 373-4, 386, 390
Chippeewa, 173-97
Choctaw, 199, 205
church, offences against, 58, 79
church and king, 80-1, 89, 111
church and law, 48-54, 66, 79, 85, 88, 90; see also religion and law
civil wrongs, 57-68, 92, 121, 167, 185-6; compensation for, 57-68, 92, 191-2, 194
clans, 163, 179-84, 190, 206, 236-7, 279, 315, 324, 337-8, 365, 367
Clovis, 29, 271, see Salic Law
codes, 20, 23, 42-154; see also Early Codes, Central Codes and Late Codes
coining, false, 79, 346
Comanches, 173-97
commendatio, 333
communications, 161, 174, 205-6, 316
concubines, 140, 149, 367
confederacies, 176, 206
confiscation of property, see forfeiture
contempt of court, 79
contract, executory, 296, 386-8

contract-tablets, 14, 383-7
conveyances, 121, *see* Deeds
corporal sanctions, 67, 92, 97f, 400;
   see also sanctions, and capital
   sanctions
corvée, 81, 103, 132
councils, 185, 193, 240, 242, 285,
   337
court fees, 269, 346
courts, 128f, 134, 187, 192-3, 238-42,
   272, 320, 330
craftsmen, 73-4, 85, 107, 353, 380
credit, 74, 84, 86, 319, 368, 380
Creek Confederacy, 199, 205, 210,
   213, 222-3
Crees, 173
criminal and civil wrongs, 101, 167,
   191-3, 218f, 269, 273, 292, 318,
   344, 346, 397, 400
criminal law, 57, 62-3, 68, 74-9, 85,
   92, 97, 101-3, 106, 191, 220f,
   228, 269, 273, 293-4, 318, 343,
   346
crops, variety of, 232, 278, 316, 337
Crow, 178
currencies, 56, 72, 84, 107, 177, 203,
   272, 316, 355, 362-3, 368, 379-
   381

Dakota, 173
damage to property, 268
damages, 65
daughters' right to inherit, 214, 258,
   338; *see also* inheritance, and
   proprietary capacity
David I, *see* Scotland
debt, 84, 86, 319, 340, 368
debt slaves, 27, 74, 81, 87, 106, 139f,
   148-9, 319, 373
deeds, written, 383-5
defamation, 66, 268, 295, 306, 345,
   400
deodand, 65, 77, 95-6
deposit, 86, 112, 137, 145, 151, 381,
   386
desertion in battle, 62, 79
Digo, 314, 324, 337, 342
Dinka, 229-70
disputes, settled in court, 320
dissolution of marriage, 164, 183,
   249, 290, 349, 390

district, or county, 237, 282
district chief, 282
divination, 170, 194, 298, 317, 346
divorce, *see* dissolution of marriage
Dobu, 198
doctors, 77, 85, 98, 150, 355, 397-8
dom, 57f
Draco, 21, 82, 92
dwellings, 157, 173-4, 200, 231

Eadric, 31, 48, 59
Early Codes, 29, 30, 31, 55-80, 106,
   297-312, 330; defined, 55-6
ecclesiastical courts, 103, 118, 136f,
   152, 327, 344, 389
ecclesiastical laws, 36, 79, 101, 147,
   327
economies, 56, 72, 83, 157, 173f,
   201, 230f, 271f, 314f, 322f, 352f,
   379-88
Edgar, 79
Edictus Rothari, *see* Lombard Laws
Edictum Theoderici, *see* Ostrogothic
   Laws
Edmund, 53, 79-80
Edward, 78, 80
Egypt, 10-13, 84, 86, 91, 353-9, 362,
   383-4
empires, 72, 84, 358
employees, 250, 361, 381
England, 47, 55-70, 73, 76, 82-4,
   89-92, 101-2, 149, 277-8, 282-5,
   291, 315-24, 333-7, 351, 354-6,
   362, 366, 373-5, 380-7, 391,
   397, 399
Eshnunna, 14, 19, 82, 86-7, 90, 92,
   99, 101, 351, 373, 375, 382
Eskimo, 173-97
Ethiopia, 350-62, 366-8, 372, 376,
   386, 389-90
Euric, 26, 301, 319
evidence, unsworn, 112, 270, 298-
   312, 390-1; written, 113; *see
   also* witnesses
exchange, medium of, *see* currencies

factions, 191, 239
Faidus, 68
false accusations, 67, 100, 125
false imprisonment, 100
family, 163, 178-80, 189, 206, 238;

family—*contd.*
  liability of for father's debts, 340, 374
father, liability for wrongs and debts of household, 375
  acquires property of household, 340, 341
  his power of life and death and power to sell members of household, 337; *see also* Patria Potestas, and proprietary capacity
  offences against him, 375
  sues for household, 375
feud, 222, 238, 261, 395
fight, injury in a, 150
fines, 62, 68f, 111-12, 263-4, 273, 340, 343, 396-8
fire, damage by, 145, 148
Food Gatherers, 157-71, 184, 379; defined, 157
food, sharing, 165, 188, 207
forfeiture of house and property, 103, 228, 260, 295, 318, 346, 400
forgery, 103; as a source of law, 49, 50
Francorum Chamavorum, Lex, 30, 43, 70, 75, 308-9
Franks, 24, 29, 48
fridus (fretus), 68
Frisian Laws, 30, 43, 70, 77, 308-9

Ganda, 313-27, 329, 331, 333, 336-346
gatherers, *see* Food Gatherers
Georgian Laws, 37, 55, 60, 61, 71, 73, 77-81, 312, 331
Germans, 24, 56, 64, 69, 228-70, 279, 285, 294, 299, 300, 312
Ghana, 349, 357, 375, 393-4; *see also* Akan Peoples
gifts requiring return, 165, 177, 207, 210, 251, 379; ritual, 202, 380
gilds, 87, 111, 316, 355-6
gild courts, 87, 355
Giriama, 314-20, 336, 338, 342-4
Glanville, 82, 102
goring oxen, 95, 143-4, 150-1
Gortyn, Laws of, 15, 22
government, 184, 205, 208, 238-242, 329f

central government, 205, 209, 235, 238, 276, 279, 329f, 339, 363
local government, 241, *see also* feudalism
grades, defined, 6, 7
Greece, 21-2, 46, 82; *see also* Athens, Draco, Gortyn, Homer
'growling', 169, 193
guardianship of minors, 258, 337
Guayakí, 157, 171
Gulathing Law, 34, 312; *see also* Norwegian Laws
Gundobad, 26; *see also* Burgundian Laws

Haida, 200, 205
Hammurabi, Code of, 14, 15, 43-6, 82-8, 91-103, 140, 351, 354-5, 359, 366-7, 373-5, 379, 382, 386
handing over or seizing persons, as sanction for wrongs, 228, 265, 268, 318, 340-4
Hawaii, 199-225
Hebrews, 19, 48, 84-7, 90, 92, 95, 101-2, 124-54, 310, 351, 354-61, 365-8, 371-400
heirs, liability of for father's debts, 319
heresy, 49
Hidatsa, 172-97
hire, 74-5, 86, 146, 318, 381-2, 386-7
Hittite Laws, 15, 17-18, 44-5, 48, 71-81, 96, 316, 320, 327, 335, 338, 340, 386
Hlothere and Eadric, 48, 59, 67, 69, 271, 311-12
Homer, 21
homestead, as basic, local, kinship, and economic and administrative group, 272, 280
homicide, 27, 61-4, 71, 75, 79, 85, 90-7, 103, 121, 137, 141, 144-5, 149, 168, 170, 186, 191, 221, 228, 249, 260-6, 273, 293-5, 318, 326, 340-3, 346, 395-7
  pollution by, 93f, 261, 263, 343, 396
  unintentional, 64-5, 68, 73, 75, 85, 95, 100, 125, 265-6, 341f, 396
  within the family, 223, 263

horse, acquisition of, 172-97, 227
horticulture, 198-224
housebreaking, 102, 144-5
household, 365, see father
houses, owned separately from land, 213, see dwellings
human sacrifice, 317, 358
hunters, early (H.1), 172-97
hunters (H.2), 199-224
hunting, 162-71, 174, 191, 201, 271, 315, 352
husband and wife, offences between, 249
Hywel Dda, see Welsh Laws

Ibo, 349
Iceland, 35-6
imprisonment, 112, 399; see also prisons, and stocks
Incas, see Peru
incest, 62, 68, 91, 103, 106, 167, 191, 221, 224, 228, 248, 260, 295, 346, 390, 400
indecent assault, 65, 100
India, 21, 48, 83, 86-9, 91, 96-7, 100-12f, 327, 332, 351, 353-9, 373-4, 382, 386, 394
Indus valley civilisation, 21, 105
Ine, Laws, of, 52-3, 56, 60, 78, 311-12
inheritance, 45, 49, 59, 69, 81, 87, 107-9, 121, 166, 190, 196, 213, 254, 256-9, 290-2, 319, 337-8, 367, 390
    and gifts, 254
    inheritance and transfer, 190, 213, 254
    obligation of heir to support family, 254
    of claims to bridewealth, 256
    of daughters, 372-3; of slaves, 373
    of widow, see widow
    rights to inherit, of women, 372-373
initiation, rites of, 160, 183, 235
interest, 74; see loan of money
investments, 349, 355, 382
Iowa, 173
Ireland, Laws of, 32, 33, 44, 70, 312
iron, 107
Iroquois, 173
irrigation, 85, 353

Isin, 82, 90, 92, 99-100; see also Lipit Ishtar
Islamic Law, see Muhammadan Law
isolation, degrees of, 161, 174, 179, 205

joint family, 86, 121, 214, 238, 373
judges, 122, 150, 240
justice, administration of, 133, 242; feudal, 330f; see also Courts
Justinian, 28, 43

Kamba, 228-70, 376
Kapauku, 198-225, 380
Kavirondo, Bantu of North, 229-70
Kavirondo, Jaluo Nilotic, 229-70
Keraki, see Trans-Fly
Kikuyu, 227-70, 376
king (or paramount chief), 56-8, 62, 68, 72, 85, 87, 107-8, 131f, 209, 238-9, 242, 271f, 277-9, 282-7, 310, 315
    as owners of the land, 212, 290, 329; of the cattle and crops, 329
    as traders, 355, 382
kingdoms, size of, 84
king's court, 80-1, 101, 103, 107, 221, 272, 293, 318
kinship groups, 178-81, 339
    ambilateral, 365
    bilateral, 206, 214, 279, 324, 337, 365
    kinship and territorial structure, 237, 279, 365-6
    liabilities of, 281
Kiowa, 173
Kipsigis, 229-70
Kitara, 313-27, 336, 342-4
kraal, see homestead
Kuma, 198-224
Kwakiutl, 200, 205

Lagash, 13
Lamba, 314-27, 333, 336-46
land, allocation of, 282, 286, 290, 329, 360-1
    cadastral surveys and registration, 11, 74
    diminishing superfluity of, 362, 370-2
    inheritance of, 69, 214, 289, 336

land—*contd*
joint holding of, 373
leases and loans of, 86, 212, 371-2
market in land, 373, 383
right of pre-emption, 87, 373
right of redemption, 87, 373
right to alienate, 212-13, 337, 371-2
right to mortgage or pledge land, 373, 382, 386
rights in, 164, 189, 201, 211-13, 252
in hunting societies, 215; in Late Codes, 368-73
individual ownership, 85, 212-215, 373
of king, 85, 212, 290; of clan, 252
of lineage, 236, 252; of small kinship groups, 212
of subclan, 252; of village, 252
sale of, 56, 74, 86, 272, 315, 383
tenure of, 86, 349; *see also* Feudalism
landless classes, 86, 107, 128, 315, 361
Lango, 229-70
language of codes, 45-58, 113, 120, 125-6, 128, 139f
languages, 160, 176, 205-6, 230
Late Codes, 17, 19, 20, 26-7, 43, 55, 75, 82-154, 301-5, 347-400; defined, 82-5, 347, 352f
law, existence of, 190, 195-6, 216f, 235, 238, 317; definition of, 195
law, words for, 57, 59, 60, 126, 243
Legis Actio Sacramenti, 391
legislation, 41-3, 45, 56, 228, 272-3, 286
legislators, 46, 273, 286
levirate, 106, 182, 250, 256-7, 289, 338; *see also* widow, inheritance of
liability for family debts, of father, 87; of children, 87
lineages, 184, 206, 236, 238, 279, 366
Lipit Ishtar, Laws of, 14-15, 46, 82, 379
literature and law, 39-54, 104, 107, 113; *see* codes
litigation, 243

loan, of goods, 146, 318, 386
of money, 74, 86, 319, 386
local variations of laws, 111, 319, 391-2
Lombard Laws, 42-3, 45, 55, 70, 74-9, 128-9, 305-6
lords and commoners, 360
lynching, 228, 260

Maine, Sir Henry, vii, 45, 47, 61, 104, 124, 378
Malekula (New Hebrides), 198, 201, 208, 213, 220
mancipium, 383-6
Mandan, 173, 178
Mandja, 272
Manu, Code of, 21; *see* India
manufactures, 201, 233, 316, 380
Mari, 16, 83, 90
market courts, 86, 316, 354
markets and market tolls and rents, 56, 73, 78, 85-6, 106, 157, 233, 272, 315, 354, 380-1
marriage, 49, 57, 59, 87, 163, 181-3, 196, 210, 244-50, 291, 336, 366f; analogous marriages, 250-1; capture, 163, 183, 210; ceremony of marriage, 88, 163, 211, 368; exchange marriage, 182, 210, 336; looser marriages, 367-8; marriage by service, 336; marriage contracts, 88; preferred marriages, 182; prohibited marriages, 163, 181-2, 208, 367; virilocal and uxorilocal, 182, 211, 228, 236, 274, 364; marriage settlements and portions, 75, 87, 141, 196, 228, 274, 289, 336, 349, 366; *see also* bridewealth
Masai, Pastoral, 227, 270
maternal uncle and nephew, 206
matriliny, 180, 206, 211, 214, 274, 324, 337, 365
Maya, 357, 395, 398-9
mayhem, 98-9
Mbuti (Pygmies), 158-71
Melanesia, 198-224
merchants' law, 78
metals, 158, 173, 200, 226, 278, 316
Mexico, 351-61, 366-7, 373-4, 389-390, 395, 398-9

military organization, 279, 286
miscarriages, 65, 150
mishpat, 57, 126
mnemonic devices, 203, 233
moieties, 179-81, 191, 200
monogyny, 106, 164, 367
monopolies, royal, 329; of the women, 354
morality and law, 47, 124, 293; *see also* religion and law
mother, striking or cursing, 87
movement of peoples, 230, 271, 275
Muhammadan Law, 83, 348-9, 367, 386, 395-7
mund, 68
mundbyrd, 52, 58-9, 68
'murder', 63, 75, 265-6, 341-3, 346; *see also* homicide
mutilations, 57, 66-8, 74, 77-9, 85, 97-103, 112-13, 318, 339, 344, 400

Nandi, 229-270
Natchez, 205
nations or states, 206, 271, 277, 314, 339, 358
negligence, 95, 112, 341, 396
Nepal, 96
New Guinea, 198-221
New Hebrides, 198-224
Ngala, 275, 314-27, 333, 336-46
Ngbetu, 275, 314-27, 333, 336-46
Nguni, 274-96, 298-300, 336, 340
Ngwato, 276, 350, 356, 396; *see also* Tswana
Nigeria, Northern, 342, 347-400
Southern, 347-400; differences between Eastern and Western halves, 349; Eastern, 348
Nippur, 14
nobility and rank, 58-9, 63, 84, 105, 107, 207-8, 272, 317, 359-61; preoccupation with rank, 207; purchase of rank, 208, 236
Nootka, 200, 205
Normans, 82
Norwegian Laws, 34-5, 45, 70, 75-81, 312
Nuer, 228-70, 320
Nupe, 348, 352-67, 370-4, 381-2
Nuzi, 16, 83

Nyika, 314, 320, 338, 342

Oath of purgation, 47, 49, 52, 75, 90, 101, 112, 135, 145-6, 148, 151, 194, 223, 270, 296-312, 318, 386-7, 390-1; procedure by oath, 391-4
Ojibway, 185
Omaha, 173, 193
Ona, 157-71
Ontong Java, 198-224
ordeals, 47, 48, 52, 75, 79, 90, 101, 103, 112-13, 139, 170, 223, 228, 270, 274, 297-312, 318, 327, 346, 386-7, 390-1
order, maintenance of, 330; restoration of, 186, 193, 218-20, 238
Osage, 173
Ostrogothic Laws, 27, 42-3, 55, 82-3, 91-2, 100-1
Oto, 173
outlawry, 76, 78-9, 111, 113, 268, 295, 318, 340, 342-3, 346, 396
'ownership', 164, 188-9, 212, 370-1

parent, offences against, 148, 375
partnership, 69, 382
pastoralists, 172-3, 198, 226-70; and cultivators, 322, 324
Patria Potestas, 87, 121, 338; right to sell wife, child or sister, 87
patriliny, 180, 206, 211, 214, 228, 236, 274, 279, 288, 324, 337, 352, 357, 365
peace, preservation and restoration of, 185-6, 192-3, 218
penances for religious offences, 101, 108, 344
perjury, 79, 125
personal execution, 319, 340
personal injuries, 59, 61, 77, 97-100, 121, 142, 150, 186, 191, 266, 273, 318, 346, 397-8; compensation for, 59, 65, 77, 266, 343; tariffs, 228, 269-70, 343
personal law, 319
Peru, 351-7, 360-1, 366-7, 376, 389, 395, 399
phratries, 179, 206
pigs, 200
pledge, 382; *see also* land

plough, heavy, 107, 353
Pokot, *see* Suk
police, 186, 193, 241-2
pollution of land by homicide, 92
polyandry, 183
polygyny, 66, 107, 141, 164, 182,
    211, 246, 280
Polynesia, 198-224
Ponca, 173, 184-5
pontifices, 117f
populations, density of, 56, 73, 84,
    159, 175, 204, 231, 277, 321,
    355-6; fertility, 246, 289; size of,
    56, 73, 84, 160-1, 175, 204-5,
    229, 277, 320, 356
poultry, 200
Powhatan (Virginia), 199, 205, 222
prices and hire charges, and control
    of, 73, 86, 316, 318, 381
priesthood, 84, 107, 134-8, 317,
    325-7, 353, 389-91; as judges, 91
'primitive', meaning, 5
primogeniture, 292, 337-8, 372
prisons, 65, 69, 97, 112-13, 318, 399
procedure, 45, 59-61, 120f, 196,
    223, 270, 296, 298, 307, 326,
    346, 391-4
property, damage to, 122
property, vested in family head, 337
property rights, 166, 187-9, 196; as
    guardian and trustee, 251; in
    cattle, 251; in goods, 166, 188,
    213, 251, 291; in incorporeal
    property, 188, 213, 216; trans-
    fers of, 188, 190, 212; *see also*
    land and inheritance,
proprietary capacity, of husband and
    father, 87, 337-8; of wife, 87,
    112, 338; of son, 87, 112, 338,
    373; of daughter, 338, 372; of
    slave, 112
Puelche and Tehuelche, 173, 176,
    185, 189-90
purification after homicide, 171,
    196, 263, 326

rape, 61, 65-8, 77, 97, 101-3, 267,
    294-5, 344, 346, 399
receiving stolen goods, 101
reference of cases to higher courts,
    273-4, 282

Rega, 272
religion and law, 47-54, 80, 87, 96,
    104, 108-10, 113, 124-8, 167,
    170, 196-7, 224, 267, 297-8,
    326, 343, 389, 396f; *see also*
    church and law
religion and magic, 83-4, 108-9,
    170-1, 175, 177, 191, 196, 204,
    223-4, 233-4, 287, 297-8, 310-11,
    317, 325-6, 328, 389
religious codes, 125
religious offences, *see* sacral crimes
religious orders, 389
religious rules, 79, 224
riht, 60
Ripuarian Code, 30, 56, 60-1, 64,
    308, 334
robbery, 66f, 97, 106, 309
Rome, 22-8, 37, 82-6, 89, 91-2, 101,
    114-23, 300, 341, 351, 360,
    365-8, 374-6, 382-7, 390, 394
rotation of crops, 85, 232, 353
Rothari, Edictus, 28, 44, 74; *see also*
    Lombard Laws
Russian Laws, 36, 43, 55, 60-1, 69-
    70, 76, 78, 312, 331

sacral crimes, 47, 49, 79, 101, 191,
    196, 223, 326, 396, 398, 400
sale, 56, 60, 69, 78, 86, 128, 272, 296,
    316; for cash, 382f; on credit,
    383-6
Salic Law, 29, 42, 44, 47, 60-1, 64,
    303-4
Salish, Coast, 200, 202, 205, 210, 216
Samoa, 199-224
sanctions, 45, 62, 64-80, 194; cor-
    poral, 67, 78, 92, 97f, 186-7,
    300, 339; pecuniary, 97, 194,
    228, 273, 339; *see also* capital
    sanctions, handing over persons,
    mutilations
sanctuaries, 49, 79, 90, 92, 135, 137,
    141, 147, 149, 185, 196-7, 223,
    261, 284-5, 319, 343, 395f
Saxonum Lex, 31, 43, 70, 74-81, 308
school books, 15, 23, 34, 44, 110,
    120-3
Scotland, 32, 60, 70, 73, 80-1, 312
scribes, 39, 48, 58, 72, 89, 105, 111,
    128-9, 317, 384, 390

sections, 181
seduction, 61, 66, 91, 102, 112, 146-147, 267, 294-5, 344
segmentary systems, 237
'sell', 382
Semang, 157-71
Seminole, 199, 205
serfs, 107, 242, 317, 322, 324, 360, 383
servants, 86
sexual perversion, 62, 260
Shangana-Tonga, 314, 342-3
Shilluk, 229-70, 293
Shoshoni, 158-71, 178-97
slander, see defamation
slave and slavery, 57, 59, 63, 66-8, 84, 142-4, 203, 207, 273, 278, 317-18, 322, 324, 338-9, 344, 360, 379-388; selling into slavery, 141; see also debt slaves
slavery, penal, 78, 102, 344, 360, 383
social classes and distinctions, 58, 63, 65-6, 73, 77, 92, 100, 112
social control, 170, 190-1, 216-18, 224, 242, 320
societies, 184, 188, 191
sodomy, 76, 221, 400
sorcery, 27, see witchcraft
sororate, 182
Sotho, 320-1, 324; North Sotho, 342; South Sotho, 272, 276, 314
specialization, economic, 174, 201, 232-3, 272, 353, 381; of the sexes, 162, 174-5, 201, 233, 272
spinning, 85
spoor law, 295
states and empires, 73, 339
stocks, for offenders, 79, 106, 318
stoning, 228
succession, 190f, 208, 214, 259, 283
suicide, 103, 400
suit and service, 273, 282f, 329f
Suk, 229, 231, 236, 257-65
Sumerians, 13-14, 47, 359, 384
suretyship, 86, 319, 392

talionic penalties, 27, 85, 95, 97-102, 113, 121, 142-3, 150, 349, 398-9
Tallensi, 227-70
Tanana Indians, Upper, 173-97
Tasmanians, 158-71

Taveta, 314, 338, 342, 344
taxation, 132, 221, 360
technicality in the law, 376, 391-2
technology, 201, 228, 231-3, 277-8, 323; see also economies
Tehuelche, 173, 185, 189-90
Teita, 314, 320, 338, 341, 343
Ten Commandments, The, 125
terrace cultivation, 353
Teton, 173
theft, 58, 61, 66, 76-9, 98, 101-3, 106, 112, 121, 125, 144, 167, 170, 186, 191-2, 221, 228, 260, 268, 273, 298, 318, 339, 343-5
Theodosian Code, 27, 43, 49
Thuringorum Lex, 30, 43; see also Angliorum et Werinorum Lex
Tikopia, 199, 205, 212
Tiv, 314-27, 336-46
Tlingit, 200, 205
Tonga, 199-224, 225
Toro, 320-7
torture, 67
totems, 179-80, 206, 236
town courts, 316
town hall, 200
towns, 73, 84, 107, 133, 206, 315, 321-2, 355-7
trade, 84-5, 107, 157, 177, 201-2, 233, 272, 354, 368, 379-88
transactions, 379
transfers of property, 190, 212-13; see also property rights, land, deeds
Trans-Fly, 198-224, 225
treason, 62, 65, 68, 78-9, 103, 295, 312, 343, 346, 400
trees and their fruits, rights to, 165
trespass by force, 67, 76, 79, 161, 164, 345
trespassing animals, 67, 122, 268
tribe, 160, 176, 178, 179, 207, 237, 277
tribute, 329f
Trobriand, 198-210, 217, 220, 222
Tsimshian, 200, 205
Tswana, 350-6, 360, 365-7, 374, 376, 380, 386, 388, 390, 395-6, 398-400
Tuscarora, 176
Twana, 199f, 205, 210, 215

Ugarit, 16, 83, 90
Ur-Nammu, 13-14, 82-3, 99-101
Urukagina, 13
usufruct of land, 371

Venda, 314, 342
Venedotian Code, *see* Welsh Laws
villages, 73, 84, 180, 206, 210, 228, 236, 280, 287, 315, 321, 357; whether compensation between, 237
Visigothic Code, 25-6, 43, 55, 82, 87, 92, 95, 97, 100-1, 304-5, 341
vouching a vendor, 69, 78, 146, 318

wager, forensic, 391-4
wages, control of, 86
wards of villages and towns, 357-8
warfare, 132, 174, 203, 234-5, 333-5, 358
warranties, 387
weaving, 85
wealth, preoccupation with, 207
week, 354
Welsh Laws, 32-3, 70, 75, 312
wergeld, 63-4, 66, 74-5, 77, 79, 92, 106
Western Europe, 24-36, 37-81, 88-91, 95, 101, 103, etc.
wheel, 353
widow, right to inherit her, 59, 66, 214, 250, 256-7, 338; *see also* levirate
her right to inherit, 87
wife, exchange of, 183; homicide of, 265; incorporeal property, 215; proprietary capacity of, 75, 87,

213, 251; right to inherit, 87, 213-14, 258; *see also* inheritance, and proprietary capacity
Wihtred, Laws of, 52, 60, 311
William I, 54, 98-9, 274, 311, 334
wills, 91, 121, 166, 215, 259, 292, 338, 376
Winnebago, 173, 184-5
witchcraft, 62, 76, 79-80, 91, 103, 122, 190-1, 196, 204, 220-1, 228, 249, 260, 295, 298, 319, 343, 346, 390, 400
witnesses, to transactions, 73, 78, 381-3; in trials, 128, 301-12, 318; *see also* Evidence
wives, number of, 246
women, as holders of fiefs, 359
as husbands, 250
as regents, 283-4
guardianship of, 112, 121
occupations of, 85, etc.; *see also* specialization
property of, 166, 188, 258, 291, 338; *see also* proprietary capacity
wergeld of, 63
wounding, *see* personal injuries
writing, 39-54, 73, 87, 104, 113, 117, 128, 384, 390; *see also* scribes

Xhosa, 273, 279-81, 284, 286, 298

Yahgan, 157-71
Yakö, 349
Yoruba, 348, 352, 356, 370-3, 376, 397
Yurok, 199-224

Zulu, 81, 273-96